COMMUNITY
IN CONFLICT

COMMUNITY IN CONFLICT

A WORKING-CLASS HISTORY OF THE
1913–14 MICHIGAN COPPER STRIKE
AND THE ITALIAN HALL TRAGEDY

GARY KAUNONEN AND **AARON GOINGS**

MICHIGAN STATE UNIVERSITY PRESS | EAST LANSING

♾ The paper used in this publication meets the minimum requirements of ANSI/
NISO Z39.48-1992 (R 1997) (Permanence of Paper).

Michigan State University Press
East Lansing, Michigan 48823-5245

Printed and bound in the United States of America.

19 18 17 16 15 14 13   1 2 3 4 5 6 7 8 9 10

LIBRARY OF CONGRESS CATALOGING-IN-PUBLICATION DATA
Kaunonen, Gary.
Community in conflict : a working-class history of the 1913–14 Michigan Copper
Strike and the Italian Hall Tragedy / Gary Kaunonen and Aaron Goings.
pages cm
Includes bibliographical references and index.
ISBN 978-1-61186-093-1 (pbk. : alk. paper) — ISBN 978-1-60917-385-2 (ebook) 1.
Copper Miners' Strike, Mich., 1913–1914. 2. Italian Hall Disaster, Calumet, Mich.,
1913. 3. Strikes and lockouts—Miners—Michigan—Calumet Region—History—20th
century. 4. Copper mines and mining—Michigan—Calumet Region—History—20th
century. 5. Working class—Michigan—Calumet Region—History—20th century. 6.
Calumet Region (Mich.)—Economic conditions—20th century. I. Goings, Aaron,
author. II. Title.
HD5325.M731913 .M525 2013
331.892'8223430977499309041—dc23
2012041056

Book design by Charlie Sharp, Sharp Des!gns, Lansing, Michigan
Cover design by Erin Kirk New

Cover art is a political cartoon that was drawn by Konstu Sallinen, a Finnish
immigrant working at the Tyomies Publishing Company in Hancock, Michigan,
during the strike. Originally published in *Lapatossu* (1913) from the collection of
Gary Kaunonen.

Michigan State University Press is a member of the Green Press Initiative and is
committed to developing and encouraging ecologically responsible publishing
practices. For more information about the Green Press Initiative and the use of
recycled paper in book publishing, please visit *www.greenpressinitiative.org*.

Visit Michigan State University Press at *www.msupress.org*

Contents

Preface

While much of the Copper Country's tradition celebrates the sheer enormity and progress of the area's halcyon copper days and the men who drew enormous profits from the industry, there was the "little" discrepancy: thousands of mineworkers were the ones who actually worked to produce all this wealth. The mineworkers who ate, caroused, lived, worked, were injured, and died underground often do not receive the credit due for their contributions to building the lore, traditions, and wealth of this industrial area.

This book works to tell a different story, not of progress and wealth, but of reality for Copper Country wageworkers before and during the great upheaval of the 1913–14 Michigan Copper Strike.

Rather than paying tribute to the so-called Copper Kings who reaped enormous profits because of their ownership of the mines, this book is a labor history of the 1913–14 strike told from the perspective of the working people of the Copper Country. We seek to chronicle the men and women who produced the wealth (both material and otherwise) of the region and their efforts to find a voice through labor organizations, political parties, and ethnic associations that sought to change their material existence. In short, this book strives to recount the class struggles waged in pursuit of industrial democracy in the face of exploitation by the kings of Michigan copper.

As a labor history, this book begins with the understanding that class struggle is inherent in capitalist societies. Workers are locked in a perpetual struggle with their employers, one in which both sides seek to gain at the other's expense. In other words, workers desire the full fruits of their labor, while employers want to have a free hand to extract as much wealth as possible. As such, this book takes into serious consideration overt forms of class conflict, such as strikes, sabotage, and picket line violence, as well as the more hidden forms of class conflict, including political corruption, struggles over "space" within the community, and the so-called industrial accidents that then, as now, are "accidents" experienced mostly, if not only, by members of the working class.

Drawing inspiration from the New Labor History and E. P. Thompson's "bottom up" approach, *Community in Conflict* places working people and their experiences at the center of Copper Country history. Throughout the text we analyze a wide range of working-class activity, including working-class politics, unionization, strikes, and material culture. Of course, class was not the only source of division among the Copper Country's residents. The region's working people were themselves fragmented by gender, race, ethnicity, skill, religion, and political beliefs, and many of the "workers' institutions" such as craft unions were comprised almost entirely of white men who labored in skilled trades. But rather than focusing on working-class fragmentation, *Community in Conflict* seeks to highlight examples of labor solidarity in Michigan's copper range, particularly those moments when class experiences and class-based activism overcame traditional divisions within the working class. Such was the case in 1913 when Copper Country workers—men and women, skilled and unskilled, and drawn from numerous ethnic groups—combined and confronted the equally unified group of Copper Country employers.

Other books, such as Arthur Thurner's *Rebels on the Range*, have told the history of the strike largely from the employers' perspective. Thurner relies on accounts from newspapers that the Copper Country strikers would have termed the "kept press." By privileging one viewpoint, that of the mine owners, Thurner's works presents a misleading view of the strike, one that ignores the perspective of the working people responsible for making the strike. *Community in Conflict*, however, seeks to shed light on the strike from the often-overlooked viewpoint of those who sought better wage and working conditions in area mines; those seeking to put more food on the family table; and yes, even those revolutionaries who sought to subvert the capitalist system.

It is this perspective, the viewpoint of working people, unionists, radicals, and revolutionaries, which is most often ignored or marginalized in standard histories such as Thurner's *Rebels on the Range*. This is regrettable because historical events are often presented in a top-down form that rewards the wealthy few with leading roles in the historical narrative. Thus, in its own way, the writing of history is itself a class struggle, and unfortunately for students of this region, employers and their intellectual assistants have succeeded mightily in this struggle. Labor history thus gives a voice to those who were silenced by exclusion, incarceration, marginalization, oppression, and suppression. It is our hope that *Community in Conflict* provides a necessary corrective to the historiography of the Copper Country Strike by returning the voices of the working men and women to the center of the strike.

As the book's title intends, community stands at the center of our analysis of the 1913–14 Michigan Copper Strike. Community is an important analytical tool for labor historians because the interaction between worker and employer occurs primarily at the local level. When a worker is fired or an employer is picketed, most of the action and interaction occurs within a single community. The 1913–14 Michigan Copper Strike was just such a grassroots endeavor between individuals and groups operating in local social halls, on busy streets, and within communities. Thus, the community study perspective best elucidates the lived experiences of working people in the Copper Country at this time.

Community can also show the diverse ways in which individuals were knitted together through networks of kith and kin, class and family, race and gender. During the Copper Country Strike, striking mineworkers sought to draw lines between themselves and their bosses, recognizing that workers shared a community of interests distinct from their employers and seeking to unite with other elements of the community. During the strike, both the mining operators and union sought alliances with ethnic groups, professionals, and middle-class merchants, each of which held a significant stake in their community and could lend material support and added credence to each group's cause.

Communities, like factory shop floors and political elections, were and are spheres of conflict, sites where groups with divergent interests struggle for influence and control. During the strike of 1913–14, both unionists and employers sought to define the other as "outsiders" to the community, thus seeking to mobilize community support for themselves. Union organizers were pegged as "outside agitators," while major employers were labeled capitalists from "back east," or more universally, "parasites" who produced nothing and lived luxuriously at the Copper Country community's expense.

Lastly, *Community in Conflict* seeks to straddle the line between local and national. Previous literature of the 1913–14 strike has been prone to provincialism, privileging what was unique about the region rather than analyzing it within the context of national and international events, such as the development of monopoly capitalism, the growth of diverse forms of working-class radicalism, and the prevalence of anti-labor violence. As a result, previous studies have focused solely on what was unique about the Copper Country Strike, without explaining how and why these events fit into and were shaped by national and international forces. These national and international forces colored how workers saw their laboring and social environment in the Copper Country, but the strike votes, picket lines, and parades were local examples of national and international solidarity.

It is perhaps clear that this will not be a traditional history of the 1913–14 Michigan Copper Strike. An expanded scope of significance, new areas of study, new documentary sources, radical scholarly foundations, and varied tools of analysis will provide a new breadth of understanding and scholarly insight into this watershed event in *American* labor history.

Acknowledgments

Gary Kaunonen would like to acknowledge and thank many people, institutions, and archives for their help in making this book possible.

First and foremost, my family: *Sofia, Niilo, and Grady, this book is dedicated to each of you.* If I can teach you one thing in life, it is that persistence pays off (and never trust "The Man"). Lindsay was patient and supportive of late nights at the keyboard and trips to public presentations. My parents, Art and Edie, who are always supportive, were interested in the work and generous in compliments.

To my friend and co-author, "AG," this was my first long-distance relationship that worked. Thank you.

I wish to give thanks to members of the academy who have steered my interests and sparked my curiosity. From very early on: Dr. Carol MacLennan has been a guiding light; Dr. Larry Lankton and Kim Hoagland have been inspirations and great mentors; more recently, Dr. Beth Flynn and Dr. Robert Johnson of Tech's Humanities Department have been incredible in guiding my academic PhD plans and considerate in providing time to finish this book. I would also like to thank Dr. Karla Kitalong for her interest in this work, "eh."

Lastly, I would like to thank "The Dynamic" and all the others at the 2011 Industrial Archaeology Field School at Cliff Mine for cutting me some slack on my research days. Nick "Young Buck" Reed and Eric "Eazy E" Pomber are about the funniest fellas I have ever met in an archaeology trench, and the other people I met there were incredible as well: Chris, Roger, Bubbles, Megs, et al. Special thanks go to Dr. Tim Scarlett and soon-to-be Dr. Sean "Messrs." Gohman for letting me skip out on the hot days to do archival research in an air conditioned building.

Aaron Goings wishes to extend his gratitude to everyone who helped make this book possible.

First, I am fortunate to have a number of supportive coworkers at Saint Martin's University. Thanks to my friends and fellow workers Roger Snider, Rex Casillas, David Price, Brian Barnes, Dick Langill, Kathleen McKain, Father Peter Tynan, Jeff Birkenstein, Olivia Archibald, Julia Chavez, Teresa Winstead, Michael Butler, Victor Kogan, Keri Olsen, Robert Hauhart, Karen Jaskar, Don Stout, Paul Patterson, Julie Yamamoto, Kirsti Thomas, Leslie Huff, John Hopkins, Joe Mailhot, Jeremy Newton, Marie Boisvert, Heather Grob, and Todd Barosky. I am especially indebted to the long-haired, wild-eyed radicals (you know who you are) among the Saint Martin's faculty who devote so much time and energy to fighting for academic freedom and workers' rights.

This project emerged from many conversations with my friend and coauthor Gary Kaunonen, and this book is the project of our true collaboration. I also wish to thank Mark Leier, Betsy Jameson, and Karen Blair for their years of generosity, kindness, and intellectual guidance.

My greatest debts are owed to my family. I am especially grateful to my parents, Chris and Mike, brothers Brad and Todd, and my late grandmother Nina, whose support guided me through this long academic journey. Thanks as well to the Archie, Goings, Utter, Clocksin, and Cardinal families for all the years of encouragement, and the good times in Humptulips and at Nina's house. And, thank you to the AmRheins and Sheinbaums for welcoming me into your families. *I dedicate this book to my wonderful wife Jess.* She is the light of my life.

We both wish to thank, applaud, and encourage support for the area's archival collections: Michigan Technological University's Copper Country Historical Collections, Keweenaw National Historical Park's Archive and Museum Collections, and Finlandia University's Finnish American Historical Archives are superb. These three repositories hold an incredible collection of materials, and the staffs at all three are first-rate. Specifically, we would like to thank Erik Nordberg, Beth Russell, and Sawyer Newman at "The Tech"; Jeremiah Mason, Brian Hoduski, Jo Urion, and Kathleen Harter at Keweenaw National Historical Park; and James Kurtti and Hilary Virtanen at Finlandia. A special thank you to the Friends of the Van Pelt Library, which awarded Aaron a travel grant to support one of his visits to the Copper Country.

We would also like to thank Michigan State University Press, especially Julie Loehr, Julie Reaume, and Kristine Blakeslee, for supporting this project. A hearty thank you also goes out to the initial readers of the manuscript who gave us great ideas that helped shape the final product.

incl. JR

Introduction

IN MANY WAYS, THE COPPER COUNTRY WAS A TYPICAL LATE-NINETEENTH AND early twentieth-century American mining region with disputes between labor and management that every so often climaxed in a divisive labor strike. Atypical, however, was one specific event in the Copper Country's history—the Italian Hall tragedy in Calumet, Michigan, on Christmas Eve in 1913. That night, during a holiday party organized for the strikers' children, someone yelled "Fire!" in a crowded labor hall, and the party's attendees rushed toward the front door to escape the fire they believed had started in the hall. Before they could exit Italian Hall, many tripped and fell, causing others to trip over recently fallen bodies. Those who fell were crushed by those who tripped over them, until the entire stairway was blocked by a pile of injured, dead, and dying victims.

The results were as horrible as any in the history of American labor: between seventy-three and seventy-nine persons were killed, the overwhelming majority of whom were children. An English-language article in *Työmies*, a Finnish immigrant socialist newspaper based in Hancock, Michigan, expressed disbelief at the sheer scale of the tragedy: "The most appalling disaster in the history of Michigan occurred last evening at the Italian Hall in Calumet where hundreds of men, women, and children had gathered to witness Christmas exercises for the strikers' children."[1]

As a horrible keystone event of the 1913–14 Michigan Copper Strike, the Italian Hall tragedy was a macabre exclamation point on an especially violent time in American labor history. The perils of striking workers in an ethnic hall near Lake Superior became etched on the national consciousness like the rough, sunken death dates "Dec. 24, 1913" on the headstones of those in Calumet's Lake View Cemetery who died in the panic. While the terrible events of the Italian Hall tragedy made their mark in national news at that time, they have come to be an everlasting, almost haunting reminder of the strike's violent past in the collective historical memory of the entire Copper Country. Dreadfully, Calumet and Michigan's Copper Country became famous for something else besides the red metal mineral being mined thousands of feet underground.

Though this memory faded over the years, the personal and social scars caused by this tragedy were deep enough to inspire a national treasure to put pen to paper in an effort to compel workers almost thirty years later to fight for a better life. Events in Calumet, Michigan, became the focus of a moving 1940s labor song:

Take a trip with me in nineteen thirteen
To Calumet, Michigan, in the copper country
I'll take you to a place called Italian Hall
And the miners are having their big Christmas ball . . .

Such a terrible sight I never did see
We carried our children back up to their tree
The scabs outside still laughed at their spree
And the children that died there was seventy-three

The piano played a slow funeral tune,
And the town was lit up by a cold Christmas moon
The parents, they cried and the men, they moaned,
See what your greed for money has done?[2]

Above are the first and last two stanzas from Woody Guthrie's nearly forgotten labor song "1913 Massacre." Guthrie is an American icon. His classic "This Land Is Your Land" is sung in elementary schools across the nation, but why might Guthrie be interested in an Italian fraternal hall in a place called Calumet, Michigan? Expressed through Guthrie's lyrics are the anger, pain, sorrow, and tragedy of this heartbreaking event. Though Guthrie penned the song in the mid-1940s reportedly after reading a

chapter entitled "Calumet and Ludlow: Massacre of the Innocents," in Mother Bloor's
We Are Many, the song provided a memorial to people who died three decades
earlier. Guthrie's song is not an especially accurate portrayal of events at Italian Hall;
rather, Guthrie's memorial to those who died at Italian Hall was a call to action for
those seeking social justice and union representation in the 1940s. To inspire the
men and women engaged in these struggles, Guthrie wrote and performed a song
about an event in American labor history that happened in a place called Calumet,
which recalled a labor strike and human tragedy of *national significance*.

Despite the national significance of the Italian Hall tragedy, writing about the
event has been missing research based on documentary evidence from first-person
sources. Lacking is "evidence" about why, or in fact if, anti-union forces targeted
the hall and its Christmas Eve festivities, full of children, for retribution as a way to
drive the Western Federation of Miners (WFM) from Michigan's Copper Country,
thus ending the strike. Here we present evidence that such was the case, and we
take the claim a step further by demonstrating via the historical record that mining
companies, a Citizens' Alliance vigilante group, and Houghton County law enforcement personnel orchestrated a December campaign of intimidation and violence
that culminated in the tragedy at Italian Hall. Thus, this book provides a new and
pointed analysis of Italian Hall and the events that set in motion the loss of so many
innocent lives.

There was, however, much more to the 1913–14 strike than the Italian Hall
tragedy. The strike was an epic showdown between organized labor and monopoly
capital. This labor conflict was also a concerted effort by organized labor to give a
voice to workers at their workplaces, workplaces that were controlled by absentee
owners who lived more than a thousand miles away in big cities like Boston,
Philadelphia, and New York. For this grand showdown, organized labor marched
some of its best-known personalities to the conflict. Mary Harris "Mother" Jones,
the famous, feisty, and fiery eighty-year-old self-described labor agitator, paraded
down the streets of Calumet and caterwauled blistering speeches to crowds of
thousands. Clarence Darrow, the progressive, celebrity-like lawyer from Chicago,
tried to act as mediator between strikers and a progressive Michigan governor.
Even the American icon (and socialist) Helen Keller donated hundreds of dollars to
the struggle to organize the Michigan copper mines. But amid all this celebrity and
national publicity, the grassroots organization of Copper Country laborers propelled
this workers' revolt.

Calumet, Michigan—this is the place Guthrie attempts to take us to in song. It
is also a place where few outside the local community understand the significance
of the area's history. This is not surprising. Frankly, Calumet and the rest of the
Copper Country are overlooked by most Americans. Peering at or into the numerous

dilapidated buildings of the Copper Country could lead people to believe that with each passing year, time has incrementally but increasingly forgotten this area's historical significance. Though there is a vibrant university community in the Copper Country, the historic significance of the region has been disregarded and forgotten by most Americans and labor historians. Yet there does exist, in the area's architecture, archival records, and local memory, a nostalgic longing to understand the past. But what of this past?

Community in Conflict restores class, conflict, and a working-class perspective to the center of Copper Country history. While these themes have been noticeably absent from earlier writings on the region, we did not need to dig very deep into the region's historic sources to uncover the "hidden history" of labor activism, unionists, radicals, and strikes. Indeed, there was something feverish, something palpable, and something revolutionary occurring in Michigan's Copper Country just after the turn of the twentieth century, and yet few institutions, organizations, or historians have understood—or even sought to understand—the context, scale, and scope of this revolutionary activism. During the early twentieth century, the Copper Country was awash in working-class struggle, and that important perspective has been lost. Lost and forgotten among the stories of copper barons and million-dollar machinery is a people's history. This book delivers that history. The project of this book is to present a history of the Copper Country's forgotten people—the working-class families that have been overlooked by traditional histories that focus on the accomplishments of mine bosses, the paternalistic set of labor relations these employers established, and the "community" life of which these men were at the center.

A Primer on Copper Country History

Michigan's Copper Country, like so many places in America, was signed away on paper from Native Americans. In 1842, what was once the home of migrating Native Americans, fur trappers, and missionaries became a mining frontier. The area was home to the first large mining boom in United States history, and promises of riches in reddish metallic wealth occasioned many a tenderfoot to charge into the Upper Peninsula wilderness. The rush to the area found three relatively standardized periods or phases of mining.[3] In the first period, initial scavenging of the area occurred from roughly the early to mid-1840s through the mid-1860s. This charge to find copper, or prospecting as it might also be termed, commenced at a rather rapid pace. Some came to find wealth, but most found nothing except black flies in the summer, snow in the winter, and intervening frustration. If a prospector was extremely lucky, mineral was discovered, oftentimes in the bottom of ancient Native American quarry pits.[4]

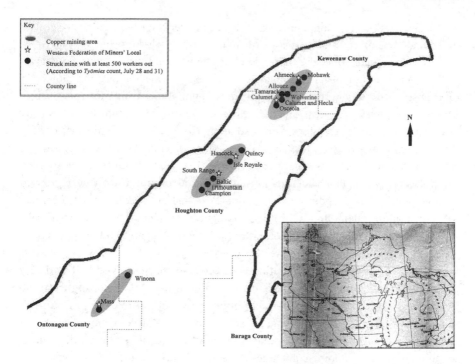

Map of the Keweenaw Peninsula showing principal copper lodes, cities, and Western Federation of Miners headquarters. The inset is a regional map. Keweenaw Map Drawn by Gary Kaunonen; inset map from U.S. Government Publication, 1914.

Once the mineral was discovered, the second phase of mining was the development of copper deposits. Development meant the marshaling and march of resources to isolated areas to remove copper rock from underground and then release the red metal from its rocky reality. This meant the building of temporary mine, milling, and, in some instances, smelting structures to ferret out a paying, minable copper lode from sometimes fickle copper deposits. In the Keweenaw Peninsula, copper generally was found in three "types." Two types of copper brought fame and people to the area, but did little to bring riches. These two variations of the mineral were float copper, which had been scraped from the earth's surface and moved by ancient glaciers, and mass copper, which was found in large, immense, almost globlike formations sometimes weighing thousands of pounds. A third type of mineral, copper rock, was not nearly as impressive or exciting to find as float or mass copper, but copper rock was in fact the red metal that made fortunes. However, due to its placement inside amygdaloidal or conglomerate rock, copper rock needed millions of dollars in capital to be mined and processed on an industrial scale for profit.[5]

In a third phase, once the copper lode was determined to be a paying endeavor, full-scale production began, which included the large-scale building and moving in of industrial resources. This involved the movement of more and more people into the area. In a number of areas, small development camps turned into small company locations beside copper mines. Soon, all along the Keweenaw Peninsula, mining towns began to spring up, and the copper boom was on. So precarious, though, were the financial fortunes of copper companies that more mining endeavors failed than succeeded. Only a select few mines, and thus mining towns, ever grew to include more than a handful of people, but those that did became raucous centers of industrial life. Bars, hotels, brothels, opulent homes, churches, fraternal halls, workers' homes, and other signs of industrial America began to fill in spaces once covered by ancient, towering white pine trees.

The first signs of white habitation were often small, sparsely settled, and very isolated mining camps. From these camps, mining "locations" sprung from the wilderness. Mining locations were community spaces in the Copper Country's machine-fortified industrial setting. These locations were on company property but did not typically house industrial machinery; rather, locations housed the human capital upon which mining companies depended. Workers, and in some instances their families, lived on company property in houses built and maintained by the company. Wealthier mining companies built larger homes, updated these homes regularly, and oftentimes built social spaces for their workers such as libraries, bath-houses, clubhouses, schools, and churches.[6] Unlike the company locations of coal operators in the Appalachians, Copper Country capitalists did not intend to indebt workers to the company by paying in company script. Instead, copper companies on the Keweenaw sought to create an all-inclusive system of social welfare that would lure committed workers and their families to become dependent on the company and the lifestyle it provided in the isolated Copper Country wilderness.

This system of welfare capitalism was in every way a highly standardized and hierarchical system of paternalism. Larry Lankton, a Copper Country historian, concluded that "many companies used paternalism as a bridge between management and labor. One hallmark of paternalism was the belief that life and work were not separate domains, but were interrelated and mutually reinforcing. . . . They involved themselves in workers' private lives by engaging in health, education, and social welfare activities."[7] Made famous by the likes of company towns such as Lowell, Massachusetts; Gary, Indiana; Pullman, Illinois; and even Hershey, Pennsylvania, paternalism was not exclusive or novel to the Copper Country's industrial setting, but like the unique, almost elementally pure copper coming from the ground, paternalism in the Copper Country was somewhat distinctive. Due to the Copper Country's relative isolation on the industrial frontier, a kind of closed-off kingdom developed that caused one observer to remark about social control on the Keweenaw Peninsula, "perhaps no more completely controlled paternalism ever existed in this country than that which developed there."[8]

While paternalism outwardly seems to be a pleasant arrangement for all involved, huge cracks were inherent in the system. In libraries built and funded by mining companies, works by those with viewpoints other than the company line were excluded. For example, a mineworker could not find a WFM union treatise on workers' rights in the stacks of the company library. Schools did not teach a progressive or even liberal education; often working-class students could expect to attend vocational programs at school in which they would be trained for employment in the mining industry while the children of the wealthy or ascending middle-class were prepared for higher education. In most cases curriculum was determined and disseminated in the shadows of giant industrial smokestacks. In one such instance, the Calumet "public" school stood adjacent to the offices of the Calumet & Hecla (C&H) Mining Company, which were located in the company's industrial core. Any talk of worker organization meant the loss of one's job and most everything that accompanied it. In short, underlying paternalism were mechanisms of social control that intended to create a pacified and subservient labor force. A worker's life was for all intents and purposes the company's life.

In general, paternalism rewarded those with roots in Anglo-European Protestant traditions, as well as others who were willing to assimilate to the dominant cultural, economic, political, and social order, while essentially punishing those with "foreign" characteristics and traits who refused to conform. The social hierarchy of the Copper Country was especially rigid. As area copper mines expanded production, more and more bodies were needed to feed the machinery. Early on, successive waves of European immigrants and native-born Americans sought employment in area copper mines and the accompanying copper processing facilities. New immigrant groups, especially those drawn from southern and eastern European backgrounds, were placed at or near the bottom of the region's social hierarchy. Mine managers and superintendents were almost always American or Anglo-European. Mineworkers, especially those on the lowest rungs of the company ladder, were almost always Finnish, Italian, or Slavic.

Once all the company houses were filled by preferred employees, Copper Country capitalists had to find shelter for the other workers. The solution was to develop community spaces off company property, but still in the sphere of mining company influence. For all the early company and town building that occurred during the early twentieth century in the Copper Country, four communities came to prominence during this era. All of these communities were commercial centers, technically not on company-owned land yet certainly and heavily influenced by the copper bosses. Of the countless hamlets, towns, and villages that went from boom to bust, Calumet, Hancock, Houghton, and South Range represent the largest and most significant urban centers in the Copper Country. To cultivate and maintain influence in these commercial and community spaces, the mining companies and men who ran them donated lands for churches, sat on school boards, held most public offices, ran civic and social clubs, either covertly or tacitly owned area newspapers, and parceled out money for endeavors deemed worthwhile.

Historically, mining companies ruled the day in the Copper Country, and this idea of ownership of the region—lock, stock, and barrel—inserted itself in many ways into the working, personal, religious, and social lives of people. This lasting influence of the copper industry can even be observed in such ostensibly benign things as the nicknames of high school athletic teams. As Calumet was once home to some of the largest and wealthiest copper deposits in the world, administered by a powerful oligarchy, what would be a fitting moniker for the local hockey, football, or basketball team? The Copper Kings, of course.

It is on this epic stage of class struggle that the historical actors introduced in *Community in Conflict* reside. Powerful men who ran multi-million dollar mining companies with sometimes iron fists were challenged, chided, and chagrined by the efforts of the local working-class community and their chosen representatives: the Western Federation of Miners. What happened in Michigan's Copper Country in 1913 and 1914 was something tremendous, terrifying, tense, and tragic all at the same time. During this period of great upheaval the Copper Country was a community in conflict and a place on the edge as an extraordinary story unfolded that captured the nation's attention. The 1913–14 Michigan Copper Strike was an incredibly important event in American history and, just like Woody Guthrie, we think Calumet, the Copper Country, and the history of the area's workers are rather exceptional.

CHAPTER 1

Context

The Calumet and Hecla corporation has been able for many years to chloroform its slaves
and others by the "benevolent feudalism" it so zealously practiced.

—*Solidarity*

ON THE AFTERNOON OF APRIL 4, 1914, JOSEPH CANNON OF THE WESTERN FED-
eration of Miners (WFM) was addressing a group of radicals and workers with
news of the great Copper Country Strike still under way in Michigan's Keweenaw
Peninsula. The well-attended speech was delivered to some of the leading lights of
American radicalism, including Carlo Tresca and Alexander Berkman. In spite, or
perhaps because, of the significance of the topic as well as the notoriety of those in
the crowd, the speech was broken up by police who clubbed their way through the
crowd, attacking and injuring some of the attendees. While the subject of Cannon's
speech was the Michigan Copper Strike, the event occurred more than a thousand
miles away in the heart of New York City. That a speaker could draw a large crowd
in the center of urban America to hear a speech about a copper strike in an isolated
corner of the country was proof positive of the strike's relevance to the nation's labor
and left-wing movements.[1]

As this incident suggests, the Michigan Copper Strike was a conflict of great national significance. However, most of the key features of Copper Country labor relations—including important aspects of the 1913–14 strike—were not unique to the region, but part of much larger historical trends sweeping across industrial America. These include the forms of anti-unionism practiced by Copper Country employers, the roles of political progressivism and socialism in shaping the industrial relations landscape, and the place of paternalism in quieting worker organization. In the Copper Country, as in numerous other industrial battlegrounds, employers and their allies resorted to mass, organized violence in order to quell worker organization. Indeed, while some scholars have analyzed the unique attributes of Copper Country labor and industrial history, the parallels between its most famous conflict and other contemporary labor events ending in violence such as the Triangle Shirtwaist Factory Fire, the Lawrence Textile Strike, the Ludlow Strike, and the various "massacres" of Industrial Workers of the World (IWW, or "Wobblies") members in the Pacific Northwest are quite striking. In many of these conflicts, including the Copper Country Strike, citizens' alliance groups—vigilante businessmen's groups formed to attack and destroy unions and radical associations—were used to disrupt the strikes and destroy the organizations leading the strike.

Despite its significance to U.S. history, the 1913–14 strike has been met with a wall of silence by those writing general histories of American labor. It goes unmentioned in most surveys of American labor history. Furthermore, evidence that the strike has not penetrated the national consciousness can be seen by its exclusion from American history textbooks.

Regardless of its exclusion from twenty-first century general U.S. and labor history texts, the Copper Country Strike was without question among the most significant labor conflicts during a decade full of labor militancy, political radicalism, and antilabor violence. The strike was waged for nine long months through a brutal Copper Country winter between an interethnic group of strikers united under the banner of the WFM and a well-organized, aggressive, and ruthless group of employers. Those employers emerged victorious in a struggle that drove the WFM deep into debt and contributed to a period of major decline in the fortunes of one of the most militant unions of all time.[2]

The strike also led to a major congressional investigation, as members of the U.S. House of Representatives conducted an analysis of labor relations in the Copper Country, trying to, in the words of Edward T. Taylor, chairman of the Subcommittee on Mines and Mining, "make a thorough and complete investigation of the conditions existing in and about the copper mines in the counties of Houghton, Keweenaw, and Ontonagon, in the State of Michigan."[3] Ultimately, the strike's greatest significance came in its most tragic episode when between seventy-three and seventy-nine members of striking workers' families were killed during the Italian Hall tragedy, one of the greatest losses of life in all of labor history.[4]

One measure of the strike's significance was the great deal of press coverage that it received. Throughout late 1913 and early 1914, the Copper Country and its labor war were the frequent subjects of articles written in national newspapers such as the *New York Times*, *Los Angeles Times*, and *Boston Daily Globe*.[5] In response to events at Italian Hall, the *New York Times* ran a long, detailed piece commenting on the tragedy, while contextualizing it as part of a wider struggle between workers and employers. The article read: "Calumet, which has been the scene of so much disorder by reason of the copper strike, is almost in a state of terror to-night as the result of the catastrophe. . . . The foreign miners of the district are enraged and grief-stricken over the disaster."[6]

While mainstream newspapers carried regular news of the Michigan Copper Strike, the struggle always remained a labor conflict, one that was widely supported by many sectors of the American labor and radical movements. Thus, the *International Socialist Review* covered the strike heavily, writing long, detailed reports of the strikers' courage in the face of employer violence. One such article read: "So far they have been unable to intimidate the miners. The men are standing firmly. Parades are held every day along the 28 miles which comprise the range. Meetings of from three to six thousand are held every day in Calumet, Hancock, South Range, and Mass City. There is no sign of weakening on the part of the men."[7]

Keen observers of the labor movement likewise understood the implications of the strike, noting that it stood to possibly reshape the nature of U.S. labor relations. Thus, national figures in the labor and leftist movements of the United States visited the strike zone seeking to investigate and report upon the conflict or aid the strike. This group included Charles Moyer, president of the WFM; John Mitchell, vice president of the American Federation of Labor (AFL) and longtime United Mine Workers of America (UMWA) official; and Mary Harris "Mother" Jones, the labor organizer known as "the miners' angel."[8] During his speech on August 22, Mitchell informed a large crowd that the AFL sympathized with the WFM during the strike and was committed "to better the conditions of life and labor for the miners in this field."[9] Mitchell also appealed to workers across the country to aid the Michigan strikers. In Butte, Montana, the labor leader asked that city's workers to stand by their fellow miners "through thick and thin," and stated that "every labor organization in the United States should really support the Michigan men."[10]

Labor and Violence in the Early Twentieth Century

The presence of Mitchell, Moyer, Jones, and other noted members of the American labor movement certainly generated enthusiasm among the Copper Country strikers, but their presence at the strike scene should not be taken as an indication that the 1913–14 Michigan Copper Strike was a uniquely climactic or violent struggle. Instead, the copper miners' strike occurred in a period of great labor tumult as strikes, labor riots, free speech fights, and tragedies occurred across the nation. The Triangle Shirtwaist Fire in New York City and the Ludlow Massacre in Colorado, two of the most notable tragedies in the history of American labor, share significant characteristics with the Italian Hall tragedy.

Just two years before the events at Italian Hall, on March 25, 1911, a fire broke out at the Triangle Shirtwaist Factory, which employed hundreds of mostly young, female laborers. The fire quickly engulfed the building as well as the workers, who were unable to escape the blaze because their bosses had locked or blockaded the exits. All told, 146 workers perished in the fire, while an untold number of others were hurt. Decrying the act she blamed on the factory owners, socialist Clara Lemlich argued that if "Triangle had been a union shop there would not have been any locked doors, and the girls would have been on the street almost an hour before the fire started."[11] A circular distributed at the victims' funeral went further, urging workers to "never forgive the enemies of our class."[12] Many Copper Country workers no doubt saw parallels between this so-called industrial accident and the deaths of their children during the Italian Hall tragedy on Christmas Eve 1913.

Three years later, at roughly the same time as the Michigan Copper Strike, 10,000 coal miners struck in southern Colorado, leading to one of the longest-running, bloodiest labor conflicts in United States history. A bitter climax to the strike was reached on April 20, 1914, when Colorado militiamen attacked one of the strikers' tent colonies, set fire to the tents, and rained machine-gun fire down upon the colony. At least thirteen people, including at least eleven children, died in the massacre.[13] The killings caused outrage across the nation, as workers, unionists, radicals, and others described the troops in terms appropriate for mass murderers.[14] The cover of the June 1914 issue of the *Masses*, a socialist magazine, featured a cartoon image of an armed Ludlow striker protecting his wife and children against the armed militiamen who killed men, women, and children during the great Colorado coal strike.[15]

The Triangle Shirtwaist Fire, the Colorado coal strike, as well as several other labor conflicts in which workers were the victims of murder or large-scale accidental killings, also set the stage for the most infamous event of the 1913–14 strike, the Italian Hall tragedy on Christmas Eve 1913. Shock and disbelief were only two of the many reactions expressed by the public at the loss of life suffered by Copper Country working families on December 24, 1913. Among the striking miners, their families, and their supporters around the globe, however, a more common reaction was anger, for these groups blamed the employers and their allies for the deaths of so many children. Charles Moyer labeled the tragedy a "mass murder," as did the staffs of *Työmies*, the Hancock-based newspaper of the Finnish Socialist Federation (FSF), and the *Miners' Magazine*, the newspaper of the WFM.[16] Even the *New York Times* reported that if the person who yelled "Fire!" was caught, he would meet a violent end at the hands of angry Michigan workers. On the day after the tragedy, the newspaper commented: "Every policeman and detective in this region is searching to-night for the man who gave the false alarm of fire, and if he is caught he will probably be lynched."[17]

The deaths resulting from the Italian Hall tragedy were without question the most painful and notorious acts of violence experienced by the strikers and their families. But those were far from the only casualties suffered by Copper Country workers during the period of the strike. Strikers Steve Putrich and Alois Tijan were shot dead by mine guards and Waddell-Mahon Detective Agency gun thugs on August 14, while Margaret Fazekas, a fourteen-year-old girl who was picketing on September 1, was shot in the back of the head by local law enforcement. Describing her injury, Fazekas commented that "Dr. Roach said some of my brain came out, but he put it back in again, and he took a bone out of it—a small bone."[18] Additionally, WFM president Charles Moyer was shot on December 26, 1913, in a Hancock hotel and deported from town by a group of ruffians he described as "New York gangsters."[19]

While these violent acts differed dramatically from the day-to-day social conditions of Copper Country residents, they were by no means unique in terms of early twentieth-century labor relations. In fact, the period of labor violence that marked the Michigan copper miners' strike can best be understood as one of the many "labor wars" that occurred across the nation between the Gilded Age and World War II. Thus, the various forms of antilabor violence experienced by Copper Country workers were only one part—albeit a significant part—of the war upon labor activists by employers and antilabor state officials across the nation.[20]

It is only within the context of these various "labor wars" that the antilabor violence experienced in the Copper Country during 1913 and 1914 can be understood. Indeed, throughout the early twentieth century, unionists, strikers, and radicals were subjected to beatings, torture, murders, arrests, frame-ups, and long prison sentences for their political beliefs and actions. Among the favorite targets for physical abuse were members of the IWW, whose activism—as well as persecution—was national in scope in the years after the union was founded in 1905. The historian and journalist Patrick Renshaw captured part of this violence in a chapter of his book *The Wobblies: The Story of the IWW and Syndicalism in the United States* entitled "Three Martyrs," in which he describes the lives, activism, and deaths at the hands of employers or anti-union state officials of Wobbly activists Joe Hill, Frank Little, and Wesley Everest.[21]

Still, Hill's, Little's, and Everest's deaths were only the tip of the iceberg of violence experienced by the IWW. John Alar, a striking Croatian immigrant mine-worker, was shot dead by company guards during the 1916 Mesabi Range Strike, while Wobblies were gunned down in the cities of Everett and Aberdeen, Washington, and lynched in Butte, Montana, and Centralia, Washington.[22] During the 1913 Paterson, New Jersey, silk strike, Valentino Modestino was killed by an imported gun thug.[23] Reacting to Modestino's murder, William "Big Bill" Haywood both excoriated the acts of the killers and praised the heroism of strikers willing to brave the dangerous picket lines: "In spite of being subjected to such indignities, the strikers are no sooner released than they go back on the picket line, there to face the assassins, detectives, and thugs employed by the manufacturers. They have not been backward about firing their guns into crowds of strikers, as was shown by the case of Valentino Modestino, who was killed by two detectives who aimed at the strikers."[24]

Strikebreakers

While violence was a common feature of early twentieth-century labor struggles, municipal police forces were only occasionally the perpetrators of the violent acts committed against labor activists and strikers. Considering that small municipal police forces were usually unable to serve as effective strikebreakers against union-ists or strikers that outnumbered them by many-to-one, local officials sometimes turned to deputizing private citizens, allowing them to break strikes—and sometimes strikers' bones—all with the sanction of the state.

These groups, which were frequently allied with employers' organizations such as local chambers of commerce, were organized throughout North America, mobilizing local "citizens" to attack strikers and uproot unions in places as diverse as St. Louis, Minneapolis, Winnipeg, and San Diego.[25] In many places, including the Copper Country, these groups were called citizens' committees or citizens' alliances, and because these forces were mobilized to break strikes, it should come as no surprise that their ranks frequently included members of the employing class. During the 1911–12 Aberdeen, Washington, free speech fight, more than 500 businessmen formed a citizens' committee and were deputized in the municipal police force. The group harassed, physically assaulted, and arrested Wobblies.[26] One of the committee members provided a report of how they handled the radicals: "We organized that night a vigilante committee—a Citizens' Committee, I think we called it—to put down the strike by intimidation and force. . . . We got hundreds of heavy clubs of the weight and size of pick-handles, armed our vigilantes with them, and that night raided all the IWW headquarters, rounded up as many of them as we could find, and escorted them out of town."[27]

These so-called citizens' committees were mobilized with great effect at rounding up and intimidating strikers and disrupting strikers' public displays. In San Diego, an informal citizens' committee consisting of vigilantes assisted local police and employers in their efforts to restrict IWW members from speaking on the city's streets. Abram R. Sauer, the editor of a pro–free speech newspaper who was attacked by the San Diego vigilantes, concluded that "the personnel of the vigilantes represents not only the bankers and merchants but has [as] its workers leading Church members and bartenders. Chamber of Commerce and the Real Estate Board are well represented."[28]

Employers utilized similar tactics in the Copper Country. Arrests and mass roundups by municipal police and members of the Citizens' Alliance were common occurrences during the Copper Country Strike, as workers were arrested and jailed for a dizzying array of "offenses" ranging from "intimidation" and "profanity" to carrying concealed weapons and inciting to riot. Certainly, hundreds of arrested strikers were charged with crimes that did actually exist in the Michigan law books, but many of these arrests were repressive tactics to remove strikers and their allies from public circulation or punish them for successfully pursuing the strikers' goals.[29] The most obvious examples of partisan arrests and jailings occurred as strikers were arrested for participating in strike parades and picket lines. Such was the case on October 8 when seven men and one woman were arrested and charged with carrying concealed weapons and "intimidation" while attempting to maintain picket lines.[30] Others were arrested and jailed based on little more than the whim of deputized citizens. Joseph A. Dunnigan, an eighteen-year-old living at Ahmeek, was arrested in his front yard and held at gunpoint by deputies on December 17 simply because he had walked outside of his home while deputies were conducting "business" in his neighborhood.[31]

Joining police officers and deputized citizens were imported strikebreakers, hired thugs, scabs, and labor spies brought into the region by mine owners and professional scab-herding services, companies that specialized in recruiting replacement workers for use in strikes. In fact, from the late nineteenth century up until the 1913–14 strike, the Copper Country crawled with labor spies from the Pinkerton, Thiel, and other detective agencies. Labor spies have nearly as long a historical pedigree in the United States as labor unions themselves. Their continued use throughout much of the nineteenth and twentieth centuries can be attributed to spies' successful infiltration of unions and their ability to destroy workers' organizations.[32]

In many states, from 1900 forward the most prominent of these detective agencies was the Thiel Detective Service. Gus Thiel, the agency's founder, worked as a Pinkerton agent during the 1860s before setting out on his own in 1873 when he moved to St. Louis and then Chicago to set up his own agency.[33] Within a decade the agency was thriving, with branches scattered throughout the United States, particularly in the West where the Thiel agents became the dominant force in their industry.[34]

In addition to labor spies, employers throughout the nation effectively mobilized strikebreakers during labor conflicts. Strikebreaking services were usually based in a single or multiple locations, but their reach was truly national. Writing of the strikebreaking firm Bergoff Brothers and Waddell of New York, the historian Stephen J. Norwood noted that the agency "promised it could supply 10,000 strikebreakers to a corporation within seventy-two hours, mobilizing probably more men more quickly than the federal government could."[35]

Copper Country workers had good reason to be fearful of the imported strike-breakers who, with no ties to the community and frequently with the knowledge that they would escape prosecution for any crimes they might commit, stood ready to perform nearly any task that got them closer to their bosses' goal of bringing about a favorable conclusion to the strike. During the 1913–14 strike, strikebreakers from the Waddell-Mahon Detective Agency and Ascher Detective Agency were brought into the embattled region beginning as early as August, and immediately set to work protecting the mine owners' interests.

The presence of these imported "thugs" proved to be a source of anxiety for strikers and their families, who were concerned both for their personal safety and for the moral affront that came with having hired ruffians, a group widely known for their abuses, occupying their communities. Frank Domegrovich, one of the mineworkers on strike in 1913–14, described in broken English, the fear he and his family experienced when their home was raided by two soldiers and two deputized citizens in the middle of a December night during the strike. He stated that the intruders "came down from upstairs downstairs, and I told them 'Don't go in the room, because they make my children scared.' They don't care anything, and they went in the room looking around. Our three rooms that was downstairs, they look around. They have revolver. Children wake up, they was make too scared, my family and children."[36]

Hired thugs were not the only group imported into the Copper Country to break the miners' strike. Large numbers of scabs were also transported into the region, as scab-herders roamed far and wide to recruit men to take the strikers' jobs. In fact, scab-recruiting agencies functioned in most large American cities during the late nineteenth and early twentieth centuries, recruiting members of what Marx called the "reserve army of labor" and shipping these workers into strike zones to break strikes. Between 1881 and 1900, more than 500,000 scabs were hired to break strikes in the United States, with more than 40 percent of the workers being imported from outside into various strike zones.[37]

One group of companies that aided and abetted the Copper Country mine owners were so-called employment bureaus, businesses that recruited and supplied scabs to companies experiencing labor troubles. The threat of strikes was so great that large Copper Country mining companies like the Quincy Mining Company were approached by "investigators" such as the Burr-Herr Company, which in 1907 had offices in Chicago and Pittsburgh, with offers to provide scab-herding services. F. C. Herr, one of the company's bosses, wrote Quincy General Manager Charles Lawton offering to "get some business in our line," and noting that "we make a specialty of handling strikes, furnishing men to fill the places of strikers, and protect[ing] property."[38] During the copper strike of 1913–14, mine companies searched frantically for men who were capable of operating mining equipment and willing to serve as scabs during a nationally known labor conflict. Thus, in December 1913 Lawton must have been pleased when the Youngstown Employment Bureau and Employment Agency, based in Youngstown, Ohio, offered to "furnish you with men of good character, no trouble-makers. Men that are sober, reliable, and willing to work."[39]

As a major conflict involving thousands of workers, the Copper Country strike presented itself as an ideal opportunity for professional scab-herders to render their services for Michigan's mine owners. In fact, during the strike, Calumet & Hecla (C&H) alone employed at least 942 scabs; more than 700 of them were working-class immigrants imported from outside the Copper Country. Men came by the hundreds from Michigan's Lower Peninsula and from Illinois, while dozens more were lured from Wisconsin, Minnesota, North Dakota, and Pennsylvania to help break the copper miners' strike.[40]

Harry T. Parks, a twenty-four-year-old native-born American living in Detroit, was recruited in that city by August Beck, who lured the prospective worker to the mines under false pretenses. Parks was told on January 14, 1914, that "all the men had gone back to work excepting a few anarchists and socialists," and "there was no trouble at all" in the Copper Country.[41] In order to secure enough scabs for the big job of breaking the strike, Beck and his associates forcibly transported the men to the Copper Country, accompanied by armed guards who prevented the men from escaping their fate as scabs. After realizing that he was headed for a strike zone, Parks tried to escape in Saginaw, Michigan, but was prevented from doing so by an armed guard. Upon his arrival in the Copper Country, Parks again noticed that his prospects for escape were limited. While he was scabbing, Parks was forced to live in a bunkhouse under constant watch by four to six armed guards who refused to let him go anywhere other than the mine where he worked and the bunkhouse where he slept.

Testifying before a congressional committee tasked with investigating the strike, Parks recalled his desire to stop working but inability to escape these guards stating: "I tried [to escape] several times. . . . I didn't care to run away. I didn't want anyone to attack me. Everyone you would see around there had a gun or a club and a gun."[42] Another man being transported in order to scab on the copper miners made a more dramatic escape attempt. Parks described "one man [who] tried to jump out of the window," but the guards "brought him back and sat him down in a seat and watched him to see that he didn't try it again."[43]

Progressives and Socialists

The Copper Country, as well as the state of Michigan at large, was fully caught up in the Progressive movement of the early twentieth century. This was most clearly visible in the realm of electoral politics, as Michigan Progressives such as Governor Woodbridge N. Ferris and Congressman William J. MacDonald were elected while championing Progressive platforms.[44] Ferris, a Democratic politician and schoolmaster originally from New York, drew significant support from working-class voters. As the Democratic standard-bearer for governor, Ferris possessed many of the key characteristics of a Progressive. The governor viewed the state as a force for positive change, a view he shared with other Progressives. Ferris's Progressive *bona fides* were testified to by numerous contemporaries, including Charles Moore, who in his book *The History of Michigan* described Ferris as

> a strong Wilson Progressive Democrat, and has shown in his general attitude toward public affairs such a spirit of insight, of co-operation, of tactful good nature, and of progressiveness that he enjoys to a remarkable degree the confidence of the people of Michigan as a whole and it is said that in the campaign of 1914 he received at least 60,000 normally Republican votes. In many ways Governor Ferris has helped lead the progressive and well-considered program of legislation undertaken in the state during the last three years, and special praise has been given to his admirable handling of the strike in the Michigan copper regions during 1913–1914. In sending the entire National Guard of Michigan to the scene, he showed a vigor and promptness and determination which at once overawed the forces of lawlessness, and handled the various problems which subsequently arose so diplomatically that not a single life was sacrificed through

any fault of the militia. Since the peaceful solution of those difficulties, practically all parties have united in admiring the impartial and straightforward stand taken by the governor.[45]

Others, including members of the Copper Country labor movement, presented an alternative interpretation of Ferris's actions during the strike, criticizing the Guard as a group of thugs and scab-herders.[46]

Ferris certainly alienated large parts of his working-class constituency by using the Michigan National Guard to break the strike, but the use of state power by "progressive" politicians to break strikes was by no means limited to the Ferris. Instead, Progressives, like their more conservative counterparts, demonstrated their willingness to aid employers in struggles with their employees. Thus, during the 1912 IWW free speech fight in Aberdeen, Washington, the noted Progressive Washington governor Marion E. Hay offered to send in the National Guard to assist local employers in their efforts to expel the IWW from Aberdeen.[47] In August 1913, "progressive" governor of California Hiram Johnson sent the National Guard to Wheatland after a mass meeting of agricultural workers led by the IWW was violently dispersed by local police.[48] One socialist writer described the use of the Guard as an attack on the working class: "It was PROGRESSIVE Governor Johnson of California who sent his soldiers to Sacramento, armed with guns, to help drive members of your class and MY class out of that city because they were unable to secure work."[49]

While at times seemingly unsympathetic to local workers' struggles, there were a number of major legislative accomplishments by Progressives. Mostly these victories included protecting working people from the depredations of unregulated capitalism. Workers' compensation and child labor laws, as well as legislation limiting the legal hours of work, were passed in all major industrial states between 1910 and 1917.[50] The Michigan workers' compensation law was particularly significant to Copper Country miners, for theirs was an especially dangerous, deadly industry, and the law was designed to provide "compensation for the accidental injury to or death of employees, and restricting the right to compensation or damages in such cases as are provided by this act."[51] Thereafter, for the first time in Copper Country history, injured workers and the families of hurt or deceased workers had the opportunity to seek recourse for injuries sustained on the job.[52]

To the ideological left of the Progressive movement were the socialists. A second major social and political movement to emerge during the late nineteenth and early twentieth centuries, socialists formed a number of national political parties, local and state branches of those parties, and foreign-language organizations within those parties.[53] The socialists gained much of their strength from hundreds of leftist newspapers, scores of social clubs and auxiliaries, and several labor unions such as the WFM, United Brewery Workers, and International Shingle Weavers' Union that had socialist leaderships and political platforms.[54] Moreover, in places as diverse as Lawrence, Massachusetts; Hartford, Arkansas; Aberdeen, Washington; and Hancock, Michigan, socialists crafted a rich cultural life, usually based at local halls, which featured a wide variety of social and cultural activities, such as sporting events, dances, picnics, and parades.[55] Indeed, the public presence of local socialist parties was often most visible during annual May Day parades or other assorted mass marches used to support political candidates or strikers, or to protest some antilabor action taken by the state or capitalists.

Among the most impressive accomplishments of American socialists was the creation and maintenance of their large and diverse press. While New York, Massachusetts, and Illinois all had lively left-wing presses, many of the most successful newspapers and socialist journals came out of the lower Midwest in states such as Oklahoma and Kansas.[56] The most successful socialist news organ was *Appeal to Reason*, a weekly published in Girard, Kansas, between 1897 and 1922. At its height, the *Appeal* had upward of one million subscribers, a number that no doubt underestimated the newspaper's readership.[57] Considering that socialist literature appealed most heavily to working people, some of whom were too itinerant or poor to receive regular subscriptions to the *Appeal to Reason* or other newspapers, it is likely that much of the Left read dog-eared, crumpled issues that were passed around the local socialist hall, factory, or saloon. The national scale of the socialist press certainly helped generate support for the struggles of working people occurring in out-of-the-way places such as Michigan's Keweenaw Peninsula.

The English-language socialist press succeeded in reaching a large part of the American socialist readership; however, across the nation and especially in socialist strongholds with large immigrant populations such as Chicago and New York City, the socialist press appeared in many different languages. A host of foreign-language periodicals were printed by a diverse group of immigrant socialists in Chicago. These included daily socialist newspapers written in Czech, German, Yiddish, and Slovene, as well as in English.[58] Large metropolitan areas were not the only places of high foreign-language readership; Finnish socialists published newspapers in Fitchburg, Massachusetts; Astoria, Oregon; and Hancock, Michigan.[59]

The diversity of languages no doubt increased the reach of socialists in the United States, and in some communities such as Hancock, the socialist movement was primarily an immigrant movement whose members, in this case, spoke, wrote, and read in the Finnish language.[60] The *International Socialist Review* remarked upon the importance of the Finnish socialist press to the Left in the Copper Country: "A

Finnish Socialist daily was established in Hancock called *Työmies* (The Working Man), and the plant is today valued at $40,000. This paper, and the fighting rank and file of Finns, are the brains and backbone of the copper strike; their strikers are always on the picket line; their paper has been an invincible barricade."[61]

Paternalism and Company Towns

While Copper Country mineworkers, their family members, and other workers did form socialist organizations and strike during the early twentieth century, it is true that only a minority of Copper Country workers mobilized to overthrow—or even dramatically reform—capitalism. Moreover, until the copper strike of 1913–14, the region's labor conflicts were relatively short-lived and minor in scope and scale. Even the more impressive labor upsurges, such as the 1905 Houghton County Streetcar Strike and 1906 Rockland Strike, which will be analyzed more fully in later chapters, were fought over bread-and-butter issues such as the right to join a union, wage increases, and safer conditions rather than a major reshaping of the ways Copper Country mining companies did business. Some scholars have interpreted the relative absence of radical class consciousness in the Copper Country as being, in part, the result of the benevolent paternalism shown by mine bosses to workers.[62]

Certainly, Michigan copper companies exercised some degree of benevolence in relations with the region's workers. Workers in copper mines, and their families, received in exchange for their long and difficult hours of labor, subsidized housing in a company dwelling, free water for that house, reduced home heating prices, as well as free trash pickup and home maintenance.[63] But paternalism had a darker side as well. Mine bosses censored the reading materials available at company-run libraries and spied upon employees to guard against union activities.[64] Taking a critical look at mine owner paternalism, T. F. G. Dougherty, a member of the IWW, criticized the system that he acknowledged succeeded at dampening workers' freedoms:

> The Calumet and Hecla corporation has been able for many years to chloroform its slaves and others by the "benevolent feudalism" it so zealously practiced. It furnished water and electric lights, schools and hospitals, old age pension funds (of which they "generously permitted" the workers to pay part) and "cheap" house rents and many other "humanitarian" tricks which had the effect of lulling the slaves to sleep and brought forth loud and prolonged praise from mealy mouthed sky pilots, hypocritical "reformers," the prostitutes of capitalist press, the readers, and all the other parasites who are supported out of the proceeds of the robbery of the workers.[65]

Employers as well as their boosters in the corporate press tended to propose kinder interpretations of the system of "benevolent" paternalism in use throughout the Copper Country. Writing in the *Engineering and Mining Journal*, an industry organ, Claude T. Rice described the positive impact that company paternalism had on the Copper Country's workforce, concluding that "the miners stay contentedly in these Lake Superior mining camps."[66]

An illustration of how the ostensibly benevolent acts of mine owners might be used to their advantage in labor relations can be seen in the case of the subsidized housing owned by the mine companies, which could provide employers with additional leverage against workers during strikes. If a mining family lived in a company house and then struck, management not only cut off the workers' paychecks but could also evict residents from their homes. During questioning at the congressional investigation of the conditions in the Copper Country and of the copper strike, one of the investigators probed Croatian immigrant mineworker Louis Zargnl for a response as to why he had a right to remain in a company-owned house while on strike against that company:

The CHAIRMAN. I will tell you, Judge, I think the committee would like to get his idea as to what he thought about remaining there on the company's property, and what he considered might be his rights, if any, concerning both light and water and the use of the property. I would like to have his ideas and his version of the matter. Possibly counsel might put it a little bit fairer to him, but, nevertheless, I want him to give us his idea.

(To the witness.) What did you think about your living in the company's house? It was the company's house, wasn't it?

The WITNESS. Yes

The CHAIRMAN. It was the company's ground?

The WITNESS. Yes.

The CHAIRMAN. And the company was furnishing you light?

The WITNESS. Yes.

The CHAIRMAN. And water?

The WITNESS. Yes.

The CHAIRMAN. What did you think about your using this property belonging to the company? How long did you expect to continue to use that? What was your idea about this matter?

The WITNESS. Well, any time I working I was willing to pay.

The CHAIRMAN. But if the strike was not settled in a year or two years, did you expect to stay there right along and use the light and water and the company's house all while without paying anything?

The WITNESS. Well, I told them if it comes tight like that. I can get out and make different. They got three-quarters of the houses empty, pretty close. I couldn't tell exactly. Pretty close. There is difference. It was tight.

The CHAIRMAN. What I want to get at is this: Did you think you had any particular length of time, 30 days or 90 days or 6 months or any particular time within which you had a right to stay there or to use this company's property? What did you think about it? Did you think you could stay there as long as you pleased?

The WITNESS. Well, I stay there so long as they chase me away; that is all. I didn't have no money to move. When they chase me away I have got to go some place.[67]

Complementing employer ownership over workers' homes was the mine owners' control of company hospitals, which enabled employers to determine the quality and quantity of health care, as well as who would receive that care.[68] The Slovenian immigrant writer and editor Ivan Molek, who worked as a trammer, or unskilled laborer, pushing around thousand-pound rock cars for ten-hour shifts, described how company-run medical care was used to maintain a degree of control over workers' lives: "Work at C. & H. imposed an obligation on one. No absence without a legitimate excuse! Declaring illness was no help, since the company controlled the health services. To be sick meant to see the company doctor. To plead a headache as cause for absence due to drink meant that, first, the person got a warming; the second time he was laid off without recourse."[69]

Neither paternalism nor company towns were unique to the Copper Country during the early twentieth century. In fact, from the mining towns of West Virginia to the mill towns of the Pacific Northwest and the infamous town of Pullman, Illinois, where Pullman railroad cars were built, employers sought to re-create feudal manors across industrial America, ones complete with corporate ownership of land, buildings, and services.[70] Responding to the power the Grays Harbor Commercial Company exerted over the lives of the residents of Cosmopolis, Washington, one area newspaper opined that the company controlled "everything from its school affairs to the extortionate water system. The manager of the company controls the vote of the town."[71] In the lead-up to the West Virginia "coal wars" of 1912–13, the socialist organizer and writer Theresa Malkiel described the large degree of employer control over most aspects of workers' lives:

The company owns the shacks in which the miners live all along the line for about twenty miles, and when a man offends in the least, he not only loses his job, but has to move; the man cannot find shelter anywhere along the line nor any work even in adjoining mines. If you bear in mind that the miner seldom sees any cash and has no means to go elsewhere, you can realize in what state of abject slavery the miners are kept. They are paid by the month and having no cash must buy the provisions from the company store and pay 100 per cent more for every article.[72]

As Malkiel's words indicate, the paternalistic control of industrial towns and mine locations were replicated from coast to coast, and were sometimes a cause of worker protests. And, as occurred in industrial towns like Pullman and the mining regions of West Virginia, in the Copper Country, employer paternalism did not prevent local workers from organizing and striking.

CHAPTER 2

Community

All afternoon and evening hundreds of people were in the grove and all had a good time. Nothing happened to mar the pleasant day, making the day an ideal one. The members of the different unions were well pleased with the success of their celebration.

—*Daily Mining Gazette*, September 7, 1909

ON SEPTEMBER 1, 1913, UNIONIZED WORKERS THROUGHOUT THE COPPER COUNTRY joined their family members and supporters in celebrating Labor Day. However, this holiday differed substantially from earlier Labor Days as it occurred in the middle of the 1913–14 Michigan Copper Strike. The *Miners' Bulletin*, the organ of the striking mineworkers, reported the size of the celebration as well as the dedication of the workers who turned out: "Labor Day at Hancock witnessed the largest gathering in its history. The miners from Painesdale and South Range formed in parade and marched in celebration, the former walking nine miles to reach the parade." The *Bulletin* continued by remarking upon the commitment of the working men and women who turned out to celebrate *their* day: "The day was devoted to education. There was no place or opportunity for games. The crowd seemed intent on learning the significance of labor day and listened to a discussion of labor's problems. The struggles in this district had put everyone in an attentive mood and it is doubtful if any group of speakers ever faced a more attentive audience."[1]

Joining the union men were a number of working-class women, members of local unions as well as the Hancock Ladies' Auxiliary of the Western Federation of Miners (WFM).[2] Collectively, the men and women, native-born and immigrant, skilled and unskilled members of the Copper Country working class, united on Labor Day 1913 to stake their claim to the public space of the region's cities and towns. By 1913, these types of working-class demonstrations were common in the region, but they were also the products of decades of class-based organizing. Indeed, beginning in the late nineteenth century, Copper Country workers formed unions, struck, and crafted a distinctly working-class culture based in public demonstrations and celebrations. By 1913, the Copper Country's labor movement, including its radical elements, was committed to protecting the workers' status as major stakeholders in the community.

In contrast to Copper Country workers, whose presence in the community rested upon their numbers, public displays through parades and picket lines, and buildings owned and operated by their organizations, employers' status in the community rested largely upon their ownership of the majority of community spaces, their control over workplaces, their ability to hire and fire workers as they saw fit, their support from the local press, and their wealth. Indeed, employers' ownership of private property throughout the Copper Country gave them power in a number of arenas. It enabled them to exert control over the mainstream press, "convince" their employees to cross picket lines, and run proemployer candidates for local office. This conception of employers and community differs substantially from that posited by the historian Arthur Thurner, whose chapter "Community Builders" from the book *Strangers and Sojourners: A History of Michigan's Keweenaw Peninsula* is entirely dedicated to extolling the virtues of Copper Country employers and their efforts to make the region's towns "almost model communit[ies]."[3] To Thurner, employers deserved their elevated positions in the community because their wealth had been responsible for developing the region, carving mines and towns out of the wilderness. Moreover, employers formed their own "unions" (employers' organizations to assert and defend their class interests) and built structures, published literature, and sought alliances with other community groups to maintain control over the community and its workplaces. After all, their money had paid the men to dig the mines, had built the homes and stores, and had connected the region to the outside world.[4]

But mine owners and high-ranking mine officers represented but a tiny minority of the Copper Country's residents, and it was clear that much of the population would have disagreed with Thurner's assertions about the community. In fact, the

Copper Country was not some peaceful backwater void of conflict, but a region rife with divisions including those of race, ethnicity, gender, and class. The divisions did not exist solely in the region's mines. They existed throughout the Copper Country's numerous towns, villages, and mine locations, all of which were organized around the principles of industrial capitalism. Workers and employers squared off along the region's docks, in its breweries, and at its building sites. Workers, and not just miners, from a vast array of trades formed unions to defend their class interests, and it was largely through these unions that Copper Country laborers laid their claims to the community.

The Early Labor Movement

The first large-scale unionization of Copper Country workers occurred under the Knights of Labor, which established at least eighteen branches in the Upper Peninsula between 1885 and 1888. Formed in 1869, the Knights sought to create a class-conscious industrial union movement, one that drew in the entire working class: men and women regardless of race, ethnicity, or skill. The historian Melvyn Dubofsky described the organization as "the only prominent, national organization in existence, [and thus] the Knights grew rapidly from 1879 to 1886. By 1886 membership approached one million."[5]

Copper Country workers formed seven Knights of Labor locals. Six of the branches were formed in Houghton County and the other one in Baraga County. Some of the unionized laborers were miners. Calumet & Hecla (C&H) mine officers exchanged hurried messages during the 1880s and early 1890s, warning against the threat posed by the Knights and discussing rationales for dismissing Knights' members.[6] However, most of the branches organized were "mixed locals," unions formed by workers hoping to accomplish many of the same goals but drawn from different industries. One of the branches, Hancock Local 6569, was formed by cigar makers in 1886 and remained an active local for two years before folding in 1888.[7] Perhaps more significant, Assembly 1128 in Lake Linden included both male and female members, establishing itself as an early exemplar of mixed-sex unionism in a region where men comprised the overwhelming majority of union members throughout the late nineteenth and early twentieth centuries.[8] The Knights were, in fact, known for enrolling both men and women in their ranks; the union had approximately 60,000 female members between 1882 and 1890.[9] Assembly 1128 persisted until at least 1895, which was nearly a decade after the national organization had fallen into a steep decline. By that point the local's leadership consisted mostly of mineworkers such as Jacob Grabenstein, the union's recording secretary and treasurer.[10]

Despite the presence of male and female Knights in the region, there is no reason to believe that the Copper Country Knights formed a mass movement or challenged the region's oligarchy. Still, the small unions did remain connected to the wider Knights of Labor movement. For example, in April 1889 the *Advance and Labor Leaf,* the organ of the Michigan labor movement based in Detroit, informed its readers that the "moulders of the Lake Superior iron works at Houghton are on a strike for eight hours as a day's labor."[11]

During the late nineteenth and early twentieth centuries, the Copper Country labor movement expanded from a handful of trade unions that had little in the way of public presence to a legitimate movement complete with mass meetings, parades, and their own union hall. This was especially true in the towns of Hancock and Houghton, where labor unionism had its deepest roots. In the Portage Lake towns, workers affiliated with dozens of trade unions met under the auspices of the Houghton-Hancock Trades and Labor Council (HTLC), a local umbrella organization for local unions that was affiliated with the American Federation of Labor (AFL).[12] The HTLC had been organized by 1902, and it remained a persistent advocate for workers' rights throughout the 1913–14 miners' strike. The HTLC included more than a dozen affiliates during the early years of the twentieth century,[13] and the labor council's officers were representative of the local labor movement's occupational diversity. It included International Typographers Union (ITU) officers Charles Balconi, William Walls, and Carl A. Parta; cigar maker Herman Meisel; Otto Simmer, a barber; Henry Webber, a miner; and John A. McGrath, a bookkeeper at Rupert and Sons General Store and thus likely a member of the clerks' union.[14] While it is not possible to determine the precise number of Copper Country union members during later years, the movement grew throughout the early twentieth century to the point where the *Keweenaw Miner* estimated that there were about 2,000 unionists in August 1911.[15]

One of the key periods in the early local labor history was from 1902 to 1903 when, according to the Michigan Bureau of Labor and Industrial Statistics, the number of Copper Country unions reported in a canvass of organized labor in Baraga, Calumet, Hancock, and Houghton ballooned from zero to eleven, with the number of union members growing from none to 290. While the 1902 canvassers likely missed a union or two, such as the Ontonagon Longshoremen's Union (formed in 1894), the labor movement's growth was nonetheless dramatic.[16] It, too, was indicative of the growth of organized labor in Michigan and the nation at large. That same year the bureau reported 253 new unions and an increase in membership of 16,179 in Michigan, while the AFL reported a growth of 442,100 new union members in 1903 alone.[17] Thus, AFL president Samuel Gompers reported in November 1903 that "never in the history of the labor movement, in this or in any other country, or, for that matter, never in the history of any movement for uplifting the toiling masses, has there been such a uniform growth in the number of unions formed, or in the number of wage-workers becoming members of existing unions."[18]

Most Copper Country unions were craft organizations, usually small bodies of workers who labored in a single craft or occupation such as cigar making, carpentry, or painting. The Hancock, Houghton, and Calumet trades were thoroughly organized during the early twentieth century. By 1908, everyone from miners to barbers and from carpenters to store clerks had unionized.[19] Among the first unions organized in the Copper Country was the Hancock machinists' union, which had organized and included twenty members by 1898, and the Calumet cigar makers, who were already meeting by September 1900.[20] However, mining, the most important of the local industries, remained only partially unionized before the strike of 1913–14. Still, certain unions did have large memberships. For example, in 1911 the Houghton County painters' union had more than fifty members.[21] Other unions had much smaller numbers of members, and yet their local craft was fully organized. Calumet Cigar Makers' Union 413 was composed of thirteen members in 1901, but that branch was among the most active in the nation, frequently writing articles for the union's monthly journal, advocating union-made products, and taking part in the Copper Country's annual Labor Day festivities.[22]

Most of the Copper Country's unions were made up of Houghton County workers, but none of that county's early trade unions matched the size of the Baraga longshoremen's union. "A big delegation of longshoremen was up from Baraga and L'Anse," read the *Daily Mining Gazette* in its 1908 Labor Day edition.[23] Baraga's longshoremen's union was only one of six local dockworkers' branches formed in the Copper Country before 1913. Also forming longshoremen's union branches were workers in Lake Linden, Hancock, Ontonagon, and Houghton, where two dock-workers' unions operated.[24]

No fewer than thirty-two trade unions functioned in the Copper Country prior to 1913.[25] This figure is especially significant because it does not include the numerous miners' union locals affiliated with the WFM that were formed by area workers between 1903 and 1913, nor does it include the Knights of Labor locals mentioned above. Indeed, during the first decade of the twentieth century, cigar makers, machinists, streetcar workers, longshoremen, painters, typographical workers, carpenters, smelters, masons, barbers, molders, iron workers, printers, tailors, bricklayers, stonecutters, store clerks, locomotive firemen, brewery workers, leather workers, locomotive engineers, blast furnace workers, and plumbers had formed local trade unions. As this list indicates, a visitor to the Copper Country in the year 1910 could, in all likelihood, venture into Hancock where he or she could visit a store and be served by union clerks, read a newspaper printed by union members, have his or her hair cut by union barbers, smoke a union-made cigar, and observe a host of union building trades workers as they constructed the town's homes and businesses.

With their labor halls, meetings, and social events, unions also served as centers of community where (usually) masculine bonding might occur. In this way unions resembled fraternities, and as with those bodies, union gatherings provided workers with places to socialize with friends, enjoy a union-made cigar or beer, and discuss issues of shared concern.[26] And, as with fraternities, many Copper Country unionists were well-established members of the community. This group included Charles Balconi, secretary of the Houghton County Labor Council, a longtime officer in the local ITU, and pressman for the *Daily Mining Gazette*; and Joseph R. Kelly, a founding member of the Hancock Typographical Union and a longtime Houghton County typesetter who learned his trade at the *Northwestern Mining Journal* in Hancock.[27] Balconi, Kelly, and others were family men who lived, worked, and purchased goods in the Copper Country. These workers, rather than any "outside agitators," did the slow, steady, and difficult work necessary to build a labor movement.

While Copper Country unionists did not publish their own local newspapers, the various crafts communicated via news organs put out by their international unions. George R. French, an organizer with the Cigar Makers International Union of America (CMIUA), wrote to the *Cigar Makers' Official Journal* in September 1904 praising the pioneering work of the unionized cigar makers in Calumet. He declared, "The cigarmakers were pioneers in the labor movement here, and they have organized many of the other trades. All members of [Houghton-Hancock Union Local] 408 are working."[28] These union newspapers also served as clearinghouses for a significant amount of news about local unions. For example, when Calumet Local 413 of the CMIUA purchased flowers for union member Gus Richards's funeral, the *Cigar Makers' Official Journal* published an expression of gratitude from the deceased worker's parents.[29]

As was the case throughout the nation, Copper Country unions federated with larger local, state, and federal umbrella organizations such as the Michigan Federation of Labor or the AFL. Most local Copper Country union branches belonged to national or international labor organizations: the Houghton County tailors' union was actually Hancock-Houghton Local 363 of the Journeymen Tailors' Union of America, and the Hancock brewery union was officially known as the International United Brewery Workmen, Local Union 65.[30] Like local, state, and national labor federations, a union's parent body could and did provide useful financial and logistical support, as well as other acts of solidarity, in times of tumult. During the October 1905 streetcar strike in Houghton County, for example, the Amalgamated Association of Street and Electric Railway Employees publicized the strike in its newspaper, the

Motorman and Conductor.[31] In 1910, several WFM locals contributed money to Hancock Miners' Union No. 200 to aid unionist Charles Waali in a lawsuit against the Quincy Mining Company.[32]

For many Copper Country workers, their unions served as fertile training ground for class struggle during the early twentieth century. Indeed, while trade unions have justifiably been criticized for downplaying class conflict in favor of harmony; promoting ethnic divisions by seeking to enroll only skilled, and thus usually old-stock, native-born American workers; and leaving the majority of nonwhite, immigrant, and female laborers in mass-production industries unorganized and thus unprotected against the their employers, unions were, first and foremost, class-based organizations formed by workers to increase their power vis-à-vis their employers. Unionized workers met with each other in a host of venues and communicated with each other through a host of media to discuss their shared concerns as workers. For example, Calumet Cigar Makers' Local 413 held meetings on the first Friday of each month at Curto's Hall located at 322 Sixth Street in Calumet.[33] By 1908, the various unions of Houghton County owned a labor hall in Houghton where all unions might assemble, as they did before the 1908 Labor Day parade.[34]

For Copper Country workers, their unions also proved useful as vehicles for reducing working hours and attaining living wages. They also provided protection against arbitrary discharge and wage reductions and gave workers the ability to bargain collectively over the conditions of their labor. Between 1902 and 1903, Copper Country unionists reduced their working day from an average of 9.8 to 9.6 hours, and drove up their average weekly earnings by a nickel, from $3.55 to $3.60.[35]

By January 1, 1906, all members of Houghton Local 596 of the ITU, which had members in Houghton, Hancock, and Calumet, had secured the eight-hour day, which gave them a rare bit of leisure time in an era when most workers labored ten or more hours each day.[36] Additionally, ITU locals signed contracts with their employers that guaranteed a certain rate of pay and other provisions over the life of the contract. On October 24, 1910, organizer B.G. Brady, an official with the ITU, joined a wage-scale committee comprised of Copper Country unionists in negotiating a two-year contract with local employers guaranteeing them pay raises, shift differentials that awarded a higher rate of pay for evening work, and a flat rate for all employees. Union wages provided a decent standard of living, and while unionists did not get rich for their labor, union contracts did guarantee something akin to living wages. Between 1910 and 1912, for example, Houghton typographical workers made $20 per week for working the day shift and $21 for the first year and $22 for the second year of working the night shift.[37]

Unions and the Community

Because of their purchasing power, high membership, and long-term residence in the region, Copper Country unionists commanded a great deal of support from other sectors of their communities. One element of the community support received by strikers came in the number of small business owners who supported their unions, their cause during strikes, and their quest for higher wages. Such was the case with Copper Country resident Charles Keifer, who owned a clothing store in Lake Linden during the 1913–14 copper strike and recalled showing his support for the strikers when he "paraded with the strikers" and argued that any workplace improvements received by the mineworkers were due to the efforts of the union. He stated that the mine owners "would never pay you much until the union got hold of them in 1913." Although Keifer supported unions, this support rested on the increased purchasing power that unions won for their members, and hence their increased buying power at Keifer's store: "you had to be friends of theirs because they were the ones who bought stuff."[38]

Other businesses supported labor by purchasing advertising space in labor and socialist publications. Thus, banks such as the Superior Savings Bank and First National Bank of Hancock, as well as Bosch Brewing Company in Lake Linden, advertised in the *Michigan Federation of Labor: Official Year Book* for 1906–07.[39] Businesses delivered an even greater level of support to socialist newspapers such as the *Wage-Slave* and *Työmies*. In 1913, more than a dozen Copper Country businesses supported *Työmies* by purchasing advertising space in the Finnish-language socialist newspaper.[40]

Even those community members who did not support unions would have had a hard time missing the symbols of unionism present throughout the Copper Country. Among the most conspicuous of these symbols were the various union labels promoted by crafts such as the cigar makers and brewers. Members of Calumet Cigar Makers' Union Local 413 were among the most vigorous proponents of the union label in the nation. According to Local 413, the label could be more effectively mobilized nationally as it had been used in Calumet, where "we have been advertising the label continuously from one end of the year to the other. We have billboards of our own, and we keep them covered with big sheet posters, and we have calendars and those signs that hang behind the bar, and stickers, and in fact we advertise the label in every way that's possible." The cigar makers' union's efforts yielded great results, not only in terms of advertisement but also for the sales of union-made products. Its members wrote, "We are up here in a mining country where there are mostly all [union] ten-cent cigars sold. In fact there are very few [non-union] five-cent cigars made up here."[41]

Some unionists used the opportunity provided by parades on holidays to exhibit solidarity and pride in their craft by turning out in droves to parade through Hancock and Houghton, and by participating in activities that followed the march. These parades also provided unionists with their best opportunity to display their commitment to their unions, as well as a pride in their crafts. Frequently the workers wore uniforms that signaled their membership in a particular trade or carried banners that proclaimed their union membership. For example, in 1911 members of the painters' union wore identical uniforms: white suits and caps to match, while two years later the Baraga longshoremen were singled out for their "natty uniforms" by a local newspaper.[42] In 1908, the Houghton typographical union built a float to accompany members on the march. While only the "Typos" built a float for the 1908 parade, other unions were distinguishable by their "banners or uniforms," according to the *Daily Mining Gazette*.[43]

On occasion, community support was manifested in the form of supportive state officials who refused to aid and abet corporate strikebreaking efforts. During the 1905 Houghton County streetcar strike, for example, municipal officials of Houghton County issued a resolution declaring that "we are not in sympathy with, and vigorously condemn the methods resorted to by the Houghton County Street Railway Company in its efforts to break the pending strike."[44] State officials also turned out to support labor's largest public displays on Labor Day each year. During the 1909 Labor Day celebrations, Hancock mayor W. Frank James joined Judge George C. Bentley in giving speeches to the region's unionized workers, while unionists chose ex-mayor W. J. Roberts of Ishpeming, a politician with wide socialist and working-class backing, to deliver the keynote address.[45]

A Day for Laborers

The most visible public displays of working-class community in the Copper Country came during the annual Labor Day celebrations. All across the nation Labor Day festivities began in the morning with a parade featuring union members marching throughout town, accompanied by supportive politicians and businessmen as well as parade standards such as local bands. Following the parade, unionists and their supporters usually held mass meetings where they were addressed by local union leaders, aspiring politicians, and other local notables. The day's events concluded with outdoor celebrations that usually included a picnic, music, additional speeches, and sporting events.[46]

Like Labor Days across the nation, those held in the Copper Country tended to be somewhat elaborate affairs. Labor Day differed from most of the rest of the year because it was a holiday and thus allowed workers to enjoy some freedom to sleep in, relax around the house with their families, and enjoy outdoor entertainments. The varied and no doubt enjoyable recreations featured during the 1909 Hancock Labor Day celebration were described in the *Daily Mining Gazette*:

> The Isle Royale band played at the park all afternoon and evening for dancing and there were other forms of amusement for the visitors. Arthur Fenn had his trick high diving dog there and gave three exhibitions. All afternoon and evening hundreds of people were in the grove and all had a good time. Nothing happened to mar the pleasant day, making the day an ideal one. The members of the different unions were well pleased with the success of their celebration.[47]

Following the 1912 Hancock Labor Day parade, which featured thirteen unions, the workers and their families engaged in a "program of sports" that included a greased-pig chase, pie- and apple-eating contests, a tug-of-war between Houghton and Hancock longshoremen, a hobble skirt race, and a 100-yard dash.[48] Joining the large turnout of Houghton County unionists were those from nearby towns. In fact, the Portage Lake Labor Day celebration became a major destination for Upper Peninsula workers eager to show their support for labor's cause. In 1910, "several members of Ontonagon and Baraga unions" traveled to Hancock for the celebration.[49] That these longshoremen "and their friends" made the special trip to Hancock each year for Labor Day was a strong indication of the significance of the holiday to the region's working people.[50]

The Portage Lake towns did not have a monopoly on Labor Day celebrations, however. Following their visit to Hancock to participate in that city's large 1908 parade, "a big delegation" of longshoremen from the towns of Baraga and L'Anse returned to Baraga to attend a ball in celebration of Labor Day.[51] Three years later the Ontonagon longshoremen were unable to attend the Houghton-Hancock celebration because a celebration of their own was being planned in their hometown.[52]

Ontonagon County residents were especially enthusiastic about their Labor Day festivities. The weekly *Ontonagon Herald* began advertising the celebration weeks in advance of Labor Day, running front-page articles encouraging "All Laboring Men and All Lodges in the County . . . to Join Big Parade," then publishing front-page summaries of the annual events. After the 1911 celebration, in which "Labor Day festivities were not marred by the downpour of water," the *Ontonagon Herald* praised local workers for putting on such a rousing success: "The Longshoremen are to be congratulated on the manner in which they conducted this affair on their day and we hope that they will live long and see many such days."[53]

The large turnout of Ontonagon and Baraga unionists at the 1910 Labor Day festivities was also indicative of the growth of these events—and in the Copper Country labor movement more generally—during the 1910s. At the 1911 parade, hundreds marched and thousands participated in what was called by the *Daily Mining Gazette* the "biggest ever" labor demonstration in Copper Country history. The march included more than fifty members of the local painters' union, only one of many that turned out en masse for the day's events.[54] The 1912 celebration broke the Labor Day parade and picnic attendance record. The *Daily Mining Gazette* reported approvingly of the workers' efforts: "The grove yesterday afternoon was the mecca for hundreds of copper country folk who congregated to help make the celebration a success. . . . Yesterday's celebration may truly be said to have been the most successful in the history of organized labor in the copper country."[55] In 1913, amid the raucousness of the great copper strike, Copper Country workers again broke records for their Labor Day turnout. That day's event brought out no fewer than eighteen labor unions as well as "many women and children in the miners' parade." The *Miners' Bulletin*, a local publication of the WFM, reported that "the line of march, four abreast, extended one and one half miles," and the number of parade participants made the event "the largest gathering in its history."[56]

Certainly, not all of the workers who turned out for Labor Day events were members of unions. Indeed, as early as 1906 employers learned that union members as well as non-union miners turned out to celebrate Labor Day. A labor spy hired by the Quincy Mining Company to keep watch over the activities of its workers had his surveillance disturbed by the Labor Day activities in 1906 when "the miners who were not working were down town to attend the Labor Day exercises." This was one indication that non-union as well as union laborers and their families supported the cause of organized labor and of working-class interests more generally.

In fact, a large number of the Copper Country's residents went out of their way to commemorate Labor Day. Even the antilabor *Daily Mining Gazette* trumpeted the efforts of pro-union community members in Hancock: "Hancock stores and private homes will be decorated with stars and stripes tomorrow as a further testimonial of the welcome which this city extends to labor organizations of the copper country."[57] However, as demonstrated below, the local press changed its tune when workers transitioned from forming unions and holding public celebrations to striking to bring about changes in the workplace.

Labor Day activities grew progressively more diverse during the early twentieth century, as immigrant workers took on leadership roles and attended the festivities in large numbers to show their support for the labor movement. The *Daily Mining Gazette* reported the presence of Finnish- and Italian-speaking union organizers urging their fellow workers to unionize at the 1911 parade. It noted, "A new phase to the program will be speaking in the afternoon by Finnish and Italian gentlemen, the talks to be along lines of organization."[58]

During the 1910s, a larger and more militant Copper Country labor movement was also a more diverse movement as large numbers of the so-called new immigrant groups—Finns, Croatians, Italians, and others—joined, organized, and led local union branches. Earlier trade unions were organized and led by native-born Americans, as well as first- or second-generation immigrants from northwestern Europe. For example, Thomas H. McNeil, an Englishman who moved to the United States in 1900 and worked in an iron foundry, served as financial secretary in the Hancock-Houghton branch of the International Molders' Union during the first decade of the twentieth century.[59] Ironically, considering the important roles played by Finns, Italians, and Croatians in organizing Copper Country WFM locals and the 1913–14 strike, some local unionists blamed workers from these ethnic groups for retarding the growth of the labor movement. In 1902, N. B. Johnson, a Houghton unionist, complained in the *American Federationist*, the newspaper of the AFL, that "we are somewhat hindered in organization by the immigration of Finlanders and Italians, who work for any price."[60]

Characteristic of this change toward a move inclusive type of labor movement was John Rasi (Ross), father of the prominent Finnish American historian Carl Ross and a typesetter at *Työmies*.[61] The elder Ross, like his fellow workers at *Työmies*, belonged to the ITU. In fact, beginning in 1904, when *Työmies* began publication in Hancock, the local typos' union received an infusion of Finnish-speaking members as the entirety of the newspaper's staff belonged to the union.[62] Many new immigrants joined the ranks of the American labor movement, including the region's tailors, who formed Hancock-Houghton Local 363 of the Journeymen Tailors' Union of America in early 1913. The founding members of Local 363 were representative of the infusion of diverse faces and voices into the movement. They included the union's first two secretaries, Adolph Wirkkula, a Finn, and E. Czernkovich, a Croatian. The surnames of the union's other founding members indicated the union's immigrant membership: Uno Klemdte, Victor Irvo, Herman M. Elonen, Charles Cornhovich, and E. Gombkoviz.[63]

The presence of large numbers of immigrants in Copper Country unions, including the WFM, during the 1910s was seen by some anti-unionists as evidence that unionism, radicalism, and labor militancy were all "imported" from outside the region by "aliens" who were not part of the Copper Country community. However, by 1910 immigrants and their children represented 89 percent of the population of Houghton, Keweenaw, and Ontonagon Counties, and thus immigrants *were* significant parts of the community.[64] These men, women, and children built the Copper Country's houses, unloaded the coal and other necessities off the ships docked on Portage Lake, provided the unpaid domestic labor that kept the region's households functioning, and mined the copper that produced most of the region's wealth.

Copper Country Unions and the Sexes

As was true of trade unions across the nation, the overwhelming majority of the Copper Country's labor organizations' officials and members were men. American trade unions were, in fact, masculine enterprises that failed to organize all but a tiny group of female wage laborers.[65] Much the same was true of Copper Country unions, which were composed of laborers in exclusively or mostly all-male occupations such as mining and the building and maritime trades. Moreover, the language used by writers describing local unions tended to emphasize their members' male-ness. The *Ontonagon Herald* praised the "large number of Longshoremen and other laboring men which turned out to help make the celebration a success" after the 1913 Labor Day celebration in Ontonagon.[66]

In spite of their relative absence from the Copper Country trade union movement, women worked in the Copper Country, performing both the unpaid, domestic labor necessary to keep households and families operational and a variety of paid forms of employment. Dozens of Copper Country women labored as domestic servants, waitresses, and laundry workers, and by the early 1910s some women entered the unionized crafts. One such female unionist was K. Peterson, a tailor who joined the Hancock local of the Journeymen Tailors' Union of America in November 1913.[67]

More important numerically and in terms of influence on the local labor movement were the members of the WFM's Hancock Ladies' Auxiliary Local 5. Formed on April 19, 1911, the auxiliary was among the first women's organizations to affiliate with the WFM.[68] By July 1911, the Hancock Ladies' Auxiliary had grown in size and significance to the point where it was able to send a voting delegate to the WFM's annual convention in Denver.[69] A second auxiliary, Calumet Local 15, was formed in late summer 1913 with a leadership cadre consisting of M. E. Mikkola, Annie Clemenc, and other working-class women.[70] Locals 5 and 15 were not ancillary to the labor movement as a whole. Their members marched in Labor Day parades and hosted fund-raisers for the union and parties for strikers' children.[71] Showing at least some commitment to gender equality, both men and women participated in Copper Country May Day celebrations, including during the 1913 commemoration of International Labor Day when one man and one woman were chosen to head the parade. The *Miners' Magazine* reported: "Heading the parade on mount was William

Toppari of Hancock and Miss Williams of Superior mine."[72] With the infusion of female voices in Copper Country unions and the WFM auxiliaries, Copper Country unions were becoming increasingly representative of the local working class by the early 1910s.

STREETCAR STRIKE!

Miners were the group most likely to strike in the Copper Country during the late nineteenth and early twentieth centuries. But not all labor conflicts emerged from among the men who labored underground. The most epic of the nonmining strikes in the early twentieth-century Copper Country was the 1905 Streetcar Strike in which streetcar workers, in alliance with a large cross section of community supporters, halted Houghton County's street railway network for several weeks.

On February 25, 1905, Houghton County streetcar employees struck over the Houghton County Street Railway Company's use of a blacklist against union members. Earlier that month, Houghton County employees began joining the Amalgamated Association of Street and Electric Railway Employees, which counted more than seventy-five members who formed Division No. 400 of that international union.[73] Responding with an iron fist, the Houghton County Street Railway Company fired the union's officers. According to one union member, the strike was "brought about by ruthless endeavors on the part of the employing companies to suppress the efforts of the employees to organize."[74] In response to their fellow workers' firing, all seventy-eight streetcar workers struck.[75]

The strike began in response to a firing of a few union members, but it erupted into a mass action as streetcar workers and community members mobilized to halt the scab-operated streetcars and protect workers' rights. The streetcar company hired scabs to replace the strikers. The *Copper Country Evening News* reported that the company had "a large number of men on hand, which it has been assembling for a number of days, for the purpose of replacing the union employees."[76] The *Motorman and Conductor* reported that the scabs were imported from Chicago and that "the extravagance of securing and harboring" the strikebreakers proved to be a great expense for the company.[77]

A large section of the community showed its displeasure at the company's union busting through the use of direct action. On the strike's first day, approximately fifty unionists paraded throughout Calumet distributing handbills that read: "Get off the cars. Wanted, everybody to know that the street railway company has discharged several of its employees because they belonged to the union. The company refused to meet the employees on any reasonable terms."[78] Scabs attempted to operate the streetcars throughout Hancock and Houghton, but their pace was dramatically slowed to one mile per hour because of obstructions, including beer barrels and large chunks of ice, placed in the streetcars' way.[79] Between fifty and sixty workers pulled a brewery wagon onto the tracks, unhitched its horses, and loaded themselves onto the wagon, placing an imposing obstacle in the way of the streetcar. Frustrated, the scab driver rammed the wagon, which destroyed it, and then pulled out a revolver to threaten its driver. Others took to greasing the streetcar rails, breaking out the streetcars' windows, deriding the scab operators, and throwing rocks and chunks of ice at the passing cars.[80]

Violence was not uncommon during the strike, and seemingly most of it occurred when prostrike members of the community sought to impede the streetcars from operating. Some protesters were met with a hail of gunfire from the scab-driven streetcars. James Rowe was shot through the chest, an unnamed man was shot through the arm, and a little girl named Fvetich was "slightly wounded by a bullet" according to the *Copper Country Evening News*.[81]

By two weeks into the strike, as the streetcar company failed in its efforts to operate its cars using scab operators, the *Evening News* even admitted that local residents refused to cross the union's picket lines because "many sympathize with the union cause."[82] Mass meetings, in which community support was demonstrated and public officials attempted to end the conflict, were held throughout the strike.[83] According to the union, even after six weeks without streetcar service, 8,000 Copper Country residents pledged to not ride scab-driven streetcars during the strike.[84]

One prominent member of the prostrike group was attorney P. H. O'Brien, who addressed a "standing-room only" meeting of strikers and supporters in Calumet on March 23. This speech by the "unselfish" O'Brien, "to the cause of right and justice," was reprinted beneath a photo of the attorney in the *Motorman and Conductor*.[85] In his speech, O'Brien delivered high praise to the labor movement and union members, and he spoke in vivid terms of class struggle:

> We all know what the union has done for the laboring man in reducing the number of working hours, the abolishment of child labor, and other evils. In the great battle between capital and labor you will find that the unions have been on the firing line. The unions have fought the battles for the workingman. Whether you are a union man or not, the unions have fought your battles. I am glad to see you all stand by the street car boys. (Applause.)[86]

According to the *Motorman and Conductor*, the importation of scabs to take the place of local union members "provoked the indignation of the citizens of Houghton and Hancock and a vigorous boycott resulted, causing absolute loss of patronage to the company."[87] As a result of the strike, the Houghton County Street Railway Company lost more than $45,000 in 1905, a rare deficit for a corporation that yielded tens of thousands of dollars of annual profits.[88]

Employers, Community Mobilization, and the Iron Fist

As these illustrations attest, there were numerous labor organizations in the Copper Country in the years leading up to the copper strike of 1913–14, and in some instances these organizations waged large-scale, community-based struggles against their bosses. In spite of the occasional flairs of militancy, Copper Country unions were, in many cases, able to operate without the persistent assaults on their ability to organize that one might expect. For example, the staffs of several anti-union newspapers such as the *Daily Mining Gazette* and *Copper Country Evening News* belonged to the typographers' and printers' unions, thus indicating at least an acceptance, if not approval, of the significance of the region's labor movement to its working people.[89] Still, some employers moved beyond acceptance and toleration of unionized laborers in the Copper Country to outright support, which was demonstrated by their leading role in Houghton County's Labor Day festivities. Thus, some employers were willing to support the right of some workers to organize a certain type of union: a craft union, which during the early twentieth century meant a union comprised of and led by mostly white, native-born or northern European men who presented no overt challenge to the capitalist system.

Not surprisingly, those Copper Country employers who bitterly opposed local unions offered the most ardent support to employing-class domination over their communities. Indeed, Copper Country workers held major numerical advantages over their bosses, advantages that if channeled into a coordinated plan of action, might prove useful in political campaigns or Labor Day demonstrations, where working-class power was sometimes demonstrated. Employers organized "unions" of their own (employers' organizations) to combat the threat of labor unions. These employers' organizations—commercial clubs, chambers of commerce, and citizens' alliances—could be mobilized during times of labor strife to stamp out unions. Thus, while employer influence and power rested upon their wealth, ownership over key resources, and paternalistic relationships with some workers, it also rested on their willingness to create class-based organizations and unleash the iron fist upon workers who struck or otherwise acted collectively.

In spite of the opposing class interests of owners and workers, and the ability of unions, especially militant ones like the WFM, to channel working-class energies into an effective program, some large employers claimed that they were not opposed to unions. James MacNaughton of C&H even suggested that he did not mind if mineworkers unionized, stating that "probably all" of his company's foundry workers belonged to a union and that he and his colleagues had no problems with that union so long as it did not seek to enforce a closed shop.[90]

MacNaughton's public displays of tolerance toward unions, however, concealed his and other employers' efforts to fire and blacklist unionists, particularly the Finnish- and Italian-speaking workers who frequently performed the long, difficult, and dangerous work necessary to unionize. The most obvious assaults on the mineworkers' ability to organize came through the efforts of labor spies who were paid to watch over the miners and other community members, and to report on their activities—especially strike, union, and radical activities—to the mine bosses who hired them. Miners also took extreme steps to ensure that their organizational activities would not be detected by employers, their allies, or the operatives who were paid to spy on their activities. When a labor spy contacted an Italian American unionist in September 1906, the spy was able to convince the union member to take him "to the woods, where they met four Austrians. They got into a conversation about the late strike."[91]

One of the many dangers faced by militant, radical, or insufficiently deferential workers was that they would be placed on a blacklist. The use of a blacklist against members of the Houghton County streetcar workers' union by the owners of the Houghton County Street Railway Company was the main reason why those workers staged a strike in 1905.[92] Unfortunately, blacklists were not confined to the local transportation industry, but instead made up a regular part of Copper Country labor relations. For example, Copper Country businesses such as Carroll's Foundry outright forbade unions from organizing workers at their plants and refused to hire any member of the Iron Molders' Union.[93] In 1914, former congressman Victor Berger reported on the pervasiveness of these lists and noted that local socialists needed to conceal their political beliefs, lest they be fired. He stated, "They very rarely admit when they are looking for work in the mines that they are Socialists, but they have often been discharged as agitators when they were found out. . . . Any man who is active in behalf of a labor organization is considered a Socialist agitator."[94]

Copper Country employers went to great lengths to obtain and maintain their blacklists. H. H. Baldwin, an officer with the Thiel Detective Service, wrote to Charles L. Lawton, letting him know that one of the local Thiel operatives was devoting "his time to ascertaining the names of the Socialists and union men that are working in the mine," and that "by checking them against your list of employees you can then tell whether or not he is reporting names of men who are employed in other mines."[95] Of course, being listed as an "undesirable" by a labor spy was a serious blow to the employment prospects of a worker. This was the case with one man named Erickson, who was discharged from employment at the Quincy Mining Company for having a "troublesome character." The desire to punish such "troublesome" workers was so great that Quincy president William Rogers Todd asked Lawton about employers forming an "arrangement with the Calumet and Copper Range to keep each other advised regarding such men, as it is important that we and they should know the names of men that other mines let go."[96] Charles Lawton admitted having a "blacklist" and hinted that C&H also kept one, but since "it is a very serious legal offense to keep a blacklist," management at the C&H and the Copper Range mines "are a little bit shy possibly in giving out any list."[97]

Employers were especially effective in their attacks on mineworkers' strikes leading up to the 1913–14 strike. During a number of the early Copper Country labor conflicts, unionists, strikers, sympathetic community members, and bystanders were caught up in waves of repression leveled upon them by employers, state officials, strikebreakers, and scabs. Violent repression was especially visible during the Rockland Strike of 1906, when sheriffs killed two Finnish trammers, and during the all-out attack on the miners by the employers and state during the 1913–14 conflict.[98]

Copper Country employers and their police allies also used deportation as a method for repressing radicals and breaking strikes. Such was the case in May 1905 when the Houghton County sheriff arrested two men for expressing their beliefs in socialism at a local church and copper smelter, and deported them to the Newberry Insane Asylum. John Iola, one of Sheriff August Beck's targets, addressed a Lutheran church in a speech "upon socialism," while Daniel Harley was nabbed for articulating that "he owns the smelters and is in position to give employment to all of the unemployed of the copper country." That a belief in socialism or workers' control of industry was a threat to Copper Country employers and their allies in the sheriff's office was made clear when Sheriff Beck transported Iola and Harley to an insane asylum to be "treated" for their "disease."[99]

During most labor conflicts, the Copper Country's mainstream (or "kept") press lined up solidly behind the interests of employers.[100] Almost without fail the mainstream press condemned strikes and strikers, and took those opportunities to fan the flames of anti-unionism among the several thousand subscribers to English-language publications in the Copper Country.[101] These anti-union attacks were not subtle, as local newspapers functioned as a near caricature of anti-union newspapers during strikes, blaming all difficulties on the strikers, accusing them of crime, violence, and community discord.

This fact was made clear during an 1872 mining strike. During the conflict, mine management refused to bargain or even meet with the miners' representatives, instead instructing the strikers "that if they are not satisfied with the wages offered to them, they will be settled with and can go elsewhere to labor." This individualistic plan was deemed to be "eminently fair, and leaves no room whatever for argument" by the *Portage Lake Mining Gazette*.[102] In contrast, the "programme of the men [strikers] . . . smacks of tyranny and unmistakable oppression, and the fact is to be deplored that there are men found in sufficient numbers to take such an arbitrary stand and attempt to maintain it," according to the *Daily Mining Gazette*.[103]

While employers were able to effectively mobilize labor spies, strikebreakers, and the antilabor press in their efforts to keep the copper mines union free, their efforts were strengthened when they organized around their class interests. The historian Larry Lankton has demonstrated that after the turn of the twentieth century, mine corporations such as C&H "recognized that they had a stake in how other companies confronted labor problems. Thus, in 1905, C&H for the first time shared employment and wage information with other companies and consulted with them on the propriety of altering existing wage scales."[104] According to Lankton, this proto-cooperation boded poorly for Copper Country workers because it "opened the door to the creation of a united front of mining companies, standing shoulder to shoulder against labor."[105] Indeed, formal networks of cooperation that facilitated their sharing of information about workers, strikes, and conditions proved to be the most effective means of fighting unions in the Copper Country. Thus, Copper Country mineworkers who were determined to organize as a collective body faced a formidable and equally organized employing class supported by powerful institutions in the community.

CHAPTER 3

Immigrants

A great struggle of the miners in Colorado and at Calumet, Michigan, is still going on.
. . . Comrades, workers, brothers! Nobody should leave for these states! Inform your
friends and comrades to look for work in other places so as to not become traitors of
those martyrs who are our brothers and whose struggle is also ours.

—*Radnicka Straza*, Croatian immigrant working-class newspaper

IN THE YEARS LEADING UP TO THE 1913–14 COPPER COUNTRY STRIKE, IMMIGRANT
laborers took on an increasingly important role in the Copper Country's labor force,
as well as in its radical and workers' movements. The presence of European-born
workers and their children was visible in union memberships, in the foreign-language
labor and left-wing publications they wrote, and in the community spaces they owned
and operated. Additionally, immigrant radicals—especially the "Red" Finns—carried
out a number of public demonstrations in which their politics and ethnicity were on
display. The best known of these parades came on July 28, 1907, during the so-called
Red Flag Parade when nearly 4,000 people lined the streets to watch as a parade
of hundreds marched through the streets of Hancock in violation of a municipal
ordinance forbidding the "carrying or exhibiting the red flag of anarchy or any flag

or symbol representing anarchy, or teaching against or toward the destruction of the organized government of the United States."[1]

During the parade, Hancock police "rushed forward like wild beasts with foam coming from their mouths," according to one of the thirteen socialists arrested during the incident.[2] Leo Laukki, a socialist and advocate of industrial unionism, a future prominent member of the Industrial Workers of the World (IWW), and a recent arrival from Finland where he "was sought by the secret police of Russia" for organizing soldiers into revolutionary organizations, was one of the "Reds" arrested during the parade. Combining his radical politics with his internationalism, Laukki expressed his views that "the economical system of the United States should be overthrown in one way or another," and that insurrection would be carried out "in Finland, Russia, and all over."[3]

Laukki's participation in the parade was characteristic of the strongly Finnish composition of the Copper Country Left during the early twentieth century. Of the twelve men and one woman arrested during the July 28 parade, nearly all had Finnish surnames.[4] Much the same could be said of other parades held under radical auspices, including the May 4, 1913, parade through Hancock and Houghton, held in honor of May Day, the international workers' day. According to the *Miners' Magazine*, "It is not too much to say that there was in parade about 3,000 men, because the parade was over one mile long."[5] The Finnish character of the parade was apparent from the fact that the notice of the parade that appeared in the *Miners' Magazine* was written by two Finns, John Välimäki and Charles E. Hietala. Following the parade, the demonstrators attended a meeting at Kansankoti Hall, the Finnish socialist hall and headquarters of the Työmies Publishing Company.[6]

Older, established groups in the region nonetheless treated Finns, the largest immigrant group in the Copper Country, as a distinct "other." This was due only partly to their status as new immigrants; it was also a product of the extraordinarily radical nature of Finnish politics in America. Still, the Copper Country's radical Left was not composed solely of Finns, but also drew in radicals from a number of the Keweenaw's largest groups of ethnic laborers, including radicals who spoke English, Finnish, Croatian, Slovenian, Hungarian, and Italian.[7] A June 1913 meeting exhibited this diversity; "a red letter day in the history of Calumet Miners' Union" was celebrated when 2,000 people paid twenty-five cents each to attend a meeting where "addresses on unionism were delivered in English, Italian, Finnish, Croatian, and Hungarian."[8] As these events suggest, the Copper Country Left during the early twentieth century was shaped by its largely immigrant composition. The diverse groups of Copper Country workers, which included labor militants and socialists, had equally diverse methods for responding to—and in some cases reshaping—their working and living conditions in the heavily industrialized Copper Country of Michigan.

Immigrants and "Race," the Racialization Process

As occurred throughout industrial America during the late nineteenth and early twentieth centuries, ethnic hostilities and conflicts were conspicuous in the Copper Country's mining towns. The capitalist system, which forces workers to compete against each other for limited jobs, likewise contributed to conflicts between "old immigrants," those who hailed from northern and western Europe and who tended to dominate U.S. immigration patterns before 1890, and "new immigrants" who hailed from southern and eastern Europe and arrived between 1890 and the 1920s. With a premium put on good jobs, those that paid the most and were the least dangerous, employers and foremen with the ability to hire whom they wanted and assign them to whatever job they pleased had a great degree of power over the lives of Copper Country workers.

In 1914, Daniel Waatti, a longtime Calumet miner, contended that all of the region's mine bosses were Scottish, Swedish, or Cornish, while there were no Finnish, Croatian, Polish, or Hungarian "captains or even second captains."[9] Arthur Thurner noted this occurrence when he wrote that "discrimination at work" was present in the Copper Country, with "Finns, Slavs, and Italians . . . often [being] relegated to the most menial jobs in mines and mills by Cornish, Irish, Scandinavians, Germans, and Anglo-Americans."[10] "The Cornish 'hold' in mining militated against hopes of Finns, Slavs, and Italians to rise in the ranks," continued Thurner, as English-speaking shift bosses and superintendents reserved the best jobs for fellow English speakers.[11] The historian Arthur E. Puotinen described the same discriminatory practices by "Cornish and Irish shift bosses" who benefited from discrimination "at the expense of newer immigrant groups such as the Finns."[12]

Ethnic discrimination occurred especially as part of the copper mining hierarchy, as even mine owners and superintendents sought to weed out certain ethnic groups in favor of others. One labor spy hired by the Quincy Mining Company during an August 1906 mine strike differentiated between "old" and "new" immigrant groups, reporting that those in the latter group were both more stubborn and militant. He wrote: "I went to the mines this afternoon. Everything is quiet there. It is difficult to get a Finn, Hungarian, or Italian to talk but I can talk freely with the Irish and Germans. . . . I met four Finlanders in the Eagle saloon this evening and they said that they would not go back to work until their terms are agreed to."[13]

In their attacks upon local Finnish immigrants, Copper Country employers and Cornish, German, or American shift bosses reflected the dominant racial ideology of their era. Finns, while light-haired and light-skinned, were not Nordic peoples and were widely perceived by early twentieth-century social scientists to be of a different race. During the early twentieth century, Americans held multiple and contested beliefs about race, and to at least some Americans, Finns belonged to a different racial group than their Anglo-Saxon and Nordic counterparts.[14] Through the mainstream press and eugenicist propagandists, dominant ideas of the "essential Finn" were able to be transmitted throughout the country, repeated by local elites and intellectuals, and judging from Finns' lack of acceptance in some craft unions and non-Finn neighborhoods, at least partly accepted by the native-born working class. As the sociologist Peter Kivisto remarked, Finns were widely perceived as "violence prone revolutionaries."[15] Eschewing stories on the rich cultural production going on at the Finn halls, in their cooperatives, and among local Finnish entrepreneurs, the Copper Country press included Finnish immigrants most often when they were the perpetrators of stabbings or the hapless victims of industrial violence, or portrayed them as drunkards engaged in reckless behaviors.

Illustrations of the treatment afforded Finns in the Copper Country, whose individual traits were swallowed up inside the "essential Finn" caricature, can be found throughout the region's mainstream press. For example, when a Finnish American laborer was injured or killed on the job, newspapers invariably referred to his or her Finnish-ness, as did the *Calumet and Red Jacket News* in March 1889: "A Finn, named Jacob Korby, aged 20, was, about 10 o'clock this morning, instantly killed by a piece of the vein falling on him in the No. 11 shaft at the South Hecla." This description of Korby, "A Finn," contrasts sharply with a second article about an "industrial accident" in Calumet in which the victim had an Anglo surname. It read: "Three miners, named Samuel Pascoe, James H. Knight, and William James, had been working in the Red Jacket all night" when James was killed in an explosion.[16]

An even more vivid example appeared in the *Daily Mining Gazette* in July 1906 when a journalist attempted to make light of a violent confrontation between groups of Finns and Croatians, or "Austrians" as the article called them:

> Ten Austrians against Two Fins [*sic*] and When Arrested Pleas of Self Defense is Made. . . . The two injured men . . . were walking with their wives toward their home in Centennial Heights when they passed a crowd of Austrians who were playing their national game. This consists of rolling a large ball, somewhat similar to bowling. It seems that Nevela happened to touch one of the balls as he was passing, deflecting its course. No sooner had he done this, so he states, than he was instantly caught by the men, who in court admitted the fact that they were intoxicated.[17]

Additionally, in August 1906, during a mine strike in Rockland, the *Copper Country Evening News* commented on the "foreign residents" of Calumet and their efforts to raise legal defense funds for the mostly immigrant strike force. That the news organ commented upon the foreignness of the strikers and their defenders was but one of many attempts to differentiate between the region's immigrant working class and its largely native-born middle and employing classes.[18]

"Red" Finns

While Finnish immigrant workers were lumped together as a single type of person in the late nineteenth and early twentieth centuries, Finnish leftists were singled out as a separate race. Finnish immigrant radicals, in fact, offer the clearest example of the relationship in the United States between political radicalism and the racialization process. Across the nation, Finnish socialists were known as "Red Finns," a reference to the color red in socialist flags, but also to the connection made in the minds of American elites between Finnish radicals and Indian "savages."[19] Indeed, before 1910 it was common for social scientists to refer to Finns as part of the "Homo Mongolicus" race and the Finno-Tatar "family."[20] After leading a strike on the Mesabi Iron Range of Minnesota in 1907, Finnish miners were castigated as "a race that tries to take advantage of the companies at every opportunity and are not to be trusted."[21] Finnish immigrants were called "Jack-pine Savages," "racially sullen," and Mongolians because of their class-conscious labor activism.[22] The last identification was so strong, in fact, that in 1907 nativist employers attempted to halt Finnish immigration into the United States by invoking Asian exclusion legislation.[23]

Thus, in the Copper Country, to be a "Red" Finn was to be the target of special abuse by local employers and some members of the middle class. The historian Alison K. Hoagland argued that Finns constituted the region's largest immigrant group, but "they were also the most discriminated against, due to their reputation for socialist politics."[24] Quincy Mining Company general manager Charles Lawton ranked workers' qualities as employees based on their ethnicity: "The Germans, apparently, are going to make better machine men than the Russians, or the Russian Polacks. The two latter nationalities are going to make good trammers, even better than the Finns. There is no use overlooking the fact that the good Finns are of the best workmen that we have." However, Lawton divided Finnish immigrant workers into "two kinds" based on their political beliefs: "the poor and Socialistic Finns are of the worst workmen that we have—there is a marked difference between the two kinds."[25]

The threat posed by the radical Finns was so acute because no group in American history has been more strongly attracted to socialist and syndicalist ideas, joined radical organizations in greater numbers, and refused to cower before the boss as often as the Finns.[26] Finnish immigrants, although one of the smaller immigrant groups in the United States, comprised the largest blocs of immigrant socialists in the nation. They formed the Finnish Socialist Federation (FSF) in 1906, one of the many language federations of the SPA. In 1912, the FSF reported 167 locals; four newspapers, three of which were dailies (none of which registered under 2,000 subscribers); ownership of the Work People's College, a radical workers' college in Duluth, Minnesota; and 13,000 members, a full 12 percent of the entire SPA membership.[27] By 1913, the FSF comprised 260 local branches that managed eighty libraries and owned at least seventy-six meeting halls.[28]

"Red" Finns were also a threat to employers' interests in the Copper Country because the radical immigrants established a strong base in the community through their political activism, clubs, publications, and halls. By supporting and running socialist candidates for local elected office, making their own literature and material culture, staking their claim to public space by building halls and holding street meetings, and striking regularly, these radicals mounted a large and public challenge to employer domination of the region.

The first efforts at constructing a radical Finnish working-class organization came in 1894 when Calumet Finns organized the Suomi Workers' club, which like the conservative Finnish organizations, offered insurance and educational opportunities to its members.[29] Working-class Finns in Calumet also published a short-lived newspaper, *Työväen Ystävä* (Workers' Friend), in 1896.[30] Still, Finnish immigrant socialism in the Copper Country received little in the way of institutional growth until 1900, when labor organizer Martin Hendrickson toured Michigan's Upper Peninsula and was warmly received by large gatherings of Finnish workers in the Copper Country. Thirty Hancock Finns set up a socialist branch called the *Jousi Seura* (Society of the Bow) that same year.[31]

In 1912, Michigan branches of the FSF had twenty-five locals and approximately 1,500 members.[32] Most of these locals were formed in the iron and copper ranges of Michigan's Upper Peninsula. By 1912, Upper Peninsula Finns had formed FSF branches in South Range, Mass City, Calumet, Marquette, Negaunee, and more than a dozen other towns. While many of the largest FSF branches lay outside of the Copper Country in places such as Detroit, Marquette, and Ironwood, the state's largest local was in Hancock, which counted 232 members in 1912. Smaller but still significant local branches were built by "Red" Finns in Ahmeek, which included 103 members, and Mass City, which, impressively, had 63 of its 64 members paid up at the time the FSF published its annual yearbook for 1912.[33] While the Chassel, Michigan, branch of the FSF did not report any membership statistics for publication in the yearbook, its members did contribute funds to the 1913 Akron rubber strike led by the IWW.[34] Another indication of the strength of the FSF was the number of Christmas and New Year's greetings sent to supporters in the Copper Country. In December 1913, *Työmies* issued 108 of these greetings to Finnish immigrant socialists in five Copper Country towns, including sixty greetings sent to supporters in Hancock.[35]

The Copper Country's Finnish socialists were linked to national organizations, which served as potential sources of support during crises such as the 1913–14 Copper Country Strike. During that conflict, local, state, and national Finnish socialist organizations donated large sums of money to the strikers' cause. Such assistance was rendered to the strikers by the National Finnish Socialist Organization, which contributed more than $1,000 to the Western Federation of Miners (WFM) Michigan Defense Fund in 1913.[36] Labor organizations with large numbers of Finnish members also contributed to the mineworkers' cause. The Central Labor Council and International Longshoremen's Association of Astoria, Oregon, donated to the miners' defense fund in November 1913.[37]

The dominant presence of Finns within the Copper Country's Left was made plain by the words of Alexander M. Stirton, editor of the *Wage-Slave*, an English-language socialist newspaper published in Hancock. While there were both English- and Finnish-language socialist publications printed in Houghton County, Stirton's words made obvious the leading part played by the Finns: "Our readers understand of course that the Finnish paper is the big paper in this establishment, a large, seven-column paper, eight pages, issued three times a week. The *Wage-Slave* does not publish *Työmies*. Työmies Pub. Co. publishes the *Wage-Slave*."[38] Members of the mainstream media likewise made the connection between the Finns' ethnicity, political radicalism, and workplace militancy. In the 1906 Rockland Strike at the Michigan Mine, which was approximately thirty miles south of Hancock, many of the strike's leaders were Finnish socialists. This fact was recognized by the *Ontonagon Herald*, which stated that "the leaders" of the strike "have very strong socialistic views."[39] In 1908, SPA presidential candidate Eugene V. Debs visited Houghton and Hancock, delivering speeches alongside Stirton, the SPA's gubernatorial candidate. While neither of these men was a Finn, they addressed "a large audience, made up principally of Finlanders," according to the *Wolverine Citizen* of Flint, Michigan.[40]

Not All "Red" Immigrants Were Finns

While Finns were the largest group of immigrant radicals and militants in the Copper Country, other ethnic radicals understood that their interests differed from those of the area's mine owners. The largest of these ethnic groups were the Croatians and Italians, two southern European immigrant groups whose foreign languages, Catholicism, and inexperience with industrial work in Europe distinguished them from the Copper Country's dominant ethnic groups.

Croatian as well as Slovenian workers formed several socialist and working-men's organizations in the Copper Country, most of which were based in Calumet, the center of Michigan's South Slav population. Croatian Americans have a strong historical identification with left-wing activism in the United States and radical Croatian immigrants formed socialist clubs across the country during the first years of the twentieth century. Along with other South Slavs, Croatians formed the South Slav Socialist Federation (SSSF) in 1909. By December 1912, the federation consisted of eighty-five active locals with 1,800 members, and had an annual income of $10,000. As the federation's name indicated, its membership was multiethnic, consisting of 926 Slovenians, 710 Croatians, and 164 Serbians, with approximately one-third of its members enrolled in labor unions.[41] Croatian socialists likewise participated heavily in the interethnic McKees Rock Strike of 1909 and the Minnesota Iron Ore Strike of 1916, and published at least three Croatian-language IWW newspapers between 1919 and 1925.[42]

South Slavs in Calumet formed an SSSF local prior to 1913. While most of the records of the Croatian socialists in Calumet have been lost for posterity, some things about the local Croatian radicals are known.[43] Working-class Croatians in the Copper Country joined their radical immigrant comrades by establishing a left-wing newspaper representing their interests as workers. The *Hrvatski Radnik* (Croatian Worker) was a weekly news organ that went through a number of editors.[44]

During the 1913–14 Copper Country Strike, Tomo Strizic began editing a Croatian-language newspaper, the *Radnicka Straza*, which joined the *Hrvatski Radnik* in voicing a worker's perspective during the conflict. Just how militant the voices of the Croatian-language workers' newspapers were was expressed in the *Radnicka Straza*, which referred to the "savage behavior" of the "capitalist slaves" who attacked, arrested, and jailed a number of strikers and their wives.[45] During the strike, the *Radnicka Straza* issued a manifesto that declared: "A great struggle of the miners in Colorado and at Calumet, Michigan, is still going on. . . . Comrades, workers, brothers! Nobody should leave for these states! Inform your friends and comrades to look for work in other places so as to not become traitors of those martyrs who are our brothers and whose struggle is also ours."[46]

Larger and more significant than the SSSF was the National Croatian Society (NCS), which, as its name suggested, was a national body with hundreds of branches, thousands of members, and hundreds of thousands of dollars in assets.[47] Founded in 1894 as the Croatian Union, the NCS grew to more than 20,000 members by the time it held its tenth annual convention in Calumet during September 1909.[48] The historian George Prpic described the impressive early moments of the NCS conference at Calumet: "This unusually long convention was inaugurated by a parade of delegates and the Croatian people of Calumet. The parade started in Osceola

Map of the locations of various organizations, benevolent societies, and businesses sympathetic to causes of organized labor between 1910 and 1913 in Calumet's downtown. Many of the buildings and organizations associated with the strike are clustered between Pine and Oak Streets to the north and south, and Fifth and Eighth Streets to the east and west. This very small spatial area was packed with thousands of immigrants who in some cases had been in the country less than a decade. These immigrant organizations—from the Finnish Socialist Federation, to the Croatian Co-operative, to the prolabor Slovenian Glasnik Publishing Company—were the backbone of Western Federation of Miners membership and support. Drawn by Gary Kaunonen.

and went through Laurium and then into Calumet to the old Opera House where the convention was held. It must have been a fine sight to see those bewhiskered delegates in derby hats parading behind a couple of bands to let everyone know that the biggest of all Croatian societies was meeting in Calumet."[49]

While the NCS was not a socialist or even an explicitly working-class organization, the society did serve its large working-class membership. At the eleventh convention of the NCS the delegates added a section to their by-laws that denied membership benefits to strikebreakers. It read: "The members who are taken ill because of drinking, immoral life, venereal diseases or because they work during a strike as strike breakers, lose their rights to sickness benefit."[50] The large left-wing segment of the NCS went further, demanding that the organization banish all Croatians who scabbed during the 1913–14 Copper Country Strike and other labor conflicts from its membership lists. While the organization's Supreme Board did not go that far, it did allow members from the Copper Country to retain their membership while on strike without paying any dues.[51] Other Croatian organizations contributed funds to the 1913–14 Copper Country labor upheaval, with Local 69 of the NCS, based in Palatka, Michigan, located on the Menominee Iron Range, donating $32.50 to the WFM's organizational efforts in the Keweenaw.[52]

Similar to other southern European immigrants, many South Slavs came to the United States intending to return to their homeland, rejoin their families and friends, and use the wages they made in America to purchase lands or otherwise aid their families. For this reason, the overwhelming majority of Croatians and Slovenians who immigrated to the Copper Country during the late nineteenth and early twentieth centuries were men, as were the most prominent members of these immigrant groups' socialist and working-class movements.[53]

One major exception to the maleness of the South Slav workers' movements was working-class activist Ana Clemenc, a member of the Michigan Women's Hall of Fame whose story has been the subject of scholarly works and children's books.[54] Her father was an immigrant Slovenian mineworker, and her mother was a midwife and cook. Ana married Joseph Clemenc, an immigrant Croatian mineworker and activist member of the WFM in Calumet. Ana was "a socialist by conviction and strong advocate of workers' rights," according to one of her biographers.[55] One socialist writer noted, "I suppose Annie Clemenc knows what it is to go hungry, but I don't believe all the millions of dividends taken out of the Calumet & Hecla mine could buy her."[56]

During the copper strike of 1913–14, Clemenc figured prominently, leading strike parades, reportedly fighting off soldiers as they tried to attack strike demonstrations, and taking a leading role in organizing the 1913 Christmas Eve party at Italian Hall that ended in tragedy.[57] One anonymous writer for the *International Socialist Review* met "Big Annie" in Calumet and lauded her activism: "'Big Annie' has been leading the parades of the striking miners to which she walked early every morning from seven to ten miles. The women have been especially brave and class consciousness [*sic*] in this copper war. And the Finns, who have been educated in the principles of Socialism, are lending a militant character to the struggle that helps much to developing [sic] the staying powers of the men."[58]

Cooperation

So-called new immigrants such as the Finns and Croatians were not the only groups to form ethnic working-class institutions. In fact, a number of older, well-established immigrant groups such as the Germans formed workers' clubs in the Copper Country and maintained these institutions for decades after their initial entry into the region While there exists a vast mythology about the vaunted independence, opportunity, and self-interestedness of Americans, immigrants as well as the native-born working class have historically been as, if not more, interested in forming networks of support that enabled them to cooperate for their mutual benefit and receive assistance during times of need.[59]

In the Copper Country, the first formal organizations formed by immigrant workers were "mutual benefit societies," which, as their names suggest, were devoted to co-operation and assisting workers in the pursuit of mutually beneficial activities. The historian Larry Lankton listed some of the reasons why Copper Country residents joined these organizations, writing:

> when their members fell on hard times, these associations did more than just encourage acts of kindness and charity; they functioned much like insurance programs and paid out specified monetary benefits, usually derived from members' initiation fees (ranging from $1 to $5) and monthly dues (usually fifty cents to a dollar). . . . Societies typically paid monthly benefits when a man was unable to work because of sickness, accident, or general misfortune. And in the event of a member's death, any surviving widow or orphan got a death benefit and help in burying the deceased, which included a trail of mourners at the funeral.[60]

As Lankton's description suggests, some workers joined mutual benefit societies partly out of self-interest, a desire to protect themselves and their families in case of a disaster.

German immigrants were among the first to form mutual benefit societies in the Copper Country. In 1859, members of Hancock's German community formed the Hancock Deutscher Arbeiter Unterstuetzun Verein (German Workers' Support Association). Fifty years after its incorporation, the group still met on the first Sunday of each month at Germania Hall in Hancock.[61] A second German workers' organization called Arbeiter Unterstuetzungs Verein of Calumet was formed in 1912 as a benevolent and death benefits society. While ostensibly a fraternal organization formed to assist its members who suffered from the perils of capitalism, the group's choice of a name highlighting its class-based membership is one indication that German immigrants and their children remained dedicated to at least some form of collective activity.[62]

A number of other German mutual benefit organizations formed during the late nineteenth and early twentieth centuries. According to the Articles of Association for the Germania Society of Hancock, its purpose was to provide "assistance, aid, and help to disabled members because of work, sickness, accident, or other misfortune."[63] Considering that few members of the employing class would be concerned with becoming disabled or injured due to work, and that they would have the resources to personally fund their own care in the case of "sickness, accident, or misfortune," it stands to reason that the Germania Society retained its significance as a working-class organization in the Copper Country.

A number of other ethnic groups followed the Germans' model of establishing mutual benefit societies in the Copper Country. These included organizations founded by the Irish, such as the Ancient Order of Hibernians in Hancock; by the Swedes, such as the Swedish Benevolent Society of Calumet in 1883; by the Poles, such as the St. John Polish Miners' Society in Painesdale and the Polish Benevolent Society of Hussars of John Sobieski the Third in Calumet; by the Hungarians, who operated five societies in Houghton County during 1911;[64] and by the Finns, such as the Finnish Benevolent Society of Houghton County and the Finnish Accident and Aid Association of the Kearsarge and Wolverine Miners in 1892; the Atlantic Finlanders' Accident Association, Atlantic Mine, in 1893; and the Finnish Working Peoples' Society of Calumet in 1895.[65] Italian immigrants were especially effective in the establishment of benevolent societies. In fact, between 1875 and 1912 Italians established no less than twenty-two ethnic organizations in Calumet, Hancock, and Laurium.[66]

Some of the Copper Country's ethnic mutual aid organizations had obvious religious affiliations, including the Society of St. Patrick of the Village of Hancock, formed in 1876. Many were, however, secular organizations that indicated their memberships were restricted to working people, such as the Finnish Workmen's Co-Operative Company of Kearsarge, Michigan.[67] A number of immigrant groups also formed cooperative insurance organizations, such as the Calumet Finnish fire insurance organization in 1878 and the Italian Mutual Fire Insurance Company in 1901, while according to the historian Arthur Thurner, Otter Lake Finns established cooperative farming, hunting, home-building, and educational organizations.[68]

As with the Finnish Workmen's Co-Operative Company, some ethnic mutual benefit societies had noticeable working-class roots as well as radical purposes for forming the organizations. This was especially true among the Finns, Italians, and Croatians, all of whom formed leftist workers' organizations between 1890 and 1910. While, for good reason, much of the scholarship on the Copper Country has emphasized the central place of Finnish institutions, including Finnish co-ops, in the region's history, Italians and Croatians likewise expressed their consciousness of class by forming working-class institutions. Notable among these groups was the Croatian Benevolent Society of Calumet, formed in 1901 for the "mutual benefit of its membership . . . and not for profit of any kind."[69] The use of communal language by the authors of the articles was illustrative of their interest in collective, rather than personal, gain for members of Calumet's Croatian community. The collective needs of the Croatian community were likewise represented by the Croatian co-op store in Calumet. According to the co-op's Articles of Association, its members consisted of "miners, mechanics, laborers, and others," a strong indication of its working-class composition.[70] An Italian immigrant organization known as the Società Italiana di Mutua Beneficenza went even further, immediately proclaiming its political purposes: "We, whose names are subscribed hereto, have, by these Articles of Association, associated ourselves together for the purpose of forming a body politic."[71]

Copper Country immigrants began forming workers' co-ops as early as the 1870s when more than 400 owner-members from Calumet, Red Jacket, Hancock, Quincy, and Allouez formed the Scandinavian Union Store, organized in Red Jacket.[72] During the early twentieth century, Finnish co-ops dotted the Upper Peninsula, founded in several of the region's "Finn Towns." Reino Nikolai Hannula, a Finnish American historian active in the co-op movement during his youth, explained that these cooperatives were founded and maintained for radical purposes:

> The Finnish-American cooperative movement was part and parcel of the Finnish-American socialist movement. . . . The Finnish socialists, the ones who were active cooperators when I was a boy . . . viewed the cooperatives as a useful tool in the struggle to achieve socialism. Look at what happens in a society when the co-ops are weak or nonexistent, they asserted. Whenever the owners of industry, the capitalists, are forced to give a wage increase to their workers, they can recapture their profit (the surplus value) by merely raising the price of their product. When the co-ops are strong they can't do that because they can't raise their prices with impunity. The competition from a strong cooperative movement will force these private entrepreneurs to keep their price increases to a minimum. Thus, they will lose part of their surplus value (profit) with each wage increase.[73]

The earliest Finnish co-ops in Michigan were founded on the Marquette and Menominee Iron Ranges. Finns first established a collective consumers' store in

Republic on the Marquette Range in 1907 and then in Crystal Falls on the Menominee Range the next year.[74] Four additional co-ops were founded in 1913, two of which, in Rock and Mass City, were established by Copper Country Finns.[75] By 1913, Finns also ran cooperative stores at Wolverine and Lake Linden.[76]

While the Finns were the most prolific hall builders and have become the best known of all the "hall" radicals, Copper Country Italians would certainly be top candidates in the prize for persistence. Formed in 1889, the Società Italiana di Mutua Beneficenza immediately set out to place its stamp on the Calumet landscape. This Italian organization built three Calumet Italian Halls roughly in the same location, all of which came to unfortunate ends: the first was blown over in a windstorm just as its construction neared completion in November 1889; the second burned to the ground on New Year's Day 1908; and the third was the site of the infamous 1913 Christmas Eve tragedy.[77] While a number of ethnic organizations with an equally diverse set of political positions met at the Italian halls, and thus it would be incorrect to equate this organization with any set of political beliefs, Calumet's Italian Hall *was* an important meeting place for Copper Country radicals as well as their more conservative counterparts. For example, the Società Italiana di Mutua Beneficenza rented out part of its hall to the Croatian Publishing Company, which published the *Hrvatski Radnik*.[78] Italian Hall also hosted mass socialist meetings, including those with unquestionably radical intentions. In March 1906, the Houghton County socialists held a meeting at the hall to pass resolutions protesting the arrests of WFM officials charged with the murder of former Idaho governor Frank Steuenberg.[79]

Immigrant Workers, Militant Workers

In most instances, members of the so-called new immigrant workers were well out in front of their native-born and "old immigrant" counterparts when it came to organizing unions, standing up to the boss, and striking. Certainly, "new immigrants" worked in some of the harshest, most dangerous conditions for the lowest wages. But their militancy can only be partly explained by the "social sores" that accompanied their ethnicity and occupations. Indeed, while other groups of "new immigrants," including Italians and Croatians, struck the Copper Country's mines during the early twentieth century, their levels of militancy paled in comparison to that of the Finns, a fact noted by their contemporaries as well as by later historians. Thus, the Finnish American historian Carl Ross observed of the 1913–14 strike that "the Finns always have considered this as 'their' strike."[80] Writing to the *International Socialist Review* in the midst of that great labor tumult, Leslie H. Marcy attributed the rise of mineworkers' unionism to the actions of the

Finns: "About four years ago the Finnish Socialists organized the first union in the copper country, that amounted to anything, at Hancock, Mich., and affiliated with the Western Federation of Miners."[81]

Employers knew full well that most of the pro-union and radical workers at their workplaces were immigrants, and they were especially concerned about the large number of Finns who worked in their mines. This fact was made most obvious in the summer of 1906, when a mostly Finnish group of trammers at the Michigan Mine in Rockland struck and "rioted" to stop underground miners from crossing their picket line.[82] In response to the Rockland Strike, as well as earlier labor conflicts led by Finns, local bosses turned to hiring Finnish-speaking labor spies with an ability to communicate and read the Finnish language to infiltrate Finnish organizations, befriend Finnish workers, and report back on what local Finnish workers were discussing. Thus, in August 1906, a Finn labor spy working for the Thiel Detective Service and known only as E. E. R. was assigned to the Quincy Mine. According to a higher-ranking Thiel agent, this assignment was made to "ascertain fully the feeling and attitude of the Finlander employees."[83]

Correspondence between labor spy companies such as Thiel and the Pinkerton National Detective Agency and the Quincy Mining Company demonstrated that there was a considerable and consistent need for Finnish-speaking "operatives" to infiltrate the organizations and investigate the activities of Finnish workers, unionists, and strikers. When a "Finnish-speaking Operative" with "experience in both gold and copper mines, and thoroughly acquainted with WF of M tactics," became available in March 1911, an executive at the Thiel Detective Service wrote to the Quincy Mining Company offering the spy's services.[84] Even with a number of Finnish-speaking Thiel operatives in its employment in 1907, the Quincy Mining Company still sought out more, including "a Finn operative" ordered by the company from the notorious Pinkerton National Detective Agency.[85]

The prominent role played by Finns in the labor movement meant that all too often the victims of class violence were Finnish immigrants, while their attackers were native-born Americans or immigrants from Anglo stock. Such was the case during the aforementioned Rockland Strike. During the strike, trammers from the mine, nearly all of whom were Finns, struck to compel their bosses to pay higher wages. Their protests soon extended to the actions of underground miners at the Michigan Mine who, according to the *Daily Mining Gazette*, "refused to join the trammers in the strike."[86]

Like their Finnish fellow workers, Croatian members of the working class frequently took active roles in Copper Country labor struggles. The significance of the Croatians to the Copper Country working class and that group's penchant for radicalism made the region's Croatian immigrants prized recruits for union organizers. As Croatian American historian George J. Prpic has argued, "a great majority of the Croatian immigrants belonged to the working class," and indeed a large number of the Copper Country's miners were immigrants or second-generation Croatian Americans.[87]

A snapshot of the lives of eastern European working-class immigrant families can be seen by examining the Butler Row Houses, an approximately 5,600-square-foot structure comprised of eight miniature boardinghouses in Calumet. Packed into the Butler Row Houses were dozens of working-class immigrants at the time of the 1910 U.S. Census.[88] The Butler Row Houses was actually a row of small, one-and-a-half-story houses connected by common outside steps. These houses were approximately 562.5 square feet each and were subdivided into two units. Within these small units lived large groups of working-class families with up to twelve residents per house. Tellingly, the row of boardinghouses was marked "tenement" on a 1907 Sanborn map, and in terms of living conditions the Butler Row Houses differed little from the tenements of major eastern cities. Eighty-one working-class immigrants and American-born children squeezed into these cramped spaces.[89]

The Millers—Louis, Margaret, and Mortiz—were one such Butler Row Houses family. Louis, the husband, father, and "head" of the family, emigrated in 1901 from Croatia. By 1910, Louis had taken a job at Calumet where he, like so many local Croatians, worked as a trammer. Margaret, Louis's wife, a Croatian-born woman who immigrated to the United States in 1908, worked as a boardinghouse keeper, tending to the family's boarders and their infant son, Mortiz, who was born in Michigan. The Miller household also included seven Croatian-born boarders, all of whom labored as trammers, as well as Annie Yalich, an eighteen-year-old Croatian woman who worked as a servant in the home.[90]

Like Louis Miller and the seven boarders who lived at "his" house, many of the boardinghouse residents were trammers, the men who performed the difficult, dangerous jobs of loading tramcars with copper ore and pushing them out of the mines. Slovenian newspaperman Ivan Molek worked as a trammer at Calumet & Hecla (C&H) during his days in Calumet, and, like many trammers, Molek "met with a near-fatal accident in the mine," which happened when he "had fallen under a car filled with rock." "As it rolled over me," he later wrote, "the flesh on my hip and elbow was torn to the bone." Molek remembered that, in order to avoid responsibility, C&H, like other mine companies, went out of its way to blame the victims of these "industrial accidents," accusing injured workers of recklessness and negligence. He described the company's policy: "I was sharply reprimanded by the C&H officials for violating their rules. Miners were forbidden to ride atop filled wagons through the shafts; and the company disclaimed all responsibility for any accident arising from this reason. It was company policy to pay five hundred dollars death claim for every worker killed through no fault of his own. Had I been killed, they would not have been under any obligation."[91]

Molek's injuries were not unusual, and the poverty and cramped living conditions experienced by the immigrant trammers and their families at the Butler Row Houses were quite common in the Copper Country. Molek, like the Croatian immigrant mineworkers living in the Butler tenements, came to the United States in hopes of achieving some sort of "American Dream." But that dream frequently gave way before a reality full of poverty, long working hours, cramped living conditions, and so-called industrial accidents.

The case of Croatian immigrant mineworker Nick Verbanac is illustrative in this regard. Verbanac was active during the 1913–14 strike as a WFM organizer who worked "among the Croatian people," and was charged in the December 7, 1913, murders of scab miners Arthur Jane, Harry Jane, and Thomas Dally.[92] Regardless of his role in these murders (which was highly contested by the WFM), Verbanac has mostly been remembered as an outsider, the classic "foreign agitator" hired by the WFM to bring revolution to the Copper Country. For example, Arthur Thurner took great pains to depict Verbanac as a corrupt, gun-toting, free-spending union official,[93] but Verbanac's story is much more complex than this caricature suggests. His path toward becoming a radical member and organizer of the WFM was much more the result of personal experience in the region's main industry, rather than that of a paycheck provided to him by an outside organization. Born in Croatia in 1887, Verbanac became a naturalized American citizen and lived and worked in the Keweenaw for eight years leading up to the Copper Country Strike of 1913–14. Despite years of hard work as a drill boy, trammer, and miner in and around the copper mines, Verbanac failed to gain access to anything approaching "the good life." He lived as a boarder in Quincy Township in 1910 and boarded in South Range three years later.[94]

As a longtime Copper Country mineworker, Verbanac was an especially prized member of the WFM's organizing cadre because of his fluency in Croatian and English, and, as with numerous other strikers, Verbanac was active in harassing mineworkers who tried to cross the picket lines. He joined his fellow workers in organizing parades to pass in front of scabs as they walked to work at the Baltic mine.[95] His militancy was further demonstrated on Christmas Day, 1913, when, at St. John's Church in Calumet, Verbanac laid full blame for the Italian Hall tragedy at the feet of the employer-dominated Citizens' Alliance. Urging violent retribution for what he no doubt considered to be a massacre, Verbanac argued that local workers should "take an axe" to members of the Citizens' Alliance.[96] Verbanac's militancy made him notorious among Copper Country mine bosses, who colluded to have him removed from employment and permanently blacklisted. Indeed, the

Croatian American radical and WFM organizer was a prized target for Quincy Mine bosses, who sought to remove him from their employment for his radical activities. However, Verbanac was able to delay his firing due to a stroke of good luck, and the unfamiliarity of Quincy's bosses with their employees. Charles Lawton, general manager of the Quincy Mining Company, could not locate Verbanac, and wrote to William R. Todd, the Quincy president: "We have four men by the same name" so "we shall expect soon to commence discharging until we get the right man."[97]

Joining Verbanac in challenging the Copper Country's mine bosses was Tony Porcar, a Croatian who first went into the copper mines as a trammer at the age of fifteen. Working at the Copper Range, Michigan, Victoria, C&H, and Champion mines, Porcar indicated that his work in the mines had weakened him so that within a few years he had tremendous difficulty pushing a tramcar. Asked why this was the case during the U.S. congressional investigation into the copper strike, the Croatian mineworker stated that at age fifteen "I was coming from the old country at that time. I didn't do much work in the old country. I was feeling good—15 years. I was feeling stout." But, continued Porcar, the combination of hard labor with the "cold down there at the thirteenth level" took a heavy toll on the trammer. After two weeks of work he would be "played out" and forced to "stay home sometimes a week or two or three weeks" to recuperate.[98]

While their working and living conditions, long hours, and poverty no doubt played into the willingness of these Croatian immigrant workers to strike, for many workers it was their experiences at the hands of state and local officials that radicalized them. For example, on July 31, 1913, Victor Ozanich, a twenty-year-old Croatian immigrant and striking WFM member, was arrested for allegedly attempting to blow up one of the shaft houses in Calumet, taken to the Houghton County Jail, and beaten. Ozanich described his ordeal: "First he hit me on the side of the eye and told me, 'What am I laughing at?' I said I wasn't laughing. Then he hit me once again, and he again asked me what I was laughing at. I told him I wasn't laughing: and then he kicked me in the shin again."[99] Two other Croatian strikers, Frank King and Tony Stefanic, were physically attacked by members of the Michigan National Guard during a strike parade in Calumet on September 13, 1913, while showing their devotion to their adopted country by carrying the stars and stripes. According to King:

> We parade on Seventh Street, and we turn on Pine Street. When we got on Pine Street, turn back again to Seventh and start on Eighth Street, and we got corner Elm and Eighth, and I was carrying the flag, American flag, but some soldiers come up there; there was good bunch of soldiers; I couldn't tell you how many soldiers there was; good number of soldiers was horseback, and afoot soldiers. One soldier says, "Go ahead, do your duty. Go through this street." Well, I say, all right. Another soldier came and swing his saber and

knock the staff out of the flag. . . . Another soldier, at same time, he knock the eagle off. Another soldier is took their bayonet and punch the flag through. One of those soldiers came out, grabbed the flag. Capt. Blackman coming and hit him [Tony Stefanic] on the left side, giving him black eye.[100]

Interethnic Organizing

By the end of the first decade of the twentieth century, Copper Country workers had begun to work in concert, forming interethnic unions and radical groups to express class interests. Some evidence indicates that the WFM provided the impetus for interethnic organization in the Copper Country. The historian Elizabeth Jameson has argued that western mineworker unionists carried successful strategies for combating ethnic divisions into the Copper Country. After traveling to the Keweenaw in 1903, WFM organizer Joy Pollard brought his experiences from the Colorado mine wars to the Copper Country and "printed circulars in Italian, 'Austrian' (Serbian), Finnish, Polish, and Swedish."[101]

Others within the WFM bureaucracy must have understood the necessity of employing immigrant organizers, as by 1908 a number of immigrant mineworkers held positions as organizers and local officials within the federation. As the historian Arthur E. Puotinen wrote, "By early 1908 a cadre of Western Federation of Miners representatives moved into the Michigan iron mining districts, and they gradually worked their way to the Copper Country. Finnish leaders such as John Välimäki, Frank Aaltonen, John Kolu, Helmer Mikko, John Hietala, and Axel Kolinen worked shoulder to shoulder with organizers from other ethnic groups in this process."[102] Building on this strategy and recognizing the significance of immigrants to the copper region's labor force, the WFM sent in yet another multiethnic group of organizers in 1910, including two organizers with Croatian surnames, two with Finnish surnames, and two with Italian surnames.[103]

In January 1913, mere months before the eruption of the strike, the Copper (Calumet), Hancock, Mass City, and South Range WFM locals elected local presidents and secretaries with Finnish or Italian surnames: Italians Peter Jedda and Peter Sculatti joined Finns John E. Anttila, Charles E. Hietala, A. A. Toivonen, Jacob Vainioupas, Arvid Viitanen, and Henry Koski in efforts to organize Copper Country mineworkers.[104] As this list shows, eastern and southern European immigrants joined Finns as leaders of the Copper Country labor movement as the region cascaded toward the great strike of 1913–14.

On other occasions, Copper Country workers with little to no assistance from labor organizations or outside agitators organized interethnic strike forces led by strike committees whose diversity represented the strikers themselves. During a summer 1906 strike at the Quincy Mining Company, several workers took note of the diversity of the strike force. One Finnish immigrant observed "the Finlanders, Italians, and Irish stuck together but that the English were against it."[105] That same strike saw the multilingual mine labor force use English as their lingua franca. Indeed, Finnish, Italian, and Croatian workers appointed "men of each nationality who understood English," who could communicate with one another and thus coordinate plans across linguistic boundaries.[106]

A key figure in advancing interethnic working-class cooperation in the Copper Country was the Italian socialist and WFM organizer Teofilo Petriella. Fluent in English and Italian, Petriella was a teacher in Italy and in his own words was "invited by the Board of Education to the city of Rome to take a position in the schools there."[107] He was a longtime labor radical, a member of the SPA, WFM, IWW, and another group he referred to as a "revolutionary organization."[108] Skilled as a writer, editor, and orator, Petriella worked as an organizer for several organizations, including the Socialist Party of New Jersey and the WFM.[109]

Arriving in Houghton County in January 1906, Petriella immediately took to the local lecture circuit, addressing English- and Italian-speaking audiences.[110] By February 1906, Petriella served as the editor of *La Sentinella*, an Italian-language socialist newspaper published in Calumet between 1895 and 1907. According to the historian Russell M. Magnaghi, *La Sentinella* was "filled with socialist philosophy and rhetoric," and regularly included militant editorials written by Petriella.[111] The editor contributed a great deal of time to *La Sentinella*, but went unpaid for his services. At the 1907 WFM convention in Denver, Petriella discussed his lack of payment for working on the newspaper and at least one of the reasons why he persisted in working on it without pay. He said that he was paid "not a single cent. Nothing but honor. . . . I have contributed to that paper as I have contributed to other papers before and afterwards, and for nothing."[112] Despite, or perhaps because of, the newspaper's radical views, it received substantial support from the Copper Country's Italian business community, whose members funded *La Sentinella* by purchasing advertising space in its pages.[113]

In April 1906, Petriella organized the Italian portion of a joint Italian-Finnish socialist meeting, social affair, and dramatic performance designed to raise awareness (and likely funds) for a local mineworkers' strike.[114] The socialist meeting was characterized by a great deal of interethnic cooperation, and indeed Petriella was known for forging fellow workers from diverse ethnic groups into a cohesive whole. For example, Petriella arrived on the Minnesota iron ranges in 1906 to help bridge ethnic divisions between the strikers and unite them under the banner of the WFM. According to landscape historian Arnold R. Alanen, one of the Italian socialist's "first actions in Minnesota" was to "replace the English-speaking leaders of local unions with immigrants and divided the range into Finnish, Italian, and Slavic sections."[115]

Guided by organizers like Petriella or groups such as the Finnish socialists, Italian benevolent societies, or Croatian cooperators, a number of Copper Country ethnic groups had, by the early 1910s, begun to unite in class-conscious organizations that bridged ethnic divisions. In this manner, members of "new immigrant" groups led the Copper Country Left as they mobilized in their struggles with the region's oligarchy. Whether motivated by common class experiences, the initiative of the WFM, or the dynamic organizational skills of local and "outside" organizers, members of diverse immigrant groups had begun to realize that they shared class interests, interests that bridged ethnic divisions and could be acted upon for their mutual benefit.

CHAPTER 4

Troublemakers

Yesterday afternoon I went to Wolverine and interviewed the Hungarian strike leader, Jimmy Kelso. I . . . was not able to accomplish anything. He is just a boy a little over 22 years of age, has anarchistic tendencies and is just a plain damn fool. He possesses the self-sufficiency of youth and one cannot naturally do anything with him.

—"Big Jim" MacNaughton, superintendent of the C&H Mining Company, to Quincy Shaw, president of the C&H Mining Company, August 26, 1913

PICNICS, PARADES, AND CONVENTIONS WERE ALL CHARACTERISTIC OF THE RICH public culture crafted by Copper Country socialists during the early twentieth century. Perhaps the radicals' favorite date for taking to the streets was the first of May, May Day, widely known as International Workers' Day. Each year working people gathered in cities and towns across the nation to celebrate May Day, a day that regularly featured such radical staples as soapbox speeches and mass demonstrations. While the holiday was only sporadically celebrated in the Copper Country during the early twentieth century, by 1913, on the verge of the Copper Country mineworkers' strike, the socialist movement had established itself to the point where thousands of working people met to celebrate a day dedicated to their interests as workers. John Välimäki and Charles E. Hietala, officials in the Hancock branch of the Western Federation of Miners (WFM), wrote to the *Miners' Magazine* detailing the May Day 1913 activities:

> A great May Day celebration was held under the auspices of the Hancock Copper Miners' Union No. 200 of the Western Federation of Miners, on Sunday, May 4, in which the miners of the copper country of Michigan turned out in a big parade through Hancock and Houghton in the morning and in the afternoon attended a meeting held in the Kansankoti hall.
>
> The parade started at 10 o'clock A.M. from the corner of Franklin and Shelden streets, Houghton, where the line was formed, and marched across to Hancock, proceeding along Hancock avenue to Lake street and thence back on Quincy street to the Kansankoti hall on Tezcuco street, where it disbanded. The parade was the biggest one ever held by the miners in the upper peninsula of Michigan. When the parade started from Houghton it numbered over 2,500 and a number of miners joined from Hancock into the parade. It is not too much to say that there was in parade about 3,000 men because the parade was over one mile long.[1]

Following the parade, a mass meeting in Kansankoti Hall was addressed by an interethnic group of WFM and socialist leaders: C. E. Mahoney, vice president of the WFM, spoke in English; *Työmies* editor A. O. Sarell spoke in Finnish; Croatian immigrant WFM organizer Thomas Strizich addressed the crowd in his native language; and Calumet WFM organizer Anton Romano spoke in Italian.[2] Occurring almost three months before the start of the 1913–14 Michigan Copper Strike, these highly energetic and ideological May Day festivities no doubt had a significant impact on the push to strike against the Copper Country mine bosses.

In spite of the undeniably radical tone set by celebrations such as the 1913 May Day parade, with a few exceptions, the Copper Country labor movement remained generally conservative prior to the rise of the WFM. In addition to the mineworkers' acts of militancy, scores of other Copper Country workers formed trade unions that were affiliated with the American Federation of Labor (AFL), took part in the rich working-class culture of the early twentieth-century labor movement, and occasionally waged strikes against local employers. For the most part, these unions were allowed to organize and maintain their memberships without stiff opposition from their employers, municipal officials, or mine bosses. Thus, with the exception of those led by mineworkers, few significant labor struggles occurred in the Copper Country as cigar makers, longshoremen, brewery workers, and others formed a lively local labor movement, but one that was not militantly opposed by their employers.

Still, as the large turnout for May Day 1913 indicated, the Michigan copper region was not devoid of radicals or radical movements. One early example of Copper Country radicalism came on May Day 1872, as the region's miners took their first concerted steps to contest their oppression by organizing unions and waging strikes against their employers. That day the miners and other underground laborers at Calumet & Hecla (C&H)—influenced by the Marxist International Workingmen's Association (IWA)—struck for higher wages and an eight-hour workday. The 1872 strike was followed up by a series of minor labor conflicts waged by the Knights of Labor. The seeds of radical discontent sown by such early labor organizations as the IWA and the Knights of Labor steadily grew into open rebellion.

Copper Country Radicals

Copper Country mine owners went to great lengths to prevent radicals from organizing in their communities and workplaces. Still, some miners and others in the region bravely defied these restrictions and threats, forming radical political parties and clubs as well as unions and revolutionary organizations. During the late nineteenth and early twentieth centuries, Copper Country politics was dominated by the Republican Party. However, politicians representing working-class interests and receiving support from workers ran for, and occasionally won, election to local or statewide political office.

One of the earliest working-class politicians seeking office in the region was C. H. O'Rourke, a teamster, blacksmith, and farmer who published a newspaper in Ironwood in 1886 that was, according to one biographer, known as the "Knights of Labor newspaper." That same year, and presumably with the support of local Knights, O'Rouke was elected Ontonagon County sheriff, an office he held for four years before serving a two-year term as county treasurer.[3] At roughly the same time, Martin Kallander, a Swedish immigrant who operated a boardinghouse in Bessemer, was elected to the Michigan House of Representatives in 1887 from the Ontonagon district. According to a compilation of biographical sketches of Michigan legislators put out by the state of Michigan, Kallender "was nominated for Representative by the Labor Party and then endorsed by the Democrats."[4] In the early 1910s, John Dunnigan, an activist in the WFM, was elected as mine inspector for Keweenaw County. Dunnigan's election, according to his son Patrick, came in spite of the vigorous opposition of mine bosses, who told local workers, "Don't you vote for Dunnigan."[5]

A more persistent institutionalized threat to the dominant two-party system came from the Socialist Party of America (SPA). In the Keweenaw, socialists hailed from many different ethnic groups. English-speaking socialist locals were formed in Hancock, Lake Linden, Laurium, and the nearby cities of Ishpeming, Negaunee, and

Marquette on Michigan's Marquette Iron Range. Members of these organizations, like their Finnish-speaking counterparts, had a rich cultural life.[6] For example, Calumet socialists hosted annual picnics at Tamarack park. While these gatherings included groups of Finnish and Italian socialists, the main event at the 1906 picnic was a speech given by A. Farmer, an English-speaking socialist. His speech was accompanied by music from the Red Jacket City Band and followed by a parade of local socialists and the band.[7] In spite of its relatively isolated location, the Copper Country was also a regular stop on the socialists' speaking tours, owing to the ability of local socialists to guarantee a large crowd of dedicated leftists. For example, on October 21 and 22, 1906, J. Walker, the SPA's candidate for governor of Michigan, and William T. Biggs, a Chicago socialist, delivered speeches in Calumet and Hancock.[8]

While immigrants played a major role in the development of Copper Country socialism, many leaders of the Copper Country's socialist movement consisted of native-born Americans who spoke and read English, and belonged to one of the many local unions. Edgar L. Glanville, a union plumber and secretary of the Lake Linden SPA local, was born in Wisconsin to American-born parents.[9] Albert L. Larsen, secretary of the Laurium branch of the SPA, was born in Norway, but by a decade into the twentieth century he was a nationalized American citizen who had learned English and had established himself as a house painter in Houghton County, one of the most heavily unionized crafts in the region.[10] Larsen's successor as secretary of the Laurium SPA was Annie M. Kline, who served as a party official during the tumultuous 1913–14 Copper Country Strike. While Kline's leadership position in the Laurium SPA was in many ways an unusual case, it was also at least a minor indication of the group's commitment to gender equality in an era when women were barred from the voting booths in Michigan, and the Copper Country Republican and Democratic Parties were closely guarded male institutions.[11]

While the best-known socialist locals in the Copper Country were undoubtedly Finnish branches, the "English" branches of the party were likewise significant forces in local politics and union activity. In 1914, Victor Berger, a socialist and former member of Congress, recalled the German roots of Copper Country socialists, stating: "Once upon a time there was even a German organization in existence in the copper country, but the German element up here learned to speak English."[12] Moreover, local socialists issued resolutions in English that were printed in the Copper Country's English-language mainstream press. Such was the case in March 1905 when socialists met at a convention in Hancock and publicly attacked the capitalist system: "The Socialist party would abolish classes in society and all would be guaranteed equal rights and opportunities which can only be brought about by the abolition of private ownership of the means of production and distribution and the establishment of the co-operative commonwealth."[13]

Like their Finnish, Italian, and Croatian counterparts, local English-speaking socialists enjoyed a set of rich political and social cultural traditions and founded numerous institutions during the early twentieth century. The Hancock local of the SPA likely enjoyed a great deal of musical activity considering that its secretary was John Surbeck, who earned his living as a Hancock music teacher.[14] However, Surbeck's musical performances were not limited to private lessons taught at his house. The socialist leader also ran the Surbeck Orchestra in Hancock, a position that indicated his leadership in the Copper Country's cultural front.[15]

Much as it did across the nation, the Copper Country SPA fielded candidates for local and statewide political offices. One of its more prominent political nominees was John Henry Johnson, a Swedish-born lawyer educated in Calumet's public schools and the University of Michigan Law School. Johnson practiced law in Houghton County between 1902 and 1906, and was nominated by the SPA for Superior Court of Michigan in 1904 and Houghton County Probate Court in 1905.[16]

Still, the Copper Country's socialist movement was largely comprised of newly arrived immigrants, men and women who came to and worked in Michigan's copper mining region but, in many cases, were not U.S. citizens and thus lacked voting rights. As a result, SPA political candidates usually fared poorly in elections, receiving vote totals that were not commensurate with their strength in the region. For example, Eugene V. Debs, the perennial presidential candidate of the SPA, visited Red Jacket in June 1904, where he addressed approximately 300 persons, including "quite a number of ladies," on the topic of socialism.[17] Debs returned to the Copper Country in 1908 and delivered another well-attended speech. Yet during the presidential election held later that year, he earned only 3 percent of the Houghton County vote. Four years later, during the 1912 election, Debs again received only 3 percent of that county's votes. The reason for the difference between Copper Country residents' public outpouring of support for Debs at social events and the lack of support for him at election time is relatively simple: only 13 percent of Copper Country residents voted in the 1908 election, including, no doubt, few of the region's numerous socialist, but noncitizen Finns and other immigrants, so recently arrived from the Old Country.[18] Four years later, only 14,958 of Houghton, Keweenaw, and Ontonagon counties' 103,904 residents cast ballots in the 1912 gubernatorial election.[19]

Copper Country Socialists and the *Wage-Slave*

The best record of the Copper Country socialist activities can be found in the remaining copies of the *Wage-Slave*, a weekly newspaper from Hancock published by the Työmies Publishing Company. The *Wage-Slave* mixed Upper Peninsula news with stories on state, national, and international events. It also published dates for socialist speaking tours and local socialist meetings, along with a weekly column entitled "Ishpeming Sparks" carrying news of that city's socialist activities.[20]

The *Wage-Slave* was sustained largely through regular subscriptions, bundle orders, and the money paid to the press by advertisers. In May 1908, the newspaper had a subscription list of 2,300, and large bundle orders were regularly sent out to Michigan socialist locals.[21] As can be said for most working-class news organs, the readership of the *Wage-Slave* was likely much larger than its subscription list indicated, as working people who were either too migratory or too poor to purchase their own copy of the newspaper could read a secondhand copy left at a local hall or saloon. Alexander M. Stirton, the *Wage-Slave*'s editor, commented on this fact, writing: "The *Wage-Slave* is probably the best English advertising medium in the Copper Country. It isn't our subscription list alone that counts, but our extra circulation also, and the fact that every word is read and re-read by every man into whose hands it falls."[22]

Somewhat surprising, perhaps, considering the militant reputation of socialists, the *Wage-Slave* was on sale far and wide in the Upper Peninsula, appearing in the periodicals sections of such family-friendly stores as W. M. Washburn's candy store on Quincy Street in Hancock.[23] The newspaper also drew advertising money from a diverse cross section of the Copper Country business community. Advertisers included small business owners with Finnish surnames, including Otto Laitinen, a tailor in Ishpeming; M. Rauhala, a Hancock tailor; and A. Nieminen, a butcher and grocer in Hancock.[24] The New Light, a lighting store with outlets throughout the Upper Peninsula; jeweler W. J. Roberts from Ishpeming; and real estate agents trying to sell land in California all contributed to the socialist cause through their advertisements in the *Wage-Slave*.[25]

The newspaper's editorials garnered favorable coverage from such notable left-wing publications as the *International Socialist Review*, a monthly Marxist journal published by the Charles H. Kerr Press.[26] In March 1908, the monthly journal reprinted an editorial titled "Socialist Political Unity," in which the *Wage-Slave* called for an end to the schism between the SPA and the Socialist Labor Party. It read: "So let's get together. Union is strength. One all-embracing industrial unionism is what we need, and one all-embracing Socialist Party, and both revolutionary to the core."[27]

As a well-known radical with a national reputation, Stirton was easily the most visible of the English-speaking Copper Country socialists. He served as a delegate from Michigan to the 1908 SPA convention in Chicago and was on the SPA national committee the following year.[28] A former schoolteacher and minister in Greeley City, Michigan, the editor was a major player in the Socialist Party of Michigan as well.

In explaining his conversion to socialism, Stirton equated capitalism with evil, an evil that he and his fellow "toilers" needed to defeat: "I am making this step because it is impossible to be sane and not revolt; be sane and be silent; be sane and not take my place shoulder to shoulder beside my comrades, the toilers in the fight to overthrow the capitalist system."[29] While still a minister in 1906, Stirton authored a pamphlet entitled *From Star Dust to Socialism*, published by *Appeal to Reason*, a weekly socialist newspaper published in Girard, Kansas. One reviewer of the work described it as "one of those broad-sweeping general summaries of cosmical and social evolution, of which the Socialist writings already has so many, but which will always be needed so long as the great majority of the population act on the hypothesis that 'things were always this way and always will be.'"[30]

Part of Stirton's notoriety came from his itinerant speaking schedule. As the editor of one of the most notable socialist publications in the country, Stirton traveled throughout the Upper Peninsula and the wider Midwest, speaking on behalf of socialist causes and supporting socialist political candidates. For example, on June 28, 1908, he delivered speeches in Red Jacket and Laurium under the title "Why Socialism Must Win the United States during the Life-time of the Present Generation."[31] Stirton himself entered the political fray during the 1908 election cycle, running as the SPA's gubernatorial candidate in Michigan and touring the state alongside the SPA presidential nominee, Eugene V. Debs.[32] Still, Stirton earned only 9,400 votes out of more than 540,000 total votes cast in that election.[33]

Like many far-left socialists, Stirton applied an ethical stamp to working-class activism, arguing that because capitalism is a socioeconomic system based on oppression and exploitation, militant deeds by the working class on behalf of the working class are inherently good. He wrote: "Whatever line of conduct advances the interests of the working class is right and whatever line does not advance the interests of the working class is wrong."[34] However, the editor's ethical opposition to capitalism also rested on his experience in the church, a fact demonstrated by his choice of phrases for the *Wage-Slave* masthead: "Socialism Stands for the Golden Rule. Capitalism Stands for the Rule of Gold."[35]

Stirton's radicalism and talents as an editor won him high praise from many elements of the American radical and labor movements, a praise that included the awarding of Stirton with the moniker "Comrade" by his fellow radicals. The *International Socialist Review* happily reported that

> Comrade A. M. Stirton, editor of the *Wage-Slave*, published at Hancock, Mich., dropped
> in to pay the publishing house a visit a few days ago. He brought good news of the work
> being done in the northern peninsula. The more we know the editor of the *Wage-Slave*
> the better we understand the continued improvement of that virile weekly, for Comrade

> Stirton believes first, last, and all the time in the wage worker. . . . That little paper devotes
> itself exclusively to the battles and interests of the proletariat.[36]

Some radicals even gave credit to Stirton for the success of the SPA in the Copper
Country. During the Copper Country Strike of 1913–14, T. F. G. Dougherty, an
organizer for the Industrial Workers of the World (IWW), reporting on the strike,
observed: "It was in this region, at Hancock, that the red revolutionary 'Wage Slave'
was published by that good old rebel A. M. Stirton and it was mainly through Stirton
that the WF of M began its work in the copper region."[37]

Stirton occupied a spot on the far left of the SPA, a position based on his advo-
cacy of industrial unionism and revolutionary working-class direct action. He was
closely associated with the WFM. In December 1908, when WFM organizer William
Tracy was forced to take leave of Michigan to attend to union affairs in Minnesota,
Stirton ran the union's affairs from its headquarters in Laurium.[38] The editor wrote:
"Let us get busy then and organize into great Industrial Unions competent TO STRIKE
AND STAY, that's the word, not to strike and leave as the manner of the Craft Unions
is. Get busy and build up the I.W.W. Let every miner in the country join the Western
Federation of Miners, and let the Western Federation of Miners swing into line and
take its place where it ought to be in the I.W.W."[39]

Stirton's attitude toward industrial unions and revolutionary activity was a
popular one in the early twentieth century, a perspective shared by such notables as
Eugene V. Debs and William "Big Bill" Haywood. To these radical socialists, industrial
unions, those that were organized around the principle that all workers within an
industry ought to belong to the same union, were preferable to trade unions because
the former enrolled members of diverse races and ethnic groups, as well as both men
and women. Industrial unions were also better suited to modern, mass-production
industry, which had proved so effective at de-skilling workers through automation.
Trade unions, so the argument went, were holdovers of a bygone era, one in which
skilled craftsmen had a great degree of leverage in bargaining with employers.
Industrial unionism was especially attractive to Copper Country mineworkers,
who frequently worked alongside men from numerous ethnic groups and whose
ethnic backgrounds were occasionally used by employers to sow divisions among
the miners.

The Wobblies

Stirton's reputation as a radical and talented newspaperman extended well outside
of the Copper Country, and in 1909 he was recruited by eastern radicals to become

the first editor of *Solidarity*, a newspaper published by the IWW, whose members were also known as the Wobblies. Founded in 1905, the IWW functioned as both an industrial union and revolutionary organization. Committed to organizing all workers regardless of sex, race, ethnicity, or skill, the union experienced its greatest successes in the textile towns of New England, the harvest fields and hard-rock mines of the American West, the logging camps and lumber mills in the Pacific Northwest, and the docks of Philadelphia.[40]

The IWW differed from both the SPA and trade unions of the day, accusing the former of placing too much emphasis on politicians and elections, and attacking the latter as the "American Separation of Labor" for their policies of organizing small, craft-based unions rather than industrial organizations. The Wobblies were also far to the left of their counterparts in the SPA and AFL, having adopted an anarcho-syndicalist platform at their 1908 convention. It read: "The army of production must be organized, not only for every-day struggle with capitalists, but also to carry on the production when capitalism shall have been overthrown. By organizing industrially we are forming the structure of the new society within the shell of the old."[41] As anarcho-syndicalists, the Wobblies placed their hopes for revolution in the hands of "the workers themselves," the only group capable of bringing forth a new society through a general strike. Addressing a crowd in New York City on the topic of the general strike, "Big Bill" Haywood argued, "If I didn't think that the general strike was leading on to the great revolution which will emancipate the working class I wouldn't be here. I am with you because I believe that in this little meeting there is a nucleus here that will carry on the work and propagate the seed that will grow into the great revolution that will overthrow the capitalist class."[42]

One of the first places the IWW established itself as a strong force was in the steel industry in and around Pittsburgh, including in the towns of McKees Rock and New Castle, Pennsylvania.[43] McKees Rock was the site of one of the first major IWW struggles—and IWW victories—in which the strikers defeated the Pressed Steel Car Company. Perhaps the most lasting gain made from the McKees Rock strike was the founding of *Solidarity*, a weekly IWW publication. *Solidarity* was owned and operated by the New Castle locals of the IWW, with its staff consisting of fellow workers C. H. McCarty, Valentine Jacobs, Earl F. Moore, Geo. Fix, B. H. Williams, and Stirton.[44]

"Big Bill" Haywood, one of the leading socialists and Wobblies during the early twentieth century, recalled that "Comrade A. M. Stirton, who had for some years previously edited the *Wage-Slave* in Michigan, a paper well and favorably known throughout the country as an advocate of industrial unionism, arrived in New Castle, where *Solidarity* was started to help in the battles of the workers in the iron and steel district. C. H. McCarthy became the manager of the paper and

Comrade Stirton editor."[45] A photo of the editor appeared in advertisements for the revolutionary newspaper, which laid out the purpose for *Solidarity*: "Aims to be the leading exponent of industrial unionism in the United States. . . . A Real Working-Class Weekly."[46]

As was true of many left-wing editors, Stirton's actions on behalf of the working class landed him in jail after being convicted of violating a law regulating publishing in Pennsylvania. Following a short term in jail by the *Solidarity* staff, including Stirton, the editor stepped down from his position. In addition, Stirton worked without pay for much of 1910 owing to the financial difficulties of *Solidarity*. He left the editorship in the spring of 1910 following his release from jail and moved to Saginaw and then Grand Rapids, Michigan, where he was praised by his successors at the newspapers for dropping "all his claims against *Solidarity* for back wages while editor of the paper in 1910."[47] Stirton remained tied to the IWW after departing the *Solidarity* staff. His radical position alienated him from his former comrades within the Socialist Party of Michigan, with Stirton informing the IWW "that he couldn't be drawn into a Socialist local with a pair of mules."[48]

While Stirton's career trajectory made a clear connection between Copper Country radicalism and the IWW, the relationship between that region and the union was more nuanced and tenuous. Several dozen Copper Country mineworkers *did* belong to the IWW during the years 1905–1907 by virtue of their membership in locals of the WFM and that federation's affiliation with the IWW during that period.[49] Two Copper Country miners' unions, Local 200 in Hancock and Local 203 in Laurium-Calumet, both affiliated with the WFM, functioned during the years of WFM membership in the IWW. Only spotty membership statistics for these unions are available, but there were forty-two members in the Hancock union in July 1906.[50] Moreover, the WFM—and, by extension, the IWW—was paying the Työmies Publishing Company in Hancock to publish Finnish-language pamphlets beginning as early as December 1906, and it was within this group, the radical Finnish immigrant population, where the IWW's most significant influence and support rested.[51]

In the years leading up to the Copper Country Strike of 1913–14, a number of IWW locals were founded in the Keweenaw, as well as in nearby Marquette County. Among the first of these branches was Local 138 of the IWW in Laurium, a mixed local founded on June 23, 1909.[52] Laurium and Calumet Wobblies impressed the editors of *Solidarity*, who praised the Copper Country radicals for "piling up a good sub[scription] list for *Solidarity* and adding to [it] right along." The radical organ continued by urging Michiganders to equal the efforts of Copper Country IWWs: "Say, you Reds in the Lower Peninsula of Michigan, especially in Grand Rapids and Detroit, are you going to let the copper country boys scoot away ahead of you?"[53]

One of the Laurium local's members was Edward Hammond, a Wobbly who moved to the Calumet area and joined WFM Local 203 in that city, but "absolutely" refused "to pay the initiation fee, claiming the [Western] Federation [of Miners] are in duty bound to accept the IWW cards."[54] Hammond apparently impressed his fellow workers in the Copper Country, since WFM Local 203 elected him as a delegate to the 1909 WFM National Convention in Denver. But upon his arrival at the convention, Hammond was greeted with a letter and resolution from Local 203, declaring his election as a delegate to be null and void, since he "was in bad standing in said union, never having paid initiation fees nor dues."[55] Hammond's Copper Country experiences did not continue after 1909, but the organizer did have a fruitful experience in the IWW. He authored the pamphlet *Two Schools of Unionism*, published by the IWW, which, according to *Solidarity*, was the "best leaflet yet on the difference between Craft Unionism and the IWW."[56]

Other IWW locals were formed to the southeast in Negaunee and Marquette on the Michigan Iron Range. Founded in August 1909, Negaunee Local 65 was comprised of public sector workers, an unusual occupation for Wobblies considering that in February 1910 it was one of only two public-sector IWW branches, the other being located in Los Angeles.[57] Significant, too, was the fact that the Negaunee IWW included both male and female members, including the sole union officer listed in the union's press: local secretary Elma Anoinen.[58]

Louis Melia was one such Marquette Iron Range Wobbly in the 1910s. Writing to *Solidarity* during the 1913–14 Copper Country Strike, Melia declared that his fellow workers in the copper district were "waging an economic struggle, a social war as it were, in their endeavor to gain an eight-hour day, higher pay, and the right to organize; which the mine owners, through economic pressure, have for 20 odd years, succeeded in stifling."[59] Although Melia did not live in the Copper Country, he was confident that the strikers would win because of the changing and increasingly radical composition of the region's workforce. He wrote: "A new and determined element, a young virile generation, imbued with the spirit of solidarity, cognizant of a bitter past, will not tolerate forever the iron heel of copper magnates."[60]

While the IWW did not present an organizational challenge to the Copper Country mine operators, Quincy mine manager Charles Lawton did receive at least one hurried warning from a colleague, H. H. Halstead, district manager of the Corporations Auxiliary Company in Chicago, who warned him that "organizers of the Industrial Workers of the World, the syndicalist organization that has caused so much industrial strife throughout the East, are now getting very active in this section and the condition that will result from their efforts will not bring joy to the hearts of employers unless preventive measures are taken to nullify the effects of their work."[61] During the 1913–14 strike, Lawton was convinced that the "Wobbly menace" had infiltrated the local workforce and was partly responsible for the strike.

Writing to the president of the Quincy Mining Company, Lawton declared: "it does appear as if we could operate the mine with entirely new men better than we could with many of the former men that have joined the I.W.W. movement."[62]

In spite of their historical relationship with the region, the Wobblies as an organization did not exert much in the way of influence during the 1913–14 Michigan Copper Strike—the strike was in name solely a WFM-led action. However, the Wobblies' decentralized industrial unionist platform colored events that occurred early in the strike—especially in the active and large population of Finnish immigrant strikers. As an organization the IWW reported on the conflict from afar, visited the region as individual organizers or speakers, harassed strikebreakers en route to the Copper Country, and contributed funds to the strikers. In spite of the strike's significance to labor history and to the early twentieth-century labor movement, the IWW as a union remained at a distance, only occasionally writing of the struggle in their two main organs, the *Industrial Worker* and *Solidarity*.[63] Thus, Clarence Andrews, a professor of technical and business writing at Michigan Tech who authored a short history of the strike, stated of the Wobblies: "No, they [the IWW] were never here, to the best of my knowledge."[64] In fact, while *Solidarity* had been founded by Stirton in 1908, when he was a Hancock resident, the newspaper issued only a few "special" reports on the strike, and those were penned by T. F. G. Dougherty, a Wobbly writing from Grand Rapids, Michigan, a city more than 600 miles from the strike zone.

The lack of coverage was not due to any ignorance on the part of the IWW about the strike's import, as Dougherty himself acknowledged: "The greatest strike and lockout ever known in Michigan is now on in the upper peninsula of this state."[65] With full knowledge that scabs were being recruited in major cities in the Midwest and shipped to the Copper Country, Wobblies in Minneapolis, Minnesota, mobilized to confront—and hopefully halt—the strikebreakers before they could leave the city. On October 14, 1913, a group of Wobblies stopped a cadre of potential scabs as they prepared to leave for Calumet. IWW member R. Reese reported on the force applied by the Wobblies in *Solidarity*:

> A lively fight ensued yesterday between a bunch of strikebreakers and IWW men. The scabs were on their way to Calumet, Mich., to take the places of the striking copper miners. They were met by some of our members, who told them not to go to Calumet to help defeat the striking miners. But these rats wouldn't listen to argument, so a more forcible language had to be applied. The IWW men gave them a dose of direct action with such telling effect that they went to a doctor instead of Calumet. During the fight one of the scabs drew a gun, but he was overpowered and the gun taken away from him. The police arrested two of our fellow workers and the gunman. The charge against Fellow Workers JOHN DELANY and JULIUS HANSEN was assault and battery. The kangaroo court today

found both of them guilty. Sentence 10 days in the workhouse. The charge against the gunman was dismissed and "His Honor" stated that scabs had a perfect right to carry guns. How is that for justice?[66]

To prevent additional scabs from being recruited in Minneapolis and St. Paul, IWW members took to picketing the employment offices and distributing handbills, "telling the slaves to stay away from Calumet, Mich."[67] Certain IWW locals, while nearly always strapped for cash, donated what little they had to the Michigan copper miners. Thus, in early December 1913 IWW branches in Detroit and Spokane, Washington, made small cash contributions to the strikers' defense fund.[68] Another minor source of support came from radicals, including Wobblies, who promoted the strikers' cause at mass meetings across the nation. At an April 5, 1914, meeting of the IWW in New York City, Joseph Cannon of the WFM was addressing the crowd on the copper strike in Michigan when the police rushed and forcefully dispersed the crowd.[69]

Thus, unlike many of the most famous conflicts of the 1910s, the IWW did not play a leading role in the 1913–14 strike. Instead, the Wobblies appeared to understand that the copper strike would be won or lost by the Michigan copper miners, and their main institution was the WFM. Acknowledging that his organization played only a small part in the strike, but hopefully predicting a future for the Wobblies in the Copper Country, T. F. G. Dougherty wrote: "When the WORKERS begin to RECOGNIZE that the only way to fight the boss is by being organized solidly in a revolutionary industrial union, the boss will wish that he had recognized the now-conservative WF of M."[70] Furthermore, most of the IWW's financial resources and its best-known organizers were tied up with equally significant conflicts in other parts of the United States, while the copper miners, led by the WFM, waged their struggle in the Upper Peninsula.

CHAPTER 5

Organization

When hard times came and the company went down, we never had any trouble with
reducing wages somewhat to keep the company going . . . the men and the companies
all worked together as friends and we paid them as much as we could.
                    —William Parsons Todd, vice president of the Quincy Mining Company
                                        during the 1913–14 Michigan Copper Strike

DUE TO THE EFFORTS OF EARLY UNION ORGANIZERS, CLASS-CONSCIOUS IMMI-
grants, and resilient radicals, Copper Country mineworkers began to believe that
there was an opportunity to collectively voice their concerns about wages, hours,
and working conditions in an attempt to exert some control over their labor. Many
laborers in Copper Country mines came to understand that there was no way around
it—mining was a dangerous job. Each and every day a mineworker went underground
there was a chance he would never see the sky again. Those were the cold, hard facts
of hard-rock mining in the Copper Country. Imagine a job where life, the essential
act of existence, was always in a precarious state of balance between going home to
see your wife and kids or being hauled out the bottom of the mine—dead. Worse
yet, there were many ways to die or become injured. In Copper Country mines,

mineworkers worked with hard rock, so entire cave-ins of the underground "roof" were rare, but the falling of thousand-pound boulders like one massive, crushing drop of rain from above was not just something to be wary of—it was somewhat commonplace.

Rock falls, electrocution, falls down a thousand-foot mineshaft, getting blown up, breathing in carbon monoxide, being burned alive underground, and being run over by machinery were all a daily concern. Adding to the logical concerns of working underground in a copper mine was the fact that the Copper Country mines were playing catch-up with younger, richer, and shallower mines in the American West. The Butte, Montana, and Bisbee, Arizona, mining regions were surpassing the production of Michigan copper at the turn of the twentieth century, and the need to compete with these mines sometimes drove Copper Country mine managers to cut corners and speed up an already dangerous industry.

Working conditions and the dangers inherent in mining were a key factor in the Copper Country push for organization—union representation for worker grievances. While the Copper Country mines were less deadly than their western U.S. counterparts, death and injury were all-too-frequent occurrences. In 1911, there were 60 deaths (more than one death a week), 656 serious injuries, and 3,974 slight injuries in Copper Country mines.[1]

It was fire, however, that was the cause of the most deadly Copper Country mining accident. On September 7, 1895, at approximately 11.30 A.M. in the Osceola Mine, twenty-nine or perhaps thirty people lost their lives as one of the hundreds of timbers used as support and structure underground caught fire. Like lighting mammoth matchsticks in a massive matchbox, the fire spread throughout the mine. Shafts that could have been used as escape routes became full of smoke, and as the fire raged it became clear that those still in the mine were in perilous danger, not so much from the lapping flames of fire, but more so from succumbing to smoke inhalation. Above ground, mining management and the crowd that had gathered around the smoldering shaft wondered what might become of the men underground. Wives and children were overcome with grief, while mine managers attempted to determine how to best put out the fire.[2]

As attempts were made to get men out, it became clear that workers in Shaft Nos. 3 and 4 were trapped. Crews of men descended into the mine looking for survivors, but were turned back due to the thickness of smoke and lack of breathable air. In the afternoon, after about five hours of fire, management of the Osceola decided to cap the No. 3 Shaft, cutting oxygen to the fire, but also effectively sealing the fate of workers still in Shaft Nos. 3 and 4. As the Houghton County mine inspector reported, "As soon as it was possible to enter the mine the work of recovering the bodies was begun. Thirteen were found the following Thursday and the last recovered the Monday following. The bodies were all discovered in or near No. 4 Shaft, scattered between the 4th and 17th levels."[3]

Undoubtedly, many looked upon the capping of the shaft as a sealing of the mineworkers in their own untimely tomb. An inquest was held to determine if any blame was to be meted out, and almost predictably the jury found that the deaths of the men were their own fault. The Copper Country, as we have seen already, was ruled by the whims and will of the mining companies and the men who ran them. Mining officials often handpicked candidates to run for county office, and county officials frequently were mining management such as Jim MacNaughton of Calumet & Hecla (C&H), who was on the Houghton County Board of Supervisors for years. Juries were often just as biased. Justice was slanted heavily in favor of the mining companies, and the Osceola Mine fire would prove the tradition of company domination in all affairs steadfast.

According to Houghton County officials, nineteen miners, five trammers, one general laborer, and four boys were dead because of their own actions while at work in the Osceola Mine. The jury declared that "the deceased did not realize the seriousness of their danger," and "we exonerate the mine officials from all negligence in this sad affair." The Houghton County mine inspector seemed to think that the men lagged underground, even in the face of impending doom, because they were "old and experienced miners, and their loss of life was doubtless due to the fact that they thought that owing to their being so little timber in the mine that there could be no fire of consequence there. . . . Their assurance of their safety made them careless and thoughtless."[4]

Thus, it became recorded in history that these mineworkers were so old and experienced yet negligent that they were unable to recognize the dire nature of their situation in a mine on fire. Never mind that these "old and experienced" workers included four boys or that the workers were found "scattered" throughout the No. 4 Shaft so as to not be able to communicate—meaning that even if the experienced workers in the shaft knew what to do in what seemed to be an ordinary fire, they were not able to communicate with those in fear for their life. In an incident such as this, blame is often difficult to dispatch, but blaming the victims to avoid fault or exonerate mining company officials was then and is now inexcusable. This was the life of a mineworker—a life filled with peril, struggle, toil, and sometimes injustice.

Death was not the only constant concern in Copper Country mines. Sanitary conditions underground were simple—makeshift in some cases, and nonexistent in others. The most sanitary mines used empty boxes for toilets, which were later hauled to the surface. The Copper Range Company provided no sanitary materials, reporting once to a federal labor investigation committee, "There are no sanitary regulations beyond requiring levels to be cleaned up from time to time."[5]

Other environmental issues were of as little concern as the sanitation in mines. Proper ventilation, stale air, noise, and light were of little consequence to mining management. Some of these sensory offenses were unavoidable. As the mines went deeper, the temperatures got hotter. There was no avoiding that simple fact, and in some of the oldest and deepest mines, such as the C&H, Quincy, and Tamarack mines, depths were sweltering at constant 80-plus degrees Fahrenheit. Imagine the shock of working in the stale 80-degree doldrums of a mine, and then walking out into blinding snow and the almost arctic below-zero temperatures of a Copper Country winter. The two conflicting meteorological phenomena had to have been mind-bending to workers. The high temperatures, stale yet moist air, literally "shitty" working areas, absence of light, and deafening sounds of heavy industry made for deplorable working conditions, but even these sad working conditions were better than the alternative for many—starvation.[6]

There was simply no way of getting around the fact that mining was a dangerous and dirty job where workers had little power in influencing their own affairs underground. The problem, then, for many of the Copper Country's working-class people was the recompense for putting lives on the line every single day while rich fat cats "back east" in New York, Boston, and Philadelphia enjoyed the fruits of their labor. The discrepancy between those with the wealth and those who made the wealth was too much to ignore. While immigrant trammers pushed thousand-pound rock cars each day, earning a little over twenty-five cents an hour while often working over fifty-five hours a week, C&H paid $3,347,000 in dividends (equal to over $76,000,000 in contemporary times) to stockholders in 1912 alone. In this same year, Copper Range paid out $788,000 in dividends, and Quincy paid out $550,000 in dividends. More lopsidedly, C&H's general manager, "Big Jim" MacNaughton, made a reported $120,000 a year in 1912.[7]

Moreover, in spite of the Copper Country mine owners' reputations for running a benevolent, paternalistic empire, poverty was a persistent problem in the lives of working families in the area. Wages for non-union workers in service industries were especially low. According to the Michigan Bureau of Labor and Industrial Statistics, in 1907 Houghton County's male hotel clerks were paid only $1 per day, while women employed as chambermaids, many working in the homes of mine managers, earned a daily rate of fifty cents, hardly enough to keep a worker out of poverty.[8]

The *Calumet Evening News* ran regular articles exploring the difficult conditions faced by the region's poor. In many of the most tragic cases, a working family's poverty was related to an act of industrial violence in a mine, as workers killed on the job often left a family with few provisions. Thus, in September 1909 a charity set up by mineworkers at C&H investigated cases where poor families needed relief. In one case, a German American widow living in Laurium with her three young children had "nothing to eat in the home," while there were "other cases of a similar nature being unearthed by the committee daily, which tends to show there is a great deal of poverty existing in Calumet."[9]

The blatant disconnect between labor and capital was a glaring feature of everyday life in the Copper Country, and no measure of "welfare capitalism" or paternalism could bridge the gap between the "haves" and the "have-nots." In trying to content workers by doling out benefits, Copper Country mining companies created a working-class dependence on, and subservience to, the men who administered the mines. This was the irreconcilable essence of paternalism—a child-like reliance on the often-fickle generosity of the men or "fathers" in power. While mining companies provided their workers amenities such as bathhouses, libraries, schools, and low housing rental rates, paternalism was perhaps *the* underlying cause of inequality in Copper Country society. Paternalism made children of grown Copper Country mineworkers, who relied on the company for their survival. Paternalism created an entire hierarchical society that was dependent on one industry that could, and often did, use and abuse its own power. Paternalism at its very core relates that one group knows what is best for the other. Mine owners were enlightened and knew what was best for their workers—the workers that in almost every sense of the word they owned. It was pure and simple wage slavery, and many of the Copper Country workers knew it. This sense of autocratic, ruling power was, by the way, what many immigrants left their home countries to escape.

William Parsons Todd, the one-time vice-president and former board member of Quincy Mining Company and son of Quincy Mining Company president William Rogers Todd, admitted this autocratic company perspective, stating, "It was up to us to look after them and so that we didn't like unions coming in and trying to tell us that they were going to look after the men. We felt that we'd do a better job."[10] At the core of this paternalism there existed a sense of ownership that permitted abuse through outright displays of power such as intimidation and union busting and more subtle means such as control and manipulation of local economics and politics.

Added to this control and manipulation was a sense of superiority that legitimized such governing actions. A healthy dose of self-imposed naivety was also sprinkled in with the paternalist perspective. Todd exhibited all of these traits when describing Copper Country labor relations: "In fact we very seldom had any labor disturbance, practically almost never. We always tried to keep a step ahead and increase wages before the men expected it. So (workers) got the habit of just depending on the company.... When hard times came and the company went down, we never had any trouble with reducing wages somewhat to keep the company going. ... The men and the companies all worked together as friends and we paid them as much as we could."[11]

The relations of power that stood at the center of Copper Country paternalism were again crystal clear in how Todd saw the company's role in protecting its workers. Previously, Todd stated that companies were the sole protector of their men's needs, no unions necessary, but when accidents befell workers on company property, apparently the company could only do so much. In fact, when asked about the cause of accidents, Todd replied, "Men being careless. We used to lay a fuse and maybe we had a thousand men or more underground altogether, somehow or other we used to lose . . . seemed to lose two men a year. Funny! I remember one year we went up until about the 10th of December . . . we hadn't lost a man and between that and the end of December we lost two men. And underground almost entirely . . . very seldom was it really anything but the men's own fault (for accidents)."[12]

Not surprisingly, due to the power and control exercised by Copper Country mining companies, those investigating deaths and accidents in area mines almost always agreed with Todd and the mining companies' perspective in regard to responsibility for casualties in mining. When poring through the Houghton County mine inspectors' reports during the last decade of the nineteenth century and into the first decade of the twentieth, it is difficult, bordering on impossible, to find one death in Copper Country mines that was attributed to the fault of the company. This sense of perspective, the company line, was the one workers were contending with, and the entrenched power the companies zealously guarded was the struggle class-conscious workers faced as they began uphill efforts to organize Copper Country workers.

Workers Respond to Company Power

Though there were concerted efforts on the part of the Copper Country mine management to quell organized labor prior to the dawn of the twentieth century, there were volatile, if not unorganized, attempts by mineworkers to control the conditions of their labor early in the Copper Country's history. The most explosive (literally) attempt by mineworkers to have a say in the operations of Copper Country mines was the 1870 Glycerin Strike. After the introduction of nitroglycerin oil into a few area mines by the Mabbs brothers, workers at the Huron Mine north of Houghton revolted by blowing the explosive sky-high using the miners' preferred blasting agent—the more stable black powder. As Larry Lankton wrote referencing an early Copper Country newspaper regarding the ensuing but short-lived strike, "Residents heard two explosions: one light, when the black powder detonated, and one very heavy when the nitro went up. They saw the explosion too: 'The country was illuminated, as by an electric flash.'"[13]

The Glycerin Strike signaled a rather tumultuous start to labor relations in the

1870s. The IWA spurred a Copper Country strike at the C&H Mine in 1872. The *Mining Gazette* referred to the strike's "ringleaders" as members of the "International League," a possible reference to the IWA, especially considering the revolutionary organization's presence in American labor history during the early 1870s. Depending on the author, this early action by organized labor was either "crushed" by the mining companies or so contentious and significant that mining officials wrote Michigan governor H. P. Baldwin for Michigan National Guard troops. Arthur Puotinen, writing on the significance and radical nature of the strike, documented that Houghton County Sheriff Bartholomew Shea pleaded with Baldwin, "Rioters have rescued prisoners from me and taken arms from my men. Want troops very badly. The situation is very alarming. My posse has failed in arresting ringleaders."[14] Within a week of the strike's onset men at the Schoolcraft, Franklin, Pewabic, Quincy, and Copper Falls mines joined C&H miners. According to the *Mining Gazette*, the strike occurred when the C&H's promise to raise workers' wages to a point that was "just" fell far short of the mineworkers' expectations.[15]

Regardless of whether or not some of the strikers belonged to or sympathized with the IWA, the scope of the strike and militant actions by the strikers caused the mine owners, mainstream press, and state officials to act in concert to quell the miners' actions. On May 13, Sheriff Shea arrested two especially active strikers for breaching the public peace, and attempted to transport them to the county jail under the guard of eighteen deputies.[16] However, while proceeding to the jail, the deputies were overtaken by between 600 and 700 men who "had formed themselves into a mob" in order to rescue their interned fellow workers.[17] While the mainstream press let out a series of screeds against "the rabble" and "cowardly scoundrels" for their "childish and threatening demonstrations," the mass actions by Copper Country miners were clearly taken on behalf of their fellow workers in opposition to the enforcement of a law that the region's working people believed was wrong.[18] Indeed, to the several hundred strikers who liberated their fellow workers, their actions no doubt appeared to have been taken in defense of their class and in opposition to those who would repress their actions.

While this early strike was a significant labor action in a nascent mining region, the strike was most notable for the reaction it garnered from C&H president Alexander Agassiz. A somewhat mythical and curious figure in Copper Country history, Agassiz was perhaps willing to deal with Copper Country labor on fair terms at the beginning of his career as C&H president. Bordering on being an absentee landlord as president of C&H, Agassiz was likely more intent on following and surpassing his father's footsteps in the field of natural history. His father, Louis Agassiz, was the renowned naturalist, having a prehistoric glacial lake named in his honor, which placed the bar for notoriety quite high for Alexander. The younger Agassiz was president of C&H only so much as it would advance his career as a naturalist, and therefore likely to be somewhat unconcerned with questions of labor.

When this early strike occurred in 1872, Alexander's initial impression was probably to seek some type of common ground with workers. He did so by offering strikers benefit programs and authorized the superintendent of C&H to issue a "My Friends" letter to workers outlining a new way to move forward. The letter and its conciliatory attitude did not have the intended consequence, and C&H workers struck with a vengeance. Agassiz saw the dismissal of the benefits and his letter as a betrayal to C&H, and perhaps to his own benevolence. This single event would shape Agassiz's and C&H's relations with workers until his death in 1910.[19]

Workers would not have to wait until 1910 to put Agassiz's newfound understandings in regards to labor relations to a test. Just two years later, in 1874, trammers led a walkout at the C&H mines. This small-scale wildcat strike led by Finns and Swedes did not receive a benevolently toned "My Friends" letter. Instead, Agassiz instructed recently appointed superintendent James North Wright to take this tack with striking workers: "We cannot be dictated to by anyone. The mine must stop if it stays closed forever. . . . Wages will be raised whenever we see fit and at no other time."[20]

Agassiz's hard line typified most copper companies' labor-management relations for the latter part of the nineteenth century. This hard line, and fluctuating copper prices, signaled a period of relative labor peace, but a single incident, a set of suspicious fires at the C&H mines in 1887, seemingly rekindled the discontent between labor and management and ushered in a quarter-century of labor unrest in the Copper Country. Strikes and walkouts throughout the 1890s at mines large and small began to set the table for a slow burn to a major Copper Country confrontation.[21] All that was needed was a catalyst—a group to organize Copper Country mineworkers. That group was coming, and it had a fiery reputation.

Early Overtures from the Western Federation of Miners

The secretive and somewhat exclusive Knights of Labor had been run out of the Copper Country for the most part by the late 1890s, but they left area copper mines with the seeds of a militant class consciousness that had previously not existed on the Keweenaw Peninsula. At the dawn of the twentieth century, the stage was set on the local and, perhaps more important, national level for a concerted effort to organize Copper Country workers. At the national level, organized labor had gained influence, numbers, and power in the afterglow of the Gilded Age—so much so that workers in virtual kingdoms and bastions of industrial capitalism, such as the

Copper Country, were open and receptive to conceptions of radical worker organization. Along with this new understanding of industrial relations came variations of discontent, both on the national scene and at the local level in the Copper Country. Where once ethnic organizations and benevolent groups paid members for sickness, injury, and death, a new understanding of liability and responsibility colored the class-conscious perspectives of industrial work. Where the Knights of Labor left off in regards to organized labor, a more radical industrial union committed to organizing just mineworkers began to challenge the wage and working conditions in the Copper Country.

Although the most radical challenge to the region's ruling class came in 1913–14 under the leadership of the Western Federation of Miners (WFM), that strike was initiated only after years of mostly failed efforts by that union to organize the region's mineworkers. The reports issued by those organizers to the annual conventions of the WFM reveal significant details about the lives of Copper Country workers, the efforts taken by employers to prevent them from unionizing, and the difficulties those men and women experienced as they sought to form unions of their own choosing.

While the WFM was the first union to begin organizing copper mineworkers as a collective body in the Upper Peninsula, there was an earlier attempt to organize Michigan's iron mining ranges by a regional union. In 1895, the Northern Mineral Mineworkers Union (NMMU) formed as the result of a strike on the Marquette Iron Range. Initial membership in the NMMU, which also spread to the Gogebic and Menominee ranges (and later to the Mesabi and Vermillion ranges in Minnesota) was close to 4,000 workers. This regional union became a national union when the membership applied to and was granted a charter as a national affiliate of the American Federation of Labor (AFL) in December of the same year.[22]

The NMMU was, however, strictly an iron mineworkers union. The NMMU did not attempt to organize the Copper Country as historian John P. Beck wrote about Robert Askew, first president of the union, "his total membership figure was set at five thousand miners, causing him to declare that [Michigan's] copper district would be organized as soon as 'assurances have been received that the effort will meet with encouraging success.'"[23] The NMMU becomes significant to the WFM's organizational efforts because one of the Federation's organizers, Joy Pollard, traced Askew's steps in attempting to found locals in the Upper Peninsula, with one important side step: the Copper Country. Where Askew left off, Pollard picked up, and found a population of Keweenaw Peninsula mineworkers receptive to the WFM. In its early stages in the Copper Country between 1903 and 1904, the WFM, through Pollard, established locals in Laurium, Hancock, Painesdale, and Allouez; a smelterman's local in Lake Linden; and District Local 10, also sited in Lake Linden. Strikes at the Quincy mine followed in 1904 and 1905.[24] Pollard was so successful in his stops throughout the Upper Peninsula that the NMMU, which had declined in membership since 1896, voted to affiliate with the WFM in 1903. Thus, union-minded Copper Country mineworkers joined with their iron-mining brethren across the Upper Peninsula under the WFM's banner.[25]

Pollard's personal life as an organizer was also captured in reports from this nascent period in Copper Country labor history. A member of the WFM's Free Coin-age Miners' Local 19 and organizer for the Federation, Pollard came to the Copper Country in September 1903 and remained in the region for nearly a year. Even prior to his involvement in Michigan mine labor, Pollard had gained prominence in the U.S. labor movement. By 1902, he was a socialist as well as a national speaker for labor's cause. In June 1902, the *Labor World*, a union newspaper published in Butte, Montana, described Pollard as "a man whose good and advanced understanding and strong positive purpose makes him of great value in any movement."[26] In 1904, he toured the Atlantic Coast helping to organize French-Canadian carpenters in New Hampshire, spreading news of miners' strikes throughout New England, and collecting funds for the WFM among New England unionists.[27]

The historian Arthur Thurner summarized Pollard's activities in the Copper Country, writing:

> Joy Pollard, union organizer, arrived in the Copper Country where strikebreakers were being recruited. Craft union members and A. T. Schmelzer of Lake Linden, brother of a WFM Executive Board member from Silverton, Colorado, introduced him to local copper workers who advised him to organize Calumet men first. As he visited iron mines in Michigan and Wisconsin subsequently he heard the same message: "Get Calumet or the Copper boys and we will all follow."[28]

Pollard's extensive time spent in the Copper Country gained him notoriety among the region's residents, as was demonstrated by the article written about him after his departure from the region that appeared in the May 17, 1905, issue of a Calumet newspaper, discussing his arrest in Cripple Creek, Colorado, for carrying concealed weapons.[29]

Following Pollard's extended visit to the Copper Country, several organizers continued his work, keeping the region's local unions in working order. The names of WFM organizers who traveled to the Michigan copper region with the intention to organize its mineworkers appeared in the pages of the WFM's annual convention minutes in the years leading up to the 1913–14 strike. These men—Frank Schmelzer and William E. Tracy—delivered reports cataloging their mostly failed attempts to enroll the masses of Michigan copper mineworkers into the union.

For three weeks in April 1907 Frank Schmelzer unsuccessfully sought out signs of support for his union in the Copper Country. Describing the region's workers as ignorant and cowardly, Schmelzer concluded that Copper Country mineworkers had little interest in unions or collectively improving their conditions, instead preferring to "go to some other place where conditions are better." He was concerned that workers who "voted with their feet" and headed into "the jurisdiction of some of the strongest locals of the Federation" would weaken the stronger unions with their lack of class-consciousness. To prevent the Copper Country's workers from diluting the WFM's militant membership, the union organizer advised "that a uniform set of books should be adopted by the Convention for all the locals," which would enable strong union locals to monitor weaker ones, such as those in Michigan, which threatened to ship their weak members out west.[30]

Some historians have viewed the lack of radical activism and pessimistic reports of organizers such as Schmelzer as a sign of general contentment by Copper Country laborers with their working and living conditions in area mines. However, the experiences of one contemporary observer of Copper Country mineworkers' activities sheds a different light on the ability—or inability—of local mineworkers to form effective unions and radical organizations in the years leading up to 1913. Indeed, the experiences of William E. Tracy, a WFM organizer and delegate from South Dakota, attest to the fact that where local mineworkers failed to form unions, join existing unions, or do much in the way to maintain an existing union, such failures were not the product of a lack of class-consciousness on the part of Copper Country mineworkers.

In the summer of 1908, Tracy set out to organize new members into the WFM, strengthen existing locals, and audit the financial records of union locals in the Upper Midwest.[31] From the start, it was plain to see that neither union organizers nor Copper Country workers in general were able to operate without fear, coercion, and the possibility of losing their jobs, their freedom, or even their lives for their union activities. Tracy's activities in Michigan were diligently recorded by two detectives who, according to the organizer, were "industriously watching my movements, taking note of the men with whom I talked, or associated, and evidently reporting on my actions to some other son of a she-wolf, who was paying well for a little information about my conduct." He understood that the spy's presence made it "likely that I should meet with vigorous opposition from some source in any attempt that I might make toward organizing."[32]

In spite of the daunting impediments set in his way, Tracy experienced far greater success in the Copper Country than had his predecessors. After months of abortive efforts to meet with local workers and have them take up the union banner, the WFM organizer's perseverance paid off in May 1909 when miners began flocking into the union fold. Tracy reported:

I returned to Laurium on the 13th [of May], and on the 16th I attended the meeting of Hancock No. 200. On the 16th, in the evening, I went to Lake Linden, where I had been advised that there was some interest awakening. I succeeded in meeting with a few of the men there who thought that there was a possibility of reorganizing at that place. I left a blank application for a charter with Andy Schmelzer, who said that he thought he would be able to secure the necessary signatures within a short time. On the 22d I went to South Range again, and that evening I organized a local there, starting with a membership of 43 men, Finns and Italians.[33]

Mineworkers throughout the region were catching the "union bug," as Tracy continued to note the dramatic rise in interest in the WFM among Copper Country workers:

June 6th to June 12th I did but little business outside of the office in Laurium. On June 12th I went to South Range and again assisted in holding the meeting of that local. I returned that night to Hancock, attended the meeting of local No. 200 on Sunday morning, and went again to South Range in the afternoon, where an enormous mass meeting was held in the skating rink. Fully 1,000 men were present at this meeting. Charles Bartolini opened the meeting with a long and powerful address in Italian; Snellman followed with a short talk to the Finns, after which I had the platform and tried to say things to the English. Still later John Korpi and John Välimäki each spoke in Finnish.[34]

The organizer concluded by reporting that he attended a pair of mineworkers' union picnics held in the Copper Country. Considering that the region was largely void of unions when he had arrived a year earlier, the presence of several local unions and a growing union culture was evidence that Tracy's trip into the Upper Peninsula had been a fruitful one.[35]

The experiences of WFM officials, whether mostly negative as in the case of Schmelzer or largely effective at enrolling members as in Tracy's example, do provide one lens into the early stages of the Copper Country mineworkers' labor movement. These experiences are especially valuable since the WFM convention minutes offer a firsthand glimpse into the lives of workers and organizers as they sought to construct a working-class movement among the men whose labor created much of the region's wealth. And if one were to rely primarily on the WFM convention minutes, supplemented in many cases by articles from the mainstream press, one would most likely reach conclusions similar to earlier historians about the nature of Copper Country labor organizing: that it was the product of outside agitators or organizers, such as Schmelzer and Tracy, who ventured into the copper mining region with little to no knowledge or experience with the region's people, its customs, its culture, or its specific conflicts. But these organizers' experiences paint, at best, an incomplete picture.

Spies and Mineworkers Report on Working Conditions

The problem with relying mostly on the statements of "outside agitators" is that these reports sometimes relegate the experiences of Copper Country mineworkers to the periphery of the story. By mainly including the viewpoints of the organizers, the workers themselves become the passive subjects of history, men and women who were acted upon by the "important" historical agents such as union organizers, socialist agitators, and employers. A closer examination using nuanced sources demonstrates a markedly different view of the Copper Country's labor history, revealing that the region's workers were themselves historical agents.

The best lens into the lives, work, and rebellions of Copper Country mineworkers comes to us through the reports of the labor spies who were paid by the region's mine owners to spy upon their employees, pay special attention to those workers who spoke of unionism or radicalism, intervene when possible to prevent unionization or strikes, and write regular reports to their employers detailing the daily, lived experiences of local miners and other working people.

Part of these (usually) men's jobs was to associate with the workers they were hired to observe, to obtain jobs in the mines, to observe conversations at local saloons and clubs, and to shadow their targets' daily activities about town. Many of the spies' reports indicated a general disgruntlement with the local working and living conditions. One major area of complaint was the various dangers of underground mining, including their fears of unsafe equipment, poisonous waters, and explosions. At the Quincy Mining Company's No. 6 Shaft in October 1906, a Thiel spy reported that "some men . . . were not satisfied, for the reason that it is a wet level, and the poisonous water runs on their hands, burning them, as well as runs on their bodies in some cases."[36] That same operative crafted a list of the workers' complaints. These included that "the cage is not run to stop at the places required," and in one instance "it did not stop at 510," so the men "had to use a ladder in going from 490 to 510, that is, two levels; and in the morning they had to go from 510 to 550 in order to get a ride in the cage up to the surface." Worse yet, in some parts "the ladder was worn out, so that there was danger of falling off it." The mineworkers also complained about the air blasts coming from the mine, which "are incessant at the present time," and some of which "shook slightly the houses in the town." Even the so-called dryhouses where workers changed their clothes were the subject of complaint, for "they are altogether too small and the accommodations of the very poorest . . . operative had to wash with cold water in a dirty bucket, without soap."[37]

The miners also differentiated between the "good" and the "bad" mines, the latter of which included Quincy No. 7 Shaft. Victor Hendrickson and J. Lumptula, two copper miners, discussed the rough working conditions at the Quincy Mine with a Thiel labor spy, stating that "the Quincy mines were very hot, particularly No. 7, which was called 'the men's slaughter' for the reason that each week something happened to the men employed there; that there were not over twelve gangs; and that of each gang every week someone was either killed or injured."[38] On occasion, a spy's own experiences with hard work served as a warning sign to employers about the difficult working conditions faced by the men in the mines. In September 1906, for example, Operative K with the Thiel Detective Service reported that he had to quit tramming because "he could not stand it" and required a lighter-duty job.[39]

Spies also discovered that mineworkers complained about their low wages, long hours, and obnoxious shift bosses. On October 3, 1906, shortly after the conclusion of a strike at the Quincy Mining Company, Quincy workers expressed that they were "not satisfied with their present scale of wages." The mineworkers' frustrations with their insufficient pay was measured against pragmatic estimations of their ability to wrest additional concessions from management after gaining a wage increase only two months earlier during their strike. The spy reported, "they are not anxious to go on another strike as they do not think they could gain anything by so doing."[40] Investigation by Operative K of the Thiel agency likewise revealed that the August 1906 strike at the Quincy Mine was the product of the mineworkers' general dissatisfaction with their rates of pay. One Italian mine laborer told the spy:

> The majority were Finns. They had a meeting and discussed what they should do. The Finns decided that they would go on strike provided they could get the different nationalities to go out with them. Of course they had a union for the last six years including some of each of the different nationalities. They all talked together and of course the union men advised the others to go on a strike telling them that they would then get a raise very quickly.[41]

Striking the Mines

Despite the previously mentioned problems experienced by the WFM and its organizers in the Copper Country, the region's mineworkers began a concerted series of steps to contest their wage-slavery by organizing at the grassroots level. This was a step taken as far back as the first major strike in 1872 and a growing tradition of class-consciousness that did not entirely rest upon the success or failure of one or two "outside" organizers. However, the actions of the sometimes malcontent WFM organizers likely had a substantial effect on Copper Country workers as the pace of labor action escalated in the first decade of the twentieth century.

A series of strikes broke out between 1904 and 1906 over wages, as striking miners and trammers demanded wage increases. In 1904, at the Quincy Mine in Hancock, 1,200 of the 1,600 miners and trammers struck for two weeks between January 17 and February 3 with demands for increased pay. According to the mine owners, the strikers used "considerable intimidation and threatened violence," but there was "no damage done and no personal injuries of any consequence" during the conflict. In early February, the two sides reached a deal providing for an additional $3 per month for miners but nothing for trammers.

In mid-March 1905, Quincy miners and trammers received wage increases from $62 to $65 and from $58.50 to $60 per month, respectively. Apparently emboldened by this raise, 280 Quincy trammers struck, demanding the same $65-per-month paid to their fellow underground workers. This push for wage parity between miners and trammers was foiled, however, after only two days; when the men returned to the job, trammers won an additional $1.50 per month, while miners gained a $2 monthly increase.[42]

In the summer of 1906, two strikes started a clock ticking toward a district-wide labor-management confrontation in 1913. A strike at the Quincy Mine lasted three long weeks, but was a stalemate for Quincy's workers. Instead of gaining a 10 percent increase, which they demanded from management, Quincy's workers accepted a 5 percent wage increase.[43] Demonstrating that working conditions were as, if not more, important than wages, the strikers also issued an extensive list of demands and resolved "to end this strike at once when the authorized officials of the said Quincy Mining Company have accepted the above mentioned terms and signed them." These demands included safety improvements to hoisting equipment, improved maintenance of the mine's water pipes, a stipulation that the company "has no right to expel any striker because of taking part in this strike," and a good faith agreement by management to "fulfill these terms under one year from the date of signing." Understanding that their jobs threatened their lives—and thus their ability to provide for their families—the strikers presented their demands in language about the family: "We make the above mentioned demands regarding our own safety as fathers and sustainers of our families, because we understand that our position without above mentioned betterments is dangerous."[44]

During this strike, Quincy managers surveyed worker sentiment through labor spies. Operative No. 5 was the main spy employed by Quincy and transitioned from workplace to recreational areas along with the company's employees. In one report,

No. 5 observed, "I talked with and listened to the miners' conversation which was principally about the meeting which the miners are to hold this afternoon to decide whether they will go back to work or continue the strike. All those who expressed themselves in my presence appeared to believe the strike would be settled and work resumed Monday."[45] How things changed with a little different perspective. At the actual meeting, which was held at 2:30 P.M. in a Hancock social hall, the labor spy reported, "I was unable to gain admittance to the hall as only miners were allowed to enter upon presentation of their card. The meeting closed at 4:30 P.M., and the crowd appeared to be excited, as they had come to no settlement. Those most excited were the men of families who wish to go back to work."[46]

The other strike during the summer of 1906, a good distance away from Hancock, was the Rockland Strike. Rockland was an isolated industrial berg on the southern end of Michigan's copper range. The labor action in Rockland was a much shorter yet more intense strike, which had sadly prophetic roots in a warning from that area's law enforcement officers given only a year before the strike. A small 1905 labor action at the Adventure Mine, which was close to Rockland proper, motivated Ontonagon County Sheriff McFarlane to state that any such future labor activity would result in gunfire on the sheriff's part. Events at Rockland in 1906 made his wicked promise come true.[47]

The events in Rockland come with some further historical background. On July 4, 1906, a WFM organizer was in Rockland, which was close to the Michigan Mine. The organizer requested to speak at a local Finnish immigrant temperance society. The organizer proceeded to pontificate and told the gathered workers to strike for better wages and industrial democracy—fitting for an Independence Day speech. The organizer's words did not take long to create action, because on July 30 the workers of Rockland walked off the job at the Michigan Mine.[48]

McFarlane immediately went to the mine to break up the crowd that had assembled. Various versions of what happened next depended on which side of the labor-management question one was on, but two facts existed after the confrontation. These cold, hard facts were the bodies of two strikers, shot dead. Reportedly one was even left in Rockland's downtown for a day as a warning that martial law was in effect. In the carrying out of law and order, two "Finlanders" received "justice" capitalism-style. "Ludvig Ojala's head was shot off at point-blank range," and Oscar Ohtonen was shot in his stomach, receiving fatal wounds to his lower intestine. Nine other strikers were wounded, but not fatally.[49]

Strangely, there were no reports of anyone wounded on the sheriff's side of the clash, even though the "unruly" mob of strikers numbered an estimated 280 to 300 persons. Rumors flew around respectable social circles that strikers had guns, and the local press, beholding to the mining companies, spun the event to make

McFarlane a hero.[50] As one might imagine, the sensational reports coming out of Rockland from both sides shook the greater Copper Country. Labor organizers portrayed events in Rockland as a call to action, a cause to kick-start lagging efforts at organization. Copper Country agitators and organizers made speeches against the power of the copper company's monopoly of the area. One labor spy recounted the oration of a Finnish immigrant organizer by the name of Maki who spoke in a Hancock meeting hall

> about the strike in Rockland. He said the men had demanded a little betterment of their condition, namely, one hour less and 25 cents increase in wages; that they had made their request without threats of any kind but that the company had called in the police officers and ill treated the men. He went into a Socialistic discourse about capital and labor and asked the men to unite together and stand up for their rights and they would surely win. The operative states that Macki [*sic*] is a radical agitator.[51]

As Copper Country labor organizers portrayed the Rockland strikers as martyrs, the general outlook in 1906 for union organization was lagging even though wages continued to be a concern, and more than ever, working conditions became a major grievance. Yet another labor spy reported, "On the previous day, about 4:20 P.M., while the operative was at the Quincy Company's smelter an air blast was heard in the Quincy mine, which shook the ground, streets and houses slightly. A man was also hurt or killed in the mine on the preceding day."[52] Despite the low pay and the deadly conditions, the effort to organize Copper Country workers seemed to be languishing. A Quincy labor spy reported in the fall of 1906 that the "fight" had left some Quincy workers in the wake of the stalemated 1906 strike.[53]

In the fits and starts of organizing activity between 1904 and 1906, one essential detail needs to be emphasized: the importance and radicalization of the Copper Country's Finnish immigrant population. In some ways and in specific instances, the socialist and unionist Copper Country Finns carried the working-class torch through rough times. As the push to organize the Copper Country moved forward, Finnish immigrants and their socialist and unionist institutions and organizations would come to play a key role in challenging the power of the Copper Country oligarchy. In both sheer numbers and in dedication to the cause, Finnish immigrants proved some of the most earnest and erstwhile supporters of working-class causes. As leaders within the WFM and as rank-and-file union members, the Finnish immigrant dedication to the American labor movement proved to be an essential part of the struggle to combat the exploitation by Michigan's copper barons.[54]

The WFM Gains Traction

In 1908, Copper Country workers seemed to get a second wind. Perhaps this renewed energy came from events like the beginning of publication of *Wage-Slave*, the Socialist Party of Michigan's newspaper in Hancock, or from incidents of direct action such as the 1907 Hancock Red Flag Parade. Regardless of the exact catalyst, in the wake of these events the WFM seized upon the opportunity to send a cadre of organizers into Copper Country mines. Five WFM locals then formed in the Copper Country between 1908 and 1910. More significantly, these locals organized in towns and cities near some of the Copper Country's largest mines. Locals grew up near the C&H, Quincy, and Copper Range mines, and later achieved large membership near the Ahmeek and Mohawk mines. Over time, a local even formed in Mass City on the southern edge of the Keweenaw's Copper Country.[55] By 1910, the WFM locals contained a total membership of over 7,000 people. Lankton documented the meteoric growth, writing, "The South Range local began at 30 and grew to 1,580 members. Hancock's local grew from 363 members to 1,450, and the Calumet local grew from 440 members to 2,048 members."[56]

By 1910, there were two major differences in the WFM's organizational efforts, which made for a much more successful drive to organize the Copper Country. First, the WFM's efforts cut across ethnic lines. Multiethnic organizers were brought in to unite the sometimes-divided working masses. At this time language, religion, and social standing segregated the Copper Country, and a key to bringing workers together was minimizing the differences in ethnicity that had divided them. Second, the WFM as an industrial union sought to bridge the division of labor and the rigid underground labor hierarchy that existed in Copper Country mines. The WFM needed to unite skilled miners and unskilled trammers, timbermen, and other mineworkers. This was something that had rarely happened before in Copper Country labor actions. There had been a disconnect between skilled and unskilled labor in area mines for a long time, but seemingly bread-and-butter issues such as wages, technological change, and working conditions united Copper Country mine workers to form a previously unknown worker solidarity.

By the spring of 1913, large numbers of mine employees from numerous ethnic groups and job descriptions were prepared to lay down their work tools and walk off the job. Skilled and unskilled, Italian and Cornish, "native" and foreigner—almost all underground workers were now onboard the "union train" and this train, proverbial as it was, was going full speed ahead. Union activity in the Copper Country began as a whimper, progressed to a mutter, and became a roar. Wages, working conditions, unwanted technological change (according to workers), and the recognition of the union as the workers' representative were the major grievances of Copper Country mineworkers.

Wages were an especially divisive topic between labor and management. When asked if the men were satisfied with their wages, Quincy Mining Company board member and vice president at the time of the strike, William Parsons Todd, stated blissfully: "As far as I know, that wasn't discussed . . . that wasn't to come up."[57] It had come up, often, in many strikes before 1913, and it resurfaced as a major factor in the 1913–14 strike. For many in the Copper Country's working class, the disparity in pay between C&H superintendent James MacNaughton, who made a reported $120,000 a year, and the average Copper Country unskilled laborer, who made $2.59 a day in 1913, was glaring.

In many ways, the strike was not just about material factors such as wages—it was also about respect. There was a lack of respect, a certain airy disconnect between labor and management in the Copper Country. Mineworkers risked their lives every day and management often ignored or mocked this sacrifice. A good example of this disrespect comes from William Parsons Todd. In an ultimate demonstration of his disconnect with and disrespect toward the area mines' working class, Todd opined that the reason for a strike in 1913–14 was that the men were after "the easy life, naturally."[58]

Prelude to a Strike

As the spring of 1913 rolled around the men were not as satisfied with the mining companies as Todd recollected. Working-class discontent simmered in the Copper Country from the very south of the copper range in Ontonagon County to the heavily mineralized strip of land between Hancock and Calumet to the northern extreme of the profitable copper-producing regions in Keweenaw County. This tension led to the WFM's opening, and surprisingly reserved, attempt to negotiate with a Copper Country mining company in late April. On April 21, 1913, the nascent Mass Miners Union No. 215 of the WFM sent a letter to mine manager Elton W. Walker that was conciliatory in tone but exacting in purpose: "The members of Mass Miners Union have on their regular meeting decided to communicate with the management of the Mass Mines. This communication is rather somewhat an appeal than anything else." There were just two appeals to Mass mines management: a full dinner hour where workers did not have to sort "drills, tools, etc. at dinner hour as we have to do at present"; and "kindly issue orders to the hoisting engineers not to run the hoist so fast while the men are riding the skip." The grievances of the Mass mineworkers were deceptively simple, but loaded with innuendo that was soon to turn the Copper

Country on its head. The letter ended with a hopeful tone: "We hope the management of the Mass Mines will agree with us taking in the consideration that we are not looking for anything unjust, and that we do not wish to go under any trouble, but we wish to continue in performing an honest days work and under those agreements are willing to, if desired, be helpful on shortage of labor hand."[59]

The response of the Mass Mining Company was to discharge and lay off men—not just any men, but union men. This move precipitated an April 28, 1913, letter from C. E. Mahoney, vice president of the WFM. Mahoney's terse letter was intended to convey the power of organized labor. The WFM charged the Mass Mining Company with discrimination by firing union men because of the letter sent on April 21. Mahoney argued that this firing of men from the Mass Miners Union constituted a lockout and that "failure on Your part as Employers to reply to this communication will be taken as A confirmation of the charge of Discrimination on the part of Your Company as Employers and Organized Labor will of Nessity [sic] take this view of it and conduct Its Self accordingly." Mahoney then asked for a meeting with Walker in the beginning of May to sort the situation out and wrote, "You may see fit to confer on this Important matter and that the same may result in an Adjustment of all elements of dispute and continue industrial Peace."[60]

While it is difficult to infer from the rather genteel language, this letter signaled and was symbolic of the great impending clash between organized labor and management in the Copper Country. Copper Country workers were asking for a change in their working lives, and copper mining management was not willing to acknowledge laboring men's concerns in a real manner, especially at the behest of the WFM. Each day, seemingly, brought Michigan's copper district closer to a strike as the pace of labor agitation and organization quickened. May Day saw large parades in the Copper Country. On June 8, 1913, workers assembled at the Calumet Theater to talk organized labor under the auspices of the Calumet Miners Union. This meeting saw thousands of workers take to the streets in downtown Red Jacket in what was labeled as a "Union mass meeting." Workers clogged Red Jacket's Sixth Street so much that the interurban trolley was hindered from moving through the excited throng of people.[61] On June 10, 1913, *Työmies*, the Finnish-language socialist-unionist newspaper, reported that 3,000 C&H mine "slaves" awakened at a public meeting during which Finnish immigrant organizer John Välimäki spoke.[62] Workers could feel the coming struggle; companies were getting ready for conflict as well.

Almost daily in June, Charles Lawton, general manager of the Quincy Mining Company, reported from Hancock to William R. Todd in Boston of the tense situation in the Copper Country. On June 12, 1913, Lawton wrote, "There is still much of the 'strike' talk going on, and, although the men are working fairly well, and there seems to be considerable new labor coming into the district, still, I am a little inclined to look at the situation with some apprehension, and feel that we ought to organize a Secret Service Department along the lines that we discussed while you were here at the mine." This apprehension led Lawton to request the establishment of a local labor spy force, along the lines of the one that C&H had already organized, "although, of course, much smaller."

On June 16, Lawton wrote bemoaning the lack of trammers, who were not showing up to work, "Captain Kendall reported this morning that there are 17 trammers in No. 8 shaft, 21 in No. 6, and 25 in No. 2, when we should have upwards of 30 or 40." Apparently C&H, with the help of former Houghton County Sheriff Beck, had already hired "38 Russian Poles that he has taken to the Isle Royale and put to work tramming." Citing the good price of copper, a need for unskilled labor, and a compulsion to act in accordance with C&H, Lawton was almost begging for a chance to hunt up employees.[63]

On June 18, Lawton gave a stern description of the situation, which he peppered with reports from a labor spy who was not living up to Quincy's standards for industrial subterfuge:

> We are confronted with a very serious labor situation, and should take serious, careful steps to control it. Number Fifteen gives but little assistance to that end, for he reports all who belong to the Federation, or who have socialistic tendencies, but cannot advise us the degree of influence that each has over the others. . . . Many of our best men have joined the Western Federation, and are at times brought into joining with and listening to the socialists; yet they are at heart neither, and we should protect them from such influences and associations, by knowing who are the active, and at heart, dangerous men to us, and not employ them, but remove them from our midst. . . . Our Captains and Shift Bosses are alive to the condition and are doing everything they can to overcome it. The trouble is not so much in the laxity of the "bosses," as it is with the men in persistently trying to carry out the teachings of agitators of the Western Federation and "Socialist" ranks . . . the "bosses" are almost powerless to overcome the troubles.[64]

By July 2, Lawton was almost fit to be tied, writing, "I am again very much concerned over the present labor situation—the revival of 'strike' talk, and the great deficiency of the Finnish labor throughout the mine. . . . The temper of the Finnish employees today is unprecedented in all of my experience, and is almost unbearable. . . . It is practically impossible to get the Finnish miners and trammers to do anything near what is right and proper—'they just simply won't.'" Lawton was clear in his writing: the Finnish mineworkers were behind the push for a strike, and in a strange sense Lawton was looking forward to a strike to "clear the atmosphere, and increase their efficiency back to normal."[65]

After Independence Day, Lawton seems to have come to terms that a strike was coming and soon, writing on July 5, "I do not think it would be hard at this time to call a strike with a 'Hurrah!' from one end of the Copper Country to the other." Instead of speculation, Lawton shifted to thinking about how to thwart the efforts of the WFM and striking workers. Lawton began his offensive against the WFM locals by instituting a system of information gathering and found from "quite reliable sources that there was a meeting of the underground men at Coburntown . . . for the special purpose of arranging to stop hoisting water from our shafts during the strike." Lawton adjudged this perceived industrial sabotage as "pure Western Federation tactics" and that the copper bosses better be "well prepared for Western Federation methods." Though Lawton seemingly deplored the uncivilized and uncouth methods of the WFM, he advocated acting "quickly and vigorously," but hoped that Quincy could, "however, avoid all vicious moves." For a time the company did, but as the strike would wear on into the Copper Country winter, Lawton's hopes to avoid vicious moves all but dissipated.[66]

Lawton's information network proved a blessing and a curse. As early as July 11, Lawton had information that a strike vote was held. "I had an interview this morning with Mr. H. H. Baldwin, Manager of this District for the Thiel Detective Service, who informs me that the local Western Federation voted on a strike Sunday last, the 6th, the result being that 470 votes were cast, of which 370 were for a strike and 40, being old employees of the Quincy, voted and talked vigorously against a strike." The workers apparently set July 15 as a date to begin striking, but here is where Lawton's information led him astray; he was under the assumption that "the strike would be at the Quincy alone, and not at any of the other mines." This caused Lawton to make the fateful predication that "should there be a strike, it will not be a unanimous move among our employees, and I doubt that it will be of very long duration."[67] As time would tell, Lawton was severely mistaken, but the march toward a strike had a few more twists and turns as both Lawton and James MacNaughton of the C&H Mining Company would come to understand.

July 15 finally came, and letters with an ultimatum from the WFM locals hit the desks of Copper Country mining management. Lawton wrote to Todd, "the special delivery registered letter from the Secretary of the Western Federation Miners' Association has been presented to me in person, and I have refused to accept it."[68] C&H's management was more thoughtful about the special mail they had received. James MacNaughton, in Calumet, wrote Quincy Shaw in Boston, "while we have not as yet formulated any definite plan, my present feeling is that I shall not acknowledge the letter in anyway whatever, for by writing a letter to the Secretary acknowledging the receipt of this one I would be in a measure recognizing the Union." Joining MacNaughton in mapping out C&H's local strategy was Rodolphe

Agassiz. For his part, Rodolphe, the son of Alexander, who had died in 1910, was even more philosophical about how to proceed: "In discussing this with Mr. Agassiz he has suggested tentatively for our consideration, the advisability of writing a letter acknowledging the receipt of this one and stating that inasmuch as the writers of this letter are not in our employ, we cannot discuss time or wage conditions at any of our mines with them."[69]

Agassiz lost out, and thus the company line was cast: ignore the WFM. C&H had bolstered its workforce already by adding speculative replacement workers in the spring and summer of 1913, but Lawton and the Quincy Mining Company's force of mining captains vacillated between fighting it out "so the miners will get it out of their systems" and attempting to postpone or delay the strike while weeding out the "malcontents" to avoid a strike altogether. As Quincy's very differing strategies imply, Lawton was a little flummoxed by the whole ordeal.[70]

None of the Copper Country mining companies responded to the WFM's letters. Therefore, from July 15 to July 22 there was a tense silence in the Copper Country.

All of that changed on July 23, 1913. "A mob of between four and five hundred is going from one engine house to the other demanding that the fires be drawn and that the men leave their posts. Thus far no material damage has been done. We are assembling and swearing in deputy sheriffs as fast as possible. Have about six hundred now and think we will have no difficulty in taking care of the situation." This was the first in a long line of coded strike communiqués from MacNaughton to Shaw regarding the "front" of the Copper Country conflict. MacNaughton's messages during the strike wired from Calumet to Boston sounded more like the descriptions of troop movements by a sergeant in the field to a general at headquarters: "Two hundred men from the north end have just marched to Centennial shooting off firearms. Centennial is working with small force but I have just given orders to close down. Every mine in the district is closed."[71]

MacNaughton attempted to downplay the severity of the strike's first day to Shaw, but it was clear that the control the copper bosses had once asserted over the workforce was gone. On July 24, MacNaughton was forced to admit that the Copper Country was in revolt, writing to Shaw, "At conference in this office after midnight the sheriff admitted he was not able to handle the strikers." He painted the parades and actions of strikers in the streets as "rioting," writing, "So long as officers of the company and deputy sheriffs keep out their way they are orderly otherwise they club whoever gets in their path." MacNaughton attempted to pin the day's rebellion as the work of outside agitators from the WFM who were advocating violence: "Strikers are undoubtedly being led by professional gun men brought into this country for this purpose."[72] Little did MacNaughton know that the WFM national had not even authorized the strike and was wholly against it. Rather, this was the action of

Copper Country workers at the grassroots level and, while MacNaughton and others sympathetic to the mining companies attempted to portray the strikers as violent thugs, in most instances striking workers simply persuaded "loyal" employees to leave or stay away from their jobs. In about a dozen cases, however, workers refusing to join the strike were physically assaulted. There was no mistaking it; the Copper Country was in the midst of a major uprising.

And just like that, the strike was on. After the first days of pitched fervor, both sides settled into a protracted class war. Mass organizations, parades, speeches, shouting matches, bar brawls, family division, street fights, and isolated shootings would color Copper Country life for the next nine long months. At stake for the mining companies and the men who ran them was a way of life, a heavily capitalized industrial utopia that they jealously guarded and protected from internal worker input and outside interference alike. For Copper Country mineworkers—well some in the labor movement would argue that they had nothing to lose but their chains, but the subtle nuances of the strike found a once-divided workforce brought together (for a time) around competing grievances, goals, and ideologies. For some workers in the Copper Country, the strike was about bread-and-butter issues: better pay; improved working conditions; the elimination of the one-man drill, which was a labor-saving device; and the recognition of the WFM as the collective bargaining unit of Copper Country workers.

For others in the Copper Country, admittedly a smaller percentage, the strike was about revolution, an absolute and total rupture of Copper Country society. For a time these competing constituencies held together in a tense union, but cracks would eventually form in the WFM's solidarity. This tension among the Copper Country working class coupled with the corruption of Houghton County officials and mixed with the intimidation and violence of outside "gun thugs," sheriff's deputies, and an antiunion vigilante organization known as the Citizens' Alliance allowed the copper bosses to muster a formidable defense against unionism in the Copper Country.

CHAPTER 6

Union

The great majority of the strikers are like children; they are being misled by the WFM media and it is so hard to get proper information to them.

—"Big Jim" MacNaughton, superintendent of the C&H Mining Company, to Quincy Shaw, president of the C&H Mining Company, August 26, 1913

As Bruce "Utah" Phillips melodically rambled in a spoken-word song on the Grammy-nominated album *Fellow Workers*, "There are so few wars of peoples' liberation, for the people have seldom risen."[1] The people were rising in the Copper Country. For many strikers, but not all, this conflict was a war—a class war—of people's liberation. To others, the strike involved bread-and-butter issues: higher wages, safer working conditions, and recognition of the Western Federation of Miners (WFM) as the official representative of Copper Country mineworkers.

To those who saw this as class war, it was easy to see the hallmarks of any such conflict. There were two opposing sides, both of which produced a deluge of propaganda; there were pitched battles like the "Seige in South Range" and the "Fazekas Shooting"; there were daily troop movements and parades through the streets of Copper Country towns and cities by opposing sides; and sadly, there was death. There were "generals" on both sides—Jim MacNaughton for the employers, Charles Moyer for the workers—and after the whole affair was over the landscape and the people of the Copper Country would never be the same again. The Copper Country, whether people like to admit it then or now, was in the midst of a class war when the rank and file of the area WFM locals decided to strike the Copper Country mine owners on July 23, 1913. In fact, the first day of the strike, according to government reports and the company-influenced mainstream press, was like an opening violent battle, as striking workers ran off loyal employees with rocks, sticks, and metal bars in an attempt to shut down the mines. This was war, and like any other war, both sides used a general strategy and carefully thought-out tactics attempting to turn the tide of each battle with a new troop movement, better organization, sharper propaganda, or more impassioned speech.

With its efforts in the Copper Country, the WFM and its rank and file were trying to overcome the entrenchment of the copper mining companies that had ruled the area for almost seventy years. This was a gargantuan task and the strike was going to be an uphill battle for the WFM and its rank and file. While the WFM organizers brought with them a standard bag of tactical tricks, there were tactics used that were specific to the economic, environmental, and social conditions of the Copper Country.

The WFM's Strategy

The WFM's main strategy during the Michigan Copper Strike was to get mine managers to the bargaining table and recognize the union as the official representative of mineworkers. The Copper Country had been so walled off against unionism in area mines that the push to organize had been fraught with difficulty and defeat at every previous turn. As we have observed, Copper Country unionism in the most general sense was not unknown. Cigar makers, printers, barbers, molders, and other skilled crafts and trades belonged to unions affiliated with the American Federation of Labor (AFL); however, the area's major industry, controlled by a powerful handful of men, was not about to give control of its men to something as insidious as a mineworkers' union. Maintenance of power certainly played a major part in the staunch efforts to keep mineworkers unorganized, but the ethnic makeup of striking unskilled workers also played a role. Keeping "foreigners" from having effective, collective representation would keep the Copper Country "white," and would allow the levers of power to remain in the hands of a minority of men, the oligarchy, which was vastly outnumbered by the area's massive collection of immigrant workers.

As has been previously discussed, the Copper Country was a place of immigrants, and while those immigrants were powerful in terms of mass—a working body—they were weak in terms of access to political power. Some of this was the burden of immigrants, who often tended to segregate themselves along cultural, language, and religious differences. Understandably then, mining companies did little to bring workers from different backgrounds together unless it was in controlled spaces such as company libraries or English-language classes. Thus, a major or perhaps the overarching strategy of the WFM was to give immigrants a collective voice, which was difficult because of all the different languages spoken in the Copper Country. Great efforts, painstaking attempts, were made to get the cacophony of immigrant voices singing the same song. This is a somewhat metaphorical statement, but the WFM sanctioned a song paired with a familiar Civil War tune to put the strategy of raising a collective voice of all Copper Country mineworkers to practical development. "The Federation Call," composed by John Sullivan and sung to the tune of "Marching through Georgia," a Union army fight song, went:

> *The Copper Country union men are out upon a strike,*
> *Resisting corporation rule which robs of us our rights.*
> *The victory is all but won in this noble fight*
> *For recognition of the union.—Chorus—*

> *Hurrah, hurrah for the Copper Country strike*
> *Hurrah, hurrah our cause is just and right.*
> *Freedom from oppression is our motto in this fight*
> *For recognition of the union.*

> *At first our task seemed rather big, but now it does seem small*
> *Since every working man respects the Federation call.*
> *For by unity we will win, divided we will fall,*
> *In this great struggle for the union.—Chorus—*

> *Hurrah, hurrah the union makes us strong,*
> *Hurrah, hurrah it shoves us right along.*
> *It will free us from oppression and rectify each wrong,*
> *For such are the missions of the union.*

> *From Calumet to Painesdale, from Mohawk to White Pine*
> *The Federation call has stirred the sturdy sons of toil.*
> *Fifteen thousand working men have fallen into line,*
> *For recognition of the union.—Chorus—*

Hurrah, hurrah, for labor's noble cause,
Hurrah, hurrah, we'll win the world's applause
If we stand united and respect the country laws
In this great battle for the union.[2]

Packed into this rather simple and somewhat forced rhyming scheme was a great deal of ideology and innuendo. In essence, the song encompassed the entire strategy of the WFM during the 1913–14 Michigan Copper Strike: mineworkers needed to communicate to the mine managers with one collective voice, a great coming together of the Copper Country working class, to recognize the WFM as the official representative of Copper Country mineworkers. The tough part was getting the Cornish, American, and German skilled miners, alongside Croatian, Finnish, Italian, Hungarian, and Slovenian unskilled trammers, timbermen, and laborers, to all rally around this grand strategy. This was a lofty goal to say the least, and it was the great burden of the WFM in organizing Copper Country mineworkers, but as a WFM strike sign would remind, "In Unity is Strength."[3]

Federation Tactics

The WFM had been around the proverbial block. It was a battle-hardened union from raucous scraps in the mountainous West, to parades on paved streets in Minnesota's Mesabi Iron Range, to high-profile arrests after the assassination of labor foe and former Idaho governor Frank Steunenberg (those WFM members on trial were found not guilty). The WFM had money, slick lawyers, and, most important, experience with organizing mineworkers. Founded in 1893, the WFM was a fighting union born out of the isolated mining camps in the American West. Originally a somewhat loose gathering of mineworkers, the WFM began to coalesce and radicalize as an organization after difficult struggles to organize mineworkers in Colorado and Idaho. By 1901, the WFM's convention was hearing calls for "complete revolution of social and economic conditions." This radical platform caused leaders and rank and file members of the WFM to help found, support, and guide the upstart revolutionary rank and file–based Industrial Workers of the World (IWW) in 1905. The WFM's affiliation with the IWW lasted only two short years, and the WFM was again on its own, but in that time it had made hefty inroads organizing the Montana copper district around Butte. Butte was, in fact, solid union country thanks to the WFM.[4]

Though it affiliated with the AFL in 1911, a sense of rank-and-file unionism ran as an undercurrent in the WFM from its days of organizing isolated, rough-and-tumble, independent-minded mineworkers in the West. The IWW's commitment to rank-and-file decentralized unionism likely added to the WFM's perceived militancy, and this radical veneer colored the tactics utilized by the union during the 1913–14 strike. While it was known for its militancy, the WFM advocated nonviolent protest during the Copper Strike. Instead of the fist or the gun, the WFM used well-thought-out tactics such as celebrity, media, union stores, and legal maneuvering to combat the power of highly corporatized and well-heeled copper mining companies.

Grassroots, Multiethnic Organization

The WFM was in some instances the "red-haired stepchild" of a number of different union movements. For a time affiliated with the IWW, then independent, and in 1911 associated with the AFL, it was a hodgepodge of ideology. Initially it was a raucous, fighting, Wild West type of union with colorful characters like William "Big Bill" Haywood, Charles Moyer, and occasional guest speaker Mary Harris "Mother" Jones, who were the stuff of radical legend. Haywood lost his eye in a mining accident; Moyer had been arrested and spent time in prison in Chicago and, along with Haywood, had been charged with an assassination attempt on the former governor of Idaho; and Mother Jones—well Mother famously said about herself, "I'm not a humanitarian, I'm a hell-raiser." The WFM had a reputation that preceded it, which had good and bad ramifications for Copper Country union organization efforts.[5]

For many workers (especially immigrant workers) who had been radicalized by Copper Country living and working conditions, by time of the 1913–14 strike the WFM's radical background was for the most part just that—a background. In 1911, the WFM joined the AFL. Though AFL unions were prone to spurts of militant direct action in defense of their members' interests, there was a conservative nature to the AFL. It was reticent to call strikes, politically bureaucratic in nature, and racist as it tended to favor organization of white, American-born workers. Even Moyer had been making overtures to becoming a permanent member of the labor bureaucracy. By 1913, Moyer was more politician and less pugilist, likely after having had the scare of his life placed in him after the Steunenberg affair, when he could have been executed if found guilty. He had drifted from radical industrial unionism toward a more "respectable" suit-and-tie unionism. He was trying to become legitimate. In some ways, this was good for his WFM presidency, but at the same time something was lost—a fighting spirit, an unpredictable nature, a wild-child attitude if you will—the WFM was working to refine its public identity, and this was a stark departure from its early militant days and ways.[6]

There was, however, especially in the Copper Country's Finnish immigrant population, a radical bent, even as the WFM drifted toward conservative AFL unionism. The Finnish immigrant proletarian population cannot by any means be painted with one broad brushstroke, but revolutionary industrial unionism was not the exception in Finnish immigrant proletarian circles; it was a strong competing ideology, and perhaps the prevailing principle of Finnish immigrant socialists in the Upper Midwest. Many of the Finnish immigrant socialist-unionists despised the AFL's conservative unionism because, according to many Finnish immigrant radicals, the AFL "groped after bourgeois support" and "opposed class warfare."[7] The upstart socialist and unionist Finns were a thorn in the side of Copper Country capitalists due to their politics and sheer number of workers employed in area's copper mines. Simply, there were many "Jack-pine Savages," as the Finns were called by outsiders, in the Copper Country; most worked in the mines, and more than any other of the Copper Country's ethnic groups, the Finns had a sizable anticapitalist element in their immigrant population.[8] This sense of radicalism was not just apparent in some of the area's Finns, but also in segments of the Croatian, Italian, and Hungarian populations.

Thus, the red WFM union card, along with all the baggage, benefits, history, and limitations that accompanied it, took its place as an oppositional symbol to the Copper Country oligarchy. Though the red WFM union card, now under the conservative AFL banner, became the symbol of organized response to worker grievances in the Copper Country, there remained, especially in the Copper Country's immigrant populations, a strong undercurrent of rank-and-file IWW ideology driving the actions of the Copper Country workers.

Evidence of the IWW's residual influence in the Copper Country was seen in the way the WFM locals went about getting down to the business of striking. In this opening volley of antagonism toward the mining companies, the Copper Country locals trumpeted a decidedly decentralized strike declaration. Motivated by the Hancock WFM local, which was heavily populated by Finnish immigrants who were thick with IWW sentiment, it appeared as if the Copper Country locals purposefully charged ahead of the WFM bureaucracy in declaring a strike. This perhaps indicates that Wobbly-style decentralization was driving the actions of striking workers. The IWW and its so-called cult of spontaneity,[9] as oppositional American Communists later described it, was opposed to the overt centralization of strike administration and directives from a distant central body to the rank and file. This eschewing of the WFM bureaucracy indicated that the Copper Country locals were not waiting for the consent of a centralized body, much in the same way that the rank and file powered previous IWW-led strike actions.

Segments of the IWW, and especially the rank-and-file Wobblies in the western United States, from the union's very earliest stages in 1905, promoted the decentralization of organization and clamored for local control. In isolated western mining areas, this likely aided the fluidity of strike actions in that decentralization made union locals highly responsive units with the freedom to act on rank-and-file demand. But in the highly corporate and tightly controlled Copper Country, decentralization made preliminary strike actions sustainable for only so long. Outside help, in monetary and organizational form, had to arrive soon, or highly solvent, not-so-distant eastern U.S. mining companies would rout the still-growing WFM Copper Country locals.

In mid-July 1913, however, the Copper Country WFM locals forged ahead against the wishes of the national office in Denver and voted to send a letter to the mining companies to pressure them into negotiations. According to WFM officials, 98 percent of the 9,000 members of the Copper Country WFM locals voted to ratify the referendum to send the letter. If the letter failed to get the mining companies to the bargaining table, a strike was the only other option built into the ballot's language.[10] Likely through information gained from labor spy reports, the mining companies had reason to think the WFM national's heart was not in the strike. Charles Lawton, general manager of the Quincy Mining Company, wrote to mining company president William R. Todd on July 17, 1913, "I am inclined to believe that the National Western Federation of Miners' Union are [sic] not in a position to maintain a strike of very long duration, and that, therefore, they are not urging it, but on the contrary, are trying to 'head it off,' though the local 'Union' is urging a strike."[11] Lawton was right. The WFM national was very much against beginning a strike in the Copper Country, but the local unions forged ahead by sending what might be called in poker an "all-in" bet. This decentralized action forced the WFM national offices to make a tough choice: support their Copper Country locals by funding a strike or cut them loose.

Such a definitive letter with decisive language was very much against the wishes of the WFM's national leadership, and thus very likely the AFL's leadership. Copper Country locals sent the letters to the superintendents of the major copper companies anyway, with the crux of the WFM locals' demands being: the right to union representation in labor negotiations, increased wages, better working conditions, and the removal of the one-man drill, a labor-saving device, from area mines. The mining companies flat out refused to meet with any representatives of the WFM or the Copper Country locals. The Quincy Mining Company's superintendent, Charles Lawton, was even reported to have sent his letter back unopened. The WFM national, therefore, really had no other choice but to call workers out, and on July 23, 1913, Copper Country mineworkers struck the entrenched and extremely powerful Michigan copper companies against the wishes of the WFM national.[12]

Thus, as the 1913–14 Michigan Copper Strike began, there was a distinct sense of two competing union ideologies fighting for expression in the Copper Country.

While the Copper Country WFM locals had a distinctly radical outlook, the WFM national was drifting toward political respectability and closer ties to AFL-style pure-and-simple unionism. The AFL's large bureaucracy likely knew the temper of the Copper Country workers, and aware of the radical nature of some of the area's Finns, Italians, Croatians, Hungarians, and Slovenes, it worked to control and confine radical impulses by immigrant workers.

And it was immigrants who took center stage in the Michigan Copper Strike. Mining companies and later the Citizens' Alliance painted events in the Copper Country stemming from the role of outside, "foreign" agitators stirring up a satisfied, idyllic mining community. In reality, there was a groundswell for the strike moving into 1913, and the supposedly contented Copper Country populace was not the peaceful kingdom portrayed by the mining companies. Mining companies and the Citizens' Alliance wanted people on the outside and local residents to believe that there was simply nothing wrong with the Copper Country status quo. There was, however, a strong bucking against the way things were, and the "famously contented" Copper Country workers had been unhappy at various points for decades. Thus, the strike was an organic movement and not solely the work of the WFM's "foreign" agitators and organizers. This sentiment was expressed well by Finnish immigrant journalist Antti Sarell, who wrote that the grassroots effort to start a union was a way to empower the local working class: "The strike was simply the consequence of unbearable exploitation that the mining companies practiced here on their workers."[13]

A number of the strike leaders were perhaps outside agitators, but the WFM's rank and file were persons involved in local working-class movements and organizations, which included folks from all walks of life. Moreover, many, of course, were originally from outside the Keweenaw Peninsula. The Copper Country was home to a large immigrant population, and the mining industry sustained itself on the cheap labor of immigrant workers. The Copper Country (and much of America) at this time was a place of immigrants—"foreigners"—who were good enough to take the toughest and most dangerous jobs in an industry, but not good enough to have a say in their working conditions or political and social surroundings. For many immigrant men in the Copper Country, the WFM was the only institution related to their working lives in which they could vote, and they gravitated to this idea of industrial democracy in large numbers.

It was, in large numbers, these immigrants and sons of immigrants who led the grassroots efforts to act in a collective, class-conscious manner, and in doing so laid the foundations for the 1913–14 Michigan Copper Strike. An article in the *Miners' Bulletin* (the English-language newspaper sponsored by the WFM) confirmed this: "You men of the copper country rebelled against unbearable conditions and brought about a strike of your own volition without the sanction of the official head of your organization."[14]

The rather long history of working-class organization that had occurred in the Copper Country occasioned this ultimate coming together of mineworkers.

To unite immigrant workers, the WFM had learned from its early efforts at organizing Copper Country workers and in other strikes in the Upper Midwest, such as the 1907 Mesabi Iron Range Strike in northeastern Minnesota, one essential thing: the power of using a multiethnic force of organizers. With surnames like Aaltonen, Hietala, Kolu, and Välimäki (Finnish); Ciagne, Jedda, and Bartalini (Italian); Verbanec and Strizich (Croatian); Arseneault (French-Canadian); Sullivan (Irish); Stodden (Cornish); Oppman (Hungarian); Holovatsky (Polish); and Shaws (Slovenian), the WFM's roster of organizers circa 1910 transcended ethnic lines and mirrored the Copper Country's vibrant cultural landscape. Indeed, a number of these organizers were from outside the Copper Country. Some came from places as close as Duluth, Minnesota, with others venturing to the Upper Peninsula from as far away as Kennett, California. More often, however, the WFM organizers had Copper Country residences. Of fifteen prominent WFM organizers identified in a 1913 edition of a Finnish-language socialist publication, *Työmiehen Joulu* (Workers' Christmas), nine had Copper Country addresses.

The addition of multiethnic organizers gave the strike actions a solidarity previously lacking. Adding to the solidarity of bringing disparate "racial" groups together was the gradual erosion of the underground laboring hierarchy. In many of the previous Copper Country labor actions, "foreign" trammers and other unskilled laboring ethnicities went on the offensive alone, without the assistance of their skilled underground brethren. The threat of the one-man drill, a drilling machine introduced as a labor-saving device, prompted established miners, usually English- or German-speaking skilled workers, to confront capital and join ranks with their fellow workers.[15]

From labor statistics at the Calumet & Hecla (C&H) mines before (July 14, 1913) and roughly two months after the strike began (September 29), an image of the most dedicated striking ethnicities emerges. By far, Finns, Croatians, and Slovenians were the most likely to walk out of C&H mines on strike. Next, Italians and Russians or Poles were the most likely ethnic groups to go out on strike. Of these numbers, Croatians were the most likely in terms of percentage to be out on strike. While their laboring population was less than that of Slovenes or Finns in the C&H mines, Croatian workers went out en masse during the strike. Before the strike, there were 131 Croatian workers in the C&H mines; in September, only eight remained. Ninety-four percent of the Croatian workers in C&H mines left the job. The world-famous Red Jacket Shaft, one of C&H's engineering marvels, was especially hit by the Croatian work stoppage. Before the strike began there were 72 Croatians working in the Red Jacket Shaft, but by September only one lone Croatian remained. In terms of the other ethnicities, Finns were the next most likely to walk from the C&H mines (63 percent), then Slovenians (57 percent), followed by Italian workers (34 percent), and then Russian or Polish laborers (31 percent).[16]

While Croatian zeal at the C&H mines was exceptional, one ethnicity's class-conscious element helped to lay the foundation for radicalism in the Copper Country by throwing everything they had into the strike. Along with opening their socialist-unionist halls and media to the WFM, Finns occupied important places both as rank and filers in the WFM and in leadership roles. Charles E. Hietala was secretary of WFM District 16, secretary-treasurer of the Hancock local, and a board member of the Finnish-language Työmies Publishing Company, and John Välimäki was a District 16 organizer for the WFM as well as secretary of the Työmies Publishing Company. Both Hietala and Välimäki were recent immigrants to the United States, yet found themselves in prominent positions taking on one of America's most powerful institutions: the mining industry. Working in tandem with the WFM locals were the Finnish Socialist Federation (FSF) locals of the Socialist Party of America. Members of the Hancock FSF, the *Jousi Seura* (Society of the Bow), rallied for money and food for the striking workers. The *Jousi* also hosted picnics for striking workers and their families: "The Hancock Local of the Socialist Party will hold a picnic at Anthony's Farm, Sunday September 14. Speaking in all languages, begins at 1.30 P.M. Admission free."[17]

The FSF locals in Ahmeek, Calumet, Hancock, Mass City, and South Range also had regular advertised meetings during the strike and rallied hard to support the WFM. While the strike was certainly a multiethnic effort, the FSF and WFM locals were so intertwined that in many instances, the FSF locals shared meeting spaces with the WFM locals. The Hancock, South Range, and Ahmeek FSF locals (composed of workers from the copper-mining towns of Mohawk, Allouez, and Ahmeek) shared meeting space with the WFM in their respective halls.[18] There was almost a complete sense of grassroots Finnish immigrant socialist-unionist solidarity with the activities of the WFM and the 1913–14 Copper Country Strike.

Union Places and Spaces

The strike stretched over sixty miles along the jagged Keweenaw copper range from southern Keweenaw County through Houghton County and into eastern Ontonagon County. *Työmies* ran large front-page headlines about the opening volley of strike events. On July 24, *Työmies* ran its first edition to come out after the commencement of the strike actions. The headline read: "Michigan Copper

Territory Mine Workers Striking," while the next day's headline was "15,000 Mine Workers Strike Copper Territory."[19]

These headlines reflected an attempt to thwart the compartmentalization of strike actions across a massive spatial distance. In attempts to combat spatial isolation of union locals and members, the WFM, *Työmies*, and the *Miners' Bulletin* took pains to portray the strike as a districtwide labor action in an effort to generate and promote solidarity between workers of various companies and ethnicities spread out across the entire Keweenaw Peninsula. Published examples of efforts to avoid compartmentalization of strike actions in *Työmies* heralded strike news from *Kuparialueella* (Copper Territory) or *Lakkoalueele* (Strike Territory). Most of the media centered on strike actions in Houghton County, but on July 24 *Työmies* addressed the swift spread of the strike into far-off Ontonagon County: "The strike has reached all the way down to the Mass Mine, Lake Mine, Algoma, South Lake, North Lake, Indiana and Winona Mines."[20]

Työmies made its first count of the number of idled workers on July 28 and estimated that roughly 15,700 workers were on strike. Two days later, on July 30, *Työmies* made another count, this time specifying the numbers for Keweenaw and Ontonagon County mines: 18,460 workers were out. This tally concluded that there were about 15,500 striking Houghton County mineworkers, 1,500 or so from Keweenaw County mines, and around 1,000 idled in Ontonagon County mines. These figures with zeros at the end may indicate some generous rounding up, but the allusion was accurate; workers were walking out of the mines by the thousands, though mining companies claimed only 15 to 20 percent of their workers joined the WFM and struck, which would put the number of striking miners at roughly 3,000.

The WFM had five centers for organization spread throughout the Copper Country: in the Calumet area, the Calumet Miners' Union, WFM Local 203, set up headquarters on Sixth Street in Wilmer's Hall. In Keweenaw County, striking workers were under the banner of the Keweenaw Miners Union Local 129, and had offices and held meetings in Ahmeek at Lesh's Hall. For workers of the Copper Range Company (Champion, Baltic, and Trimountain mines), the South Range Miners' Union, WFM Local 196, had offices and held its meetings in Kämäräinen's Hall, while using the Saima Finnish Temperance Hall for speeches and other functions. Farther south, in Mass City, the Mass Miners' Union, WFM Local 215, apparently did not have a dedicated meeting space, but rather listed the name of the local's secretary to gain information about union activities. The Hancock Miners' Union, WFM Local 200, held its meetings and had offices in Kansankoti Hall.[21]

WFM locals and halls were places of concerted effort to organize workers. Most often, the way to reach the masses, other than a newspaper, was through speeches. The WFM paraded out a number of big names to give special speeches in packed halls: Mother Jones, John Mitchell, and John L. Lewis to name a few. There was also a devoted cadre of local organizers who put it all out there in rousing speeches weekly. The WFM's speechmakers attempted to champion the cause of organized labor, while pointing to specific aspects of Copper Country work and life that were exploitative. Like most other WFM tactics and coinciding with the WFM's overall strategies, the speeches had to be in multiple languages to reach the listeners of a number of ethnic backgrounds. The *Miners' Bulletin* ran speech schedules hoping to keep the striking population and public informed of the dates and times of orations in various languages. In late August, in less than a week, local WFM organizers traveled hundreds of miles from Dodgeville in Houghton County, some forty miles to Mass City in Ontonagon County, then back again through Houghton County, up to Keweenaw County, and back to Houghton County again. It was a dizzying schedule:

UNION MEETINGS WITH SPEECHES IN MANY LANGUAGES
Tuesday, August 19, Dodgeville
John H. Walker, English
Frank Aaltonen, Finnish
Alex Susnar, Croatian

Tue. Aug. 19, Ahmeek or Mohawk
Guy Miller, English
Yanco Terzich, Croatian
John Valimaki, Finnish
Mor Oppman, Hungarian
Ben Goggins, Italian

Wednesday, August 20, Palestra, Laurium
Guy Miller, English
Joseph Cannon, English
Yanco Terzich, Croatian
Mor Oppman, Hungarian
Frank Aaltonen, Finnish
Ben Goggins, Italian
William Holowatsky, Polish

Parade at union headquarters in Calumet and march up to the Palestra, starting at 1 o'clock

Thursday, Aug. 21, Mass City
Laura Gregg Cannon, English
Schaws, Slavonian [sic]
Frank Aaltonen, Finnish
Jos. D. Cannon, English

Friday, Aug. 22, Hancock
Laura Gregg Cannon, English
Yanco Terzich, Croatian
John Valimaki, Finnish
John C. Lowney, English
Ben Goggins, Italian

Saturday, Aug. 23, South Range
Frank Aaltonen, Finnish
John C. Lowney, English
Alex Susnar, Croatian
Steve Oberto, Italian
Jos. D. Cannon, English[22]

While all the union locals' halls were important places of action, the WFM centralized its efforts at Kansankoti Hall in Hancock. Serving as central strike headquarters, Kansankoti Hall was where the WFM held union meetings, votes, and fund-raisers, and started or ended parades. WFM locals announced meeting times and office hours, which *Työmies* and the *Miners' Bulletin* published.[23]

Much of the passion and pageantry of the strike played out on Copper Country streets. With the advent of the strike, mining operations in the Copper Country came to a standstill, and the streets of the region's mining landscapes filled with the voices of raucous strikers. This "streetscape" level of organization was perhaps one of the best tactics for the union. The parade, strike-watch processions, and overflowed meetings in buildings were powerful ways of creating a sense of radical community in the Copper Country's conservative socioeconomic landscape.

One of the WFM's most frequently used and effective tactics was the aforementioned strike parade. Often the particulars of a strike parade included getting up before the crack of dawn (sometimes in terrible weather); meeting at a preselected site, which was oftentimes a union hall or other structure partial to the WFM; organizing into long lines that stretched for blocks; and then walking for hours while sometimes holding a sign. Strike parades could attract hundreds if not thousands of marchers, though there was a high degree of danger involved in these strike actions that catapulted the strike parade into an exercise of bravery and fortitude. Armed Michigan National Guardsmen—and worse, armed Houghton County sheriff's deputies and hired gun thugs—often shadowed the strikers on their parade route. At times, the parades became violent.

As the strike stretched over three counties, each county had its own peccadilloes and problems for the WFM. While Houghton County was bought and sold to area copper companies (which is explored in depth later), Keweenaw County proved a far more contested geographic space for the WFM. Keweenaw County became a hotbed of WFM activity, and before long the WFM was running the place. The WFM even made edicts to Keweenaw County copper companies, such as the one sent on July 26, 1913, to the management at the Ahmeek mine: "In behalf of the Western Federation of Miners, you are hereby authorized to keep sufficient [mine de-watering] pumps operating for the purpose of Fire Protection, and the Electric Light Plant running. In case you determine that the two men are not sufficient you are authorized to hire four." This permission note was especially significant because it was signed by a committee from the Keweenaw Miners Union Local, which included a brash Irishman by the name of John Dunnigan.[24]

The Dunnigan "clan," as they became known to the mining managers, were ardent supporters of the WFM, Irish, Catholic (an undesirable element among the Protestant oligarchy), and, according to C&H General Manager Jim MacNaughton, damn near the wickedest people in the world: "The worst point, however, to the north of us is Ahmeek. The strikers there are led by an Irish bunch called Dunnigan; they are perfect fire-eaters and knowing them as well as I do, I do not care to approach them for I realize nothing could be gained and they would probably put a wrong interpretation on everything that was said."[25] Likely to the chagrin of MacNaughton, the Dunnigans, John and Pat, were also law enforcement officers in Ahmeek during the strike.

The local kept press in Keweenaw County, the *Keweenaw Miner*, related just how the Dunnigan Clan came to power. Village president Kenel had allowed the Michigan National Guard's cavalry to quarter in Ahmeek. The large striking population of that village did not support Kenel's decision and called for the village president's resignation, which Kenel gave. In Kenel's place, the village president pro tem, another Irishman by the name of Reilly, along with the Village Council (apparently comprised of mostly pro-union members), called for the resignation of the village marshal. The village marshal acquiesced, and then the Village Council, under the leadership of Reilly, appointed Patrick Dunnigan as top peacekeeper in Ahmeek. Patrick then appointed his brother John as a deputy along with five other WFM members.[26]

It was also rumored that Keweenaw County Sheriff John Hepting was an honorary member of the WFM, and thus Keweenaw County was rife with tones of revolution. This situation worried MacNaughton. He and the Copper Country oligarchy had carefully crafted a rigid and almost total sense of control regarding the area's law enforcement and legal system. For MacNaughton, the world made sense this way, but in Keweenaw County, and with working-class advocate Patrick O'Brien as circuit court judge deciding crucial legal cases in the county, the world was turned upside down. Worse yet, the Keweenaw County mines were just miles away from the once-thought perfectly protected C&H mines. Houghton County's system was rigged for the mining companies, MacNaughton saw to that, but now Keweenaw County was coming under the control of organized labor. In an ultimate display of hypocrisy, MacNaughton described to C&H president Quincy Shaw the danger of a union organized Keweenaw to the control of the mining company:

> As a living illustration of the miscarriage of justice let me detail a case before the Circuit Court in Keweenaw County. A man called Abramson who worked at the Ahmeek was assaulted by strikers one morning when on his way to the mine. . . . The picketers were arrested, bound over to the Circuit Court by a local Justice. They appeared in the Circuit Court at Eagle River before Judge O'Brien one day last week. The Judge is a Socialist, openly says that all his sympathies are with the strikers. The Public Prosecutor is the legal advisor of the strikers and belongs to their Union. . . . The defendants were Croatians and required an interpreter. The Public Prosecutor selected Oppman the Hungarian Jew, paid organizer for the Union, as interpreter. It is needless to say the defendants were promptly found not guilty. I have come to the conclusion there is no such thing as law in this part of the Upper Peninsula.[27]

Women as Members of the WFM

"Women have been one of the great factors in the strike," concluded an article in the September 11, 1913, issue of the *Miners' Bulletin*. The article continued, "They furnish the answer to all the statements that this was a strike brought on by imported agitators. No agitator could ever induce women to get out on the picket duty five o'clock in the morning, march miles to be in attendance at the big meeting . . . or to endure the insults of scabs and deputies and meet the bayonets of soldiers without wavering."[28] Indeed, women were at the forefront of the strike, providing not only support but also leadership during picket duty, meetings, and parades. Though a mineworkers union, the WFM created auxiliary locals for women in the Copper Country. Calumet's Ladies Auxiliary organized around September 11, 1913, holding its first informal meeting at Italian Hall.[29] Hancock also had a Ladies Auxiliary, WFM No. 5, which met at Kansankoti Hall.[30]

Perhaps most notable of the Copper Country's union women was "Big" or "Tall" Ana Clemenc, branded in the labor press as an "American Joan of Arc." Now an enduring part of Copper Country mythology, Clemenc became the stuff of legend. In one heroic tale, she was said to have faced down the Michigan National Guard cavalry. Recounted in the pages of the *Miners' Bulletin*, Clemenc's bravery was used as a call to action for the WFM:

> The day when the soldiers rode down the [American] flag Annie Clemenc stood holding the staff of that big flag in front of her, horizontally. She faced cavalrymen with drawn sabers, infantrymen with bayoneted guns. They ordered her back. She didn't move an inch. . . . She was struck on her right wrist with a bayonet, and over the right bosom and shoulder with a deputy's club. . . . "Kill me," she said. "Run your bayonets and sabers through this flag and kill me, but I won't go back. If this flag will not protect me, then I will die with it."[31]

A striking recollection of a tense and valiant moment, but where mythology ends and actual events begin is at times difficult to discern with Clemenc. Perhaps the event did not transpire just as recounted in the labor press, but Clemenc's devotion to the cause and her larger-than-life persona were important aspects of the push to organize Copper Country workers. Clemenc was a media darling, and her plight, symbolic of the plight of many Copper Country women, was picked up in newspapers for the world to read. More concrete were her run-ins with Houghton County law enforcement officials—she was arrested three times, twice for "assault and battery" and once for "intimidation." She appealed each conviction.[32]

Also "notorious" in the eyes of Houghton County law enforcement officials were four Finnish immigrant women arrested for "rioting." The four women were arrested on October 3, 1913, and bound over to circuit court. They spent time in jail and became a sort of cause célèbre in the pages of the Finnish immigrant press. Frank Aaltonen, an editor at the Työmies Publishing Company, wrote of the women and their incarceration:

> They were transported like some evildoers to the same dirty jail where they put the thieves, crooks, robbers, and murderers too. The old mouldy prison walls might have felt then that the group differed from the usual ones and even the grim grates were certainly smiling when song melodies arrived through the narrow grates to the ears of wondering listeners from the girls' young chests: "My country, 'tis of thee, sweet land of liberty." . . .

Listeners smiled quietly. Songs of freedom echo most beautifully, where tyrants are nearest.[33]

Union Media

While getting organizers on the ground, bringing women to the forefront of the struggle, and housing union activities in halls all were very important, using the media was perhaps the most crucial tactic in the effort to organize Copper Country mineworkers. Union media had the ability to connect people from across wide distances in the strike territory and to trumpet successes and advise of the dangers workers faced to folks outside the Copper Country. In short, union media had great "legs" and could cover more ground faster than any human being could ever travel. Greatest of all media sources in this era was the newspaper because it could travel far distances and was much cheaper than sending union speakers to tout events in the Copper Country. Publication of the *Miners' Bulletin* began on August 14, 1913. As a triweekly two-page (and later a four-page) publication, it was a seven-column newspaper that devoted space to national news about the labor movement, Copper Country strike-specific news, legal news such as strike depositions and affidavits, messages of solidarity from other union organizations and workers, updates on other strike actions across the United States, and announcements regarding parades and speeches in the Copper Country.

The publication of speakers' schedules and parades was perhaps one of the newspaper's most important functions. It literally got union folks on the same page regarding collective action among the Copper Country's striking mineworkers. Publishing the results of a parade on August 14, the *Bulletin* boasted, "The parade and assembly at the Palestra [in Laurium] Wednesday broke all previous records. Joseph Lesch of Ahmeek, Mrs. Mikko and W. J. Rickard led the parade of fully six-thousand people."[34]

A major function of the prounion newspapers was bridging ethnic divisions in the Copper Country mineworkers' population by publishing articles written in diverse languages. The Copper Country was a polyglot of mother tongues, and a number of these languages had expression in working-class newspapers. Croatians, Finns, and Slovenes had presses that were supportive of striking miners. Italians, another large ethnic group with a formidable striking population, also had a press, but the editor of the newspaper, *Il Minatore Italiano* (The Italian Miner), was proclaimed a Judas to striking workers in the pages of the *Miners' Bulletin*. Thus, after August 23, 1913, the *Miners' Bulletin* began publishing Italian-language articles to combat the clout of *Il Minatore Italiano*. The *Bulletin* also began publishing Hungarian-language articles on its back pages in addition to English-language reports throughout the newspaper. Along with carrying general strike news, it published the names of scab miners, attacked mining companies for importing scabs from outside the region, and, to create revenue, published advertising in the Croatian, Hungarian, Italian, Finnish, and, of course, English languages.[35]

The battle for the hearts and minds of Italian workers was especially prevalent in the *Miners' Bulletin*'s pages. Italian strikers published the names of those Italian Americans who scabbed in an article conveniently titled "List of Scabs Quincy Mine." This was a commonly used tactic of labor writers, who published scabs' names so as to shame the scabs into either abandoning their offensive practices or increasing their discomfort while continuing to cross picket lines. The November 1, 1913, issue of the *Miners' Bulletin* ran the names of seven Italian American scabs: Giuseppe Colombo, Fasana Adolfo, Devo Giusti, Quido Giusti, Masini Alfredo, Giovanni Paterne, and Peter Cartupane. The article also included the author's perception of the physical and mental characteristics of the scabs, referencing the men's treachery, stupidity, and cowardice. The article's writer even published the scabs' names in all-bold lettering, thus going great lengths to guarantee that readers would be able to identify the members of the local Italian American community who betrayed the strikers' cause. A similar list published in January 1914 concluded its description of Natale Coppo by declaring that he was a "stinking scab!"[36]

Admittedly, the WFM's newspapers, the *Miners' Bulletin* and Finnish-language *Työmies*, stretched the boundaries of factual journalism during the strike. In some instances the newspapers printed downright caustic and callous stories, cartoons, and poems about scabs, gunmen, and mining company managers. The penchant to use sarcastic humor to lampoon serious issues ran deep through the organizational structure of the WFM. In one instance after both C&H and Quincy attached giant searchlights on the tops of mining structures, the *Miners' Bulletin* ripped into the devices and the people using them in a column titled "As Seen by the Search Lights." In one instance, the column printed a December poem by "A Strike Sympathizer" that read in part:

> At Six o'clock in early morn,
> Behold the deputies quite forlorn;
> Sleepily walking the Quincy hill,
> While Waddell sleeps as babies will.
>
> From out the sheriff's branch office great
> Shea and his crew emerge quite late,

Dreaming still, of the night before
When love he made to the girls galore.

Passing the dry comes the odor of suds.
The scabs stayed home to clean their duds.
The Quincy furnished their wardrobe lean.
For on washday none of the men are seen . . .

If the search-light could turn to New York state,
A Christmas story, we would relate;
Where the wives of the gunmen angrily wait,
For the men to come home and cut out their "dates."[37]

In addition to the *Miners' Bulletin*, the Finnish immigrant socialist-unionist press got the union's message out to a regional Finnish-speaking audience—the Copper Country's largest immigrant population—via the Finnish-language press. Severi Alanne, editor of the *Työmies* newspaper, which was a daily publication at this time, had a significant strike coffer to work with during the labor unrest. On August 16, 1913, less than a month after the strike began, the capital stock of the Työmies Publishing Company jumped from $15,000 to $100,000.[38] With this influx of strike capital and the influence of IWW radicals in the Finnish immigrant ranks, *Työmies* became the most combative media advocate of the strike.

The newspapers read by striking workers also featured brilliantly subversive political cartoons. Nationally syndicated progressive and socialist cartoonists such as Ryan Walker and Art Young appeared on the pages of the *Miners' Bulletin* and even *Työmies*. Usually the political cartoons had the union logo of the International Photo-Engravers Union (IPEU) in the bottom corner, assuring striking workers they were not alone in the push for collective action. For the readers of *Työmies*, these labor cartoons were their first introduction to American culture, and a biting, class-conscious introduction it was. The Työmies Publishing Company also had its own cartoonists on staff, and the likes of Konstu Sallinen and Henry Askeli lampooned area mining companies with less-skilled but perhaps more sarcastic drawings. Sallinen especially caught the working-class plight of Copper Country miners in many of his drawings that were featured in a Finnish-language satirical magazine, *Lapatossu*. A little like *MAD* magazine today, the artwork in *Lapatossu* was designed to catch the ire of the Copper Country oligarchy—and no topic was sacred.

A familiar audio tactic used often by the IWW, which was known as the "Singing Union," was also a staple of WFM organizing in the Copper Country. The WFM published a song for Copper Country strikers overlaying an old, beloved tune with new, union-sympathetic lyrics. "The Federation Call," discussed earlier in the chapter, was one example of organizational aurality. While the *Miners' Bulletin* published "The Federation Call" to unite English-speaking or dual-language strikers, the Finnish immigrant socialist-unionist press printed another tune to rally Finnish immigrants. This song was set to the familiar Finnish folk tune "Varsovalainer." The "Kuparialueen lakkolaisten marssi," or "Copper Territory Strikers' March," was a song penned by "Jukka S." and printed in editions of *Työmies* during the Michigan Copper Strike. The first verse and chorus contained vivid proletarian imagery:

> *Copper miners have gallantly risen*
> *To fight against oppression and exploitation*
> *From a long dream like a wintry bear*
> *To demand human rights*
> *We have slept enough already and been slaves*
> *Just kissing MacNaughton's whip*
> *Let's rise brothers and throw the chains*
> *Into the dirty oppressors' faces*
>
> *To the fight for human rights*
> *For our bread*
> *Off, off miners off you go!*[39]

Celebrity and Solidarity

As August events festered, the Copper Country gained national attention. Famous champions of the working class such as Clarence Darrow, Helen Keller, Ella Reeve "Mother" Bloor, and Mother Jones appeared in the Copper Country. Keller, who was an ardent socialist, donated money to support the WFM's efforts during the strike. However, Mother Jones really stirred up emotions in the Copper Country. An especially welcome figure, she received accolades from Copper Country workers:

The mineworkers' friend, famous throughout the land, Mother Jones arrived to the strike area on August 3rd, welcomed by a group of thousands of strikers in the Calumet railway station. This white-haired 81 years young fighter walked to the union offices through the alley of strikers as they greeted her with cheers. Mother gave fiery speeches to the strikers in different localities of the strike area. When Mother really got into describing the wretchedness of the workers' position, the listeners' eyes filled with tears.[40]

Perhaps the ultimate compliment was the devotion Mother Jones inspired from the people who heard her: "The Copper Country strikers will always remember Mother Jones with love."[41]

Jones's rhetoric went well beyond verbally accosting the Copper Country oligarchy. She was in the Copper Country to bolster the union's strategy to bring together an often-divided working class. She did it well, as a quotation in the *Miners' Bulletin* recalls the near caterwauled pitch of Jones's invective: "This nation was founded as the result of a strike. Lincoln brought us all on a strike against black slavery; we are out on a strike against wage slavery and feudal bonds. Sweep away all differences of nationality. You are all Americans. We are going to quit developing muscle and develop a brain for the working class. Stick together! Wake up! The hour is here! The dawn has come!"[42]

Once she had left the Copper Country, Mother Jones continued to fight for the striking Michigan mineworkers. Her celebrity induced solidarity, and this solidarity meant financial prosperity to the WFM's Copper Strike coffers:

> Mother Jones, 81 years old, who says her home is wherever labor is in trouble, thrilled the delegates to the street car men's convention yesterday with a vigorous appeal for the striking miners in Michigan. As a result of the fiery old woman's appeal the street car men unanimously appropriated $1,000 for the relief of the Michigan miners and passed resolutions denouncing the methods of the Michigan mine operators and forwarded the resolutions to President Wilson.[43]

National labor organizations such as the AFL and the United Mine Workers of America (UMWA), which was affiliated with the AFL, also offered assistance to the Copper Country strikers and their families. These offers created a sense of national labor solidarity, and demonstrated to immigrant workers isolated in Michigan's Copper Country that they were not alone. It also vaulted the famous men associated with the U.S. labor movement to celebrity status with Keweenaw copper workers who were looking for working-class heroes. According to Sarell, "The Illinois State Coalminer's Association was the first to offer help, sending the strikers $100,000. The quick aid was of course due to the fact that their former President, J. H. Walker, who was elected as the Worker's Union President for the same state, was here almost from the beginning of the strike giving powerful speeches at strike meetings." The prestige of having national organizations interested in the happenings of Copper Country workers lifted spirits, even as the specter of a freezing winter loomed large over strike actions: "In addition to this the Socialist Party of America is planning to collect a strike aid for the Copper Country strikers. Even though the Copper

Country's winter is hard, the fact that America's organized workers have taken on an aid collecting of such a wide scope makes the position a more hopeful one."[44]

Donations from all across the United States were coming in, and people in downstate Michigan joined in the cause. From an August notice in the *Miners' Bulletin*, titled "Protest from Bay City, Mich.,": "The friends and sympathizers with organized labor are getting busy throughout the state. . . . The following extracts from a speech at Bay City, Mich., by Joseph Smith, President of the Michigan United Mine Workers, with the resolutions passed unanimously, at the meeting, will afford some idea of the temper of the people."[45] Workers in Flint pitched in as well, as a December 16, 1913, article recorded: "A mass meeting of the citizens of Flint was held Sunday night December 7th when the G.A.R. hall was well filled. The meeting was called by the Flint Federation of Labor for the purpose of discussion, and in securing funds for the striking miners of the Upper Peninsula. Former mayor John A. C. Menton presided. Music was furnished by an orchestra of eleven pieces from the Musicians Union and Mrs. W. H. Winchester sang solo."[46]

Donations came from as far away as Astoria, Oregon, a hotbed of Finnish immigrant socialism, where workers thought of creative ways to aid striking workers in the Copper Country. In an article titled "Salmon Fishermen to the Rescue," the *Miners' Bulletin* proclaimed on November 11, 1913, "A mass meeting of the [Astoria] fishermen was held at the Finnish Socialist hall Thursday night, to formulate a plan of direct action in aiding the striking miners of Calumet, Mich." The original plan was to freight carloads of the salmon catch to the Copper Country, but the cost and logistics of moving so much fish overland caused the fishermen to rethink the plan. Instead, the fishermen "decided to dispose of their catch to the local canneries and forward the money to the strike committee here."[47]

The solidarity did not just go one way toward striking mineworkers. In an attempt to engage other Copper Country workers, the WFM called for a boycott of non-union beer in the Copper Country. Workers at the Park Brewing Company in Hancock were striking against the locally owned suds trade, and having a tough go of it. In the first issue of the *Miners' Bulletin*, the WFM made sure to reach a hand out in solidarity to these fellow workers, proclaiming, "The Brewery Workers at the Park Brewery Co., Hancock, Mich., went out on strike July 11 because that firm absolutely refused to consider the fair demands made by the Local Union No. 65 of the International Union United Brewery Workmen." The WFM then wrapped the plight of the Park Brewery workers with its own, opining, "The Brewery proprietors of Houghton County, Michigan have organized for themselves what is called the Upper Peninsula Brewer's Association. (Mr. Foley, owner of the Park Brewery) denies the men a right to organize and better their conditions. The same as the mine owners refuse to recognize the Western Federation of Miners." The article went on to list union breweries—Blatz, Schlitz, and Pabst—followed by a great ideological mantra provided by the Brewery Workmen's local, "If you are a friend of organized labor, think, speak, act and drink accordingly."[48] This was likely a heartily welcomed slogan from organized labor, to which many tired, aching, and thirsty mineworkers could easily respond, "Solidarity Forever."

The Law and the WFM's Legal Team

While the Copper Country's legal environment was especially slanted toward the mining companies, the WFM spent what was likely an impressive amount of money on legal representation. The WFM's Copper Country legal team included local attorneys as well as nationally recognized labor lawyers. Men such as Angus Kerr from Calumet (who once practiced law in Calumet with Albert E. Petermann, the C&H company lawyer) and Edward Legendre from Laurium provided local knowledge, while attorneys such as O. N. Hilton from WFM headquarters in Denver provided needed expertise in national labor law.

Thus, the WFM had a high-priced and well-seasoned legal staff of local and national lawyers, but that did not change the fact that the Copper Country's bench was mostly hostile or unfamiliar with organized labor, yet quite sympathetic to the area's oligarchy. A number of local judges served in local political posts with either James MacNaughton, general manager of C&H, or Charles Lawton, general manager of the Quincy Mining Company. The legal deck was somewhat stacked against the WFM, but one Copper Country jurist was sympathetic, bordering on loyal to Copper Country workers.

Circuit Court Judge Patrick O'Brien was born to working-class Irish immigrant parents near Phoenix, Michigan, in 1868. Phoenix, a gone-bust mining location north of Calumet, had little in the way of a future, so O'Brien's family moved south to the booming Calumet-area mines. O'Brien had been schooled in a mining company's educational facility, and then tried his hand at teaching in Copper Harbor, but left to study law at Northern Indiana College in Valparaiso. He came back to the Copper County, never forgetting his working-class roots, and plied his trade as a criminal defense lawyer.[49] Lured by the call of the Progressive movement, as a defense attorney O'Brien became a champion of the workers in a region dominated by employers. Among O'Brien's best clients by way of notoriety were Finnish immigrant socialists, whom he defended with great zeal on more than one occasion. Perhaps O'Brien's most infamous case was his defense of the "Red Flag 13" in July 1907 when Finnish socialists ignored an edict by Hancock's city government to abstain from carrying the red flag of socialism in a summer parade. They did anyway and were summarily beaten and arrested in downtown Hancock.[50]

O'Brien was chosen to defend them, and a spirited defense it was as he attempted to turn the day's chaos on those who beat the Red Flag 13 and later, even on the arresting officers, arguing in court that "the citizens were anarchists last Sunday when they destroyed the red flag of the Socialists. The latter were not disorderly he said; the people began the riot" and that "the police of Hancock were the trespassers [against the Red Flag 13] and should be punished for it." O'Brien's 1907 defense of the Red Flag 13 also included a minitutorial on the symbolism of the socialists' red flag, which he described as "the universal flag of the down-trodden and oppressed people, the international flag of an international people."[51]

Given this rather colorful history, it is easy to understand that O'Brien may have been seen as a problem for Copper Country mine managers. He openly advocated, in a 1907 courtroom, tenets of socialism, including government ownership of industry. For his working-class advocacy, he was elected circuit court judge, but his tenure in that position was fraught with difficulties. He was no longer a defense attorney and had to at least appear impartial. He often struggled at this, giving strikers brought before him a generous benefit of the doubt. This did not escape the watchful eyes of the Copper Country oligarchy, and on more than one occasion they were outraged by O'Brien's decisions.

The most noteworthy of O'Brien's rulings during the strike revolved around an injunction he granted against picketing. While O'Brien granted the injunction in mid-September, he dissolved the injunction on September 29, 1913, on a technicality—writing that the original application for the injunction did not contain affidavits from the mining companies' lawyers. Jim MacNaughton of the C&H was spitting tacks on hearing that the injunction was dissolved and wrote to Quincy Shaw in Boston, "The truth of the matter is O'Brien's Socialistic tendencies have mastered him and he has gone into the hands of the enemy. Mr. Rees is getting the necessary papers ready and will apply to the Supreme Court for a mandamus compelling O'Brien to issue an injunction. . . . In the meantime everything is perfectly quite [sic] although I expect that tomorrow picketing will begin again with renewed vigor."[52]

While O'Brien did much of what he could for strikers, a man from a working-class Croatian background drew the ire of Copper Country strikers. Supposedly a friend to organized labor, the elected prosecuting attorney for Houghton County, Anthony Lucas, came to be especially reviled by the writers and editors at the *Miners' Bulletin*. During the strike, Lucas cultivated a tense relationship with strikers. For a while it appeared as if he was a friend to organized labor, but as conditions worsened in the Copper Country and as mine managers tightened control on the area's striking population, Lucas appears to have chosen his occupation over his commitment to striking mineworkers. One especially sarcastic and caustic article about Lucas in the *Miners' Bulletin*, titled "Our Beautiful Prosecutor," questioned the ethical nature of having two fallacy-inspired professions (politician and lawyer) competing for voters' attention: "It is not strange when a good politician comes to the voters before the election time and offers anything on God's earth. The Prosecuting Attorney of Houghton County offered even that he would make iron rings from wood. After the election his actions sounded louder than his words."[53]

While WFM lawyers were certainly up against it in the Copper Country, perhaps the best-known legal mind in America, Progressive jurist Clarence Darrow, took up the cause of the striking workers, visiting the Copper Country seeking a meeting with C&H lawyers. Reportedly at the bequest of Governor Woodbridge N. Ferris, Darrow initiated contact with C&H's vaunted legal firm of Rees, Robinson, and Petermann, but was rebuffed in his efforts as there was supposedly a "Nothing to Arbitrate sign hung out" on their offices.[54]

Feeding and Entertaining Striking Workers

As the Copper Country days grew shorter, winter loomed on the gray autumn horizon. Public sentiment, after the shootings of striking workers by company thugs and the importation of scab workers (who in some cases were held against their will in train cars and boardinghouses), was teetering toward the side of the strikers. The mining companies hoped the harsh, snowy Copper Country winter and deficiency in WFM funding would combine to wear the strikers' resolve down to nil. The WFM promised and delivered strike benefits as early as mid-August, and to the chagrin of the mining companies, with massive donations of money from across the United States there was ample funding to support striking families into and perhaps beyond the looming Copper Country winter.

In mid-November, the WFM put this funding to use by opening its own stores. A November 15, 1913, article in the *Miners' Bulletin* announced the establishment of "Union Stores":

> The Western Federation of Miners has established stores at Calumet, Hancock, Ahmeek and South Range with John L. Hennessy as general manager and purchasing agent. Each store is manned by a competent and able set of clerks. These stores have been opened within the last week and the business being done is phenomenal. A great many persons not belonging to the union have made inquiry as to whether they would be permitted

to purchase goods at these stores and for their information we will say yes, bring your cash and you may purchase all you want. The stores are filled with principally staple groceries.[55]

The "Union Stores" were shops where strikers and their families could pay for food, clothes, and other dry goods with WFM stamps. In essence, the WFM created its own token economy in the Copper Country, and as part of the strike relief, the WFM distributed $3.00 a week for single men, $7.00 a week for family men with five or more children, and $9.00 a week in cases of emergency.[56] John Palosaari, a member of the Hancock WFM local, remembered, "At that time [during the strike] they gave a kind of coupon book—for three dollars a week—to get your food on and they had a union store down there in Hancock. They had tickets from $.10, $.05 and $.25, and $.50—something like that. You had to bring coupons to get your food at the union store."[57]

Other individuals and organizations chipped in where the WFM stores left off. Area farmers aided strikers by donating potatoes and other products off their land. In one instance a farmer pulled up his wagon right outside of the Ahmeek union store and distributed an entire load of produce.[58] Timely December food donations were coming in from as far away as Wisconsin, as "The citizens of Brantwood, Wis. have donated a car of fine potatoes to strikers of this district and the car arrived last Saturday in charge of Nestor Aaltonen. The citizens of Brantwood as well as the citizenship in general are giving financial, material and moral aid to the fighting men and women of this country who are leading the van of the industrial army which will sweep this country of gluttons, graft, and greed."[59]

The material support provided by WFM stores was in addition to locally owned stores and companies sympathetic to the strikers' cause. One such store was the Finnish Workmen's Co-operative Company in Kearsarge, which ran this ad in the *Miners' Bulletin*: "Boys we have stood with you from the start and will continue to do so. Our store is a co-operative store made up of workingmen. Our business rests upon workingmen, your cause is our cause."[60] There was a feeling of amicability with many small businesses within the community, until the establishment of the union stores, and these stores became very controversial. Operating the union stores was, however, a necessary approach to providing leadership during the strike. An essential tactic in the struggle to make the Copper Country a union district was relating the fact that the union could perform the vital function of taking care of its members' stomachs. Thus, the WFM stores were an attempt to show the mining companies that the WFM could provide sustenance as well as organization for its members.

Along with strikers' stomachs, the WFM wanted to show that it could also provide for the rank and filers' hearts and minds. Thousands upon thousands of dollars were being pumped into WFM District 16 to bolster the efforts to provide mental and recreational stimulation. Dances were held in union halls, literature was pumped out by the thousands of sheets daily, picnics occurred in area green spaces, and meetings were scheduled daily. Union leadership was attempting to bolster the drudgery of strike parades and watches with entertainment such as dances because, as Emma Goldman is said to have stated (though there is controversy regarding if she ever uttered the words), "If I can't dance, I don't want to be a part of your revolution."[61]

WFM tactics—material, ideological, and recreational—were meant to bolster the confidence of striking workers and their families. The WFM needed to prove to Copper Country workers that it could take care of its own because the strike was happening in a region that was dominated by entrenched, ensconced, and sometimes enormous mining corporations, which had a stranglehold on everything in the Copper Country from politics to education to religion. Area mining companies had their own strategy and tactics for dealing with the WFM and the clash between organized labor and capital in this great struggle.

Violence

Violence has been a part of the U.S. labor movement from its inception, and organized labor argued that capitalists just were not going to give away the power, privilege, and profits they received without a fight. Perhaps the key component to understanding labor violence is that those with the power will not give it up peacefully. Many a great debate was had about the merits or downfalls of labor violence or the benefits and detractions of peaceful protest. This was the greatest problem confronting the nascent push to organize the Copper Country. Did violence have a place in the Michigan Copper Strike, or would peaceful protests convince copper companies to sit across the bargaining table from insubordinate, mostly immigrant mineworkers?

According to a report by the federal government, the first days of the strike were violent: "After the rioting which occurred on the first two days of the strike, 16 men who tried to go to work were injured by the strikers badly enough for hospital treatment."[62] *Työmies* and journalist Antti Sarell put their own spin on the first day's volley: "At first, it seemed almost incredible that these mine slaves, who had toiled in content for decades, would really have the courage to fight for their rights. But it was true!" There was a good deal of strong proletarian rhetoric in Sarell's writing, and the "reporting" was closer to propaganda, but there was no mistaking the great fits of energy and passion emanating from Copper Country wage-slaves: "The mines of the whole Copper Country stopped on the aforementioned day [July 23, 1913] as by magic. The cocky bosses of the mines watched with amazement as the group of mine slaves, who before had submitted contently, determinedly rose from the perpetual darkness of the mines to daylight to fight for those relatively small demands to which their whimpers weren't even bothered to be answered."[63]

While the WFM did not advocate violence, there were apparently individual and isolated acts of violence as striking workers ran off loyal workers from their shifts during the opening days of the strike. C&H's general manager Jim MacNaughton secured the C&H dynamite magazines and beseeched the Michigan National Guard's Calumet unit to safeguard its ammunition reserves because he feared the WFM had brought bomb-makers as well as sharpshooters into the district. This never happened. As the strike gained momentum, however, and after a bit of cajoling from Sheriff James Cruse, MacNaughton agreed to invite the Michigan National Guard to the Copper Country. The U.S. Labor Department's report stated that with the arrival of the Guard, things quieted considerably into a relative stalemate between the WFM and the mining companies.[64]

Työmies correspondent Sarell's assessment of the situation did not see the arrival of the Michigan National Guard as a benefit to anyone but the mining companies: "Two or three days after the declaration of the strike, the entire Michigan army arrived to protect 'the property and lives' of the mining companies. Calumet, whose name is said to mean peace pipe in the Indian language, resembled the most heavily equipped war camp." The sudden transformation of the Copper Country into a heavily armed and garrisoned military encampment did not just preoccupy the attention of union sympathizers. In his coded messages to Quincy Shaw, MacNaughton's descriptions of the National Guard's movements to control strike parades and watches sound like narrations of Civil War battles. Similarly, Sarell's descriptions of the Guard's maneuverings sound like those of a battle correspondent: "All the roads that had been in common use before were blocked from the public by these strike breakers, the proud 'defenders of Michigan's fatherland' dressed in yellow soldiers' uniforms." In some instances, Copper Country immigrants viewed the Michigan National Guard as the "same old same old" from the Old Country—enforcers utilized by monarchy and absentee rulers to oppress the peasantry. As Sarell reported: "Yours truly saw it with his own eyes how these Michigan Cossacks attacked the peaceful strikers and other people in the streets of Calumet. . . . Like the wildest Russian Cossacks, these seemingly drunken cavalry soldiers rode along the sidewalks knocking down a couple of wives and their baby carriages."[65]

Whether people liked to admit it or not, violence was a large part of the Michigan Copper Strike, on both sides. Many members of Copper Country WFM locals believed, like John F. Kennedy almost fifty years later, that "those who make peaceful revolution impossible, will make violent revolution inevitable."[66] Whether it was the actual violence associated with the occupation of mine buildings and lands on the first day of the strike, or the ambient specter of revolution, riots, or reprisals, physical altercations were a regular part of the Michigan Copper Strike. The merits of violence as a strike tactic are controversial, but the simple fact is that the WFM never officially or openly advocated the use of violence in the Copper Country. Mother Jones explicitly condemned it. Thus, the huge difference between the violence supposedly perpetrated by the WFM and the violence of the procompany Citizens' Alliance vigilante group, Houghton County law enforcement officers, and the copper companies' private police and hired gun thugs, was that the violent acts attributed to the WFM were isolated incidents disavowed by the WFM's leadership; the Copper Country oligarchy, however, institutionalized violence, and, as we will see in the next chapter, committed to a campaign of violence that would attempt to rid the Copper Country of the WFM.

Members of the International Molders Union Local 322 in a Labor or May Day parade across the bridge spanning the Portage Waterway and into Hancock, ca. 1900. Image courtesy Michigan Technological University's Copper Country Historical Collections (MTU/CCHC).

Brewery workers, Park Brewery, Hancock, Michigan, ca. 1905. Workers at the Park Brewing Company went on their own strike in 1913. The WFM encouraged mineworkers to support Park's workers via a boycott of non-union beer. Image courtesy of MTU/CCHC.

Takimainen rivi (seisova), va-
semmalta oikealle:
  Peter Jedda, italialainen,
    Laurium, Mich.
  Mor Oppman, unkarilainen
    Laurium, Mich.
  Victor Brander, suomalainen
    Duluth, Minn.
  Tom Strizich, kroatialainen
    Calumet, Mich.
  Dan Sullivan, irlantilainen
    Hancock, Mich.
  Helmer W. Mikko, suomalainen
    Calumet, Mich.
  C. E. Hietala, suomalainen
    Hancock, Mich.
  W. T. Stodden, englantilainen
    Butte, Mont.
Keskimäinen rivi:
  Frank Shaws, slavonilainen
    Chicago, Ill.
  Helmer Erickson ("Iso Helme-
    ri"), suomalainen
    Hancock, Mich.
  Wm. J. Rickard, Laurium, Mich.
  Charles Vernetti, italialainen
    Collinsville, Ill.
Etumainen rivi:
  Ben Goggin, italialainen
    Kennet, Calif.
  Louis Arseneault, ranskalainen
    Laurium, Mich.
  Wm. K. Holovatsky, puolalainen
    Winnipeg, Canada.

Ryhmä "palkattuja agitaattoreita" (Lännen Kaivosmiesliiton organi-
seeraajia ja virkailijoita), joiden syyksi kaivostenomistajat
lukevat lakon puhkeamisen.

This image dispelled allegations that WFM organizers were all brought in from the outside to stir up Copper Country mineworkers. A majority of the multi-ethnic organizers had local addresses. Published in *Työmiehen Joulu* 1913.

Organizers' work paid off as thousands took to the streets of Copper Country towns and municipalities in the fall of 1913. This parade included the strike placard, "Papa is Striking for Us." In many cases, the strike was a family affair.

The *Miners' Bulletin* was used as a means to combat the local press's message and to keep WFM members updated and connected. The paper was published in Hancock by the Työmies Publishing Company. Image courtesy of MTU/CCHC.

LEFT: Strike parade, Calumet, Michigan, 1913. The placard held by this striker reads "The mines of this district can consolidate, why not its workingmen?" The placard was an effective, mobile method of communication. RIGHT: Another strike placard read, "Calumet Hecla Headquarters Boston." This slogan was likely used to indicate that mine managers were absentee landlords. Images courtesy of MTU/CCHC.

Strikers' parade, Hancock, Michigan, September 13, 1913. Parading and striking were in and of themselves a form of communication. As workers paraded through Copper Country streets, singing, chanting slogans, and yelling often accompanied the march.

"Mother Jones Day" in Calumet, Michigan, August 5, 1913. The WFM used a number of working-class celebrities to bolster the morale of striking workers and their families during the strike. The most beloved of these labor celebrities was Mary Harris "Mother" Jones. Image courtesy of Keweenaw National Historical Park (KNHP).

"John Mitchell Day," Calumet, Michigan, August 23, 1913. Mitchell, then former vice president of the American Federation of Labor and current vice president of the United Mineworkers of America, visited the Copper Country to encourage striking workers. Image courtesy of KNHP.

Women at the head of a strike parade, Quincy Hill, Michigan, 1913. Women were often at the front of strike parades, demonstrating their crucial role in the 1913–14 Michigan Copper Strike. Published in *Työmiehen Joulu* 1913.

Ana "Big Annie" Clemenc among fellow union faithful, with WFM organizer Ben Goggin to her right. Clemenc gained fame far and wide for her exploits during the strike. She was arrested at least three times during the strike. Image courtesy of KNHP.

ABOVE, RIGHT: To those against organized labor and with a racist view of immigrants, this image encapsulated the problem with America: strange people in strange dress. Xenophobia was widespread in the Copper Country at this time. Image courtesy of KNHP.

LEFT: Finnish immigrant women jailed for their participation in strike actions, Calumet, 1913. A Finnish-language publication extolled the virtues of these four women, writing that while in a dark Calumet jail, they sang like songbirds for all to hear outside. Published in *Työmiehen Joulu* 1913.

Outside of WFM headquarters, 6th Street, Calumet, 1913. The crowd of people, which includes many hanging out of second-story windows, includes a heavily skewed jumble of strikers and Michigan National Guard members. Image courtesy of MTU/CCHC.

Looking down Calumet's 6th Street, 1913, at a gathering of people likely assembled for a strike parade, with many in the crowd carrying placards and flags. In the center of the photograph is a man identified as "Chief of Police." Image courtesy of MTU/CCHC.

Strike parade through downtown South Range's main thoroughfare in 1913. South Range, a municipality off company property, was the main commercial center for workers and families employed at the Copper Range Company's mines. Published in *Työmiehen Joulu* 1913.

A large audience attends an outdoor meeting of WFM representatives in South Range. Commercial centers off company property, such as South Range, were the only places striking workers could congregate for meetings. Image courtesy of KNHP.

Strikers from Keweenaw Miners Union, Local 129, parade down a Copper Country street in 1913. Parades were often very organized and orderly, allowing vehicles to travel down the center of major streets. Image courtesy of KNHP.

This image of a strike parade in Calumet, Michigan, 1913, demonstrates the festive, musical, and organized nature of most WFM parades. Image courtesy of MTU/CCHC.

STRIKE CARTOONS

These rare cartoons show the power and wit of a localized cartoonist who had sympathy toward the WFM. In most of the scenes, workers dressed in simple clothing are besting mining company management depicted in fancy dress.

Kun Kuparisaari herää eli Vapun vietto Hancockissa 1913.

Translated, the caption of this triumphantly toned cartoon reads, "When Copper Island priests [at the conservative Suomi College] woke up to May Day celebrations, Hancock, 1913." Published in *Lapatossu*, June 1, 1913.

Ja katso: ne, jotka eivät ole apinasta kehittyneet, rakensivat sillan, auttaaksensa McNaughtonin Kuparialueen lakon yli.

This cartoon's caption reads, "And behold, those monkeys built a bridge and helped McNaughton [*sic*] over to the Copper Island." MacNaughton, or the monkey, rather, then says, "The bridge is great, the question now is to see how long it lasts." Published in *Lapatossu*, December 15, 1913.

MORAALIN EDUSTAJA.

This cartoon, titled "The Moral Authority," featured this ghoulish "Copper Trust" character sarcastically quipping, "We cannot accept the WFM because it is a murderous organization." Published in *Lapatossu*, January 15, 1914.

CALUMET MICHIGAN

Drawn by nationally syndicated leftist cartoonist Ryan Walker, this cartoon addressed the sinister part that Copper Country law enforcement officials played in the strike. This cartoon first appeared in New York City's *The Call*. Published in *Työmies*, January 11, 1914.

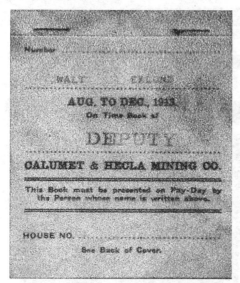

Pay book of the Calumet & Hecla Mining Company deputy Walt Eklund. Calumet & Hecla hired a number of men directly from the Michigan National Guard to bolster their private police force, which included mounted officers. Artifact on display KNHP Visitors Center.

Strikers in a parade holding a placard that read "Waddel Thugs Headquarters Sing-Sing." In this case Sing-Sing refers to the prison in New York. This slogan symbolizes strikers' portrayal of Waddell men as violent, criminal outsiders. Image courtesy of KNHP.

"Star" and revolver of Houghton County deputy sheriff. Arming poorly trained deputies with guns led to a number of deadly outcomes, most notably the shooting of Margaret Fazekas and Alois Tijan and Steve Putrich. Artifact on display KNHP Visitors Center.

A medallion given to Waddell-Mahon employees who had been employed in the Copper Country. Featured prominently are the three wise monkeys, who speak no evil, hear no evil, and see no evil. Artifact stored KNHP Museum Services building.

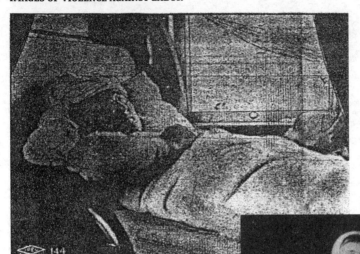

Nationally syndicated photograph of WFM president Charles Moyer in a Chicago hospital bed after being beaten, shot, and deported from the Copper Country. Published in *Työmies*, January 3, 1914.

Portrait of Margaret Fazekas. At only fourteen years of age, Margaret was an unlikely working-class martyr, a victim of the strike's violence.

Published in *Työmiehen* Joulu 1913.

The shot-up home and boardinghouse of the Putrich family in Seeberville, located next to Painesdale, Michigan. The image gives a good feeling for the conditions in which some Copper Country workers and their families lived. Image courtesy of KNHP.

Exterior view of Italian Hall. To the left sits the building where the seven- and five-year-old Sneller brothers walked to safety across an ironing board.

2   The disastrous stairway, Italian Hall, Calumet, Mich.
Tuhoisa porraskäytävä, Italialaisten Haali, Calumet, Mich.

The exterior doors in the front of the Italian Hall are two large, standard, outward-opening doors, but this photo also shows the hinge of a second set of interior "doors," which is actually a single, folding double door. Image courtesy MTU/CCHC.

Two photographs of those who died in Italian Hall. These images were nationally syndicated and brought the tragedy of Italian Hall into people's homes across the country. Published in *Työmies*, January 8, 1914.

Interior view of Italian Hall, the day after the fateful event. A baby carriage on snow runners sits in the middle of the image, and we are sadly left wondering if the baby made it out alive. Image courtesy of KNHP.

Images of the actual prints that were hung on each side of the Italian Hall's stage during the tragedy. These prints are now preserved in the KNHP's Museum Services Division building.

Cartoon indicating whom the area Finnish-language labor press thought perpetrated events at Italian Hall. The Grim Reaper figure is gesturing into the common grave where many victims of Italian Hall were buried in simple, pine boxes.

Published in *Lapatossu*, January 1, 1914.

Headline from *Työmies* newspaper, December 26, 1913. The newspaper's staff, like many affiliated with organized labor in the Copper Country, believed that the events at Italian Hall were no accident.

A coroner's storefront in the background, a line of pine boxes out front. The differing sizes of the crudely made coffins indicate the relative age of those about to be laid to rest, as well as their economic circumstances. Image courtesy of KNHP.

A step from the tragic Italian Hall stairway. On display in the KNHP's Calumet Visitors Center, this step is a physical link to the emotional story of Italian Hall.

Close-up of one of the chair backs, which has the initials "CCS." This CCS perhaps stands for Cristoforo Columbo Societa, or the Christopher Columbus Society, one of the many Italian fraternal societies that held meetings at Italian Hall.

Italian Hall chair on an exhibit at the KNHP's Calumet Visitors Center. The chair acts as a tangible object that links visitors to the center with the emotional stories of the men, women, and families who had loved ones who died at Italian Hall.

Headstones, Lake View Cemetery, outside Calumet. They mark the final resting place of the three Klarich sisters who lived on Waterworks Street in Calumet. According to the headstones, Kristina was twelve, Maria was ten, and Katarina was eight.

CHAPTER 7

Company

They chased the strikers far and wide, and all were surprised that the strikers were such
good runners. Quite a number of them were caught, but we thought it was useless to
arrest them, and some of them were made fit subjects for the hospital—in fact, they
were very roughly treated.

— Charles Lawton, general manager of the Quincy Mining Company, describing a
December 12, 1913, police break-up of a peaceful strike parade on Quincy Hill

IT WAS RIGGED. IT WAS ALL RIGGED. THE ENTIRE KEWEENAW PENINSULA WAS
bought and sold a long time before anyone with a red Western Federation of Miners (WFM) card stepped onto the Keweenaw's copper-rich ground. Documentary
evidence demonstrates that from the gerrymandering of local elections, to the
thumbs-up or thumbs-down of naturalization decisions by mine managers, to
the December 1913 campaign of violence orchestrated by mining companies and
the procompany Citizens' Alliance, the strategy and tactics to "rid the Copper
Country of the WFM and its foreign agitators" were a brutal but well-orchestrated
presentation of mining company power and manipulation of local politics, press,
and peacekeeping forces.

The struggle to organize Copper Country workers into a collective body was an uphill battle. Copper Country mining companies and the men who ran them had unfettered, unregulated, covert, and even overt influence on the cultural, economic, and social actions of the land they "ruled." Living in palatial homes, as Quincy's Charles Lawton did on the top of a hill overlooking a feudal-like kingdom, the barons of the Copper Country were checked only by their own scruples. James MacNaughton, the general manager of Calumet & Hecla (C&H), described by Finnish immigrant reporter Antti Sarell as "the emperor of the Copper Country" and by the newspaper *Työmies* as the *Tsaari*, or czar, of the copper territory,[1] ran Michigan's Copper Country like an isolated fiefdom. However, this allusion in the Finnish immigrant press to a monarchical system in the Copper Country just scratched the surface of the power mining companies exerted during the strike.

While copper companies initially attempted to ignore the strike and go about the business of mining, there was a certain fight, persistence, and pride in the WFM's rank and file that would not go away. It was only after months, and when there was no end to the strike in sight, that copper mine managers began to take the strike seriously. In some instances it was too late for the copper barons to reverse the advances of the WFM; to many supporters of organized labor it appeared that the WFM was winning, and at the very least those with anti-labor sentiments would begrudgingly admit that the WFM was holding its own. There seemed to be a real chance that the Copper Country could become WFM territory. However, in December, after a cold winter should have broken the strike (the mining companies were depending on this), area copper bosses and their supporters resorted to using two time-tested techniques to break the strike: intimidation and violence. These were the last, desperate tactics in a mining company strategy to control the maximum amount of power on a finger of land that was a protected bastion of wealth for a few, but the site of a daily struggle for many.

Company Strategy

Copper Country mining companies and the men who ran them used proven techniques to combat the influence and gains by the WFM during the strike. Control of the media, establishment of a citizens' vigilante group, hiring of strikebreakers and scabs, and intimidation and violence were all old tricks that management had at its disposal. C&H and "Big Jim" MacNaughton were especially adept at breaking strikes. In fact, many of the Copper Country mining companies looked to C&H and "Big Jim" for direction, recognizing that, given its size and resources as a company, C&H would lead in this time of tumult.[2]

Short of actually beating, shooting, and shipping WFM officers out of the Copper Country (which the Citizens' Alliance eventually did after the Italian Hall tragedy), the copper companies' main strategy during the early stages of the strike was to ignore the WFM and try to go about the business of copper mining as best they could. The general idea with this strategy was to let the carefully crafted oligarchy, which included control of Houghton County political offices, law enforcement, and legal authorities, handle the situation. Mass arrests, suppression of free speech, and a general attempt to wear down striking workers' resolve supplemented the overall strategy to simply not acknowledge that there was any such thing as the WFM. As the strike wore on, however, the strategy shifted to a more ominous display of raw power that included systematic terror and violence, which was all sanctioned by local officials, mining management, and the Copper Country's "good citizens."

Company Tactics

In order to implement their overall strategy, the mining companies used traditional union-busting tactics to rid the Copper Country of the WFM and its "foreign" agitators. There were no newly developed strategies to deal with organized labor devised by Copper Country mine management; they dipped into a bag of steadfast anti-union and anti-immigrant tricks that included bringing in imported workers or "scabs," rigging the local justice system, deputizing crews of loyal citizens and workers, hiring gun thugs from major metropolitan areas, employing labor spies to perform covert operations, organizing a Citizens' Alliance to do the companies' bidding, and creating a climate ripe for violence against striking workers and their chosen representatives.

In some ways, for the kings of the Copper Country, the mine management, it was all a sort of game, especially in the early months of the strike. There was talk of waiting out the strike, employing attrition tactics that were dependent upon importation of scabs, and waiting for the nullifying winds and snow of a Copper Country winter. However, if all else failed, if the labor spies did not spy, if they gun thugs would not shoot, if the local kept press could not print company propaganda, and if the bosses' political machinery failed to confound working-class solidarity, Jim MacNaughton and Quincy Shaw of the C&H planned to imprison strike leaders on an island in Lake Superior, Napoleon Bonaparte–style. In a letter he sent to MacNaughton in early October, Shaw wrote, "I would suggest that the island near Isle Royale in Lake Superior that you, Mr. Morrison and Mrs. MacNaughton once owned would be an ideal place (to prevent strikers and strike-leaders from disturbing the community). It seems to me that with this crowd as inhabitants and the appointing of Moyer,

Mahoney and Darrow as President, Vice President and counsel, you could probably secure a large income from the mineral rights."[3] This tongue-in-cheek tactic probably demonstrated the dismissive attitude companies originally had toward their striking workers and the WFM. Other tactics were more steadfast and deadly.

Friends in High Places

The WFM and the Copper Country rank and file were up against powerful forces. At times, it even seemed like the WFM's own national union was against the strike. There is documentary evidence that this may have been the case. A letter from the national offices of the American Federation of Labor (AFL) in Washington, D.C., to Swaby Lawton, attorney for the Quincy Mining Company in Hancock, demonstrates that the AFL was in communication with Copper Country mining companies. In one such letter, there is evidence that the AFL's national secretary gave materials on the WFM's radical past to Swaby Lawton, who also happened to be the brother of Quincy Mining Company general manager Charles Lawton. The materials sent by the AFL to Swaby Lawton were rare copies of U.S. Senate reports on labor trouble in Colorado from 1880 to the end of the Cripple Creek Strike in 1904. A letter in the Quincy Mining Company Papers from the AFL's national secretary to the Quincy Mining Company's lawyer closes with the AFL official asking for timely return of the documents due to the rare nature of the materials.

In early December, Swaby Lawton received a letter from the AFL asking for the return of the materials. Swaby responded that he gave the materials to "a friend," but that he would try to get the materials back to the AFL posthaste so that he would not "prevent any future favors" from the AFL. This is very intriguing, but there is more to the story—the "friend" Swaby Lawton gave the sensitive AFL materials to was "Progressive" Democratic governor and supposed friend of labor Woodbridge N. Ferris. Ferris got the materials from Swaby Lawton via Jim MacNaughton, who was "downstate" visiting Ferris in Lansing at the time. The same day that Swaby Lawton answered the AFL's letter by writing that he did not know exactly where the materials were, he penned a letter to Ferris stating that he needed the materials back because the AFL wanted them, but that of course he did not let the AFL know that "his friend" was the governor of Michigan. Thus, this correspondence contained in the Quincy Mining Company papers seems to indicate that the AFL was helping the very group its own industrial union was organizing against and sharing the ostensibly anti-WFM documents with a supposed "Progressive" friend of labor.

It is perhaps no wonder then, that Ferris was quick to send Michigan National Guard troops into the Copper Country. While the troops were there to be neutral peacekeepers, it was quite clear whose side they were on. Immediately strikers knew that the Guard was partial to the interests of the mining companies, and the Finnish immigrant labor press referred to the Guard as the "Michigan Cossacks," evoking a term from feudal Russia. While designed to be polemic, this assertion was not far off. The Guard was no friend of organized labor, and especially not a friend of "foreigners," as an incident just one year earlier in downstate Jackson, Michigan, suggested.

On the orders of then governor Chase Osborn, five companies of the Michigan National Guard were sent to Jackson State Prison to quell a rebellion in early September 1912. After things had quieted at the prison, a number of troops were kept in the area to "protect life and property." On the evening of September 13, off-duty Privates Howard Jackson and Clare S. McArdle were approached and accosted by two strangers described as "foreigners." The "foreigners" asked if Jackson and McArdle would sell them two Springfield rifles, according to the privates. The stalwart guards of Michigan naturally refused to do so, but noting a chance to put in place a sting operation, they made a deal to meet up with one of the strangers the next night, a man by the name of John Eisy, and sell Eisy the rifles. The plan was to meet Eisy by his home in a back alley late at night to finalize the transaction.[4]

Upon hearing of the great detective work of his two privates, Captain Frank L. Blackman, a prosecuting attorney for the city of Jackson who was familiar with the "many suspicious and even dangerous" characters of Jackson, instructed Privates Jackson and McArdle to indeed meet with the "foreigner" and pretend to make the sale, but then arrest Eisy on site. Captain Blackman and a Lieutenant Smith would tag along, hide behind bushes, and then pop out and arrest Eisy. However, Blackman's plan quickly went awry. According to findings of a hearing to determine if Blackman had murdered Eisy (a little foreshadowing here), while Privates Jackson and McArdle announced to Eisy that he was under arrest, Eisy took the stock of one of the rifles brought for sale and was going to hit the privates with the gun. Recognizing that Eisy was "a large, powerful man" (though outnumbered four to one), Captain Blackman shot Eisy—dead—with his revolver while hiding under a wagon that was twenty feet away at midnight in a dark, back alley. This explanation was good enough for Michigan's attorney general. Captain Blackman and his crack sting operation were cleared of any wrongdoing.[5]

Amazingly, Blackman was in the Copper Country during the 1913–14 strike. For the purposes of the 1913–14 Michigan Copper Strike, Blackman's guilt or innocence in Jackson is of great concern because less than a year after shooting a "foreigner" and then being exonerated for it, Captain Blackman was stationed in the Copper Country with a whole lot of "foreigners." Perhaps not surprisingly, Blackman had several notorious run-ins with the Copper Country's immigrant population. For example, during a heated interaction between scabs and "Finlander" strikers, some of whom were part of a "Broom Brigade" that reportedly used brooms to poke at scabs and guardsmen, Captain Blackman tied a woman to a horse stating, "I'll fix you so that you won't handle a broom anymore."[6] In yet another fracas with immigrant strikers, this time Croatian, Blackman reportedly punched Tony Stefanic in the eye. When questioned later as to why the situation devolved into chaos, Blackman blamed the riotous nature of the "foreigner."[7]

Blackman's conduct during the strike appeared unseemly to many. Reports filtered into Michigan National Guard headquarters in Calumet that Blackman had shot up a Calumet bar and that a number of his interactions in Centennial Heights had been "rash and belligerent." Soon after the Stefanic incident Blackman left the Copper Country, but with nary a public censure for his actions.[8] The wanton and blatant use of the term "foreigner" to somehow excuse and justify Blackman's acts in Jackson, Blackman's actions in the Copper Country that again went unpunished, and the general racism toward "foreigners" that seemed to exist in the Michigan National Guard gives insight into the social standing and public perceptions of immigrants by members of the Michigan National Guard and perhaps even native-born Americans in the state at large.

Absolute Power (Corrupts Absolutely)

Mine bosses ruled the Copper Country. The king of kings in the Copper Country was Jim MacNaughton, general manager of C&H. C&H's general manager even had the opportunity to weigh in on the citizenship of hopeful immigrants. In one letter, a bureaucrat at the U.S. Bureau of Naturalization, which was part of the Department of Labor, wrote to MacNaughton at C&H:

> Herewith I enclose you a partial list, in duplicate, of applications for naturalization filed and pending in the Circuit Court, Houghton County, Michigan. In the interests of good citizenship it is requested that you, or such person as may be conversant with the facts, express your opinion as to the desirability, or, what is more to the point, the undesirability of such of the applicants as have, by the conduct, their habits, and otherwise, shown themselves to be of that class of persons who should not be admitted to citizenship.[9]

Once the folks in the Bureau of Naturalization had names of undesirable persons, the process of getting them out of the country was paramount, and one of the WFM's organizers was targeted as such a case. Another Bureau of Naturalization letter asked C&H attorney Albert E. Petermann to assemble a case against "Hungarian Jew" Mor Oppman: "It may be worthwhile to keep a watch on Oppman and we shall appreciate any information that may lead to his conviction on that ground [of claiming to be a U.S. citizen], or any ground. . . . P.S. I enclose you a few addressed and franked envelopes for your use in communicating with our office."[10]

Mining company control of workers was not just at the federal or state level. While organized labor had friends during the Progressive era at the federal and state levels, there were very few elected officials at the local level in the Copper Country that the WFM could count as allies. Local politics was dominated either by men with great sympathies toward the mining companies or actual employment in upper-level management at the mining companies. Take, for instance, the Houghton County Board of Supervisors, which was dominated by wealthy mining men. Of the fourteen supervisors, six were management at area mining companies. Jim MacNaughton and Charles Lawton, general managers at C&H and the Quincy Mining Company, respectively, were both Houghton County supervisors, as were Adelbert Edwards, who was a clerk for the Atlantic Mining Company; R. R. Seeber, a superintendent at a mining company; A. L. Burgan, a superintendent at a copper mine's stamp mill; and Ed Koepel, who was another stamp mill superintendent. The other eight, with the exception of Richard Rourke Jr., "the Socialist," from Quincy Hillside, were professional men, such as bank officials or merchants.[11]

Especially influential in Houghton County politics was MacNaughton. He sat on Calumet Township's Board of Review and was a supervisor for Calumet Township. Not to be outdone, Charles Lawton maintained a very close relationship with Hancock's official bureaucracy; his brother, Swaby, was the city attorney.[12] In the Copper Country, which was thick with working men, not one mineworker served on the Houghton County Board of Supervisors.

This beneficial arrangement to the area's copper companies was especially problematic during the strike. When Special Prosecuting Attorney George Nichols submitted arrest reports to the Houghton County Board of Supervisors, it was like giving a play-by-play of the strike's legal happenings to the mining companies. Probably the most egregious example of a rigged legal system was the coerced composition of a December 1913 Special Grand Jury. When it was thought that the grand jury was underperforming in the early months of the strike, Nichols wrote to the Houghton County Board of Supervisors, "At this term of court (September) conditions were such that we found it almost impossible to get a conviction as the juries seemed to line up on the question of their views of the strike, rather than upon the actual facts in the case presented, and undoubtedly that was the reason that the court continued the cases over the term."[13]

Not surprisingly, by December Nichols had a new Special Grand Jury to work with, and they found true bills, or reasons to continue prosecution, against most of the strikers who came across the legal docket. This new grand jury was almost handpicked by the copper companies. Files in both the C&H and Quincy Mining Company collections have documentation of strategies, questionnaires, and notes regarding the selection of the Special Grand Jury. The results were a grand jury that was filled with respectable Copper Country citizens amenable to delivering justice to the mining companies: Thomas Dunstan was a foreman for C&H; A. F. Heidkamp, foreman of the grand jury, was the vice president of the Citizens National Bank; F. C. Schubert was a master engineer at the Hancock Consolidated Mining Company in 1912 and would later become the mine's superintendent; James W. Shields was the superintendent of the Quincy Mining Company's stamp mill; Michael Messner Jr. was the vice president of the fervently anti-union Haas Brewing Company; and so on and so on.[14]

Much like the Houghton County Board of Supervisors, of the twenty special grand jurors, eight were management or upper-level employees in area mines; eight were area businessmen, seven of whom were owners or upper-level management in banks or railroads; two were local officials (one a village clerk and the other a superintendent of sewers and plumbing); and the remaining juror was a farmer who was also on the Houghton County Board of Supervisors—and worked as Jim MacNaughton's personal chauffeur. Again, no miner, trammer, or unskilled laborer was on this grand jury, and it included no persons of Croatian, Finnish, Italian, or Slovenian background. How could members of a grand jury like this be picked from a county whose population mostly consisted of mineworkers and naturalized or second-generation Americans?

With all of this power in steering the wheels of local politics and jurisprudence, it is no wonder that something as simple but powerful as the area's newspapers were also in the pockets of the mining companies. It was no secret that the area's English-language press served the needs of the mining companies. A special relationship existed between the heads of mining companies and the owners and editors of area newspapers. Newspapers such as the *Calumet News*, Hancock's *Evening Journal*, and Houghton's *Mining Gazette* had a decidedly pro–mining company stance. This support of the Copper Country's oligarchy even led *Mining Gazette* publisher E. G. Rice to declare to Jim MacNaughton, "the idea of the [*Gazette*] organizers was to have a paper which would be devoted to the interests of the mining companies in the Copper Country."[15] The area's kept press was so devoted to the mining companies that they moved in lockstep with mining management, leading the historian Larry Lankton to write that the *Mining Gazette* "never met a union organizer, striker, or socialist that it liked."[16]

This attitude toward the WFM was clear in the editorial policies of the area kept press, and when the local press did a good job, the mining companies threw them a bone, as this letter from MacNaughton to Shaw evidenced: "I wish you would read the special edition of the Houghton Mining Gazette issued this morning . . . and when you have done so drop Homer Guck, Editor, a letter congratulating him on his efforts. His paper and the Calumet News have been with us in this dirty fight from the very first. They have done everything in their power for us and I am very sure he would highly appreciate acknowledgment from you."[17] It is clear that Houghton County law, politics, and media were bought and sold and under the control of the men who ran the Copper Country mines.

Cloak and "Daggerism"

The above instances were perhaps the most blatant and insidious ways mining companies could control the local labor force, but there were myriad other ways in which the copper bosses controlled the workers. Perhaps one of the most sinister yet effective and steadfast anti-union tactics was the labor spy, or more euphemistically, the company operative. There is documentary evidence that the C&H, Copper Range, and Quincy Mining Companies used labor spies to monitor the men they employed both in the workplace and in social settings off company property. Sometimes the vocation was even a family affair. As one Thiel operative wrote, "I have a letter from the Finnish operative. . . . He informs me that his wife found out that the union officials had a private meeting one night in Hancock recently, and they are afraid that the Austrians and Finns will soon go back to work if the strike is not settled within a week."[18]

Through labor spies and business connections or personal positions, mining companies also monitored the finances of the WFM. MacNaughton used his personal connections in the Copper Country business community to keep tabs on the WFM's bank accounts. In another instance, a mining company used a labor spy to survey the WFM's financial coffers. The operative recognized, as did C&H's MacNaughton, that the strike's success hinged on the WFM's Copper Country locals getting outside financial and moral support: "A circular issued by the Denver officials (stated) that the entire copper mining district of Michigan is tied up and all mines closed and stating that an assessment of $2. has been levied by the executive board of the W.F.M. for the month of August and asking that the locals remit this assessment from funds on hand."[19]

MacNaughton loved the intrigue created by labor spies. In the initial phases of the strike, he was nearly giddy reporting to C&H president Quincy Shaw about the cloak-and-dagger activities and intrigue created by the mysterious work done by the labor spies. MacNaughton and Shaw liked conspiring so much that at the start of the strike they began sending coded messages to each other via Western Union.

On the first day of the strike, July 23, 1913, MacNaughton in Calumet sent this coded message to Shaw in Boston:

> A monstrosity of blanket vekin and version horrify is going fragile occult envy hustle to the other depth that the fervors belle drawn and that the men levity ten precedes. Thus far nutmeg mediterranean daunt has been dredge. We are aught and suppressing imperious dementia sibyls as fast as possible. Have about verth horrify now and territory we will heavy nutmeg deter imperious taking crater of sleight.[20]

Decoded, the message read:

> A mob of between four and five hundred is going from one engine house to the other demanding that the fires be drawn and that the men leave their posts. Thus far no material damage has been done. We are assembling and swearing in deputy sheriffs as fast as possible. Have about six hundred now and think we will have no difficulty in taking care of the situation.[21]

The two got quite good at figuring out the strike's angles while playing junior spy games, and began to develop funny little terms for groups or people they felt beneath them: mobs of strikers were "monstrosities"; Michigan National Guard troops were "treachery"; and the troublesome WFM was code-named "water-lily federation misdo."[22]

Scabs

Two especially guarded secrets in MacNaughton and Shaw's coded messages were the numbers of replacement workers brought into the Copper Country, and the points of origin for these scabs. As voiced by the indefatigable labor advocate Mother Jones, who visited the Copper Country in early August 1913, scabs were especially disliked by strikers. Speculation fueled by the Copper Country's Finnish-language labor newspapers displayed a typical type of racist characterization of scabs. On August 22, 1913, *Työmies* ran a front-page article that stated, "*Neekereitä* will be appearing in Calumet."[23] The paper indicated that along with "gun hounds," "nigger" scabs would surely follow. The importation of black workers as scabs was a standard practice by employers of this era, and sadly, rather than reaching out to these workers in solidarity, white workers fell into the planned company trappings of letting racial hatred win out over working-class cohesion. However, despite the predictions of *Työmies*, Copper Country mines did not hire black workers as scabs, but rather

Scabs Brought in by C&H during 1913–14 Strike

August 1913	3	January 1914	97
September 1913	14	February 1914	98
October 1913	410	March 1914	81
November 1913	102	April 1914	39
December 1913	98	**TOTAL**	**942**

SOURCE: Calumet and Hecla Employee Records, "Ellis Spreadsheet," Copper Country Historical Archive, Michigan Technological University, Houghton, 2004.

eastern Europeans and Germans. By September, with the help of a scab workforce, the big three mining companies—C&H, Copper Range, and Quincy—were in limited but substantial production.

For the big mining companies, who were the major importers of scabs, the search for replacement workers was a very exacting, precise, and rigorous effort. C&H sent "feelers" out to gauge the labor situation, first to the west, as Jim MacNaughton wrote to President Quincy Shaw: "At the present time I have three different parties of scouts out looking up men. . . . Potter is making a general tour of cities in the Northwest; Superior, Duluth, Virginia, St. Paul, Minneapolis, etc. . . . As you know, they are through now with harvesting and a great many men are flocking to the cities looking for work." Then to the east and Canada: "I have also sent a man over to the Soo [Sault Ste. Marie, Ontario, Canada, or Sault Ste. Marie, Michigan]; a large contract employing some 1200 men will be completed there in a short while now and I am in hopes we can get some of them deflected this way." This comprehensive labor search was not just to fill the mines with bodies but also to scare the men back to work. As MacNaughton wrote, "I feel that the only way we can make inroads on the Union at the present time is by importing men. If anything will cause the Union ranks to break that will."

And import men the mining companies did. C&H began importing men even before the official beginning of the strike, and continued to bring in men at a breakneck pace. During the strike, C&H imported almost 950 men (see table). Most of these men were recent immigrants coming from other industrial places in the United States. In terms of geographic area, eastern Europe, and especially Poland, was the point of origin for many scabs. In fact, a quarter of all scabs, 242, were of Polish ethnic origin. The second largest group of scabs came from closer to home and could identify as "Americans." To round out the top five origins of scabs: Russians came in third with 137 imported men, while Germany and Hungary tallied far less.[24]

Number of C&H Scabs by International Region

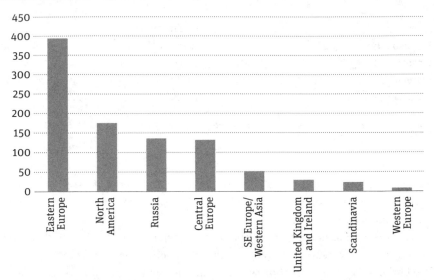

This graph shows the lopsided distribution of where scab or replacement workers came from in the Old Country. Modern regional affiliations are used to simplify the very difficult historical empires and associated ethnic backgrounds. This shows that most immigrant scabs were born in areas of Eastern Europe such as Poland and the Balkan countries. Based on data assembled by Jean Ellis from Calumet and Hecla Mining Companies employment records archived in the Michigan Technological University's Copper Country Historical Archive.

When examining where these scabs came from in the United States, two states and two mighty industrial centers stand out: Michigan and Illinois and, not surprisingly, Detroit and Chicago. While 260 of C&H's scabs came from Michigan, Chicago was the largest city of origin, with 128 scabs blowing in from the Windy City. This latter number does not include the almost 70 scabs coming from the heavily industrialized southern shore of Lake Michigan from the cities of East Chicago, Gary, and Indiana Harbor's Inland Steel Plant. Second only to Chicago was mighty Detroit, which was the place of employment for approximately 115 scabs, some of whom came from automobile plants such as Ford, Dodge, and Packard. While these industrial centers were likely the usual suspects for scabs, C&H found imported workers in some unique areas. After the wheat harvest in North Dakota, and early in the strike, C&H imported thirty-eight workers from the flat fields of North Dakota. Later in the strike, and closer to the Copper Country, men came from Kenosha, Wisconsin. These men, mostly Lithuanians, were factory workers and largely unfamiliar with mining.[25]

Places of Employment in North America for Scabs before C&H

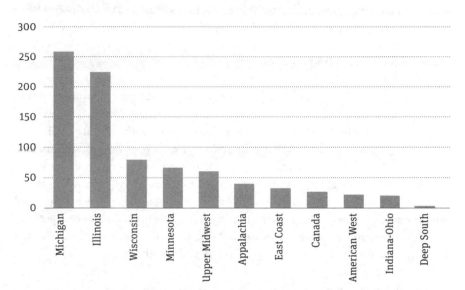

This graph shows where scab or replacement workers lived in the United States immediately before they were hired as replacement workers in the Copper Country by the Calumet & Hecla Mining Company.

Based on data assembled by Jean Ellis from Calumet & Hecla Mining Company employment records archived in Michigan Technological University's Copper Country Historical Collections.

Where scabs were coming from was important; where they were not coming from was just as, or more, important. Scabs were not coming from other mining areas. A handful of mineworkers came to scab from the nearby Marquette Iron Range. Radiating out westward from the Copper Country, very few came from the iron mining Gogebic Range; a handful more came from the Menominee Iron Range; and even fewer came from the Minnesota iron ranges. Amazingly, but perhaps not surprising, no scabs came from the WFM stronghold of Butte, Montana, which was one of the Copper Country's greatest competitors in terms of copper production. Similarly, only two imported workers came from the Copper Country's other great competitor, Bisbee, Arizona, which was beginning to surpass the Copper Country as a producing district, and few replacement workers came to the Copper Country from the far more deadly coal mining region of Appalachia.

In fact, C&H recruited scabs with mining experience primarily from other Copper Country mines. Workers at lesser-producing mines apparently saw the strike as an opportunity to get in good with the always productive and higher-paying C&H.

In all, C&H hired twenty-three scabs from other area mines.[26] For C&H, and likely other mining companies, this meant that a mostly unskilled and unproductive labor force was going to have to carry them through the strike. This slump in production, even as mines were running with close to normal numbers of replacement workers, was a constant and important drain on productivity.

The Quincy Mining Company, after consulting with C&H's head scab wrangler, former Houghton County sheriff August Beck, brought in its first scabs on September 19, 1913. Quincy, like many of the other area mining companies, tried to bring workers in on the sly. Charles Lawton, caught in a ploy to bring workers in from Chicago, wrote to Quincy president William R. Todd, "Yesterday afternoon about three o'clock, Mr. Marquardt, General Freight and Passenger Agent of the Copper Range Railroad, called me up, inquiring if the party of men that was to leave Chicago last night on special car was for us. I had to plead ignorance." Lawton was concerned with the quality of men being brought in and did not have good reports on the scabs, or "strike-breakers," from a Pinkerton guard who was either keeping the scabs from running from the train or protecting the scabs while on the train:

> The Pinkerton man that brought them here, a Mr. Pauler, states that they are typical "strike-breakers" picked up on the streets of Chicago, that he could not vouch for them in any way, and about half of them are Austrians. They are a motley-looking crew, but some good-looking Germans among them. However, they come without any baggage whatsoever; and, as Mr. Pauler says, are merely a temporary batch, and he assents to their being practically a lot of Chicago "bums."[27]

Quincy's scabs, throughout the strike, were mostly from the Austro-Hungarian Empire, and were always transported into the Copper Country via train. Always eager to extract as much wealth from its workers as possible, the company deducted the replacement workers' train fare from New York from their wages.[28] William Parsons Todd, who helped recruit replacement workers for the Quincy Mining Company, recalled the problems getting New York scabs into the Copper Country: "First batch we sent up, we lost the whole batch the third day they got there. . . . Well they went, the union got them another job down near Chicago. They got . . . induced them all to leave. . . . It taught us a lesson though." The lesson learned by Quincy—to schedule the train carrying the scabs to arrive just in time for the beginning of morning shift work in the mine "because we wanted them to land there Monday morning by six o'clock and we had them underground about an hour after we got them there. Didn't want anybody getting next to them. We'd not wanted them to see what the conditions were."[29]

Law(lessness) and (Dis)Order

Along with Copper Country politicians, law enforcement officers were decidedly pro–mining company. This became glaringly true during the strike, and court records as well as a report submitted to the Houghton County Board of Supervisors relate the stark reality of mining company bias. This report to the board of supervisors is especially interesting because it was developed by Special Prosecuting Attorney George Nichols, who was brought in by Governor Ferris to help Houghton County Prosecuting Attorney Anthony Lucas with the large influx of criminal cases due to the strike. The report is interesting in and of itself because of the incredible data it gives on the over 500 arrests made during the strike, but also because Nichols's report was made to the Houghton County Board of Supervisors, which included Jim MacNaughton and Charles Lawton.

Reflecting back on Nichols's report, with all the beatings, shootings, and attempted murder cases being adjudicated in Houghton County during the strike, fewer than thirty cases were brought against deputy sheriffs, company police, strikebreakers, or gun thugs. The see-no-evil, hear-no-evil, speak-no-evil morality of the Waddell-Mahon gun thugs became a running joke among the men hired to help police the Copper Country. On gold-painted medallions, wrapped with text declaring the gift a "Souvenir" from the Copper Country, the "Always on Duty" promise sat just below the three famous see no evil, hear no evil, speak no evil monkeys—the intention being that no matter what happened, what crimes they might commit, the Waddell-Mahon men kept their mouths shut. These were the men, by the way, who were hired by Houghton County Sheriff James A. Cruse to act as supposedly unbiased enforcers of Houghton County law.[30]

Strikers were arrested in Houghton County for everything from "assault with intent to murder" to "indecent language." The top five acts that would get a striker in front of a judge were: "intimidation," with eighty-eight arrests; "rioting," with eighty arrests; "assault and battery," with sixty-one arrests; "carrying a concealed weapon," with fifty-eight arrests; and "assault with intent to murder," with thirty-six arrests. There were a terrifying eighteen "murder" cases before Houghton County judges and thirty-six cases of "assault with intent to murder." Twelve of the eighteen murder cases stemmed from the two counts of murder alleged against six men associated with the shootings of Alois Tijan and Steve Putrich by Waddell-Mahon thugs and sheriff's deputies in Seeberville. So, it became clear that in order for someone associated with the company or Houghton County law enforcement to be charged with a crime, they must have committed murder.[31]

Almost as many of these cases against strikers were dismissed (143) as were passed on to the circuit court (175). This near one-to-one ratio between cases dismissed and cases bound over to the circuit court perhaps indicates a time-tested tactic used by Houghton County law enforcement forces: arrest at will and let the judges sort it out. This tactic was useful as it removed WFM leaders as well as the rank and file from the struggle going on in the streets. Key WFM organizers Victor Brander, Peter Jedda, Ben Goggin, Yanco Terzich, Heimer Mikko, Dan Sullivan, John Välimäki, Nick Verbanac, and Mor Oppman were arrested at some point during the strike. Ben Goggin was arrested a whopping seven times. More telling is that of the seven times arrested, five times the charges against Goggin were dismissed or discharged, or he was found not guilty. Of the two times when the charges did stick, one was for a "noise and disturbance" beef, in which Goggin paid fines and court costs, and the other was a case bound over to the circuit court for "assault and battery" on December 26, 1913, a day after the tragedy at Italian Hall.[32] This last arrest was quite possibly a way for Houghton County law enforcement forces to keep Goggin off the streets during the tense period in the community immediately after the horrible events at Italian Hall.

Women were also involved in the never-ending turnstile of Houghton County injustice. Over seventy women sympathetic to the WFM were arrested during the strike on charges ranging from rioting to indecent language to assault stemming from incidents in the "Broom Brigade."[33]

At one point, Houghton County Special Prosecuting Attorney George Nichols tried to arrest much of the WFM's leadership when he brought to trial *The People v. Charles Moyer, et al., Criminal Conspiracy* case in December. Moyer and thirty-seven other members of the WFM's leadership and cadre of organizers were served bench warrants and/or subpoenas for trial in Houghton. Of course, the handpicked Special Grand Jury returned a true bill on the case, and Moyer et al. would now stand trial. The case dragged on through the course of the strike, and was later given up altogether after the strike, but strategically filed in December as it was, many WFM officials and organizers stayed out of the Copper Country to avoid arrest or questioning due to the conspiracy charge.[34] For a pivotal time in December, when the Citizens' Alliance went aggressively on a campaign of intimidation and violence, only the WFM's lawyers remained in the Copper Country, as most of the organization's leadership was charged in the conspiracy case. Planning like that could hardly be coincidental.

Perhaps the most egregious but least known of all Copper Country legal actions were the thousands of evictions slated throughout the Copper Country during the strike. The WFM's legal team fought mining company lawyers to a stalemate on most of these cases, but the perpetual fear of losing something as essential and vital as housing was hanging over the heads of entire families and must have been incredibly stressful, especially as the Copper Country winter was increasingly on the horizon. In most cases, mining companies owned the homes of workers and could in theory evict people as they saw fit, and for any reason deemed necessary. When mining companies found themselves unable to evict striking workers due to an injunction, they grew angry. Frederick Denton, general manager of the Copper Range Mining Companies, had been very diligent in drawing up housing contracts with mineworkers just in case of a strike, but even "Mr. Denton over at the Copper Range has an ironclad contract, in which he thought he could summarily evict the men in fourteen days, but the Western Federation steps in and nullifies all this by obtaining an injunction." Perhaps realizing the public relations hit, many companies accepted the housing plight, especially early in the strike as a C&H attorney concluded on September 22, 1913, "Mr. Rees advises, after going into the matter exhaustively, that it will consume about twelve months to go through all the various legal steps that the Federation can put up."[35]

Thus, for the most part, Copper Country mineworkers and their families stayed in their homes throughout the strike. There were some cases where strikers just left rather than put up a fight, and there were other cases when mining companies aggressively pursued eviction cases in special instances. Such an occurrence was the number of December raids on suspected socialist and "evil" strikers' homes by the Houghton County sheriff, deputies, and hired Waddell-Mahon gun thugs. As Charles Lawton noted, "They expect to clean up on searching a total of forty-three houses on the Hill today. I think it is wise to get these rifles and shotguns out of the hands of the vicious strikers. These houses are largely the ones from which we are trying to evict the striking miners."[36]

Gun Thugs

As it became clear that the strike was no short-term affair, the mining companies began to employ force to deal with union organizing efforts. This included the hiring of "peacekeeping" forces and the importation of armed strikebreakers, as well as deputizing men loyal to the mining companies as Houghton County deputy sheriffs. The English- and foreign-language labor press were well aware of this tactic, and the Finnish-language press described the most notable of the company's detective services, the Waddell-Mahon Detective Agency, as "*Kenraali* Waddell's *Pyssyhurtia*," or "General Waddell's gun hounds." The Waddell-Mahon agency, much like the more infamous Pinkerton agency, specialized in union busting and strikebreaking. Interestingly, it was not only the mining companies that were hiring union-busting agencies; the sheriff of Houghton County, James Cruse, hired them as well.

An October 1913 issue of *Työmies* featured the headline "The Waddell Menace."

Under this headline the newspaper reprinted excerpts from a circular the paper claimed to have procured from the Waddell-Mahon company that lauded the union-busters' own efforts: "We point with great pardonable pride to the fact that this corporation has been selected by James A. Cruse of Houghton County—the storm center of the strike—to aid him in maintaining the integrity of the law. We are now engaged in 'policing' the 1,019 square miles of territory contained in Houghton County." General Waddell left no indecision regarding the task Cruse hired him to do: "We are safeguarding the property of the mine owners against intrusion and violence. . . . We are sure of defeating the Western Federation of Miners in this operation because we have met and defeated them before. . . . We ask you to watch the progress of the present strike . . . because we know it will be a triumph for the mine owners."[37]

Antti Sarell, a reporter for the Finnish immigrant socialist-unionist press, reported on the connections between Houghton County law enforcement forces and the Waddell-Mahon agency. Sarell quipped, "In addition to the soldiers, the officials held on a leash, the mining companies hired Waddell-Mahon's Detective Agency gun hounds to be the so-called 'guardians of order' in the strike area. They were assembled from the major cities' most crooked elements and as far as their fees; Houghton County had to pay and is still paying tens of thousands of dollars monthly as this is being written."[38] In addition to the Waddell-Mahon men, C&H and the Mohawk Mining Company hired "gun thugs" from New York's Ascher Detective Agency. If the "Waddell Menace" was not bad enough for strikers, an article in the *Miners' Bulletin* opined that the Ascher men were "as tough a looking bunch of men as have ever applied a sandbag to their victim."[39]

Even Quincy Mining Company administrators such as Charles Lawton struggled to find a good word about the Waddell-Mahon men. Initially receptive to bringing Waddell-Mahon men in, Lawton cooled, writing to Quincy vice president William Parsons Todd on October 6, 1913, "We have had some trouble with the guards that he [Waddell] has brought in, but we have made him ship them out of the country and replace them." More problematic was that the Ascher Detective Agency had hired the discarded Waddell-Mahon guards and shipped them back to the Copper Country. "Now in the case of the Ascher Agency and the men that it has shipped into the county, we find some of the condemned Waddell men that we had refused and shipped out of the county," Lawton noted.[40] While Lawton determined that the Waddell-Mahon men were good at breaking a strike, when Quincy president William R. Todd hired some Waddell-Mahon men to look after Quincy's New York offices, Lawton wrote, "The Waddell guards that have been here and are now in New York, are men that we would now hardly allow to stop over night in Houghton County. Moral, do not employ any ex-Waddell men in New York City."[41]

Early Violence against Labor

When ignoring the WFM did not produce the intended results, after bringing in thousands of scabs to take area jobs had no effect, when legal threats to evict strikers faltered, and after hiring hundreds of strong-armed men did not intimidate the WFM or its rank and file, the mining companies' gun thugs and Houghton County law enforcement reverted to the most steadfast and effective measure against the Copper Country's striking workers: violence. Dreadful, deadly incidents in August and September galvanized the striking workers and the public's response to the tactics of mining company gun thugs. Two of the especially violent episodes were the Seeberville shootings and the almost fatal shooting of teenage girl Margaret Fazekas. While General Waddell's men were at center stage in Seeberville, Houghton County deputy sheriffs were culpable for shooting young Margaret Fazekas.

The crowded, hardscrabble back streets of a ramshackle mining location was the setting for possibly the most notorious of the Waddell-Mahon men's exploits. This ghastly event occurred in mid-August 1913, and the labor newspapers were quick to print a nuanced recounting of the event: "The character of these bloodhounds dressed as humans revealed itself for the first time on August 14th when they executed one of the most cold blooded massacres known to the history of the American workers' battles in Seeberville location near Painesdale."[42]

Antti Sarell further described the event:

> For absolutely no reason six crooks identified as sheriff's deputies, of which four were Waddell-Mahon's Detective Agency gun hounds, attacked the men of Croatian Joseph Putrich's boarding house, driving the men from the courtyard to the inside of the house and after that shooting in through the house's windows with their revolvers. The consequence was that 18-year-old striker Aloiz Tijan was instantly killed and a striker named Steve Putrich died from gunshot wounds some days later. Two other strikers and the infant who was in the arms of the house's lady suffered gunshot wounds, with a shot of the revolver burning the child's face. After they had committed this cruel deed, the gun hounds went to the road in front of the house where they loaded their revolvers again and jeered amongst themselves "we wonder how many dead bodies there are in the house."[43]

Naturally, Sheriff Cruse, who had hired the men, did as much as possible to hinder efforts to locate the assailants and bring the shooters to justice. After finally rounding up the suspects, the sheriff ordered the arrests of six "murderers": James Cooper, Arthur Davis, William Groff, Harry James, Edward Polkinghorne, and

Thomas Raleigh. According to Sarell, "The hounds that had committed the massacre were let to be on the loose for a long time before the sheriff, pressured by public opinion, saw that it was better to take them 'under his surveillance' in the county jail where they weren't treated like other prisoners at all, but were allowed to live like kings."

Reports of the shootings in the *Miners' Bulletin* and *Työmies* were heartwrenching. The *Bulletin* eulogized the two slain strikers: "You shall not have died in vain. You shall be an inspiration in all of freedom's battles. You shall live in all of freedom's sons, your grave, a shrine for all her lovers. On your tombs we will write the words: 'They died for us.' In our hearts we shall carry the high resolve to be worthy of your sacrifice." Accompanying the eulogy was a short stanza of verse from Lord Byron's "Marino Faliero, Doge of Venice" for the fallen fellow workers:

> *They never fail who die in a great cause,*
> *The block may soak their gore,*
> *Their heads may sodden in the sun,*
> *Their tribes be strewn from city gates and castle walls,*
> *But still their spirits walk abroad and overwhelm,*
> *All others in advancing freedom.*[44]

The funeral for the slain strikers occurred on August 17. Sarell estimated that there were 12,576 men, women, and children at the funeral.[45] At a large WFM meeting in Kansankoti Hall that followed the funeral, Frank Aaltonen politicked for a resolution calling for the dismissal of the Waddell-Mahon men from the area.[46] Though the union members passed the resolution, it did little to dissuade Cruse from working with the hired "gun hounds." Neither this resolution nor the public outcry against the hired gun thugs did anything to dissuade Copper Country mining companies or law enforcement from depending on the strong-arm tactics of the Waddell-Mahon and Ascher agencies, which became more frequent and pointed as the strike went on.

In fact, C&H knowingly protected the whereabouts of Thomas Raleigh, even though he was wanted for murder. Not only did the company protect Raleigh, it used information obtained by him to spy on WFM activities in New York City. While four of the six shooters at Seeberville were found guilty of manslaughter, Harry James was acquitted under direction of the court, and Thomas Raleigh supposedly fled the Copper Country. Special Prosecutor George Nichols later wrote to the Houghton County Board of Supervisors that it was thought that Raleigh had indeed left the country, but labor spy correspondence reveals that Raleigh was in hiding in New York by January. In fact, he was spying on the WFM's New York offices for

C&H, providing the fruits of his work as a labor spy to Mr. Robinson, a lawyer in the firm of Rees, Robinson, and Petermann, which was on C&H's payroll. Robinson then forwarded Raleigh's correspondence to O. F. Bailey, a claim agent with C&H. Raleigh's letters to Robinson give further example of the character of men hired by the Waddell-Mahon agency and seem to indicate that while in New York, Raleigh continued to act violently. On one occasion after confronting a competing detective agency that was working with the WFM to get affidavits from former Ascher men, Raleigh wrote, "I raised hell in 80 Wall St. yesterday where I went looking for Martin, he was out and the four Jew detectives there would not fight."[47]

While Raleigh's absconding to New York made it somewhat clear that the Waddell-Mahon men could act with impunity in regards to legal action, Houghton County deputy sheriffs had much of the same carte blanche. In one tragic instance on Labor Day, September 1, 1913, "as a result of a clash between deputy sheriffs and a body of strikers and women, a girl 14 years of age, named Margaret Fazekas [of Hungarian ethnicity], was shot in the head at North Kearsarge."[48]

There were various reports in a number of languages about the events surrounding Margaret Fazekas's shooting, but most witnesses seem to agree that a large group of strikers began to have words with a smaller group of Houghton County sheriff's deputies. There was a lot of provocative language from both sides. According to the testimony of eyewitness Andrew Szeles, "The women at this point began shouting 'scabs' at the deputies and yelling at them to go home and eat their breakfast, while the latter retorted in the same tone to go home and cook theirs."[49]

Although differing in exact detail, a number of witnesses concluded that a woman from the strikers' side walked up to meet a deputy sheriff in the middle of the small dirt road, which was surrounded by miners' houses. After reaching to touch the deputy's Houghton County sheriff's star badge, the deputy sheriff hit her arm away with a billy club. The deputy backed up into the posse of armed men, who had drawn their guns. The order of "Shoot!" was barely spoken into the morning air when a single shot rang out, followed by more gunfire. A massive cloud of gunfire began wafting over the neighborhood. Word was that the guns were pointed in the air, but obviously one deputy sheriff had not pointed his weapon into the air because a bullet found the back of fourteen-year-old Margaret Fazekas's skull—indeed, the bullet entered the back of her skull as she was running away. According to a federal report on the strike, the deputy sheriffs fired over ninety rounds at the strikers and then ran with the strikers in pursuit, who only then began to throw rocks at the armed but "ammunitionless" deputy sheriffs.[50]

As we are able to infer from a number of the remembrances of people who witnessed the event, a good deal of the morning's chaos was precipitated by the charge that women should be at home cooking and not out in a strike action. This conflict between steadfast Victorian norms and a progressive labor movement came to a head in this escalating altercation, the result of which left a teen-age girl on her deathbed. Margaret was brought to a little storm shed at the back of a neighborhood house, and Dr. Andrew C. Roach provided her much-needed medical attention. He reported, "Upon examination found that she had been shot back of left ear . . . the wound was a clean cut one showing no jaggedness . . . bullet penetrated the skull and carried a good deal of brain matter, some oozing through her hair."[51]

Margaret's life was doubtless in mortal danger. Once in the storm shed turned emergency room, Margaret was propped up on a chair, unconscious, with people looking on. The report of events went on to disclose that "the girl was semi-uncon-scious for four or five days afterwards, but on Saturday of the same week the Doctor removed a piece of bone from the base of the girl's brain and the girl had shown remarkable improvement. . . . He further stated that the future of girl's sanity was problematical."[52]

The shooting of this fourteen-year-old girl created massive headlines. Not only was she a female but also a child, and while women according to the Victorian-era conventions were not supposed to be outside of the home, they especially should not be shot. Public sympathy swayed toward the striking workers, and in the very sensitive and important arena of public opinion, the shooting of an unarmed girl by a band of "thugs," on Labor Day no less, was an unadulterated calamity—a horror that sadly went unpunished. A single deputy sheriff, John Lavers, was offered up as the guilty party and charged with "assault with intent to murder," but his case was transferred to the December Special Grand Jury, and this jury, almost on cue, entered a no true bill, indicating that there was not enough evidence to convict Lavers of the shooting of Margaret.[53] Thus, a fourteen-year-old girl was shot in the back of her head, but no one was held accountable—one wonders if the same would have been true if "Big Jim" MacNaughton had been shot?

In early fall an injunction was put in place, which seemed to have a general calming effect on the Keweenaw. However, the calm was short-lived. The injunction was rescinded, and late fall brought more arrests and isolated acts of violence and retribution, which included dynamitings and isolated incidences of shootings. Mining companies were certain it was the work of the WFM, while the WFM asserted it was the work of mining company agent provocateurs. There was a lot of propaganda making its way around the Copper Country.

Sarell concluded in late October that Finns were working hard at creating ethnic solidarity: "The Copper Country Finns have to this day fought so gallantly in the strike that they have become especially hated among the mine bosses, but at the same time they have earned the respect of the entire organized labor of America. The other nationalities as well have stood gallantly in the battlefront, except for the 'Cousin

Jacks' [Cornish]." Even though Sarell emphasized the strike's Finnish immigrant component, he noted the importance of ethnic solidarity and the labor press:

> Even hours before the arrival of the newspaper, the workers have been waiting for the 'Miners Bulletin,' which has had writing in the Italian language too, alongside the English language. . . . The reading of these papers [*Työmies* and the *Miners' Bulletin*] and the speeches that have been held for example in the Kansankoti in Hancock every morning after the strike watch procession have surely had their influence on the striker's view of the world.[54]

There was a sort of mounting tension creeping over the Copper Country in October and November. Perhaps people knew that the cold winds off Lake Superior would bring changes. The mining companies welcomed winter as a sort of great equalizer, surmising that strikers would not want to walk through snow, women would stay inside with their children, and the need for clothing and food would drive workers back underground. This appeared likely to happen, but it did not. The resolve shown by striking workers frustrated the companies, and as rumors of outside investigations from federal agencies and Congress swirled around Copper Country social circles, putting an end to the strike became of paramount concern to copper companies.

Good Citizens

Perhaps the most powerful tactic the mining companies used in the Copper Country was the establishment of procompany businessmen's associations. The first such association was the Copper Country Commercial Club (CCCC). Formed early in the strike, the CCCC functioned as one of the many wings of the mining companies' strikebreaking force. The club went so far as to draft and send a long report on conditions in the Copper Country to Governor Ferris in early October. The report, complete with idyllic photos of perfectly preened company housing, was nothing more than a propaganda piece for the mining companies. Seeing the con in making, the WFM refused to submit materials to the CCCC for the report, and thus the report landed on Ferris's desk with little influence to guide his attempts at arbitrating the ever-lengthening strike.[55]

Because of the CCCC report's failure to sway political favor toward the mining companies, and as it became clear that the strikers were making inroads into the public's sympathy, the establishment of the Citizens' Alliance came about in December. It was time for the mining companies, respectable citizens, and all the associates that they could muster to do something to stem the tide of the strike. In this movement to rid the Copper Country of the WFM, powerful forces converged. At this point, the connection between Copper Country mining companies, the Citizens' Alliance, and the kept press became obvious. Newspaper stories in the *Mining Gazette, Calumet News,* and *Hancock Evening Journal* kept English-language readers abreast of the Citizens' Alliance's ideals and activities.

The copper companies relished the help given by a riled-up population of "good citizens." On December 8, 1913, two days before a Citizens' Alliance mass meetings kickoff event, Charles Lawton wrote William R. Todd, "All mines and many business houses have agreed upon a half-holiday with pay for employes [*sic*], to attend the Citizens' Alliance mass meetings Wednesday. . . . It was the consensus of opinion that they had better call a day for the general mass meetings throughout the district to take measures by which we should rid this country of the agitators of the Western Federation of Miners."[56] C&H's MacNaughton mirrored those sentiments regarding the Citizens' Alliance's December 10 meeting: "Object of meeting to protest against the action of county officials [mainly Houghton County Prosecuting Attorney Anthony Lucas and, though not a county official, circuit court Judge P. H. O'Brien] in not enforcing law and a general protest against the existence in this community of foreign agitators . . . the public is thoroughly aroused and this looks like the beginning of the end of the Western Federation of Miners in this country."[57]

Perhaps the most influential, yet dubious, of all Citizens' Alliance members was Albert E. Petermann. A lawyer, Petermann's eloquent delivery of speeches at Citizens' Alliance meetings excited crowds and drew distinct barriers between "good citizens" and the Copper Country's foreign population. Petermann was also a lawyer on C&H's payroll, a Houghton County deputy sheriff, and a onetime representative to the Michigan legislature. He was a powerful man who had the connections and money (the family owned a number of retail stores in the Copper Country) to rile up thousands of people against the so-called foreign agitators of the WFM. Petermann worked, in some cases, hand in glove with people writing propaganda against the WFM. In one mysterious letter received from a "Bill," Petermann helped to edit the content of an article in the *Leader* designed to unite members of the Citizens' Alliance in devoting "all of our energies directed toward wiping out the Western Federation of Miners. *Get Busy!*"[58]

A December Campaign of Intimidation and Violence

December changed the face of the strike. Industrial and social relations became very bitter, and that bitterness turned into more violence—and a particularly sinister type of violence: a campaign of orchestrated violence to beat the WFM out of area strikers and their families. The Citizens' Alliance, Houghton County law enforcement forces, and the mining companies' hired thugs embarked on a carefully planned violent winter campaign to rid the Copper Country of the WFM. This campaign, its participants, and the hopeful outcomes were common knowledge to the Copper Country oligarchy, who often wrote of the intended violence in unnerving terms. On December 9, 1913, Charles Lawton wrote of the proposed action, citing a mining district on the edge as fair game for retribution:

> The Citizens' Alliance members are in a very high state of tension at this time. Everybody is working for a rousing mass meeting tomorrow, and I expect some definite action will be taken in regard to ridding this country of the Western Federation agitators. I fear that any further overreactions on the part of the Federation strikers will be met with every summary action in the future. Everybody is very much wrought up.[59]

Seemingly, the strikers set the deadly December tone. On December 7, 1913, there was a shooting into the house of Thomas Dally, a Cornish scab miner. As the ammunition flew into the mining company–owned house in Painesdale, Arthur and Harry Jane, who were boarders at the Dally house, died immediately from gunshot wounds. Thomas Dally died as well and another non-fatal casualty of the gunfire was a thirteen-year-old girl who lived next door.[60]

The WFM contended the shooting was a frame-up intended to implicate WFM organizers in murder, and officials in the WFM repeated that they had called for nonviolent protest in media outlets and speeches. If it was a WFM member or members acting on their own volition, it was an act of sporadic violence. There was no indication that the WFM, its leaders, or local unions ever advocated violence against anyone, despite many efforts to pin such outrages on the WFM. The *Miners' Bulletin* was so strong in its conviction that non-union men had shot Thomas Dally and the Jane brothers, it published a December 13, 1913, poem by J.H.H. of Mohawk, Michigan, lamenting what had become of Michigan with the deaths of the miners:

"MICHIGAN MY MICHIGAN"
Oh, Michigan my Michigan,
Your head is bowed with shame
What have they done, those men
  Who should
Uphold thy honored name.
They listened to the call of wealth,
Your honor they forgot.
Three striking miners, shot to death;

Michigan, Oh Michigan, what a
     crimson blot.[61]

Almost in lockstep with the area mining companies, the area's kept press, Houghton County law enforcement agencies, and the Citizens' Alliance all put the blame on the WFM and four of its organizers, but not before Houghton County law enforcement officers arrested two other men for the bloodshed in Painesdale. Originally, Special Prosecutor Nichols charged Thomas Rossman and Isaac Gronzonovich, who were likely WFM members, with the murders of Thomas Dally and Arthur Jane. Strangely, after turning the case over to the December Special Grand Jury, they came back with a no true bill. Rossman and Gronzonovich were freed. The Citizens' Alliance, however, used the Dally-Jane shootings as a rallying cry to call for the obliteration of the WFM in the Copper Country. Yet no one had been convicted of the shootings, and in fact a rigged grand jury found that there was not enough evidence against Rossman and Gronzonovich to move forward with a case against them. Nichols, beguiled by the findings, wrote in his report to the Houghton County Board of Supervisors, "No action has been taken in the court in the Painesdale murder case, although at any time steps may be taken to apprehend certain parties now under investigation."[62]

Those certain parties were John Huhta, secretary of the WFM local in South Range; Nick Verbanac, a well-known WFM organizer; and "two Finn" union members, Hjalmer Yalonen and Joseph Juntunen. The main suspect, John Huhta, took center stage after the Special December Grand Jury decided they had the wrong two men earlier. Nichols had decided, after not being able to convict Rossman and Gronzonovich, that the case went even deeper—not only was it a four-man job, but the shootings at Painesdale were tantamount to a WFM conspiracy. While still only charged with the shootings, the complaint against the defendants in the Dally case read like a conspiracy by the WFM to assassinate all vestiges of law and order from Houghton County. In reality, it was not Huhta, Verbanac, Yalonen, and Juntunen who were on trial; it was the WFM. It became clear that the Dally-Jane shootings were going to be used by Special Prosecutor Nichols in the conspiracy trial against Moyer et al., to allege a WFM plot to bring violence to the Copper Country. The charges against the defendants read:

> And the said John Huhta, Nick Verbanac, Joseph Juntunen and Hjalmer Jalonen, together
> with other members of the said Western Federation of Miners, the names of whom are to
> the said prosecuting attorney unknown, with force and arms, unlawfully and wickedly did
> conspire, combine, confederate and agree together, wickedly and feloniously and unlaw-
> fully, with malice aforethought, with violence, force of arms, threats, intimidations, riotous

conduct, assaults, beatings, shooting, killing and murder, and by other unlawful means, to drive, force, coerce, intimidate, interfere with, molest and prevent the employees of the said mining companies who were not members of the said Western Federation of Miners, from the quiet and peacable pursuit of their lawful avocations.[63]

The contention that the Dally-Jane shootings were a frame-up came early from organized labor. The labor press was, understandably, quite vocal in the refutation of WFM involvement. Rumors swirled around the area that Huhta, who later confessed to the shooting, recanted, and then "reconfessed," was a dupe used by Cruse, Nichols, and others to implicate the WFM. WFM official Charles Tanner claimed that "he expected that Huhta would do something like this. The mine officials gave him plenty of money to make this confession. He has been spending a lot of money lately. Claims he had the snakes [shakes—alcohol addiction] and it is easy to get a man in that condition to say almost anything. All trumped up."[64]

The labor spy who reported Tanner's claim also reported that Paul Tommei, a member of Calumet's WFM local, added about Huhta's arrest: "This man that [Houghton County Prosecuting Attorney] Lucas was after [a man who the WFM alleged to be the shooter and employed by Waddell to frame the WFM] got fired by Waddell and he tried to tell his story to the Grand Jury and they wouldn't listen to him. While Lucas was away looking up this man, the Citizens' Alliance got busy and got after Huhta and filled him full of booze and he got the d.t. [delirium tremens] and they got him."[65] Tommei reportedly got the information from Lucas himself, who was talking with the WFM. According to the labor spy, Lucas later became upset with Tommei for leaking the information about Huhta, "Paul Tommei said that Lucas went after him about the rumor getting out in regard to the Waddell man that Lucas told Tommei about. Said he thought that when he was talking to Tommei he was talking to a friend. This was in regard to blaming the Waddell men for the Painesdale murder."[66]

Regardless of Huhta's guilt, innocence, or "railroading," shortly after the shootings the Citizen's Alliance used the event to practice some vigilante-style justice in the Copper Country. The alliance began an orchestrated campaign of violence against anyone or anything associated with the WFM. The first target was WFM headquarters in South Range, where alliance members, Houghton County deputy sheriffs, and other "good citizens," conducted an old-fashioned siege on the building. On December 10, Sheriff Cruse deputized 100 men, many of them members of the Citizens' Alliance, and brought the mob to South Range by train. Twelve WFM men outside the South Range offices were arrested. Cruise cordoned off the building and sent for reinforcements. Three hundred or so men responded from Houghton.[67]

The standoff lasted until three in the morning, when the 300-pound sheriff's deputy John Chellow knocked on the door, announced he had a search warrant (but did not), and threatened to bust down the door. An anxious hush and then a female's sobbing was heard. Breaking the silence, a male voice from behind the door replied, "Why don't you come around in daylight?" This blatant disrespect apparently voided the need for a warrant, and the hefty Chellow threw his weight into the door. Bang! A shot through the door nonfatally wounded Chellow. Stunned, the thick Chellow and the 400 or so members of the posse retreated, but at daybreak they raided the building once again. For their "gallant" siege, the Houghton County minions found three men in the union offices, unarmed but near six rifles without ammunition. A further investigation of the building found another thirty guns in the WFM offices along with a good amount of socialist paraphernalia. The posse arrested forty people in all. Charges against those arrested were later dropped, with the exception of the shooter.[68]

Työmies rightfully described the South Range raid as an unlawful break-in, but the area's kept press reported rumors of half-crazed, armed strikers (not sheriff's deputies) looking to shoot up the Copper Country. Race, or ethnicity, played a vital part in this characterization. This was a final dastardly tactic the mining companies and now the Citizens' Alliance were using to scare the Copper Country citizenry. Throughout the strike, mining company officials and their English-language newspaper organs, like the *Mining Gazette*, painted WFM officials and various immigrant organizers as outside or foreign agitators; never mind that it was the companies that had imported thousands of immigrant workers to work as scabs during the strike. The Citizen's Alliance went so far as to print a resolution condemning the strikers and claimed that strike violence was a "repetition of the numerous outrages that have been perpetrated at the instance of the non-resident agitators of the Western Federation of Miners." A headline in the *Gazette* the next day was more to the point: "Foreign Agitators Must Be Driven from District At Once." The South Range raid set in motion other raids across the Copper Country, and on December 11 *Työmies* reported: "Kansankoti and Työmies menaced by law and order." Automobiles stopped at the Hancock offices of the Tyomies Publishing Company and attached Kansankoti Hall, and a number of gun hounds raided the complex. Five days later, *Työmies* reported that "the Citizens' Alliance had threatened to blow-up the WFM store in Calumet," which was on the site of the former Croatian Co-operative Store.[69]

In an oral history interview, Lillian Lahti (later Gow) recounted a cold winter morning raid of her home in Ahmeek. Lillian's father had given the use of his wood-floored basement to WFM Local 129 to store supplies for the union store in Ahmeek. Lillian's father was not a mineworker, but he was sympathetic to the WFM's cause. The Lahtis' basement thus became a very important place for the WFM as a storage facility for food staples to keep strikers and their families fed and energized during the strike. Their basement was so important to the cause that John Brinkman was designated as a night watchman over the precious food. For the most part, in the early days of the strike Brinkman's job as food watcher was uneventful, with the notable exception of one night when a shot came through the glass of a front basement window.[70]

The Lahtis' food storage area was an innocent place, until winter. Just six years old at the time of the unlawful search, Lillian remembered of the early dawn raid: "One cold, cold winter morning, these officials came without a warrant, and they searched up in the attic and down in the basement for ammunition, which we didn't have. We, Dad, never had a gun in the house. . . . What are you going to do when they come, you know, several of them, you can't uh, fight them all." This episode was especially memorable for six-year-old Lillian because as the officials searched her home, apparently not needing a warrant, they manhandled a boarder at the Lahti house and refused to shut the home's door. As Lillian recalled:

> When we were just coming out of bed, and it was so cold . . . these men came in and had the door open. . . . [The boarder] said to go up and tell his wife not to worry, you know, about these officials being there. . . . Then one of the men put him down, saying, 'You stay put,' you know. Mother asked [an official] if he would close the door, because there we were in our night clothes and huddling around the stove to keep warm and they [kept] the door open.[71]

The December raids on WFM members and locations were just the opening volleys of intimidation and violence that led into a two-week-long campaign of terror by the Citizens' Alliance and Houghton County law enforcement forces. A letter written by Charles L. Lawton to William R. Todd on December 12, 1913, provides evidence of the close relationship between mine management and local police forces. As is clear, the two groups coordinated their efforts to break the mineworkers' strike:

> They [WFM members and their families] seemed determined, said that they would parade and began forming. Everybody was on hand; the police patrol was there in the saddle and gave the signal to advance by shooting their guns in the air, and the "scrap" was on. They chased the strikers far and wide, and all were surprised that the strikers were such good runners. Quite a number of them were caught, but we thought it was useless to arrest them, and some of them were made fit subjects for the hospital—in fact, they were very roughly treated.
>
> We understood that the parades would be started again this morning, and that the strikers would be prepared by being armed, and we were again prepared for them; but

not a striker not a picketer was seen on the Hill. If any had shown up, I think they would
have been badly treated.[72]

Houghton County law enforcement forces, which up to this point in the strike
were all but bumbling, had made a definitive switch toward partisan, violent strikebreakers. Almost everyone in the copper mining community knew it. Emboldened
by the influence and power asserted by the Citizens' Alliance, mining company
managers now began giving edicts to Houghton County officials, including District
Judge Patrick O'Brien, the last of those willing to give organized labor a fair shake
in the Copper Country. According to Lawton, "It transpired that great pressure
had been brought to bear upon Mr. O'Brien, the Sheriff, and Mr. Nichols, that they
would better see the Western Federation officers at once and advise them to at once
use their influence in stopping all picketing and parading, else there would be no
telling what would happen."[73]

The Citizens' Alliance used its money, power, and privilege to swing the momentum of the strike toward the mining companies. The establishment of the alliance
and its open advocacy of ridding the Copper Country of the WFM and its "foreign
agitators" was an all too familiar attack on immigrants—those good enough to work
and die in the mines, but not good enough to be viewed simply as human beings. The
alliance was on the offensive, and this strategy was apparent to and welcomed by the
mining companies. Lawton wrote Todd on December 15, 1913, praising the alliance:

> The parades of Wednesday [Citizens' Alliance] have opened the eyes of the whole com-
> munity to the large percentage of citizens that are against the Federation. They have given
> confidence to each and every one that is not in favor of the Federation; and, on the other
> hand, has [sic] depressed and frightened the strikers. They have had a wonderfully good
> effect throughout the whole district. Take it all in all, it looks as though Wednesday, the
> tenth, was the turning-point.[74]

The strike was quickly devolving into an attack on "foreign agitators." The
Citizens' Alliance took pains to credit the hard work and American attitudes of
true *citizens*. A distinction was being made between those who had the right to be
in the Copper Country and those who were outsiders. The message was becoming
clear—if you were a "foreigner" and a striker, you were a second-class citizen and not
wanted in the Copper Country. Where this violence against the WFM and the Copper
Country's foreign population would end was not certain at this time, but a fatigued,
faltering, and frustrated oligarchy that was used to getting its way was looking for
a definitive action to once and for all rid the Copper Country of the WFM and its
foreign agitators. To their credit, however, the striking population of the Copper

Country did not give up the fight, even in the face of seemingly insurmountable odds. They pushed on; strikers' collective voices would be heard, and they had a right to organize—even something as simple and innocent as a Christmas Eve party for the children of striking workers in Calumet.

CHAPTER 8

Tragedy

One little girl who was jammed in the hallway in a dying condition begged one of her rescuers to save her. She grasped his hand, kissed it, then her little head dropped upon her breast and she was dead.

—*Miners' Bulletin*, December 28, 1913

THE 1913–14 COPPER COUNTRY STRIKE WAS A BITTER CONFLICT BETWEEN THE burgeoning strength of organized labor and the entrenched power of American industrial capital. Like many of the bloody labor conflicts that came before, there were casualties in the Copper Country: Alois "Louie" Tijan and Steve Putrich gave their lives and became martyrs to the cause, while Margaret Fazekas came within an inch of martyrdom. The strike caused bloody class conflict in many cases, but one event more than any other has come to symbolize the acute bitterness present in the Copper Country during the 1913–14 Copper Country Strike: the Italian Hall tragedy.

Built in 1908, the Italian Hall was designed to be a showpiece for the Copper Country's Italian population. Though two other wooden balloon-frame Italian Halls preceded this building on almost the same site, this pressed brick structure was built to last. The hall consisted of three floors, and had a roof covered with a fireproof material. In addition to the fireproof roofing material, the *Calumet News* reported on the building's opening in October of 1908, that "particular attention has been paid to the safety of the public in the design of the building and in addition to the ample main stairway a large iron fire escape has been erected on the side of the building [and] also one from the stage, both of these are built into the solid brick walls, all doors open outward." The newspaper also described the important extras of the building's exterior: "The front is trimmed with sandstone and the cornice work is of heavy Galvanized iron." The building's interior was just as ornate. Especially fancy were the auditorium hall, stage, and balcony. According to the *Calumet News*, the auditorium was "forty feet wide by seventy one feet in length with an eighteen foot ceiling, finished in Georgia pine, maple flooring, and a highly ornamental steel ceiling"; the stage's "proscenium arch was eleven feet by twenty two feet"; and the balcony "was ten feet wide by sixty feet long, well trimmed with a neat balustrade and ornamental columns."[1]

After reading the *Calumet News'* glowing report on the construction and design of the hall, few could have imagined that some five years later the Italian Hall would be the site of one of the nation's greatest tragedies. On Christmas Eve of 1913, at a party for striking mineworkers' children sponsored by the Calumet Women's Auxiliary of the Western Federation of Miners (WFM), disaster struck. The Christmas Eve party at the Italian Hall was supposed to be a chance for the children of strikers to be "kids" again in the war-torn Copper Country, if only for a short time. After the distribution of presents, funded in part by the WFM national and in part by donations procured by the Calumet Women's Auxiliary, there was to be a Mother Goose–style play that evening. That all turned tragic in a few short moments. A call of "Fire!," a panicked exodus from the second-floor hall, and an unparalleled loss of life all changed the tenor and tone of the 1913–14 Michigan Copper Strike. The Italian Hall tragedy came to signify the depths of the accrued acrimony in the Copper Country.

In many ways, the human element has been assigned much of the blame for the loss of between 73 and 79 lives in the Italian Hall. This chapter probes the role people played in this tragedy, but the design of the building itself can also assist in explaining some of the reasons for the terrible loss of life. A primary problem was that an estimated 400 to 500 people were squeezed into a 40-by-71-foot social hall.[2] Even though most accounts concur that as the evening wore on the crowd in the

OPPOSITE: This drawing of the Italian Hall's first floor shows the large storefront windows of Vairo's Saloon and the A&P. The first floor was commercial space, while upper floors were halls or dwellings.

Drawings of the three floors of the Italian Hall by Gary Kaunonen, based on Kevin Harrington's 1975 Historic American Building Survey drawings, historical photographs, and an October 1908 *Calumet News* article.

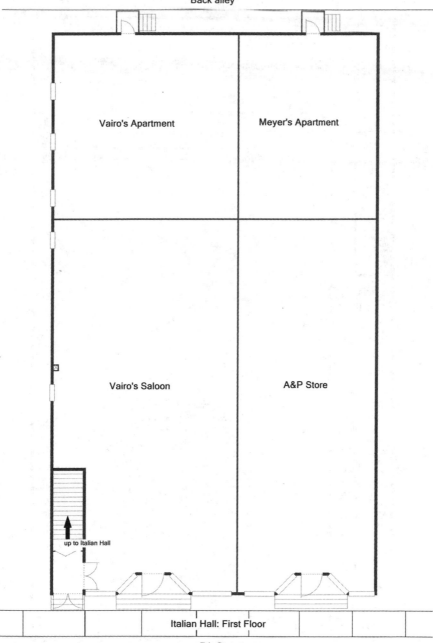

Back alley

Vairo's Apartment

Meyer's Apartment

Vairo's Saloon

A&P Store

up to Italian Hall

Italian Hall: First Floor

7th Street

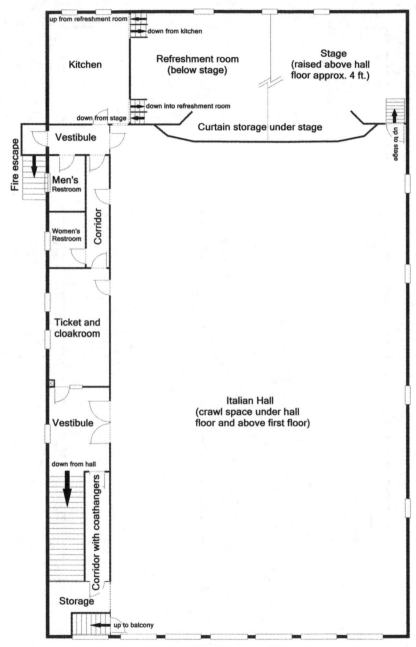

Italian Hall: Second Floor

hall thinned, this meant that an alarming number of people were tightly packed into less than 3,000 square feet. Increasingly troublesome, when the cry of "Fire!" rose above the crowd most people knew of only one way to get out—the 22-step stairway they climbed up to the second floor—and to make it to this stairway people had to first pass through a set of double doors that led from the hall into the second-floor vestibule, which was tiny (at 75 square feet) in comparison with the cavernous hall.

During the panic, few of the partygoers knew of or utilized the hall's two fire escapes described in the *Calumet News* article. For many, and especially the children, this was their first time in the Italian Hall. Additionally, and though it was a strength of the WFM's unionization efforts and a testament to the solidarity of striking Copper Country mineworkers, the night's festivities were attended by a diverse group of people who spoke an equally diverse number of languages, which must have made communication in this time of crisis quite difficult. The mentioning of these factors is not, however, intended to blame those who died in the Italian Hall or the building's architects and designers; these details are provided to lend a better understanding of the tragedy.

One factor that has never been fully examined, and thus is especially problematic, is, "Why this building on this date?" This chapter gives such context and an answer to the question, "Why the Italian Hall?" Research into the tragic events at Italian Hall has uncovered previously undiscovered documents that give valuable insight into a group, the procompany Citizens' Alliance, that, at the very least, was able and willing to cause the social climate for such a horrendous event, and, at the very worst, orchestrated the entire event.

Here, research and writing offers firsthand, primary evidence that the Citizens' Alliance, the bitter enemy of the WFM and the "foreign" element of the Copper Country, had direct links to creating the tragedy that occurred on that fateful Christmas Eve night in 1913. Further, this chapter argues that there is sufficient documentary evidence to conclude that the events at Italian Hall were no accident. There are four pieces of previously unknown material that provide support for the assertion that Italian Hall and the children trying to enjoy Christmas in a strike-ravaged copper district were the targets of a wicked plan to turn, in one final instance, the tide of the strike against the WFM.

The four historical pieces are first, the mining companies and their advocates in the Citizens' Alliance were becoming frustrated by continued and successful union

OPPOSITE: Kevin Harrington remarked in his report that the second floor of the Italian Hall was nearly unaltered in layout. This was a rather typical setup for social halls. The corridors, small spaces, and doors all gave an almost mazelike effect to the hall and its surrounding rooms. Drawing by Gary Kaunonen.

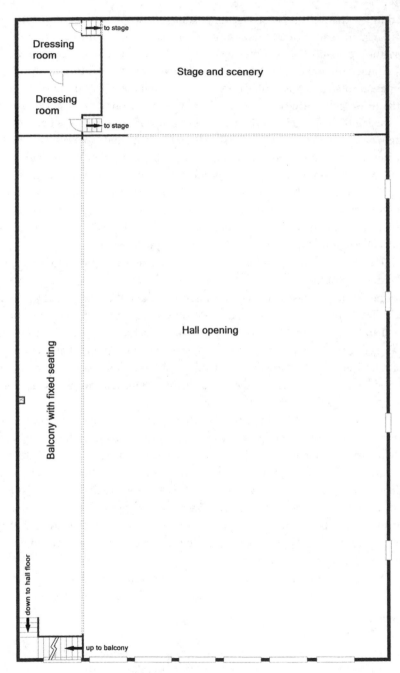

Dressing room

to stage

Dressing room

to stage

Stage and scenery

Hall opening

Balcony with fixed seating

down to hall floor

up to balcony

Italian Hall: Third Floor

OPPOSITE: The third floor of the Italian Hall was mostly open space, but dressing rooms and stage and scenery areas provided important square footage for cultural performances. Drawing by Gary Kaunonen.

efforts during the strike. The pro-mining company factions, including Calumet & Hecla (C&H), thought the strike would be over by December, and the resolve that striking workers were demonstrating caused the Citizens' Alliance to escalate the tactics used to break the strike. Second, there was the publication of material by procompany sources that targeted Italian Hall as a place of radicalism that needed to be shut down. Third, through the reports of a C&H labor spy, there is documentary proof that Italian Hall received threats against it shortly before the tragic events of Christmas Eve. Finally, the blatant xenophobia that existed in the area created an "Us vs. Them"

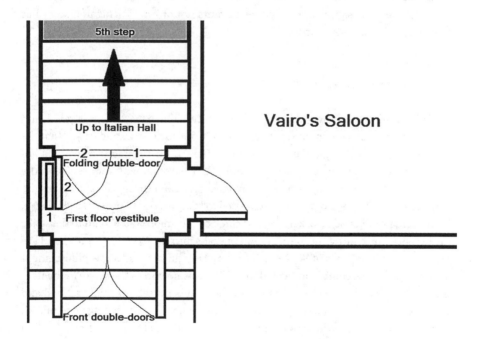

ABOVE: This drawing details Italian Hall's first-floor vestibule. The exterior doors are the iconic doors featured in many photographs. The interior door was likely a single folding double-door that was open during the panic. Research by Keweenaw National Historical Park archivist Jeremiah Mason, architectural historian Kim Hoagland, Keweenaw National Park historian Jo Urion, and Ph.D. student (Michigan Technological University) Scott See indicates that this was indeed the probable historic configuration, use, and detail of the first-floor vestibule. Drawing by Gary Kaunonen, based on a hand-drawn sketch by Jeremiah Mason.

dialectic that occasioned the targeting of Italian Hall as a place of "foreigners" and the people therein not as second-class citizens but as second-class human beings.

These four claims support an argument that the Italian Hall had been targeted by procompany forces as a place of "foreign" agitation that housed dangerous events and people. Even early in the strike, the Italian Hall was marked as home to what the good citizens of the Copper Country perceived as ungrateful immigrants. Comments on the back of a photograph from a melee in front of the Italian Hall indicate that in September of 1913, just two months into the strike, "strikers were accused of tearing up [an] American flag maliciously, during a parade."[3] Perhaps it was from this point on that the Italian Hall became a focal point of contempt, hatred, and eventually retribution in Calumet. In the eyes of the Copper Country's elite, the lovingly constructed fraternal hall was home to foreign people who needed discipline and punishment to understand what it meant to be a good citizen, loyal to the hands that fed them. The information that follows provides new perspectives on one of the most significant yet horrific events not only in Michigan history but in American labor history as well.

Context for Tragedy

The WFM and the rank and file of the union continually befuddled, frustrated, and stupefied the mining companies with a bend-but-do-not-break solidarity. What the mining companies thought would be a short affair in the summer and early fall of 1913 turned into a protracted class war, and this frustration with the resolve of the strikers irritated the mining companies' management and those who sided with the companies' perspective. Winter was supposed to bring an end to the strike. However, the cold did not dissuade workers from sticking to the union, and no end to the strike was in sight. The continuous importation of scabs into the Copper Country and the steady number of arrests of WFM members by Houghton County law enforcement officers well into December indicated that there was no end to the strike in the near future. The strikers were not giving up the fight. This caused normally refined and self-controlled, well-to-do, proper-type men to resort to name-calling and childish taunts, which likely provided the strikers with evidence that they were successful in stirring up the Copper Country power structure. The agitprop (agitation and propaganda) actions of the WFM and its rank-and-file solidarity confused, confounded, and frustrated the mining companies and especially C&H management.

This vexation was clear as early as October of 1913. The so-called "Emperor of the Copper Country," "Big Jim" MacNaughton, had been rattled so much by the strikers that he fell into a deep funk, writing C&H President Quincy Shaw, "I have written two very doleful letters on the subject of the Strike. I get so blue and depressed myself at times that I either cannot write letters at all or if I do feel I must tell my troubles to everyone else."[4] This was the most powerful man in the Copper Country writing his boss to admit that he was "blue." The strikers were deeply affecting not only the production of area mines, but also the temperament of area mine managers.

A further indicator of the WFM's success in agitating the Copper Country's mining and civic upper echelon comes from the very establishment of the Citizens' Alliance. It was an organization formed to roust the WFM from the Copper Country, but what exactly were the boundaries of behavior for such a group? According to the Citizens' Alliance's founding manifesto reprinted in the November 11, 1913, issue of the *Miners' Bulletin*, the organization formed because "of the spreading of its (WFM) poisonous propaganda of destructive socialism, violence, intimidation, and disregard of law and order must be brought to an end; and that the time has come for good citizenship to assert itself." Its members believed "that the presence of the Western Federation of Miners is a menace to the future welfare and prosperity of this district, and that therefore in the interest of Law, Order and Peace, the Western Federation of Miners must go."[5]

While in public, speakers for the Citizens' Alliance called for peace, at its very core the fundamental pulse of the alliance was to rid the Copper Country of the WFM using whatever means necessary. "If its pledges mean anything there are ten thousand people already enrolled in the copper district against Moyer, Mahoney, Miller, Terzich and their principles. *Something definite in the form of aggressive action against the Western Federation should result.*"[6]

WFM people and locations were being targeted. In Calumet, one of the most prominent and prolific centers of union organization was Italian Hall. Italian Hall was known, as was published in a November 29, 1913, *Miners' Bulletin* article, as a place of "Splendid Meeting." "A monster strikers meeting was held in the Italian Hall last Sunday night made up of Croatians, Slovanians [*sic*] and Servians [*sic*]. The hall was packed to the doors. Fully one half of the audience was made up of women. . . . Instead of speeches, a two act drama was presented. . . . The ladies belonging to the dramatic club are members of the Ladies Auxiliary of the W.F. of M. At last the giant has been awakened and in the future we will see, 'who should worry.'" In addition to meetings, Italian Hall was a popular dance spot during the strike, where a "large crowd attends the union dances on Saturday evenings."[7] If the WFM knew Italian Hall was a place of "splendid organization," it would not take long for anti-union forces to come to the same conclusion.

They did. In a December 3, 1913, letter from the mysterious "Bill," who was likely a member of the Citizens' Alliance, to C&H lawyer and Copper Country business magnate Albert E. Petermann, "Bill" includes an article slated to run in the

Leader. The article, titled "Do You Still Doubt," identifies Italian Hall as a place of foreign radicalism that shapes the WFM's secretive socialist agenda: "In Calumet, for instance, on Sunday, November 30th, 1913, there was a parade of strikers and Federation sympathizers, followed by meetings at the Opera House, the Italian Hall and Dunn's Hall. The meeting at the Opera House was for the general public and the conservative class among the strikers."[8]

The article's author then goes on to identify Italian Hall as home to radical activities. As evidence for this assertion, the article refers to the presence of radical Italian labor organizer Carlo Tresca as a featured speaker at Italian Hall on November 30, 1913. Tresca was a well-known radical who was often associated with the anarcho-syndicalist wing of the Industrial Workers of the World (IWW). Tresca was not, however, likely to have been a member of the WFM. If he was indeed at Italian Hall, he was likely there on his own volition and not as a speaker in the WFM's lineup of organizers. Tresca was a proud and open radical, and the bane of the author's argument that the WFM preached destructive socialism. "This man addressed the meeting of strikers [in Italian Hall]. Among other things he told them 'that they had just begun their fight and that they could only call themselves victors when they had planted the red flag on the mining properties.' Then [Tresca] said, '*Non la straccio con le stele e le strappo, ma la bandicra rossa del riscatto.*' In English this reads, 'Not the rag with the stars and stripes, but the red flag of our redemption.'"[9]

Tresca's oratory led the article's author to conclude:

> Do all members of the Federation hear the kind of speeches that Carlo Tresca made on Sunday last? No. Many of the men now on strike would not tolerate such a man in their midst if they had the least idea as to the doctrine he was preaching. By what means does the Federation separate the conservative members from the radical members who will listen to this socialistic doctrine?
>
> Maybe you have heard of the [WFM] red cards for admission to certain meetings [at Italian Hall]. At any rate it would be an easy matter to select the members to whom Tresca's doctrine would appeal. Some of these radical members are among all nationalities engaged in this strike.[10]

Finally, the article outlined a course of action that called for the destruction of the WFM and the people most likely to receive its "radical" message:

> It may take years to complete this task but we have years ahead of us and we can think of nothing that we can do that will be of a more lasting benefit to the citizens of this community than to expose the Western Federation of Miners. This does not include the misguided members but is intended especially for the Federation officers, agitators

and hirelings, including many of the little local parasites. . . . With this knowledge can any good citizen in this community fail to recognize his duty in joining hands to rid the Copper Country of Michigan of the Western Federation of Miners?"[11]

The Italian Hall's activities and people: secretive, radical, parasitic, foreign, and host to socialistic agitators like Carlo Tresca—something needed to be done at Italian Hall. In addition to Tresca, and as the Citizens' Alliance and Houghton County legal forces were putting the heel to strikers, the Finnish immigrant press ratcheted up the rhetoric. Especially pointed was the work of the Työmies Publishing Company's artists, who made every effort to lampoon and beguile the Copper Country oligarchy. Perhaps the most derisive piece was a December 15, 1913, cartoon in which Citizens' Alliance members drawn as simians span Portage Lake connecting the Copper Country's mainland (Houghton and points south) to Copper Island (Hancock and points north). The cartoon's caption exclaimed, "And behold, those monkeys [Citizens' Alliance members] built a bridge and helped McNaughton [*sic*] over to the Copper Island." The bridge of monkeys connected a bare cliff on one side to another cliff with an apple tree, branches heavy, almost breaking with a wealth of apples—the point being that the Citizens' Alliance was the bridge that was giving MacNaughton, and thus C&H, the support needed to gain access to untold wealth in the Copper Country. The monkey as the "McNaughton" character then posed this comment while getting ready to cross the simian bridge to the plump apple tree: "The bridge is great, the question now is to see how long it lasts."[12] While seeing himself depicted as a monkey was likely enough to make "Big Jim" boil, the caustic comics and quips coming from the labor press sustained an idyllic sense of purpose and resolve in the striking population.

No matter the vitriol from one side for the other, the children of striking miners deserved a time to just be kids again. When it was determined that a Christmas party was needed to bring a little joy into the lives of children in a literal war zone, Italian Hall, a place of frequent and successful use, was selected for such a party. Most everyone knew that the Christmas Eve party at Italian Hall was going to host a lot of kids, as an article in the December 16 *Miners' Bulletin* indicated, "'Notice:' The Ladies Auxiliary of the W.F. of M. No. 15 have decided to give a Xmas entertainment for the strikers children of the Copper Country. Any persons wishing to donate to a fund appropriated for this cause will kindly send same to: Xmas Entertainment Committee, Care W.F. of M. office 6th St., Calumet, Mich."[13]

That work of thwarting the WFM and its radical, foreign members by *"good citizens,"* though, was already in the making, and the resolve of strikers was a thorn in the side of mine managers. In a letter from MacNaughton to Quincy Shaw on December 17, 1913, MacNaughton begrudgingly wrote of the frustration he had with the WFM's resolve: "From all indications there is a great deal of discontent in the ranks of the strikers. Notwithstanding this discontent the leaders are holding them together very well and but few of them are returning to work." The WFM's ability to keep the strike from faltering was beginning to wear on those in power, and the general sentiment from the mining companies and the Citizens' Alliance was that something needed to be done—and soon, as MacNaughton indicates in the same letter: "A determined effort will be made in the next two or three days, in fact has already started, by the business men, to get the strikers to return to work. I am not so hopeful of the success of this move but some of the business men think it is worth trying, and the Lord knows they are willing to help do what they can."[14] On the same date and similar in tone was a letter from Charles Lawton of the Quincy Mining Company to William R. Todd: "Should the sheriff and Citizens' Alliance be successful in riding [sic] this country of the paid agitators, I will at once take steps to still further reduce the force [of Waddell-Mahon men at Quincy Mine]. However, I do not think it wise to run any chances of taking action prematurely."[15]

With the mining companies frustrated by the strikers' resolve and the members of the Citizens' Alliance and their minions having placed a virtual "X" on Italian Hall's doors as a place of radicalism, host to such noted radicals as Carlo Tresca and "many of the local little parasites," it is no wonder that on the same day as MacNaughton's letter to Shaw reported a coming decisive action, a Calumet labor spy reported back to his handlers: "*Two letters threatening union store and Italian hall.*"[16] Both Italian Hall and the WFM union store had, according to a labor spy who was partial to the company, received threatening letters, just a week before the tragedy at Italian Hall.

In addition to threats of violence, on December 18, 1913, a slew of Western Union "night letters" cluttered the desks of members of the House of Representatives' Committee on Rules in Washington, D.C. The letters came from concerned members of the Copper Country oligarchy, including a letter from the Citizens' Alliance that was signed by Michael Messner (remember this name) and James A. Cruse (Houghton County sheriff), and the entire Copper Country Commercial Club (CCCC) (signed by Joseph W. Selden, president, and G. L. Price, secretary). The letters were very dramatic. As an example of the tone of these letters, one from CCCC president Selden read: "The entire citizenship of the Copper District and the united sentiment of your whole congressional district calls upon you to cease any further efforts in the interest of Moyer, Mahoney and other leaders of the Western Federation of Miners. . . . This is from those who know the real sentiments of the entire district." J. H. Rice, owner of the *Daily Mining Gazette*, wrote, "The strike and disturbing conditions in this section are over. A majority of the men are at work and the remainder are preparing to go to work. An investigation at this time will retard rather than clear up the situation, and knowing that you want to aid and assist the workers, the business men and in fact all the people in your district, I strongly urge you to use your influence against the introduction of a resolution for an investigation of this district."[17]

What the Copper Country oligarchy, mining companies, and the Citizens' Alliance feared in a federal investigation, which did occur after the events at Italian Hall, was a peeling back of the veil that could expose the true rigid and hegemonic nature of Copper Country society. Such an investigation could reveal a copper mining district tightly controlled by a single group of men, and that was bad for business in the Copper Country, let alone any federal regulations on the copper mining industry passed as a result of a federal investigation.

Then on December 20, 1913, just four days before the tragedy at Italian Hall, Houghton County Sheriff James Cruse offered a subtle but ominous warning. In a statement printed in the *Daily Mining Gazette*, Cruse notified the Copper Country populace:

> Houghton County for the last four months has been the scene of lawlessness and disorder. Working men have been assaulted and intimidated, and the *sacred right of citizenship* violated.
>
> Every man who wants to work will be protected, and the Sheriff and his deputies, with the co-operation of the *citizens*, will make this guarantee effective.[18]

Perhaps the most telling phrase in Sheriff Cruse's warning is "with the co-operation of the citizens, will make this guarantee effective." Seemingly, Sheriff Cruse was implying that he would unleash the power of the Copper Country's "citizens" on the "foreign" strikers. This was a somewhat obvious reference and restatement of the aims to action advocated by the fervently pro–mining company Citizens' Alliance. Seemingly, the Copper Country's "citizens" were honing the sharp blades of their discontent at the area's "foreign" population, and one of the particular targets of those with the "sacred rights of citizenship" was Italian Hall.

A final indication that some type of violence was coming to Calumet appears in a December 22, 1913, letter from Nathan Drew of the National Erectors' Association in New York to C&H lawyer Albert Petermann in Calumet. This letter, composed just two days before the tragedy at Italian Hall, presages an act of impending violence. In discussing the merits of a female labor spy from Foster's detective agency set to be deployed to the Calumet area, Drew wrote Petermann, "I have assured her that she will not be called upon to do any work that is unwomanly, and also that she can rest assured that whatever she accomplishes is for the real and best interests of the miners themselves, that no one will be injured by whatever she does except a group of criminal and lawless labor agitators."[19]

All of this firsthand information from labor spies, from the documents of the Citizens' Alliance, from declarations of Houghton County law enforcement officials, from WFM media, and from correspondence between mine management points to the conclusion that Italian Hall was the likely target of retribution by members of the Citizens' Alliance, who were acting in collusion, on some level, with the mining companies. The Citizens' Alliance, the mining companies, and the Copper Country oligarchy had had enough of the strike. This much was clear. Something needed to be done, and it was clear to these men that action needed to be taken to end the strike. This is not to state with absolute certitude that the Citizens' Alliance, with the knowledge of the mining companies, sent someone to the hall to commit a mass murder, but a good deal of firsthand documentation would indicate that the "foreign" agitators who often assembled in Italian Hall were being targeted for "something definite in the form of aggressive action."[20]

Unaware or undaunted, plans were made accordingly for the festivities, which promised one of the most important things for a Copper Country winter—clothes. A December 24 *Miners' Bulletin* article titled "Miners' 'Kiddies' Christmas" reported that presents from Santa Claus were coming from as far away as Chicago:

> A number of societies about the country are preparing to make the Christmas of 1913 a memorial one for the children of the striking miners of this district. Christmas toys and substantial gifts such as clothing and shoes are being gathered at several different points and will be forwarded as soon as possible. Some of these good things may be a little late in arriving, but they are coming and will be here within a few days. The following from the "Chicago Daily News" gives some idea of what is going on in the way of making a "Merry Christmas" for our little tads.
>
> "Santa Claus promises to come, after all, to the children of the miners in Calumet, Mich., who are out of work," said Miss Agnes Nestor, president of the Chicago Women's Trade Union league. At the office of the league, 166 West Washington Street, little wooly hoods, stout shoes, warm flannels and coats are daily coming in.[21]

Christmas Eve was shaping up to be a remarkable time in the angst-filled and violence-spotted strike, though there were several ominous signs popping up just hours before the terrible event. In the same edition of the *Bulletin*, an article titled "Guerillas Raid Union Store" recounted a raid on the Keweenaw Miners Union store in Ahmeek. Keweenaw County Sheriff John Hepting, a former friend to the WFM, accompanied a "mob of Citizens' Alliance" men in raiding, searching, and shutting down the WFM store for hours. This raid apparently was conducted without a search warrant, just like the siege at South Range on December 10. As the article indicated, the December campaign of orchestrated intimidation and violence continued unabated and was actually openly sanctioned by law enforcement officials in the Copper Country.[22]

There was even an implication that people were directly warned of trouble at Italian Hall hours before the actual tragedy. In the investigation of a labor spy in regards to the events at Italian Hall, a man by the name of Borchgrevink told the operative that a Mr. Marson warned some children of danger at Italian Hall a few minutes before the disaster. Marson advised the children that it would be better for them to go home "because there is much trouble in getting the candys" and that "there might be some trouble."[23] This was not the only report of a last-minute warning. *Työmies* reported on December 26, 1913, that "a certain mining captain called Kolli, had told a relative of his in the morning [of December 24] that something terrible would happen, what was going to happen the captain had not said but it seems his statement had some connections with the happenings of the afternoon."[24] According to these sources, there were rumors of trouble at Italian Hall hours before the event, but to those inside the hall on Christmas Eve, the party was on, and the upcoming tragedy was likely the last thing that would have entered their minds.

The Tragedy Firsthand

After the notorious call of "Fire!," as people inside Italian Hall were scrambling about for their lives, panicked partygoers headed in a mass toward the hall's five-foot-nine-inch wide stairway. Mrs. Lesch, an organizer of the party, later told a C&H labor spy posing as a journalist that there was reported to be a problem with the fifth step (from the bottom) of the stairway ❶.

Further recollections of the tragedy from those who lived it follow:

> I went in the Italian Hall look for my baby, my boy; I had a boy up there. I was tired and dry and was in the saloon for about fifteen minutes with my friend Batista Rastello. Then we was there, take a glass of beer sat down by the table and I hear upstairs big noise, running of children, something like that. I was going to see for my baby. . . . Then I opened the door [from the saloon into the stairwell of Italian Hall] and I see the stairs full of people coming down; chuck full from the bottom to the top.[25]

This was the experience of Italian striker John Sandretto ❷, from Wolverine, a mining location north of Calumet. He was not in the hall, having been at a funeral earlier in the day. While drinking in the saloon on the lower floor of the building that housed Italian Hall, his world must have stood still while he heard the panic upstairs and could not get to his son.

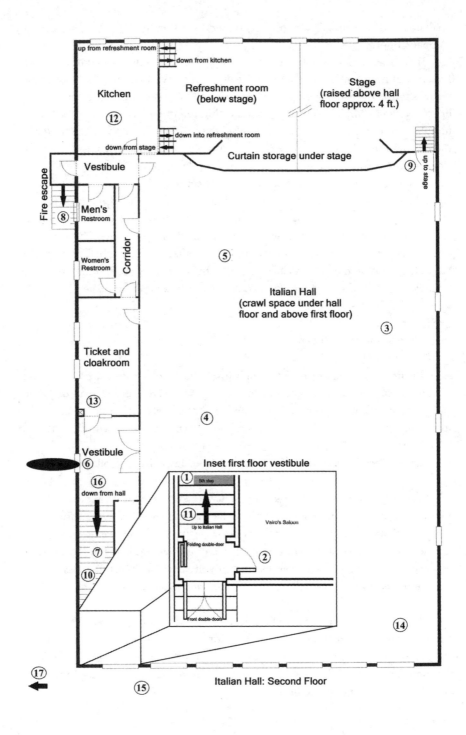

up from refreshment room

down from kitchen

Kitchen

⑫

**Refreshment room
(below stage)**

**Stage
(raised above hall
floor approx. 4 ft.)**

down into refreshment room

down from stage

Curtain storage under stage

⑨

up to stage

Vestibule

Fire escape

↓

Men's
Restroom

⑧

**Women's
Restroom**

Corridor

⑤

**Italian Hall
(crawl space under hall
floor and above first floor)**

③

**Ticket and
cloakroom**

⑬

④

Vestibule

⑥

⑯

down from hall

Inset first floor vestibule

① 5th step

⑪

Up to Italian Hall

Folding double-door

Vairo's Saloon

②

↓

⑦

⑩

Front double-doors

⑭

⑰

←

⑮

Italian Hall: Second Floor

For others in the hall who experienced the panic firsthand, the sweet sounds of children receiving candy, clothes, fruit, and presents from members of the Calumet WFM local's Women's Auxiliary was interrupted by absolute chaos. Charles Olson ❸, a Finnish immigrant, was in the hall for just moments before he heard the call of "Fire! Fire!":

> [I was] in the middle of the hall on the north side looking up here to the door leading to the stage on the north side and then looking at the same time out to the main entrance door, that's the door going to the stairway to see whether or not my children and wife were passing through. When I was standing a fellow come through the door, quite a big man, sealskin cap on and shook his hands and hollered, "FIRE!," "FIRE!," and turned back, and a lady took hold of him by the shoulders and wanted to keep him back but they [the crowd] got so excited they started to run.[26]

Olson was not the only person to see the man who cried "Fire!" Anna Lustig ❹ and John Burcar ❺ both gave vivid descriptions of the man, who passed through the big double doors from the second-floor vestibule into the hall, made the fateful cry, and then ran back down the stairs and out into the street. Lustig's and Burcar's descriptions of the man included the color of his coat (dark blue or black), a dark mustache, a hat pulled down over the eyes, and a Citizens' Alliance button by a coat pocket.[27] All three witnesses to the event indicated that the man cried "Fire!" at least once and maybe twice into the crowded hall. This cry of fire created an epic panic. The festivity's participants were thrown into an extremely excited situation, and a type of flight response rushed over the crowd, which included hundreds of vulnerable children.

John and Frank Sneller ❻, age seven and five, respectively, were sons of Croatian immigrants. The two boys were sitting close to the hall's stage waiting for a rare treat in the Copper Country's winter food fare: oranges. The cry of "Fire!" came, and chaos ensued. Due to their placement by the front of the stage, John and Frank were thankfully late in being pulled in the rush to the top of the stairs. What they witnessed in the vestibule area above the stairs was sadly remarkable. John saw a woman pulling her hair out in clumps, no doubt due to the panic and stress of the unfolding events, while also seeing two "young" parents pass their baby on top of the crowd of people to safety.[28]

OPPOSITE: The numbers in this drawing of the Italian Hall's second floor and first-floor vestibule correspond with the recollections and testimony of those who witnessed events, to provide a spatial understanding of people's experiences during the panic. Drawing by Gary Kaunonen.

The two young parents were Abram and Mary Niemalä ❼, who lived by No. 4 Shaft in Wolverine Location. Both parents were in their midthirties. Swept into the mass of people in the hall, Abram and Mary held their baby above their heads as they plummeted into the mass of bodies clogged on the hall's steep stairway. The child survived; Abram and Mary Niemalä did not.[29]

John and Frank managed to survive in a miraculous manner. A stranger from the building next to Italian Hall broke a window in the hall's second-floor vestibule area where the stairs ended, giving way to Italian Hall's second floor. Placing an ironing board from the building next to Italian Hall over to the sill of the window in the vestibule area, the stranger invited John and Frank to safety. Offering his hand to John and stating, "Take the little boy's (Frank) hand and walk to me," the stranger guided John and Frank over the ironing board suspended above the ground and to safety. The two young boys ran home to their family.[30]

Edwin Juntti ❽, age eleven in 1913, was also in the hall as the cry of "Fire!" rose from the crowd. Being a working-class boy unfamiliar with the finer things in life and possessing a one-track mind, Edwin and a few other children ran to the stage as people were theading for the stairs and filled their pockets with candy. This likely saved their lives because as they finished heaping handfuls of candy into their pockets, they noticed the plug of people around the door to the stairs and headed for the fire escape at the back of Italian Hall. They were successful in shimmying down the fire escape. After the Italian Hall tragedy, the Juntti family left the Copper Country, settling on a farm in South Dakota "far away from the Copper Country."[31]

Mary Lantto ❾, who was at Italian Hall for much of the day, was able to keep herself from being caught in the mass of people moving toward the fateful stairs. "I was knocked off [the chair] with my baby from that stage," she later stated, "and went on my knees near that heater. Got up from there as fast as I could and tried to hold my baby with one hand and the heater with the other so the crowd would not bring me down with them."[32] Hilda Foster ❿ was not able to avoid the crowd, and she was among the first people swept down the stairs. "I was about halfway down the stairway," she said, "and fainted there between the wall and the people. Then I found myself sitting here on a chair and a man on side of me said not to be scared, but I fainted every little while after that."[33]

Andrew Saari ⓫, who was in the hall with his two boys, one who was almost six years old and the other almost eight, heard the cry of "Fire!" and witnessed the panicked exodus toward the hall's stairway:

> I hear something like that [cry of "Fire!"] but I did not take notice of it. I had a newspaper
> and started to read that and then I looked inside where they give the candy and see no

fire. I thought they were fooling and started to read again but the people were going out so fast I thought there must be some kind of trouble. . . . Yes, looks to me as though everybody was going out.[34]

Andrew was caught in the rush. He later remarked that he tried to keep his boys "in front of me trying to keep them back so nobody would step on them." As they were swept to the stairs, people began falling in and on the mass of bodies in the stairwell—body piled on body—and Andrew, along with his two boys, was swallowed up in the heap of bodies at the bottom of the stairwell. Andrew stated that he made it about six feet away from the door at the bottom of the stairs. "There was a clear place by the door. I was laying with the rest of the people." He remembered that the mass of people "pushed me down. I hollered as long as I could but I fell down and stepped over the two boys." He had to wait for people to be taken from the top of the pile, and then some men plucked him from the mass: "One of my boys dead. I thought they would be both dead; but when they were taken up one was living."[35]

Anna Wuolukka ⑫, who was an organizer of the Christmas party, recalled that the WFM'S Women's Auxiliary did not buy candles for the festivities in the hall because the women were "afraid the children would catch fire." During the panic, Anna yelled to people that there was no fire, but this did not stem the tide of the mass heading toward the stairway. As the dead piled up, she tended to a number of children and tried to revive others who were likely already dead:

> I hollered to the people to come back that there was no fire, and they were all rushing, I could not say no more. After that my little girl come and said, "Ma, everybody is going out the window and there's a fire here" . . . [I] saw they were carrying the dead, but then I did not know what they were doing, and felt those that were dead and cold and tried to carry them and try to make them come to as much as I could.[36]

John Aho ⑬ and his family were in Italian Hall immediately before the rush to the stairs, and John recalled trying to extract people from the fateful stairway:

> I went into that stairway. I pulled some of the people into that little room and when I got in I pushed the crowd back and told them to go back in the hall that there was no fire, to go inside. As I got the crowd stopped enough I started to empty the stairway. I had been carrying the boys up into that little room, I don't know whether they were dead but they were injured; great crying done, and they were lying down. I looked there about twenty minutes and I got decided, I went and looked for my own children and wife. I found them. I stood with them and got them water.[37]

The image John portrays is one of horror as bodies piled upon bodies became a single mass of one tangled, lifeless mess: "[When trying to pull bodies from the stairway] it was all filled up. . . . They [bodies] were all laying against each other's back, crushed, and just as soon as you would take them away some would fall down and some would get stuck, just pick them away from them. Most of those that I carried were children."[38]

Oscar Hietalahti ⑭ kept his wits during the panic and attempted to open a window to get his wife and children out. When that failed, he waited for about half an hour amid the panic and screams. While in the hall at the top of the stairway, Oscar saw a man with a white button, which he described as a Citizen's Alliance button. Oscar described witnessing a monstrous act:

> [I] saw a man with a blue coat and an Alliance button, had the child under his arms and he placed his hands upon the child's neck and threw the child on the floor. I can't say whether he was alive or not, but he hung like [he was dead] from [the man's] arms. [The man] just came up through the doorway and threw him in. When my wife and I came they came in and threw a man the same way on the floor. They carried him by the neck, that's around the throat.[39]

Two previously undiscovered depositions in the Copper Country Historical Archive taken on December 29, 1913, and not affiliated with the coroner's inquest, indicate that at one point the double doors that led up to the second floor of Italian Hall were wide open, and then later closed at some point during the panic. Jenevive Sandretto ⑮, who was at Italian Hall with a friend, remembered four days after the event that

> Mrs. Renaldi and I started down stairs and when part way down I heard a lot of noise up-stairs and I said to Mrs. Renaldi: "What is all that noise?" and she said "I guess they are giving the candy to the children." We went down the stairs; the door at the foot of the stairs was open and we went out onto the side-walk, then we heard people running down stairs and we turned back to see what was going on. The doors were still open and there were some firemen there and they put everybody off the side-walk.[40]

According to another deposition from Mari Chopp ⑯, she recalled looking down the stairwell, over the piled bodies, to Italian Hall's doors at the foot of the stairwell:

> I was standing near the stage and had my (five) children with me when I heard a lot of people cry "Fire!" I did not see any fire, so was not afraid. The people rushed towards the stairway and I went after them with my children, but when I got to the head of the

stairway I saw that the stairs was full of people, piled up. . . . I could see that the door at the foot of the stairs was shut.[41]

If Sandretto's and Chopp's depositions are accurate, it is clear that the front doors, which guarded the entrance to Italian Hall, were at one point open. Then at some time after the panic ensued were closed. Perhaps there was no ill intention in closing the doors. It is very possible that officials on the scene shut the doors to keep bystanders on the sidewalk from becoming entangled in the mass of bodies piling up in the stairwell. Or, as *Työmies* indicated, perhaps there was a concerted, intentional, and nefarious attempt to trap people at the hated Italian Hall in the stairwell, effectively sealing them in a death chamber. In an oral history interview in the early 1970s, Herman Kallungi ⑰, who was in Red Jacket (Calumet) when the fire whistles blew, remembered that there was a definite attempt by a group that he identifies as Waddell men to limit the help of outsiders:

> I got up by that big Austrian Church by the depot there and I heard the fire whistles start blowing and I could tell where the fire was by the time they blew. The location . . . I stopped there because I could tell by the whistles it was in town. When I got down a little ways I could not see the smoke. There was no smoke. There was a big crowd of people in front of the Italian Hall on Seventh Street.
>
> They had a strike breaking gang there. . . When I got there . . . [the] Waddell [men] were strikebreakers. When I got there one of them on horseback was riding in front of the door. There was a narrow stairway coming down there. People were piling down. There was a door going into the tavern and they pulled a lot of them in there. But those that come down they could have saved a lot more but that goddamned Waddell man was riding back and forth in front of the door. Wouldn't let anybody help out.[42]

Chronicling the Disaster

The *Miners' Bulletin* and *Työmies* were quick to print the workers' version of the event. *Työmies* printed a rare English-language article in a special impromptu edition published on Christmas Day. The beginning of the English-language version of the article read:

> The most appalling disaster in the history of Michigan occurred last evening at the Italian Hall in Calumet where hundreds of men, women and children had gathered to witness Christmas exercises for the strikers['] children. The program which was quite lengthy had just begun when a strange man ascended the stairway, yelled "fire" and quickly made

his escape to the street. Several persons who stood near the entrance where this man appeared, state that he had his cap pulled down over his eyes, and that pinned to the lapel of his coat was a Citizen's [sic] Alliance button. At the cry of fire the great crowd arose as one and made a mad rush for the exit in the front of the building. In the rush down the stairway many fell and being unable to regain their feet were trampled to death, their bodies acting as stumbling blocks for others who followed, until the hallway was entirely blocked by the dead and dying. The fire alarm was soon sounded and those responding were forced to gain entrance to the hall by ladders at the front windows. Firemen entered the building in this manner and stopped the panic stricken crowd from further crowding into the hallway upon the dead bodies of their friends in a frantic effort to escape. The bodies in the hallway were so tightly packed that they could not be released from below, and firemen were compelled to remove the dead from the top of the stairway carrying the dead and dying back up into the hall before the stairs could be cleared. At the time the cry of fire was sounded in the hall Mrs. Annie Clemenc was making a talk to the little ones present who naturally were crowded as near the stage as possible, their little faces beaming with happiness, their hearts bounding with Christmas cheer. In less than three minutes afterward fifty of their frail little bodies were jammed and crushed in the hallway being used as a roadway over which their companions were vainly endeavoring to escape. The scene was a horrible one, and will never be effaced from the minds of those who witnessed the terrible tragedy.

The bodies of the dead were taken to a temporary morgue established in the town hall as soon as they were removed from the building. As soon as identifications were made, the bodies were removed to their homes. In some homes the mother and all the children lie cold in death, the husband and father crazed with grief. In others the mother being the only one spared has been plunged into despair and sorrow that yet dazes her, the full truth not yet dawning upon her terrified brain.[43]

It took *Työmies* and the *Miners' Bulletin* a while to collect their staff and regain their collective wits after the tragedy, but as soon as the union media outlets got their bearings, a frantic effort to collect information and data on the events at Italian Hall commenced. From this collection of information and firsthand stories, a devious picture began to emerge from the labor press on the actual events at Italian Hall.

On December 26, *Työmies* led with the headline "83 MURDERED: Christmas Celebration of Strikers Children in Calumet Made into a Criminal Sacrifice for Capital." The newspaper indicated that "a hooligan of the Citizens' Alliance yells 'FIRE' and gunmen block the passage of the panic stricken people." As we have seen from the testimony and depositions from persons with firsthand information, there was reason to believe that the events of Italian Hall were premeditated and purposeful.

The newspaper, however, went further by giving details of the preparation and staging for the event, reporting:

> We now have obtained descriptions and explanations from people who were witnesses to the happening and who verify the seemingly impossible idea that this massacre had been planned and was executed by human brutes, gunmen, and that they executed it purposely and knowing its terrible consequences. From these explanations it would appear that about twenty gunmen had gathered into the saloon below the hall, one man was sent to raise a cry of "Fire" another to turn in the fire call to the nearby fire station and when the people rushed out in terrible fire panic these monsters collected at the front door and stopped for a moment the egress of the building.[44]

The *Miners' Bulletin* was less intimate in its details of the preparation and staging of events, but did proclaim in a headline that events at Italian Hall were "A HARVEST OF DEATH: Striking Miner's [sic] Children in Christmas Joys Are Called by the Angel of Death." The article went on to report that "the fiend who caused this terrible disaster made his escape and is still at large. From persons who stood near the door it is learned that he was rather stockily built, a little under medium height, and wore his hat well pulled down over his countenance. Upon the lapel of his coat he wore a Citizens' Alliance button, is a statement made by several who got a good look at him."[45]

Työmies reported much the same—that a man dressed in good clothes donning a sealskin hat screamed "Fire!" at the door twice, which created a panic and sent people rushing toward the stairway. As a result of this, children and women formed about a four-foot-high heap in the stairwell, and a couple of questionable testimonies stated that something was dropped or left in the women's and children's path before they began to flow down the stairs. The article then indicated that men from the Citizens' Alliance and Houghton County deputies pushed away onlookers trying to help, and in a couple of instances deputies did not begin to help where aid was needed foremost by untangling the heap, but actually restrained others who were helping to untangle the heap, so that more and more victims crashed into the heap. The article also asserted that deputies held the doors closed, so that the rescue work could only be made from the top; as a result, the heap had to be there for a long time and therefore people suffocated. The article went on to state that deputies and Citizens' Alliance members stood around jeering and shaking their heads at strikers plugged up at the bottom of the pile, while upstairs in the hall a deputy twisted a five- or six year-old child's neck and dragged a man by the neck so to strangle the man's last breath of life, leaving thumbprints around his throat.[46]

The Grisly Aftermath

Who yelled "Fire!"? Were the doors held shut by company thugs? How many people died? Did a fire whistle blow in Calumet? The mystery around events related to Italian Hall swirled almost as soon as people began to realize that a tragedy of epic proportions had just occurred. Now the daunting task of dealing with the dead settled over the entire Copper Country because by the sheer number of familial relations, the Italian Hall disaster brought incredible misery to thousands of people. Upon visiting the undertaker's office on Christmas Day, Charles Moyer, president of the WFM, was reported to have fainted and a day later, on December 26, said in the "Finnish" funeral parlor, "This is a sorrowful thing, boys. I have witnessed all kinds of experiences. I have been in the bull pen in Colorado and it won't be long before I will be buried too."[47] Moyer's words were almost eerily prophetic because just hours after uttering those words he was bum-rushed, shot, and "deported" from the Copper Country.

In attempting to sort out the final toll of the Italian Hall's misery, even an accurate count of the dead is difficult to determine because of the enormous amount of confusion surrounding the event. Along with the chaotic circumstances of the actual event, lackluster documentation processes of the time add to the difficulty in determining just how many people died from the panic at Italian Hall. Generally, many agree that seventy-three or seventy-four people died, but research into the local press provides alternative calculations of the gruesome toll of the dead. On December 25 and December 26, *Työmies* printed a list of names of Italian Hall dead. On December 31, the *Miners' Bulletin* followed suit. The *Calumet News*, part of the kept press, even published names and a toll of the dead. *Työmies*'s accounting of the dead got as high as eighty-three, while the *Calumet News*'s toll began at eighty but was later lowered.

From the quickly organized lists of the area's press, combined with the official record of those who perished in Italian Hall from the Houghton County coroner's inquest, a revised and frustratingly vague figure of seventy-five to seventy-nine persons deceased is possible. These numbers could possibly be even higher as some news outlets claimed that a number of the dead were taken home instead of being brought to the haphazardly organized morgue in the Red Jacket City Hall. The *Calumet News*, the first media outlet on the scene, reported, "More than seventy-five dead have been accounted for, and it is estimated there are from six to eight others who were removed to their homes by parents and friends before the authorities arrived on the scene."[48] There was, indeed, great confusion even two days later, as the *Calumet News* reported on December 26, "While authorities have done their utmost to make the list of identified dead published below as accurate and complete as possible, the total, seventy-two, does not correspond with the total number of dead bodies reported from the morgues, which is seventy-five."[49]

Of course, the lists of the dead do not include those who barely escaped being crushed in the mass of bodies. As with the dead, many of those injured and convalescing in Calumet-area hospitals were children. Worse, a number of the injured children's siblings had died in the panic. According to the *Calumet News*, "Irene Ala, aged 7, daughter of Herman Ala, who was killed; Mellie Tolvi, aged 8, Raymbaultown; Lempi Kenttala, aged 9, Raymbaultown; All of the above are in the C&H hospital. Their injuries consist of bruises received in the crush and nervous shock sustained. Waino Saari, aged 7, Pewabic street, Laurium, brother of Yalmer Saari, who was killed. Patient in the Laurium hospital; One patient in the Tamarack hospital, whose name could not be ascertained."[50]

Statistics, gruesome statistics, bear witness to the horror of the night. Of the deceased working-class folks, fifty or more were children under the age of thirteen; at least two of the fifty children were babes in arms. Twenty-nine mothers and children died together on the stairway. Five groups of siblings died in the hall: the three Heikkinen brothers, the three Klarich girls, the three Mihelchich siblings, the three or possibly four Montanen siblings, and the two Myllykangas boys sadly all were crushed to death in Italian Hall's stairwell.[51]

The deaths of the above groupings of neighbors, youngsters, and brothers and sisters, and the untimely demise of other children, were perhaps the greatest source of the misery at Italian Hall. Naturally, a union party featuring candy and presents had hundreds of children who were hoping to be kids once again amid the very adult realities of living in a violent strike zone. As heart-wrenching as the loss of a child's life could be, Houghton County Prosecuting Attorney Anthony Lucas, who was questioning people during the coroner's inquest, further denigrated the children who were at Italian Hall by blaming them for causing the panic. During his questioning of Mrs. Louis Lesch, he asked, "The purpose of this jury is to find out what caused this and what brought it on and *probably the children themselves are to blame?* We got to get all the facts we can."[52] Lucas, who was of Croatian background, had a difficult job. Prior to the events at Italian Hall, Lucas had been seen, much like Judge O'Brien, as a friend of labor. However, while O'Brien gave a sizable donation of $1,000 to the Italian Hall families, Lucas berated a witness and disparaged the children who died in Italian Hall. His actions during the coroner's inquest placed him squarely at odds with his working-class background and constituency. A labor spy reported, "A Croatian said in Dunns [the Calumet union hall] that he was going to lay for Lucas some night in an alley. I will fix this _____. He is no good."[53]

Another feature of the Italian Hall casualties was that because of the successful efforts at multiethnic organization by the WFM, the Italian Hall dead were a multiethnic contingent. Persons of Finnish background, however, were numerically the most affected by the ghastly events. Approximately fifty of the Italian Hall dead were of Finnish ancestry. Many Finns had sorrowful tales, but the Manleys were especially affected as they lost three persons and one future family member. While her husband, Herman, stayed at home with the couple's youngest son, Elina Manley (who was pregnant at the time) and her four-year-old son, Wesley, along with Elina's ten- or eleven-year-old sister, Saida Raja, went to the hall. All were caught in the crush of humanity.[54]

As can be imagined, after reading descriptions of the events at Italian Hall in the *Miners' Bulletin* and *Työmies*, union folks were furious. The copper companies, Houghton County law enforcement personnel, and the Citizens' Alliance were bolstering their forces and battening their proverbial hatches for the worst. On December 27, 1913, Quincy Mining Company general manager Charles Lawton, living in the strike zone, wrote William R. Todd, safely tucked away in New York, of a mining district on the brink: "The Copper Country is again in an over-excited condition. The great calamity at Calumet on Christmas eve, where seventy-two poor people lost their lives naturaly [*sic*] has wrought the people up; and Mr. Moyer's every step since to make capital out of that great calamity has added fuel to the flames, until everything is in a very boiling condition."[55]

It was difficult for the WFM, and President Charles Moyer, to know exactly what to do. The initial instinct was to close off and turn inward, as a C&H labor spy reported:

> Moyer addressed the meeting today in regard to burying and helping the strikers whose families were killed. 'We, the entire labor union of the United States, are going to look after them all.' (Moyer) appointed committees to see them all tonight and instruct them not to accept one cent from the Citizens' Alliance or anyone else, that he would see that every one was taken care of. Committees are composed of 38 Finns, 6 Swedes, 4 Italians, 8 Croatians and 4 Hungarians.[56]

Though innuendo and rumor swirled around the Copper Country's winter sky, and accusations in the labor *and* kept press indicated that someone or some group was culpable for the events at Italian Hall, no named instigator of the disaster was even so much as arrested. There was even a Houghton County coroner's inquest held in late December, but this perhaps added more confusion than clarity to the events at Italian Hall. Oddly, with all the innuendo implicating them, no one with a known or open association with the Citizens' Alliance testified at the coroner's inquest. Houghton County legal officers never called anyone associated with the Citizens'

Alliance or even the sheriff's deputies to dispel allegations or clear up misinformation, even though certified statements in *Työmies* and eye witnesses directly implicated the Citizens' Alliance and/or the deputies with the terrible events of that night.

In reading over the text from the coroner's inquest, it is clear that it was a "show trial," designed to confuse and confound rather than confront the complex occurrences of that fateful night. This does not dismiss the brave actions of those who testified at the inquest. Given the December campaign of intimidation and violence, testifying was an act of heroism by those affected by the horrible events at Italian Hall. However, it was apparent that Houghton County officials were simply going through the motions. The inquest was conducted because something needed to be done to quiet the angry Copper Country workers and give the outside world an impression that Houghton County officials were taking action with regard to the tragic events. Thus, and quite sadly, little can be taken away from the testimony at the coroner's inquest. In most cases, Houghton County officials did not even bother to hire qualified translators for the inquest, and thus testimony was mostly taken from those who could speak English. Additionally, of the hundreds upon hundreds of people in Italian Hall that afternoon, only seventy testified.[57] Houghton County legal officials had no intention of trying to find the man who cried "Fire!" in Italian Hall; the inquest was just a way to feign action, fake empathy, and frustrate the facts.

If the above seems too far-fetched to imagine, that local Houghton County officials would purposefully bumble and confound the investigation of such a horrible event, consider local Houghton County law enforcement officials' treatment of violence in three other high-profile incidents. In the Seeberville shootings, the accused gun thugs were able to avoid arrest for a time, and only after public outcry were they jailed. Of the six arrested for murder, four were sentenced to manslaughter, one was set free, and the one who supposedly fled the country—Thomas Raleigh, mentioned previously—was actually still working as a gun thug and labor spy for C&H in New York. In the Fazekas shooting, though not deadly, a group of Houghton County deputy sheriffs faced no justice because of the rigged Houghton County grand jury. Even though one sacrificial lamb was sent forth from the gang of deputies that shot into a group of striking workers, the grand jury sent a no true bill to Houghton County prosecutors, thus ending any search for the man who shot (in the back of the head) and nearly killed a fourteen-year-old girl in broad daylight. Lastly, in the tally of injustices for the Copper Country's workers, Houghton County officials charged two men with murder in the Dally-Jane shootings, but could not get a true bill through a rigged grand jury, so they arrested a person who was an alcoholic and later charged the entire WFM with conspiracy. If the families of those who had loved ones die at Italian Hall thought they were getting an actual inquest or a sincere effort to bring somebody to justice for the night's event, they were sadly mistaken.

There was no way the Copper Country oligarchy—mine managers, lawyers, businessmen, and "good citizens"—would allow a sincere attempt to get to the bottom of what happened at Italian Hall go public. There was too much risk in the truth. It was standard operating procedure for the mining companies and Houghton County officials to impede justice—just ask fugitive Thomas Raleigh in New York—and the tragic events at Italian Hall were no different. Most everyone in the Copper Country not partial to the mining company perspective was looking for someone to blame, someone to jail, or someone to lynch for the events at Italian Hall, but that never happened. Even a hundred years later, people are still looking for answers, and these answers cannot be found in trying to tease facts out of a "show trial" like the Italian Hall coroner's inquest.

People did go to jail for the events at Italian Hall, but it was not anyone associated with the Citizens' Alliance. Instead, Copper Country law enforcement officials put employees from the Työmies Publishing Company in jail for publishing accounts of the events at Italian Hall. *Työmies* explicitly blamed the Citizens' Alliance for orchestrating the event in at least three editions. *Työmies*'s special issue Christmas Day extra directly accused the Citizens' Alliance of planning and carrying out the event. Then, on December 26, as a fund for families affected by the events at Italian Hall was gathered by the *good citizens* of the community, *Työmies* printed: "The money offered from the Citizens' Alliance will not be accepted," ostensibly because "a Citizens' Alliance thug [*huligaani*] yelled the fire alarm and gun hounds closed the exit path, which was overrun by people in terror."[58]

Finally, on December 27, *Työmies* published oath-sworn certification, gathered by WFM organizers Mor Oppman and Heimer Mikko, of a damning ten-point list that fully implicated the Citizens' Alliance and sheriff's deputies in fostering the tragic events. For the Citizens' Alliance and affiliated *good citizenry*, this ten-point list was apparently the limit. That same day editor Severi Alanne and four others from the *Työmies* staff were arrested and charged with sedition for publishing a labor perspective on the tragic events at Italian Hall. *Työmies*'s readership responded by sending thousands of petitions to the desk of Michigan's governor Ferris. Not wanting to add fuel to the already fiery situation, Ferris facilitated the dismissal of the case, though Alanne and the others paid $1,000 for bail, which was a large amount of money at that time.[59]

Funerals for the Italian Hall victims took place in a solemn, somber setting. For organized labor in the Copper Country, and for Charles Moyer who was in Hancock at the time of the panic but had been "deported" from the Copper Country on December 26, it was important for union men and women to bury union men and women. The *Miners' Bulletin* assured its readers, "The wants [of those affected by Italian Hall] would be attended to by the organization at whose head [Moyer] stands.

. . . The funerals will be held under the auspices of organized labor, and no funds other than those donated by such organizations will be accepted." A special train delivered people from points south in the Copper Country north into Calumet, and yet another train came from Negaunee, traveling over 100 miles from the Marquette Iron Range. Services for the dead were held in five different churches: St. John's, St. Mary's, and St. Joseph's Catholic churches, and the Finnish Apostolic and Finnish Synod Lutheran churches.[60]

With only a four-month respite from the funerals of the victims of the Seeberville shootings, the streets of Calumet were, once again, the scene of absolute misery as a long funeral procession of around 5,000 mourners moved through an estimated 20,000 people who watched as the caskets of the Italian Hall deceased moved through the city streets and out to Lake View Cemetery. The *Miners' Bulletin* described the march from Calumet to the cemetery in detail: "The sad procession was headed by fifteen hearses, an automobile following carrying three caskets. Forty of the little white coffins coming next in line being borne by members of the Miners' Union." The somber march led to graves in Protestant and Catholic sections of the cemetery. Altogether, thirteen undertakers assisted in preparing the bodies for burial. The ceremonies at Lake View Cemetery lasted until nightfall.[61]

The Tragedy on Film

A "motion picture" outfit ordered by the union from Chicago to film the woeful events of the parade from "near the No. 5 Tamarack Shafthouse," where they had an "unobstructed view," captured the parade in all its somber significance. Luckily, the union had the foresight to create "dummy films" of the crew's work, because someone or some group stole the dummy films and filming machine from the cameraman's hotel room in Red Jacket. The *Miners' Bulletin* triumphantly remarked about the dastardly event, "January 7, 1914, "Film Thief Foiled": "The two legged skunk who stole some film reels from the Michigan hotel room in Calumet, thinking they were the films of the funeral and parade held there on Sunday December 28th had all his pains for nothing as the genuine films were locked in the safe of the miners union office until a few days later when they were safely transported to Chicago." As indicated in the article, the real reels of the funeral footage were stored in the Calumet local's safe. Union members and sympathizers pinned the heist on the Citizens' Alliance, leaving many to wonder if "the Citizens' Alliance would stop at nothing." The images and moving pictures captured by the cameraman in Calumet and at Lake View Cemetery toured the county as a way of soliciting funds to help families of the Italian Hall tragedy, and raise funds for the strike and for the WFM.[62]

A known copy of the film is not in existence, so the gripping moving footage of the funeral parade has been lost for 100 years, but recent research unearthed the next best thing: a full and vivid description of the film from Victor Talking Machine Company executive S. W. "Harry" Goldsmith.

Before examining the contents of the moving picture and the associated images and lecture that went along with the production, it should be noted that Goldsmith was hostile, very hostile, to organized labor. From his Chicago offices at the Victor Talking Machine Company, Goldsmith offers this primary critique of the film before giving a more formal appraisal of the union presentation and film production: "The picture is punk indeed. I would not give a nickel for it or its drawing value. The lecturer gives out a bunch of rot which will take with a class, but no thinking man would believe half of what he heard."[63]

Viewing the presentation and moving picture show in Chicago's Empire Theater, Goldsmith, who presumably imagined himself to be a "thinking man," explains that the venue is at the heart of what he refers to as "the very vortex of a so-called labor district" on the corner of Madison and Union Streets. Impressed with the theater, Goldsmith compares it to the Calumet Theater, and relates that the entrance is well billed with a "touter" out front shouting, "Pictures of the Calumet Disaster." Admission to the presentation and film was ten cents. In the theater's lobby are a "half-a-dozen or more photographs of scenes up there and also one [photograph] of about a dozen bodies lying close together ready for the undertaker's work."[64]

Goldsmith then goes on to describe in detail the hour-long presentation of events in the Copper Country, which consists of a lecturer presenting lantern slides of the Copper Country landscape, being careful to point out the differences between the houses of miners and the houses of mining company executives. Noting that the presenter uses a "modulated tone" with "good English," Goldsmith writes that after the depiction of wealth disparity in the Copper Country, the "climax" of the slide presentation is the ending, which features "a group of bodies naked except for a sheet thrown over them, leaving exposed the faces and lower limbs." These are images of the Italian Hall dead, and as Goldsmith recounts, "The desire to develop a truly human interest story is pronounced. With a shaking voice the lecturer concludes his address with attention called to the film which is to portray unmistakably the recital of the war now under way between capital and labor in the Calumet region."[65]

When describing the film, Goldsmith goes into detail: "The very introductory title to the motion picture is in contradiction to the speaker's words. It mentions the disaster costing seventy-four lives, whereas the speaker in his talk calls attention to the loss of eighty lives by the cry of fire by a man who eight witnesses in an inquest testify wore the button of the Citizen's Alliance." He continues the description of the film's content: "The picture of the Italian Hall is shown and also the Finnish church with large numbers crowding their way into the edifice. Next is shown the bodies being taken out and finally the long parade with the story of the disaster told in the sight of scores of coffins being carried on the shoulders of men, and they plod along through the snow mutely, even sullenly, as though driven along by some unseen hand—possibly a Moyer."[66]

Quite predictably, as an executive of a media technology company, Goldsmith gives a pointed critique of the production quality and value of the moving picture:

> The titles are far from attractive. They appear to have been made by amateurs and contain absolutely nothing of an inflammatory nature. Were it not for the fact that so appalling a tragedy as occurred up north was pictured and my personal interest in that community, I do not believe I would walk across the street to see so uninteresting a film.
>
> The picture as a whole is not one that could be called a credit to a camera man. It is rather poorly developed—lacks that clearness essential to high grade work. It is much too long for the subject it portrays and will likely be a very poor drawing card. It will attract a first audience but one who has seen it will never suggest that others do likewise because of the interest it holds.[67]

So, assuredly not a rave review from this film critic, Goldsmith advises his contact, who is assumedly either a member of the Citizens' Alliance or a mining company higher-up, that a stenographer should be brought down to Chicago and a full documentation of the presentation and film should be made.[68] Goldsmith's review does give some very interesting and intimate details of a lost treasure. It also documents the efforts of the WFM to raise funds for the families of the Italian Hall disaster. Despite Goldsmith's lackluster review, attempts by the WFM to raise funds using such new and innovative technology were significant: here was the labor movement using state-of-the-art media to get out its message. This was a very significant venture in the movement to bring the class struggle to people at a distance. People in far-off places like Chicago and New York were watching moving pictures of the struggle of efforts to organize the Michigan copper miners.

People back in Calumet were also watching union activities, but in person, and in addition were infiltrating those activities as the region's workers attempted to pick up the pieces after the Italian Hall disaster. In a dastardly ploy to monitor and subvert the union after the events at Italian Hall, the mining companies hired at least two labor spies to infiltrate the WFM in Calumet. The first spy, code-named "Operative #1," had an ingenious cover; he was a socialist writer from Denver, home of WFM headquarters. He gained almost immediate and unfettered access to WFM activities in Calumet. The other operative, code-named "Operative #2," had a unique and manipulative mission. She, a comely looking Mexican woman, was to pose as a relief aid worker to the families of those who lost loved ones in Italian Hall, while spying on union activities in Calumet. There was a lot of cloak-and-dagger activity going on around Calumet, and the spies hired by the mining companies were very good at their job. At one point when Operative #2 thought she had been "made" by the WFM, she wrote her handler asking, "Could you work it to have me arrested? It might aid sympathy. Charge me with being a conspirator or agitator and have no evidence to hold me. I wouldn't fancy being held long."[69] Eventually, Operative #2 had an apparent breakdown in light of her subterfuge. Robert J. Foster, head of Foster's Industrial and Detective Bureau, wrote C&H Attorney Albert E. Petermann (and sent a copy of the letter to Jim MacNaughton of C&H) of #2's problems, "The operator is practically played out and a nervous wreck, and I have discontinued her services."[70]

In addition to these two operatives who were "planted" at roughly the same time, there was another spy who was apparently spying on the other two spies. A January 16, 1914, report from this third spy detailed the arrival of the Operatives #1 and #2: "A new man, writer for a Socialist magazine, description; Five feet ten, well dressed, black suit, gray checkered long overcoat, high turned down collar, horseshoe pin in the tie, light complexion and is a German from Denver. Also a Spanish woman here, going around with Rickard, stopping at Central Hotel."[71] While Operative #2's mission was to spy on the WFM, and especially William Rickard, the president of Calumet's local, Operative #1 was charged with the task of finding the man who cried "Fire!" at Italian Hall.

CHAPTER 9

Fire!?

I took the chance and started about the Christmas disaster and he seemed to become nervous and his action was very like [that] of a man who is afraid to be detected, he felt his hat and his collar as if he would feel nervous at once, and I also saw his face is become more red as before but I could not swear.

—Operative #1's report from an interview with the man
suspected of crying "Fire!" at Italian Hall

THE ABSOLUTE CHAOS SURROUNDING THE HORRIBLE AND TRAGIC EVENTS AT Italian Hall had no precedent in Michigan history and was on disastrous par with tragic events in American labor history such as the deaths at the Triangle Shirtwaist Factory in New York City. A massive crowd gathered around the hall minutes after the events unfolded, and a morbid interest surrounded the events thereafter. Shock waves registered and radiated from the epicenter of the tragedy in Calumet to other locations in the United States as well as internationally. Newspapers in Chicago, New York, and Boston (among other places) carried news of the tragedy, the "disaster," in Calumet. As we have already seen, the Western Federation of Miners (WFM) distributed filmed footage of the funeral parade and funeral. Calumet, and the victims of the events at Italian Hall, had sadly taken center stage in the class struggle of one of Michigan's greatest strikes.

This chapter addresses the issue of who cried "Fire!" at Italian Hall. The person who supposedly yelled the dastardly word (or words) at Italian Hall has never been brought to justice, and the mystery surrounding this event has grown over the years. Through all of the mystery, one thing has been lacking—firsthand accounts of the search for the man who cried "Fire!" This, perhaps, has been *the* glaring omission of past works written on the Italian Hall tragedy. This chapter provides not one but two accounts of the search for the person who yelled "Fire!"

Almost immediately after the events at the hall, word was getting around that the terrible events were precipitated by a rogue assailant who had yelled "Fire!," maybe once or maybe twice before fleeing the hall. The English- and Finnish-language labor press printed versions of the events, and laid culpability directly at the door of the Citizens' Alliance. Charles Moyer nearly lost his life for this assertion, and the Työmies Publishing Company paid the price for printing this perspective with at least five of its staff arrested. The hunt for the man who cried "Fire!" at Italian Hall was on in the Copper Country.

The reasons for an absence in identifying the man who cried "Fire!" are many. As can be imagined, there was absolute chaos immediately after the event, and that sense of chaos, tinged with heartbreaking confusion, has lasted for over 100 years. Rumor and innuendo implicated many; it is likely, given the imperfection of human nature, that almost everyone at the time of the event had heard of someone who was probably the person who yelled "Fire!" Some guesses as to who made the fateful utterance were more likely than others to have merit depending on social affiliations, connections to area officials, and ties to organizations like the WFM or the "Company." Unionists were sure that someone in the employ of the mining companies, possibly via the Citizens' Alliance, had done the dirty deed. Names of culprits were likely on the lips of every person in every blind pig, gin mill, and saloon in the Copper Country. However, sifting out fact from fiction in finding the man who yelled "Fire!" became the crucial and ultimately unsuccessful act in attempting to find closure in this terrible and tragic event. There was an active and dogged search for the man who had screamed "Fire!" into a crowded social hall, but names of people who may have cried "Fire!" have evaded the historical record—until now.

The problem was not so much discerning whether there was a man who cried "Fire!" at Italian Hall; most people agreed that the call of "Fire!" went out. It was identifying who it was and then finding the man that presented the main problem. There were two decent and quite similar descriptions of the man. These descriptions were reported in the labor press and were given during a coroner's inquest shortly after the event. In this inquest, at least two different people who stood within a stone's throw of the man gave good characterizations regarding his appearance. Anna Lustig, who was only nine or ten feet from the hall's double-door entrance, testified about the man, "A man called 'FIRE!' and then another man, I did not hear, it was not so loud; and a man with a 'Citizens Alliance' button on . . . (the button was) right here on his left side. A little above his pocket . . . twice I heard [the call of 'FIRE!'] . . . he was a good built man and dressed up good and had a cap on . . . he was fair [in complexion] . . . had a rather dark, but not black (coat)."[1]

John Burcar, a thirteen-year-old boy, had a very definite description of the man: "I was halfway [between the stage and a window] and saw the man come in and looked at him and saw he was kind of dark in the face and had a dark mustache, had a long overcoat with the collar turned up and had a christy [hat] and put it down over his eyes and the pin put in his pocket." Burcar went on to testify that the man's coat had a turned-up fur collar, that his mustache was a black color, that the man was short and stout, and that he had a Citizens' Alliance pin on his right side coat pocket.[2] Added to these descriptions, on December 26 *Työmies* reported, "The man who ran from the saloon yelling 'Fire' is not known nor has he been found but several will testify that he wore a button of the Citizens Alliance on his breast, and he was a deputy or some other volunteer who had sworn to drive the Western Federation from this district as the oath of the Citizens Alliance explains."[3]

The management at Quincy mine, which was some ten miles away from Calumet, was also looking for information on the events at Italian Hall. A December 26, 1913, letter from Quincy's president, William R. Todd, to general manager Charles Lawton indicated that Quincy's force of labor spies should be on the lookout for information: "In connection with the unfortunate disaster at Italian Hall, Wednesday evening, we mentioned to Mr. Davis to-day that possibly No. 15 might be able to secure some information regarding this situation, and asked that they instruct this man to do what he could along this line."[4] The Copper Country was consumed with finding the man who cried "Fire!"

Some six months later, the search for this man was still on most everyone's mind, and especially those sympathetic to organized labor. A labor spy reported on June 6, 1914, that "socialists had a meeting in the back of Tommei's store. The man who sold shrubbery for years was at the meeting. The meeting was in regard to the detective who said he saw the man run out of the Italian Hall."[5] This was not much to go on, but this bit of documentary evidence shows that this man and the events of Italian Hall were still on the Copper Country's collective consciousness, and neither was going away anytime soon.

Speculation on just who cried "Fire!" at Italian Hall continues to this day in the works of author Steve Lehto. His reconstruction of the events in two works is largely a combination of guesswork and embellished writing. In his first work on the events at Italian Hall, *Death's Door: The Truth behind Michigan's Largest Mass Murder*, Lehto claims to unravel Michigan's largest mass murder without offering a person or persons to be held accountable for the cry of "Fire!" Via a loose playing with sources and poor documentation, Lehto's work perhaps confuses the question of who cried "Fire!" at Italian Hall more than it advances an understanding of the context for the event and the search at that time to identify and locate a person or persons responsible for the event.

In a more recent offering, *Shortcut: The Seeberville Murders and the Dark Side of the American Dream*, about the strike-related shootings in Seeberville, Lehto offers a curiously placed three-page chapter on the events at Italian Hall. Buried in the middle section of the book is a historically fictionalized reconstruction of Lehto's vision of the Italian Hall disaster. With the creation of a brief narrative containing intimate details of the events at Italian Hall, Lehto lays out assumptions for why he thinks Edward Manley, the captain of the Waddell-Mahon strikebreaking force in Calumet, is the man who cried "Fire!" at Italian Hall. The problem is there are no sources for the intimate details Lehto provides. According to Lehto:

> A few hours into the party, a Waddell Mahon strikebreaker from New York named Edward Manley decided to break up the party. . . . Manley entered the Hall at the street entrance and climbed the flight of stairs to the second floor. There were still some people milling around in the vestibule at the top of the stairs. . . . Manley stepped into the main hall through a pair of doors which swung both ways. . . . The room was still quite crowded even though many people had already gone home. . . . Manley turned toward the stage and shouted, "Fire! Fire!" He paused to make sure that his voice was heard over the din. It was. . . . People in the hall rushed toward the door. Manley turned toward the door as well and got through them but found himself tangled in the mass of people at the top of the stairs.[6]

Interesting reading, but how did Lehto know the intimate details of this event, and how did he know about Manley's decision making in the process of yelling "Fire!" into the crowded hall? Lehto does not provide a single source in this entire chapter until the last two paragraphs, and the single, short original reference is from the *Calumet News*. Likely noticing that he is on shaky ground, Lehto then attempts to qualify his assertion in the last sentence of his three-page chapter on Italian Hall by writing, "Of the few names history has given us as possible culprits at the Italian Hall, Edward Manley is the most likely to have been the man who cried Fire."[7]

It is difficult to pin something this serious on a man with such limited research and documentation, but finally, in an endnote in the next chapter, we get the actual "truth" from Lehto regarding the events at Italian Hall. In referencing the kidnapping of WFM president Charles Moyer in endnote 473, Lehto writes, "Regardless of blame, the fact that more than six dozen people—mostly children—were killed at a Christmas Eve party by *an unknown person* would have drawn attention to the area from outside with or without Moyer's actions."[8]

The scenario depicted in *Shortcut* is highly unlikely because if Manley would have cried "Fire!" and then rushed out of the hall, as most people say the man who cried "Fire!" did, how would he get caught in the mass of people? There were numerous people who made it safely from the hall before the people started to pile on the stairs, and we can assume that Manley, after having made the call of "Fire!," left the hall in a hurry. John Burcar, who gave testimony at the coroner's inquest, stated as much after being questioned. When asked about what the man who yelled "Fire!" did after he cried the fateful word or words, Burcar testified, "He went downstairs . . . all the people were running after him . . . he hollered and then went downstairs and the people [went] after him."[9]

Most likely Manley was not the man who cried "Fire!" There are myriad reasons as to why Manley could have been in the hall that fateful evening. On one hand, he could have been there to help people to make up for all the truly awful things he had done during the strike. On the other hand, there was, according to Oscar Hietalahti's testimony during the coroner's inquest and as reported in *Työmies*, a strikebreaker in Italian Hall who twisted the neck of a child under his arm and then tossed the child "on the floor under the feet of the panic stricken people." This same man wearing a blue suit with a Citizens' Alliance button reached for an "escaping man and grabbed him by the throat and crushed him under his feet."[10] Maybe this was Manley doing the morbid work of a gun thug. He could have gotten in the hall up the ladder early after the cry of "Fire!" and then began the abuse of people in the hall while the panicked partygoers were still trying to get down the stairs, as Hietalahti indicates. Then, after committing the terrible crimes, he was swept into the mass of bodies and caught in the crush as the pile of human bodies extended from the stairwell and into the second-floor vestibule area. It could have been just as likely that someone saw Manley's mistreatment of people and gave him a drubbing. Upon hearing the news about Manley's nefarious deeds, perhaps the *Calumet News* tried to spin Manley's dastardly acts into heroism. These scenarios would explain him being injured just as well, while also placing him in the hall during the time of the event. There are any number of reasons why Manley could have been in Italian Hall, and to indict him as the person who cried "Fire!" when there is no documentary evidence to directly support such an assertion is bad practice.

The remainder of this chapter, however, provides the search for the man who cried "Fire!" with something it has never had: firsthand documentary evidence. We present two new perspectives to contemplate, which offer concrete analysis of the intriguing and flurried attempts to identify and locate the man who cried "Fire!" Additionally, the chapter provides the much sought after names of Italian Hall suspects that come from the time of the actual event. Perhaps most interesting is the fact that both the union and the company were trying to identify and locate said person. This chapter details those efforts and does not rely on nonhistorical conjecture and deduction; rather, this chapter relies on the historical record, the firsthand accounts as detailed by those who lived through the strike, to give a new perspective on the man who cried "Fire!"

A Wanted Man

One can almost imagine the whirling dervish of implication, innuendo, and inconsistency regarding the assignment of blame for the events at Italian Hall. As we have seen, union members and their supporters blamed the Citizens' Alliance—no one specific, but rather the group in general—for carefully orchestrating the fateful events in an antilabor conspiracy. There is certainly evidence for this assertion, and we provided that evidence in the preceding chapter. *Työmies* and the labor press made certain, and public, their contention that events at Italian Hall were no set of happenstance occurrences; rather, they asserted that the tragedy at Italian Hall was one more act in the Citizens' Alliance December campaign of intimidation and violence against striking workers.

There was, however, as much or more intrigue behind the scenes regarding the search for the man who cried "Fire!" Both Calumet & Hecla (C&H) and the WFM had secret searches on for this person, and in the case of the mining companies, the search was methodical and exacting, carried out by a professional detective. Thus, there was, unbeknownst to previous writers, a concerted effort to find the man who cried "Fire!" The union and the company, both with a vested interest in finding this person, had identified a person or group as having culpability for the events at Italian Hall.

The *Calumet News*, identified as the "kept press" by the union, laid the fault for the events on a "man who cried 'Fire,' [who was] supposed to be drunk as he came from [the] saloon on the lower floor."[11] Therefore, from this quote, it is clear that even the kept press thought the events at the hall were not the simple act of "bad luck," but had a very different conception of who might be culpable. The *Calumet News* was so convinced of the need for someone to blame the newspaper even promised that arrests for the evildoers were in the offing. In a December 26, 1913, special issue, the *Calumet News* printed in an article titled "Arrests Are Expected":

Ten detectives and a number of special operatives of outside agencies are conducting an investigation into the cause of the disaster, which, it is asserted may lead to arrests at any moment. . . . Rescuers who were among the first to reach the Italian hall tell stories of the conduct of the men in the saloon beneath the hall. A physician, the first to respond, found nearly a dozen bodies strewn about the floor in the bar room. Men, apparently intoxicated, hung about the bar and clamored for liquor . . . the men yelling hilariously while the lives of children, women and men were being crushed out, less than twenty feet from them. None of the men made any effort to assist in the rescue. Officers arrived and prohibited the sale of liquor.[12]

The *Calumet News*'s affiliation with the mining companies and the Citizens' Alliance proved problematic throughout the strike for many reasons, but perhaps the paper's bias was no more glaring than in its coverage of the Italian Hall tragedy. As events unfolded early in the disaster, the coverage of the *Calumet News* was relatively evenhanded. The paper concentrated on reporting the grief, misery, and sorrow associated with the event. The newspaper even contained stories of union members on the scene as it quoted Ana Clemenc in her capacity as president of the Women's Auxiliary of the WFM. However, as time passed between the event and the realization of the event's significance to public opinion, the *Calumet News*'s coverage of the events at Italian Hall began to take a more pointedly procompany and Citizens' Alliance perspective.

The Company's Search

The *Calumet News* was absolutely correct on at least one fact—there were a number of detectives and operatives sleuthing around looking for a person to identify as the man who cried "Fire!" There were probably many other people doing the same. There was, however, one person in particular with a mandate from C&H conducting his own investigation into the man who cried "Fire!" His handwritten reports were given to Captain Robert J. Foster, general manager of Foster's Industrial and Detective Bureau, who then forwarded them to Albert E. Petermann, a lawyer for C&H. These reports provide an always intimate, sometimes tense, and almost daily chronicle of a search for the man who cried "Fire!" at Italian Hall.

Reasons why C&H paid an operative to search for the man who cried "Fire!" are unclear. Motivation is sometimes difficult to determine. Perhaps C&H and Albert Petermann were genuinely interested in bringing this man to justice. Documents analyzed earlier in this book suggest otherwise, but an altruistic motive is not entirely out of the question. More likely, C&H, the Citizens' Alliance, and Petermann were attempting to decipher if anyone else could tie an assailant back to them. As we have seen earlier in this book, Jim MacNaughton, Quincy Shaw, and Petermann loved the cloak-and-dagger aspects of the strike, and if a hired operative using C&H's vast amount of resources was not able to connect the twisted dots in a plot to disrupt the Christmas Eve activities at Italian Hall, it would likely be difficult or nearly impossible for others with the same goal.

This investigator hired by C&H through Petermann, "Operative #1," assumed the guise of a socialist journalist hailing from Denver. From his written reports, there are small but noticeable variations in English attributed to Germanic speakers; the operative was likely a German immigrant or a second-generation German American whose parents spoke German in the home. Denver was also the headquarters of the WFM, and with that set of credentials, Operative #1 had almost complete access to union affairs in Calumet. His first day of "work" was likely January 5, 1914, about two weeks after the terrible events at Italian Hall. Like any other fellow starting a new job, he was nervous, but he also had good reason to be downright terrified. His first contact with the union was a tense one: "Today in the afternoon, I went to the 'Union Hall' . . . every man looked at me suspiciously. . . . Later on a fellow came to me asking if I belonged to that Union. I said, 'No, I am a correspondent for two Socialist newspapers in Denver, Colo.' and showed him my card."[13]

Intrigue was high. If caught in his ruse, who knows what the union men would have done to the operative. The operative's reports back to his handler, Captain Foster, read like some of the best cloak-and-dagger fiction ever imagined, but one indisputable fact remained: he was in Calumet to detect, discover, and identify the man who yelled "Fire!" at Italian Hall. Captain Foster's description of Operative #1's job in relation to Italian Hall was explicit: "He is making his headquarters around union headquarters and McNally's office and is working along the lines laid down by me to find one responsible for the panic Christmas eve."[14] This was the grim reality of his subterfuge.

Operative #1's almost unfettered access to the union hierarchy is clear from his first report back to his handler, dated January 7, 1914:

> One of my best friends of the members of the W.F. or M. invited me to a drink today, and I went with him to a saloon and had a good time. He asked me if I would like to join the meeting today of the Women's Auxiliary of the Western Federation of Miners. I said yes, and we went to the Italian Hall, where the meeting was going on. He introduced me to the Assistant President (the President is ill at present), and to a large number of women members, as a press correspondent sent by the Colorado newspapers.

Welcoming the reporter warmly, the women of Calumet's WFM Women's Auxiliary undoubtedly saw this man as a comrade, and the operative played the part: "She asked me to speak a few words. I did so, assuring them of my sympathy in the disaster on Christmas eve in the Italian Hall, and in a few words gave the copper barons and mine owners 'hell' and assured them that I would do all in my power to protect the W.F.M. in any way, asking for kindly assistance in my work. I had a big applause."[15]

Just like that, it seemed as though the operative was a part of Calumet's union community. The intrigue continued to be high—perhaps heightened further because, in essence, he was being scrutinized and watched by two groups: the union and procompany factions that were unaware of the operative's association with C&H. This operative was the new kid in town, so to speak, and everyone wanted to know more about him, as a report from January 9, 1914, indicates: "Tonight the maid of my hotel told me that yesterday morning when I went out, a Gentleman who occupy's [sic] the room No. 9 at the hotel went in my room locked the door and remained in there for some time. I tried to find out who that man is, but the proprietor of the hotel refused to tell me the name. I am going to force it tomorrow."[16] Was this a union man checking up on this newspaperman from Denver to see if his credentials were accurate, or was it a company thug checking up on a new agitator, wanting to see if he could find him alone to show him a little Copper Country justice firsthand? This was the peril of being a paid phony; this was the job of a labor spy.

On the Trail of the Labor Spy

For this section on the company-sponsored search for the man who cried "Fire!" we will journey along with this labor spy as he loiters in bars, talks with union folks, prowls the streets of Calumet, and hunts down leads. We are going to let him tell the story as we follow his tracks in and out of the lives of people who had information about the man who cried "Fire!" at Italian Hall. In essence, we will be spying on the spy as he attempts to hunt down the most wanted man in Michigan, and possibly the country, in the winter of 1913–14.

Once the labor spy settled in, he began hunting down leads. One of the most difficult parts of his job was contending with the polyglot of languages in the Copper Country. The operative would be running into, drinking with, and trying to extract information from people who did not speak English as a first language: Italian, Croatian, Finnish, Slovenian, and a multitude of other languages would be a significant hill to overcome as the operative struggled to gain a foothold in the community. On his first day of actual work on the case, January 11, the operative got a taste of dealing with the multiethnic nature of his unsuspecting informants:

> On Sunday the 11th I overheard a conversation of 2 Italian fellows. . . . I set close to them and acted as I would sleep, it was at the Union Hall. I never saw these men before up there. These two also spoke about a woman who claimed she saw the man who gave the false alarm her name is Lech and she lives at 6th Street as I found out. When the 2 men left the hall I followed them for about 20 m[inutes]. But in case of the terrible snowstorm lost there trail when they turned in a other street it was between 10–11 o'clock at night.[17]

Immediately, the name Lesch comes to the forefront. Mrs. Lesch gave testimony at the coroner's inquest and was a well-known member of the Calumet WFM Women's Auxiliary; she was an informant, not a suspect.

The operative then went to track down Mrs. Lesch. Her testimony was interesting during the coroner's inquest, but she did not have much then to say about the man who cried "Fire!" Did the operative think she had more to tell? "I then went back to Calumet and called at Mrs. Lech, the woman the 2 Italians spoke about, but when I asked her she said that she did not see the man but named me t[w]o women Mrs. Foster and Mrs. Lustig and a 13 years old boy John Burzer [Burcar] which stated that they saw the man and they also can give a description of him."[18] There was nothing new from Lesch, but she did provide the operative leads to three other people who had a description of the man. All of these people gave testimony at the coroner's inquest, and both Mrs. Lustig and John Burcar gave very detailed descriptions of the man who cried "Fire!"

Then Lesch reveals to the operative two important pieces in the overall Italian Hall puzzle. "Mrs. Lech said that one of the 2 women says that she saw the man who gave the false alarm deployed powder in the air before he went out."[19] A mysterious powder was mentioned during the coroner's inquest as well, but had received little attention since. The operative's report leaves us wondering about the significance of this seemingly out-of-place powder. Family recollections of experiences in Italian Hall shed some light on the mysterious powder. According to Annie Grentz, who was in the hall and witnessed the event, the same man who cried "Fire!" also reached into his pockets and pulled out something resembling flour, a white powder, and threw it into the air. Annie, who was approximately thirteen years old at the time, surmised that this white powder was used to simulate the appearance of smoke, acting as a material warning sign of fire in Italian Hall to supplement the audible call of "Fire!"[20]

The operative's report continued: "Mrs. Lech and her husband, also 2 other men who where [sic] present when I spoke to her, stated that a very great number of the children and the women died when they came down the stairway and reached the fifth step counted from downstairs. She said they died standing up, also up in the hall. I wish to say that I heard this from other men before. And I think if there is any truth about that powder it will be possible to find that man."[21]

A mysterious powder and a suspicious fifth step: was there something wrong with the fifth step, which may have tripped people up? Common mythology about the event, even continuing into the present day, is that the doors at Italian Hall swung inward, and thus people trying to open the doors were not able to do so because of the crush of humanity behind them. However, as we have learned from the deposition of Jenevive Sandretto, the doors were open, perhaps later to have been shut, according to the deposition of Mari Chopp. So which way the doors opened, given the depositions of Jenevive Sandretto and Mari Chopp, is somewhat inconsequential, but this fifth step: was there perhaps something wrong with the fifth step that tripped people up—maybe a loose board or a nail sticking out that caught someone's clothing, causing them to fall and begin clogging the stairwell? There is very little information in the coroner's inquest about what actually happened in the stairwell, so here *perhaps* was an explanation for how the bodies began to pile up in the stairwell.

In Calumet, on January 15 the operative went about town trying to locate the two women who had a firsthand description of the man reported to have stuck his head into the hall to yell "Fire!," not once, but twice: "This morning I tried to locate Mrs. Lustig and Mrs. Foster but could not find them. I then joined the meeting held by the Ladies Auxiliary and had a chance to see the sister of Mrs. Lustig this lady could not give me any information but said she will try to connect with her sister so I can meet her."[22]

No luck in locating Mrs. Lustig, but the operative did get the chance to make a face-to-face contact with a man who was in Italian Hall at the time of the panic. The operative then interviewed Peter Pichittino and did a serious sit-down session of "Question" and "Answer." The results of the interview were that Pichittino did not believe that anyone had yelled "Fire!" In fact, he was quite adamant that the call of "Fire!" did not occur until after the panic started: "Qu: Did you hear the call fire or [unreadable word, maybe 'water' as there was a rumor in the *Calumet News* that a call for water was misconstrued to mean that water was needed to put out a fire]? Answ. No, and I am sure there was no one in the hall who called fire. I only saw the people trying to get out of the hall and then everyone called fire." In addition to this statement, Pichittino stated that no strangers were allowed into the hall: "Question: Did you see any stranger in the hall? Answ: No, we had door guards and no stranger had admission."[23]

This revelation would have made it unlikely that any person would have been able to get into the hall to yell "Fire!," but this is a contested statement—contested from a pro-union source, the *Miners' Bulletin*. In the January 7, 1914, issue, the *Bulletin* was refuting the findings of the coroner's inquest and the jury's findings that no "person or persons" were allowed inside the hall without a union card. The *Bulletin* refuted that statement: "Many persons in the room were not members of the union, nor were they vouched for by members of the union. A man was stationed at the door but his business was more in the nature of keeping order and the passage way clear, than to inspect those who entered the hall. Furthermore it would have been an easy matter for a man to come into the doorway and cry fire regardless of a doorkeeper."[24] What the *Bulletin* and the WFM were likely arguing against was the idea advanced in the kept press that it was a union person who, because of despicable trick or sad fate, cried "Fire!"

The operative had located Mrs. Lustig by January 16, and quickly met with her at her home in Raymbaultown for a sit-down interview, where Lustig gave the operative the following statement:

> I went with my [difficult to read handwriting of number] children to the Italian hall at 3.10 pm. The hall was full. A few minutes later a man about 5 f. 7 inch fair compl. Dark hair a well built man with a dark blue coat and a Citizens Alliance Button on the outside pocket and I also think a mustache, with a dark cap turned in his face came in the hall and called 2 times fire and went out again. The Deputys and the member of the Citizens Alliance were for the building before the fire whistle was blown. It was not noisy in the hall before the fire was called. My husband who came through the window in the hall was choked by a funny smell. They had no candles on the tree. Mrs. Lustig also informed me that the door down stairs was blocked by Deputy and no one could go out but when the stairway was full. She also said that the coat of the man looked very much like the once the Deputys are wearing.[25]

The operative's false identity as a reporter suited his work as a spy very well. In the interviews conducted with the unsuspecting informants, he could, because of his duties as a newspaper reporter, take notes and ask very pointed and intimate questions without seeming out of place or suspect. This ability to take notes no doubt greatly increased the accuracy of his reports back to his handlers, and gives a rather pure rendition of the information he was collecting.

The interview with Mrs. Lustig proved helpful, especially when she gave the operative another invaluable lead when she "told me the name of Mr. Erwin a barber, to him came a man at the same night. The man was very nervous and asked the barber to shave his mustache he was in a very hurry. I am going to get a statement of that barber."[26] The few descriptions of the man who cried "Fire!" all indicate that he had some type of facial hair. Lustig seemed to be indicating that after putting out the horrible false fire alarm, the man went to change his appearance to avoid identification. This was a significant lead.

When the operative returned to his hotel room in Calumet for the night, he had a chance meeting that would change the whole direction of his investigation. "When I came home to night at 11 pm I met a roomer Mr. A. H. Telset [could also be Telsett or Telseff] he says he is the Vice President of the North Star [unsure of the correct spelling of the company name] Co., Minneapolis Minn. I find him very suspicious because he is a friend of P. Framhols [Framholz]."[27] Something piqued the curiosity of the operative, and experience or intuition caused him to strike up an intense conversation:

> I made him talk and he mentioned he has some doubts about the Christmas Disaster and he said that a man told him that after misfortune at the Italian hall Mr. Messner a former Deputy [and the] nephew of Mr. Giever, who is a Deputy now, came home very nervous and [unreadable word] and said what can we do, they did not [k]now what to do they send one of these children to get the [unreadable word] news and after reading it Mrs. Giever said it is only to good that they have no good description. Mr. Messner left town the next morning before daylight.[28]

Someone the operative referred to in his report as "Captain" interrupted the conversation between the two men. This "Captain" was Robert J. Foster. After the operative went to see Captain Foster, who was staying in the same Calumet hotel, Telset came back to the operative's room, and the two men talked about the "case" until three in the morning.[29]

There was a new name, or suspect, in the operative's list of suspects. The name Messner is a familiar one. As may be remembered, Messner was the surname of one of the men who signed and sent the Western Union night telegrams to the House of Representatives to stop or halt a bill to investigate the Copper Country strike; he was also the fervently anti-union vice-president of the Haas Brewing Company. Would this Messner, a well-known public figure, attempt a deed such as crying "fire" into a crowded hall? Perhaps it was a relative with the same surname? Messner climbed the operative's ever-lengthening list of people he wanted to interview, but was he a suspect?

The next day, Operative #1 went to Emil Erving's barbershop on Calumet's Fifth Street to inquire about a mustache being shaved. The interview with the barbershop employees proved very remarkable, as the operative's January 17 report revealed. Emil Erving, the owner of the barbershop, remembered, "It was on Christmas eve between 8–9 P.M. when a man came in my shop and asked me to shave his mustache, he was very nervous and excited and seemed to be in a very hurry, he had to wait because I and my assistant were busy. He did not take his coat off. He asked me 4 or 5 times to shave his mustache. When he came on the row [of barber chairs] my assistant shaved him."[30] Erving's assistant was working in the barbershop that night, and gave the nervous, hurried man the actual shave, and remembered only details that a barber could convey: "I also have been asked several times to take his mustache away. He had a very well trimmed mustache very dark brown more black."[31] The operative included a description of the man from the assistant's recollection of the man, and some of his own notations of the man:

> He is about 40 years of age 5 f. 7 or 8 inch well built figure, dark hair but thin brown eyes and dark eyebrows, he had a round mark on his forehead about a ½ inch and also a blue mark on the right sight [sic] of his face. He [the barber's assistant] remarked it is a mark as many coal miners have. His nose bone came out a little. [In the sentence, the operative drew a picture of a face with a nose that had a little bump coming out from the nose.] When he was through with shaving I asked the man if he wants his neck shaved it didn't need it very much but he refused, paid and hurried out, he did not even put his coat on in the shop. He had a dark coat blue or black was a ¾ coat. The name of the assistant is "Larenzo Laudrillo."[32]

That same day the operative located the Giever house, which was the residence where Messner and his wife were reportedly boarding: "I also located Giever at 434 8th Street but have not been able to locate the man who made the statement I reported in my last report. The name is J. Olson. I looked 4 Olsons up but no one was the man I am after. I hope to find him Monday." Operative #1's attention increasingly turned to Messner and the Giever house. As the operative reported on January 18, "This morning I spent [sic] in watching the house of Gievers, because I wanted to get acquainted with a daughter of Mr. Giever wich [sic] know all about it."[33]

On January 19, the operative turned to Mr. J. Olson to find more information on the mysterious Messner. Finding that Olson was out for the day, the operative went to Houghton to track down a lead about a suspected union turncoat by the name of O'Grady, but found that O'Grady was supposedly out of town. The operative then went back to the Calumet-Laurium area in an attempt to track down another lead. "On my way back I stopped at Laurium to see Mrs. Polwic. I was told by Mrs. Lustig that she could give a good description of the man who gave the alarm, but she said when I asked her that she did not see the man or hear the fire call, but she remarked she smelled something funny."[34] At the coroner's inquest, there was mention of strange smells, the strange powder, and then of course the very loud call of "Fire!" The operative was sifting through a plethora of sensory evidence as well as human recollections.

That evening the operative called again at Olson's home; this time Olson was in and gave the operative a physical description of Messner. Olson also provided tantalizing information about Messner's connection to the reported thugs who had been blamed by union folks for the events at Italian Hall:

> [Olson says Messner] is about 5 f. 6–7 inch, well built, dark hair and dark mustache, but he saw the man one week ago with out a mustache. He remarked that this Mr. Messner left town the next morning before 6 A.M. after the Christmas eve. He did not take himself time to take a breakfast he came back about two weeks later. He was a Deputy and quit his job. A boy of Giever's, the familie [sic] where Mr. Messner boarded, brings milk to Olson's and one day the boy had a false mustache on, when he was asked where he got this mustache from he said we have a number of them at home. It was a black mustache the boy had. . . . P.S. Mr. Olson asked me to sign a note saying that I would [not] publish his statement before proved. I did.[35]

A shaved mustache, and then a boy with a false mustache from a home with a number of false mustaches—was the operative following Calumet's rumor mill down a rabbit hole? Messner—who was this man—and the dizzying array of angles, intrigue, and people in this case were complicating the operative's investigation. Undaunted, the operative kept chasing the proverbial rabbit down the hole, keeping a vigil for information on Messner, who was becoming the operative's main suspect on a one-man list. The operative focused most of his attention on Messner: "I kept a close watch of Giever's house in the hope to see Mr. Messner, but I only saw an old man going and coming home again, it must have been Mr. Giever."[36]

Interspersed with the surveillance of the Giever house, the operative spent time tracking down other leads, and one such lead brought the labor spy into a seemingly dangerous situation:

> When I called at Borchgrevink he was not in his house, he was in a very little house next to his big one. When I knocked at that little house, a man opened the door about 3 inches. I asked for B. and he came than and he seemed to me a little nervous, he said he is working. When I asked him what his is working he waited a few second[s] then he said I am working on a patent. But I can not understand how he can work in a room as dark as the one was w[h]ere he came and I saw a machine in there. On the door he has 'No Admittance.'[37]

The rabbit hole got a little deeper—and a bit stranger.

On January 23, in an attempt to meet with the thirteen-year-old Burcar boy who had been in Italian Hall and stated that he saw the man who cried "Fire!," the operative's cover was nearly blown while he was at the WFM's Calumet offices talking to William Rickard. "Then [Rickard] said what's the matter with you, one of the boys saw you running around with that Detective. I [acted] as I did not understand and so he explained that this land agent Mr. Telset is a Detective, well I told Rickard than that I did not have an idea about that and Rickard believed it. [I told Rickard] I did not go with that Mr. T. I only meet with him on the corner of 6th Street and copper range together with Torson and he spoke a few words to me."[38]

After this narrow escape, the operative went back to meet with the man who was working on the "patent" in a darkened room. This man, Borchgrevink, provided information that indicated that the Capular children were warned to stay away from Italian Hall before the tragic events occurred:

> Borchgrevink said that Mr. Narum, who is relative of Capulars, went to them and asked for their storie and the children told him that a Mr. Marson told them at the hall few minutes before the disaster, it would be better for them to go home because there is much trouble in getting the candys and the children went. Borchgrevink says this is the truth, he saw that Marson told them to go home because there might be some trouble. Borchgrevink is foreigner and don't understand well English also the Capular children. He could not tell me if the name Marson is right spelled as wrote it.[39]

Then, on January 24 the operative went to the home of the Gievers with the intention of interviewing, maybe even confronting their boarder Messner. The operative went, however, with a backstory to fool the Gievers into thinking that the operative was an old friend of someone with the name "Merkner," in an attempt to hide any suspicion the Gievers or Messner might have in relation to the operative's true reason for visiting the house: "In the afternoon I went to Giever's house at 434 8th Street and asked for a Mr. Merkner. Mrs. Giever told me there is no man in the house with that name there is only man boarding her of the name Messner. Than I told her that I got the name from a friend of mine at Denver, he was living in Calumet some time ago and this Mr. Merkner is a good friend of him and I forgot the exact address I only remember that the house is near Pine Street and 8th Street." The ruse worked. After getting in good with Mrs. Giever, a person who introduced herself as Mrs. Messner appeared at the door to help clarify any confusion in locating the operative's fictitious long-lost friend from Denver: "Then Mrs. Messner joined our conversation and said it may be Messner, I said, well I am not sure but I always said Merkner but I saw a photograph of the man I am looking for, and I think I would recognize the man I have in mind and I gave her a description I have heard about Messner, and his [Messner's] wife said, so is my husband looking and she told me to call Sunday noon to see him it may be [he] is the man I am looking for."[40]

Finally, and with rapport established with the ladies of the house, on January 25 the operative got a chance to confront the man—Messner: "After dinner I called at Gievers house to see Messner, he is 44 years of age. 5 ft 11 to 6 ft. well built full smooth [hairless] face dark brown hair and light blue eyes, his hair is thin and he seems to be a Jew, he also has pimples all over his face and so far red complexion." The description of the man does not seem to fit the restless nature of the search for him. He seems, from the operative's description, a little underwhelming. Regardless, the operative stayed in "character," making Messner think he was still looking for the fictitious Merkner: "When I looked at him I said I don't think you are the man I am looking for and asked him if he is acquainted with a Mr. Joe Simon of Denver, he started thinking and said: 'No,' and I told him the same storie I told his wife and Mrs. Giever yesterday."[41]

The operative was "in": "He told me to sit down and we spoke about the strike and the conditions up here. He sticks to the Comp.[any] and I gave them hell. He told me that he is for 4 months a Deputy for the Comp. and that his home is at Point Mills."[42] The picture now becomes a little clearer: Messner and his wife were boarding with the Gievers in Calumet where he was working as a member of C&H's company police or as a Houghton County deputy sheriff, but he lived full-time in Point Mills, which was close to Hancock. In addition, it becomes certain that the operative was highly skilled in his craft; he was deceptive and able to get people to trust him. While perhaps his report writing was not the best, he was a mastermind in the field of labor spying.

As the operative could feel Messner getting more comfortable, he waited and then proverbially pounced. What ensued, and what is documented in the report, was a breaking down of Messner's character and body language, and a summation:

After we talked for 20 m[inutes] I took the chance and started about the Christmas disaster and he seemed to become nervous and his action was very like of a man who is afraid to be detected, he felt his hat and his collar as if he would feel nervous at once, and I also saw his face is become more red as before but I could not swear. I said that my opinion is that the man who gave the alarm is dead. He joined me, and he said he might have been living [leaving] town the next morning / that's what Messner did / he meant that it is impossible to find that man because no one can give a good description of him. I said I am glad that I have not been here, because if I had seen all this dead bodys I never could forget them, he said he did not see them because he was working at that time. I don't believe it because the panic was about 3.15 or 3.20 and he works from 4 o'clock to 12 P.M. and so he had time enough to go there or pass the Italian hall on his way to work. If he is the man I am looking for than he certainly did not go there after he was up here and gave the alarm. He has a black overcoat that what his wife mentioned when I said that I saw a photo of the man I have in mind as Mr. Merkner, his wife than said he had a picture taken as a Deputy in his black coat. He turned our conversation in asking me what I think about the federal investigation I gave my opinion. He invited me to call again when I left. He is a German born and raised in Michigan.[43]

While the operative did not note it in his report, the address of the Gievers' house at 434 Eighth Street was only a few houses down a back alley from Italian Hall, which was located at 405 Seventh Street. Exactly what this short distance between the Giever house and the hall, and likely familiarity, meant to Messner's probability of being the man who cried "Fire!" at Italian Hall is uncertain. Perhaps it is just a coincidence that the man the operative was questioning in relation to the events at Italian Hall was living almost in the hall's backyard; or perhaps it would be sheer stupidity for a person living so close to the hall to commit such an act so close to where he was boarding; or just maybe the hall's proximity to the house he was boarding at provided easy access for Messner to stage and pull off the deadly event.[44]

January 25 was the date of the second-to-the-last report in the historical record. The very next day, the operative was still at work, but perhaps had moved on to other topics related to the events at Italian Hall: "When I went back [from attending the proceedings of the Congressional Investigation] I meet Torson at the store of Framholz and he gave me a tip, he said that he knew a man who is informed that the fire engine was ready before the alarm was given, and Torson advised me that I shall go and see the man himself. His name is Tommei and he has a candy store at 5th Street."[45] This "tip" refers to the earlier accusation made in the December 26, 1913, issue of *Työmies* that the tragic events at Italian hall were planned and that the use of a fire whistle was intended to call Citizens' Alliance members to Italian Hall for retribution.

Sadly, our trail scrutinizing the investigations of Operative #1's search for the man who cried "Fire!" ends here. We are left wondering if the operative was certain Messner was the man who cried "Fire!" in Italian Hall, if he ever identified other suspects, or if he ever made a final report to C&H regarding his search for the man who cried "Fire!"

The Union's Search for the Man Who Cried "Fire!"

The search documented here for the man who cried "Fire!" by the Calumet WFM local was not much of a search per se; rather, it was a quick jump to a conclusion and then an attempt to act. The union's identification of the man who union members believed cried "Fire!" was much more direct but no less full of intrigue and, again, we rely on reports filed by a labor spy to document the WFM's search for the man who cried "Fire!" This time, however, the reports are from an unknown operative. The "trail" begins with the operative noting that the Calumet local had identified one of its organizers, a man named "George" who was seen with a company detective, as a union turncoat. Initially, there was only an identification of the man in surveillance records; the union was surveilling a curious fellow named George as early as March 2, 1914: "Hungarian detective and this man George were in Lake Linden today. George is wearing a black suit, gray overcoat, black hat, chain on the outside coat pocket."[46]

It appears that "George" was working with the union to organize men, but after being seen with a "Hungarian" detective, he was assumed to be a traitor to organized labor and a spy. A March 14 report from the unidentified labor spy indicated that George Servaski (the operative was likely incorrect in the spelling of George's last name) was working with Fred Kiskila to organize men for the Calumet local. The two WFM organizers were working on getting imported scabs out of the Copper Country, and had promised to get "between fifty and sixty men out" of the Copper Country by Sunday.[47]

Something happened between March 14 and early April; either George's cover was blown or he gave himself away, because Patrick Dunnigan, Ahmeek Village sheriff and WFM supporter from Keweenaw County, had sniffed out George and did not like what he smelled: "Dunnigan is after this man George, planning to do away with him. Threatened to put him out of the union. Going to send a petition tomorrow signed by a number of men to Anttila to put this man George Sartoskila [the labor spy is struggling with this last name] out of the union and give him a chance to get out of the Copper Country or they will get him. They planned to kill him in Lesh's saloon. Joe Naima, working in Mohawk is the one who put Paddy wise that he had a [Houghton County deputy's] star on his shirt. Paddy told George to get out and not come back anymore. Huber wants to get a crowd of men to come up to Calumet and get him."[48]

It did not take George long to get the hint. He was a wanted man by the WFM, and his outing came from his WFM union organizer partner: "The Croatian that was working with George is the man who gave him away. Rickard telegraphed all over to the different Federation officers in regard to this man. He has gone to Stillwater, Minn." By April 10, the hunt was on. The operative's report clearly indicated that the WFM was after this man named George, though the operative was struggling with the spelling of his last name: "April 10: Picked four men to look up George Bartoski. Claim he is the man who is responsible for the Italian hall disaster. This was told in Crow's saloon in Houghton by the bar tender. This is a good place to have a man. Said they are planning some dirty work at South Range."[49]

George was, in the union's collective eyes, the man who had cried "Fire!" at

Italian Hall. By April 13, there was a full-on manhunt for George, and the mission was to bring him back to the Copper Country for some kind of justice: "Fred Kiskela received a letter from George. He is in Clear Lake, Minnesota. Rickard and Antilla telephoned to the Editor of the Tyomies to send and find him. Going to try and bring him back, accusing George of being the cause of the Italian Hall disaster."[50] It seems that the union was quite sure that "George" was the person who cried "Fire!" at Italian Hall. The union was willing to devote a good deal of resources, had tapped into regional media, and was willing to almost suspend actions in the strike to hunt this man down. The union wanted to bring George back for some justice, but just what this justice would entail we will never know.

As with the company's search, there are a number of questions regarding the WFM local's search for the man who cried "Fire!" First and foremost: did the union ever get George? Frustratingly, this is not part of the historical record. Another question that remains is whether George Bartoski and George Sartoskila are the same person. Maybe Sartoskila was a strikebreaker or spy who got into good graces with the WFM and then double-crossed the union, maybe made it into Italian Hall with a red card (which takes care of the notion that someone needed a red card to get in) and perpetrated the disaster? Or are these two different people? Or maybe Sartoskila is just a hated and identified former deputy? The union's search for the man who cried "Fire!" leaves us with many questions as well.

Final Thoughts on the Man Who Cried "Fire!"

Who, then, was the man who cried "Fire!"? When we leave Operative #1 on January 25, 1914, it seems like he believes that Messner has some connection or something more to tell about the events at Italian Hall. While Messner looks like a very credible culprit for the terrible act because of the compelling firsthand labor spy reports that seem to pull us in the direction of his guilt, the WFM also had its own person of interest. It was so sure of its assertion that it was threatening to send people to Minnesota to get "George." There are, however, problems with "convicting" Messner or George for crying "Fire!" in Italian Hall.

In the case of Messner, the operative's report contains some confusion as to the time of the panic and whether Messner was working. Also, did the operative read the nonverbal communication of Messner correctly? There are simply a lot of questions that still need to be answered before anyone can conclude that they know who cried "Fire!" in Italian Hall that fateful night.

However, another intriguing piece of documentary evidence from May 30, 1914, attained from labor spy reports, indicates that this man, Messner, from Point

Mills who was boarding with the Gievers in Calumet at the time of the Italian Hall tragedy, was seen running into and out of the Hall by the person known as the "old man selling shrubbery" introduced early in this chapter:

> The old man who has been selling shrubbery for a number of years around Calumet is a union man, came up today to union headquarters and said a detective was talking with the deputy who was standing near the Calumet store when the Italian hall disaster happened and saw the man run up and come down the stairs. This deputy is working at Point Mills now. Oppman took this man's story and put it in the safe to give to Judge Hilton.[51]

Perhaps the old man selling shrubbery was right, maybe Messner was the guy? Or, perhaps the point here is not to conclude that Messner was the man who yelled "Fire!" or that the WFM Calumet local had identified the turncoat as the perpetrator of the tragic events at Italian Hall—the point is perhaps that people were looking. The fact that C&H paid an operative/spy to look for the person who cried "Fire!" in Italian Hall likely means that MacNaughton and Petermann believed, as did the union, that this was a *planned, purposeful event.* In addition to the contexts for why Italian Hall was targeted for retribution by the mining companies and the Citizens' Alliance, C&H's bankrolling of a search for the man who cried "Fire!" adds further documentary, primary evidence that the Italian Hall tragedy was likely *premeditated.*

However, no matter how much people want a name to assign to this terrible event, there are simply no easy answers. No matter how many people claim to know the name of the person who cried "Fire!" at Italian Hall, it is very likely, almost to the point of certainty, that the name and true rendering of the tragic events of that night will forever be cloaked and shrouded in mystery. There can be assumptions, inferences, and suppositions regarding the man who cried "Fire!" and the events that set in motion the terrible tragedy, but anything resembling a definitive answer to the above questions is not now or likely ever forthcoming. Anyone who claims to have such answers is not being truthful with readers. There was simply too much chaos and human error in the event and later reporting to give the Italian Hall dead, their families, and "history" a definitive answer for the tragic events of that night. Perhaps human nature leads us to look for a concrete answer to such a fluid and historical question, but the firsthand materials presented here are the closest anyone or any group has come to assembling a direct account of the search for the man who cried "Fire!"

CHAPTER 10

Cave-In

There are still men in the Copper Country who believe they were sold to the companies and believe that the Federation [WFM] had enough money to support them until the battle was won.

—Charles E. Hietala, WFM district secretary, to WFM national offices

IN MINING LINGO A "CAVE-IN" IS THE FALLING OF A MASSIVE AMOUNT OF EARTH on the top of a person. In coalmines, this could mean an entire mountain would collapse on top of people, stranding or killing hundreds of people; but in the Keweenaw, cave-ins generally happened when a section or rock from the "hanging" wall or overhead "ceiling" fell to the bottom of a work area known as a "stope." In this situation, most times, one, two, or three persons died under such singular, thousand-pound rockfalls. Area ground shook fiercely with earthquake force, rattling windows and causing feet to tremble with the collapsing rock. A parallel problem with Copper Country cave-ins were the accompanying air blasts created by the displaced air from falling rock. This air was sent rushing in a whoosh throughout the underground web of tunnels (or drifts in mining lingo) and stopes. As this air rushed through the underground workings of a mine, it extinguished the mineworkers' "sunshine" lamps, leaving the miners in absolute darkness.

This is essentially what the Italian Hall tragedy was to efforts to organize the Copper Country. Not only did the tragedy create heartbreak and misery for those affected by the disaster, but as the event was a cave-in of sorts to union efforts, it also sent a proverbial rush of wind, an air blast, through the Copper Country, casting a dark shadow on efforts at unionization for almost thirty years. The sheer tragedy and heartbreak of events at Italian Hall bewildered the Western Federation of Miners (WFM). The WFM and strikers struggled to regroup and looked to the home of Hancock's Finnish immigrant socialist-unionists to do so: "Protest Meeting: A meeting of the strikers is called for tomorrow afternoon at 2 P.M. at Kansankoti Hall. This meeting is to be held for the purpose of protesting against the tyranny of the mining companies and injustice of Houghton County Officials. Prominent speakers will be present."[1] Could the pieces be put back together again after the dreadful event at Italian Hall? The answer: a resounding no.

While hundreds of families attempted to deal with premature death, sometimes of multiple members from one family, Charles Moyer, WFM president, almost lost his life. In the aftermath of the Italian Hall tragedy, Moyer arguably made one of the biggest missteps in the history of his WFM leadership. Moyer refused to accept any public monetary donations of sympathy unless they were from card-carrying union members.[2] This act likely alienated thousands of people who had no affiliation with the mining companies—people who were potential sympathizers of the union, especially in light of the tragic events at Italian Hall. While this was an attempt to provide strong leadership in a troubled time, it infuriated the local citizens. Mining companies and the Citizens' Alliance then attempted to capitalize in the arena of public opinion on Moyer's rejection.

Sitting miles away from the epicenter of the tragedy in Calumet, Charles Lawton wrote William R. Todd complaining of Moyer's rebuke of the money: "I keenly regretted to see that Moyer, the so called President of the Federation, should endeavor at once to make capital out of such an appalling disaster; and we shall try to checkmate its effect all we can. I have advised Messrs. Rice and Black, of Houghton, that they could call upon me to stand with them in whatever they thought best to do."[3] The competence of Moyer's actions in refusing money from those without a WFM card is debatable, but what happened to him next for this decision was reprehensible. What Messrs. Rice and Black (presumably), along with other members of the Citizens' Alliance, did on December 26, 1913, was to beat and nearly kill the president of the WFM. A number of men, thirty or more, many of whom had some association with the Citizens' Alliance, rushed Moyer's hotel room in Hancock and beat and nonfatally shot him, along with WFM auditor (or bodyguard according to some sources) Charles Tanner, and then placed both men on a train to Chicago.[4]

Moyer's fateful December night started off fine, however. Sheriff James Cruse had asked for a meeting to discuss events after Italian Hall and to ask for Moyer's cooperation in calming the area. Moyer initially told Cruse via telephone that he would be at the WFM's union store in Hancock, but the two then agreed to meet at the Scott Hotel in the evening around eight o'clock. No sooner had Cruse and a "Mr. Black" sat down to begin the discussion when a man, identified by Moyer as Calumet & Hecla (C&H) lawyer Albert E. Petermann, followed by a group of men, busted into Moyer's room at the Scott and "announced their business as concerned with the question of whether the Citizens' Alliance would be permitted to aid the families of the victims of the Christmas Eve tragedy." Also on the plate for the forced discussion was getting Moyer to retract his statements regarding the Citizens' Alliance's culpability for the Italian Hall tragedy.[5]

Moyer restated his position on the WFM burying its own, and then declared that he did not "positively" state that someone with a Citizens' Alliance button had called "Fire!" According to Moyer, "The committee became very indignant, blustered around, and said I had no right to come in and advise the people of *their* community. . . . I reminded them of their meeting a short time before in which they had condemned the people they now wanted to help." Moyer's refusal to take back his statements and his unwillingness to prostrate himself before the Copper Country oligarchy caused Petermann, who had been doing much of the talking, to state, "In taking this position, you will have to assume responsibility for anything that may occur to you after this."[6]

The committee of men headed by Petermann left, and it was just Moyer, Tanner, Cruse, and Black in the room. They all talked a bit further. Moyer reiterated his willingness to cooperate with Cruse in maintaining peace in the light of events at Italian Hall, and then Cruse and Black left. Moyer then got to the telephone and was in the process of making a call to the Calumet WFM local when the door swung open and the room "filled with men." These men were not there to talk and, according to Moyer, "piled on to me like a pack of wolves, kicking and striking and cursing. 'Hang the son of a b——. Kill him.'" Two men grabbed Moyer; he lurched forward, then a gun went off; one of the thugs had shot Moyer. The union leader thought he had been shot in the head, but, still alive, he was conscious. He was alert as he was dragged from his room, out of the hotel, and across the bridge from Hancock into Houghton amid chants of "Hang him" and "Throw him off the bridge."[7]

The destination of the mob—likely made up of Citizens' Alliance members—was the railroad depot. Moyer recalled that he heard three or four men at the depot say, "There is MacNaughton," and Moyer was dragged over to this man by the depot.

Moyer recounted that "while two men held me by the arms [Jim MacNaughton] grabbed me by the throat, cursed me, and then said, 'We are going to let you go this time with your life; if you ever come back here again, we will hang you.'" The man identified as MacNaughton then went through Moyer's coat pockets and, when satisfied, was ready to put Moyer's pocketbook back in his coat when someone said, "You'd better keep it, Jim, it might have valuable papers." According to Moyer, MacNaughton took $10 from the pocketbook, leaving $30, and then returned it and some notes to Moyer's pocket.[8]

While this was occurring, the train had arrived, and Moyer and Tanner were forced aboard. Two armed men, who identified themselves as deputy sheriffs, were assigned to watch the beaten and bleeding Moyer. While waiting at the depot, Moyer asked the two guards if they would wire for a doctor down the line; they did, and the train pulled out of Houghton. In Winona, some twenty or more miles south of Houghton, a doctor boarded the train and examined Moyer. Keeping his wits about him, Moyer asked the doctor for "a statement as to my condition" and "from whom the doctor received summons to attend me." The doctor obliged and wrote:

> C. H. Moyer was treated by me for a gunshot wound of back, apparently superficial in nature, also for lacerations of scalp. J. W. Story, M.D. 12/26/13. Was called by station agent at Winona by request of W. D. Hensley.[9]

The two guards hopped off the train at the Michigan state line, and Moyer was transported to Chicago, where he was taken immediately to a hospital.

Thus, if Lawton's words to Todd on December 26, 1913, were eerily prophetic and full of innuendo, a letter to Todd on the 27th was damning. Lawton penned:

> You will undoubtedly learn from the newspapers ere this reaches you, that Mr. Moyer and his body guard very precipitately left his room in the Scott Hotel last evening without even stopping to pay his bill, but caught the Copper Range train in Houghton and left this country for good. He had the proper escort across the bridge, and he had an escort out of town. He will never come back to the Copper Country; should he, he is apt to be lost and never found.[10]

The president of one of the most influential unions in the United States had just been beaten, shot, and deported by a mob of representatives of the Citizens' Alliance.

The local kept press and even the Associated Press downplayed events in the following days. Sheriff Cruse contacted Governor Ferris, giving a report on the event, explicitly stating that "his investigation had thus far failed to show that MacNaughton had any part in the deportation." Ferris seemed to want the whole incident to disappear, declaring, "they see no reason for federal action, and that Moyer has recourse to the Houghton county courts, or an appeal to the state if Houghton authorities do not give him satisfaction." Moyer's assessment of the situation was far more realistic when he "points, however, to his account of the deputy sheriffs, declares that the grand jury includes eight avowed members of the Citizens' Alliance as well as one mine manager and Manager MacNaughton's chauffeur."[11]

Who were these people then who had beaten, shot, and deported Moyer? Rumor and innuendo implicated some of Houghton County's biggest names in the assault and deportation. In addition to rumors implicating various members of the Houghton County elite, a number of men were brought up on charges of "great bodily harm, less than the crime of murder," in Moyer's beating. In the case of *The People of the State of Michigan v. W. B. Hensley*, Special Prosecutor George Nichols accused sixteen men of the savage beating and accidental shooting of Moyer, starting with W. B. Hensley, the deputy sheriff who had wired for a doctor. In addition to Hensley, Peter Murphy, H. Stuart Goodell, John MacNaughton, R. B. Harkness, John Hicock, Ferdinando Petermann, Edgar Rashleigh, James Wills, Harry Reid, Leigh Swift, Paul Swift, John Michaels, Mart Haas, William Bilkie, Joseph Hodgson, and John A. McAuley were charged.[12]

With the defendants including some of the prominent Copper Country elite, among them a MacNaughton and a Petermann, it was unlikely that the trial would go Moyer's way. It did not. Even more laughable were the names of witnesses for "The People": John Echlin, Elizabeth Coyne, George Harris, Fred R. Bowles, Thomas Hutchinson, *John W. Black*, *James A. Cruse*, Ben F. Johnson, Henry Hollister, Archie Hall, Lorenzo Barsi, Elmer Johnson, Aloysius Newman, Anton Kovoch, Anton Krugac, Edward Marcotte, J. H. Rice, Charles H. Moyer, *Albert E. Petermann*, Charles H. Tanner, Joseph Wills, Mrs. Archie Hall, H. S. Brock, Edward Brasseau, J. W. Story, Dr. M. A. Thometz, and George Marcotte.[13] The witnesses for the prosecution called by Special Prosecutor Nichols included many of the men advocating the demise of the WFM, such as Albert Petermann and James Cruse. Furthermore, J. H. Rice and John W. Black were, according to the letter from Lawton to Todd, the ones associated with the plot to "checkmate" Moyer's efforts in the Copper Country after Italian Hall.

Months later a labor spy reported on May 18, 1914: "Rickard got a number of names who are claimed to be the ones who deported Moyer. John MacAuley, John MacNaughton, Pete MacNaughton, James Wills, Joe Wills, Heidecamp [*sic*], Hensley, Murphy, Albert Petermann and John Mann. Mikko got these names from someone in Hancock."[14] This was perhaps not a very credible way of sourcing damning anti-company information, but more so an indication of who people thought were behind the conspiracy to rid the Copper Country of its WFM leadership. More damning, if Mikko's information was accurate, some of Houghton County's biggest names were among the vigilantes: the MacNaughtons, Albert Petermann, and Heidcamp—the foreman of Houghton County's December Special Grand Jury and the group that returned a no true bill against W. B. Hensley et al. It is perhaps no wonder (again if Mikko's information is true), then, that a Houghton County grand jury inexplicably chose to exonerate the group of men responsible for the beating and shooting, though many of Moyer's assailants had been identified.[15] Justice was undoubtedly a backward concept in the strike-ravaged Copper Country.

Moyer's termed "deportation," an act probably thought to quiet the Copper Country, seemed to have the opposite effect. Lawton again wrote Todd on December 27, fearful at the state of tension that existed in the Copper Country:

> The Copper Country is again in an over-excited condition. . . . Mr. Moyer's every step since to make capital out of that great calamity has added fuel to the flames, until everything is in a very boiling condition. I understand Mr. Moyer was planning to make a great grandstand play and speech on Sunday during the several en masse funerals. . . . Further tragedies were very narrowly averted last evening and last night; and I am very fearful at any moment something may break out. You cannot realize the pitch to which the people are wrought up. . . . With Moyer and his body guard out of the way, and with a great likelihood of the balance of the paid agitators leaving soon, it is quite possible that, by the end of next week, we will be able to dispense with a number of guards and, I trust, even the mounted police—that is, I expect a general settling down to take place.[16]

In retrospect, while what happened to Moyer and Tanner in today's parlance was more like assault with a deadly weapon, attempted murder, or kidnapping, there has been some consternation in the semantics of referring to what happened to him in Hancock as a "deportation." Here, we are comfortable calling what happened to Moyer a deportation because of the special connotation and significance the term holds in labor history. In some way, to be "deported" in labor history is a badge of honor. First, and most generally, it usually means an agitator, organizer, or labor leader has done something right. A person does not get deported for being a lackluster union advocate or supporter—good radicals are "deported"—not to suggest that Moyer was even that radical at this time. He certainly had a radical background, but he was in Hancock and the Copper Country because he believed that he had been "lawful" throughout the strike. The WFM had shipped most of its other nonlocal organizers out of the area in anticipation of a coming indictment from the Houghton County grand jury. Moyer stayed.

Moyer was not the first person to be "deported" from the Lake Superior basin area; he was not even the first person during the fall and winter of 1913–14 to be deported along the shores of the lake. At Duluth, Minnesota, in September 1913,

International Workers of the World (IWW) organizer F. W. Little was taken from a train car, placed in an automobile, and "incarcerated" in a house some twenty miles south of Duluth for his efforts at organizing men in the Duluth-Superior shipyards. Members of Duluth's union community rallied, traveled the twenty miles, and confronted the gunmen holding Little in the house. After being shot at, the union men from Duluth summoned the Carlton County sheriff, and Little was released without further incident.[17] This completely heinous affair with Little was referred to in the labor press as a "deportation." The same is true with Moyer.

Further evidence for "deportation" comes from perhaps the most infamous and possibly largest deportation of union men from an area: the Bisbee Deportation. In this absolute miscarriage of justice in 1917, just three years after the Moyer deportation, some 1,000 members of the IWW (or assumed-to-be members) were rounded up around the copper mining environs of Bisbee, Arizona, by a large posse of armed vigilantes. The vigilantes then herded the men like cattle into livestock train cars and shipped them to the middle of the southwestern desert. Almost all of the deported men survived, which was the good news. The bad news was that none of the vigilantes ever faced jail time for this heinous act.[18] It is often tempting to place modern meaning on historical events, but most people, including the labor press of the time, referred to what happened to Moyer on that fateful evening as a "deportation," and it should remain that way because of the term's long history in regards to labor studies.

Regionally, the lawlessness of pro–mining company factions did not go unnoticed. On January 21, 1914, the *Miners' Bulletin* ran an article titled "General Strike Threatened," which outlined a resolution promising a solidarity strike on the Upper Peninsula's Marquette Iron Range. Members of the Negaunee and Ishpeming miners' union locals passed resolutions designed to compel an investigation by the U.S. Congress regarding the "conditions in the strike district of the copper regions." Wording of the resolution left no doubt regarding the disgust felt by the Negaunee and Ishpeming unions. Citing the brutal assault and deportations of Moyer and Tanner, the deaths at Italian Hall, the persecution of *Työmies* staff, "black hand" letters being sent to WFM officials, and the general lawlessness of the oligarchy, the Ishpeming and Negaunee miners' unions resolved that something needed to be done to curb the violence and brutality of the Houghton County sheriff and the Citizens' Alliance.[19]

Työmies also mobilized national support for a congressional investigation. J. W. Sarlund, translator and secretary of the Finnish Socialist Federation, penned this message in Chicago to U.S. socialists: "National Secretary Socialist Party calls upon all locals to hold mass meetings immediately and send resolutions to the President and their Congressman demanding congressional investigation of Michigan strike.

Secretaries of all foreign speaking federations do likewise. Recent developments, Calumet catastrophe as one, prove we must take nation wide action in name of million socialists and of their respective organizations. National Secretary and foreign secretaries have each wired President Wilson."[20]

The month of January, however, proved to be the beginning of the end for Copper Country strikers. The WFM was a little snake-bit, and Moyer's refusal to accept funds for Italian Hall victims that were not directly related to organized labor alienated the WFM and its members in the Copper Country. Adding in the extreme measures of intimidation and violence perpetrated by the Copper Country mining companies, Citizens' Alliance, and Houghton County law enforcement officials, the wheels were slowly falling off the WFM machinery. The WFM was hemorrhaging money, men were walking back on the job, and the Copper Country winter exacted an icy toll on both bodies and morale. The WFM's epic struggle, catalyzed by immigrant workers, was ending in a slow burn.

Efforts to extend the strike languished to the point of extinction. In retrospect, the exact catalyst for the strike's end is unclear. Whether it was the intimidation and violence of the Copper Country oligarchy, Moyer's comments about the WFM burying its own, the tragedy at Italian Hall, disillusionment with the course of the strike, or just plain exhaustion on the part of the strikers, it seemed that the proletarian surge had been turned back. In January 1914, nearly 8,000 men went back to work. The mining companies had not changed their stance throughout the strike, as Puotinen wrote: "On March 2, a Calumet and Hecla superintendent reiterated a company position stated forty years earlier by Alexander Agassiz during the strike of 1874. Die-hard union men 'can find employment elsewhere. If they do not want to subscribe to the conditions that we impose, they are perfectly free to go to other places.'"[21]

There were small hints of an emerging end to the strike, bolstered by admonishments to listen for official union news only from official union sources: "Attention Striking Miners: The strike will not be 'called off' by the Daily Mining Gazette, Copper Journal, Calumet News nor by bulletins posted in the 'Rexall Drug Store.' Any information relative to the strike will be forthcoming from authoritative sources. DO NOT BE DECEIVED."[22] Even union-perceived concessions from the mining companies in April seemed to indicate that strike actions were close to ending: "Another Victory—Abolishment of the heavy one-man drill better known as the widowmaker. Every demand except the recognition of the union has now been granted." According to the *Miners' Bulletin*, mines were switching to the lighter Baby Leyner drill, which weighed approximately 90 pounds—down from previous models of the heavier one-man drill (150–190 pounds) in use before the strike. The *Bulletin* added, "Not only is the Baby Leyner lighter, but it is dustless and easily operated."[23] The WFM's

April rhetoric and rather technical machinery descriptions were much different from the heavily inspired proletarian-themed rhetoric that had come at the beginning of the strike; energy was lost, no matter how the WFM tried to spin it.

Every indication seemed to point to the strike ending in April, and on April 14, it did. The *Miners' Bulletin* reported that two propositions were put before the Copper Country WFM locals. The first was to make further sacrifices regarding strikers' benefits doled out by the WFM or return to work. The men, in large numbers, chose to return to work.[24] WFM district secretary Charles E. Hietala divulged that a vote on continuing the strike found that of the 4,740 men voting, the overwhelming majority 3,104 voted to go back to work. Mining companies required that strikers turn in their red WFM union cards to regain employment in the area copper mines. For many, giving up the fight and returning to the mines was just too much to bear. There are no statistical analyses of the out-migration from the Copper Country during this time, but it is common knowledge that many strikers left for other mining districts, such as the Minnesota iron ore ranges; left for Detroit factories; joined logging operations deep in the Upper Peninsula forests; or moved to rural agricultural areas on the Copper Country's industrial periphery.[25]

With the culmination of the strike actions, the *Miners' Bulletin* sounded a conciliatory yet defiant tone, advising the men to "Return to your work with a firm determining to do your full duty to your employer, an Honest days work for the compensation agreed upon. Give him full value of service, but do not permit yourselves to sink down into dumb indifference as to your future welfare, and the welfare of your children." The *Bulletin* implored the men to never give up on the coming "battle . . . fought for your own freedom . . . triumph over the bulwarks of capitalism which will join its predecessors of chattel slavery, serfdom and feudalism, to be buried forever in the past." This was impassioned writing from the *Bulletin*, but perhaps needlessly didactic in the midst of what was occurring at the time.[26]

It was in this last hour of concession that the Finnish Anti-socialist League officially organized in the Copper Country. The first formal meeting of Hancock's Anti-socialist League was on April 9, 1914, in Rouleau Hall. Calumet Finns organized a branch of the Anti-socialist League on May 10 of the same year, holding a large gathering in the Calumet National Guard Armory.[27] Twenty-two people attended the Hancock league's first meeting. The second meeting saw Swaby Lawton, Hancock city attorney and brother of Quincy Mine Company superintendent Charles Lawton, join the group as a new member of "good social standing." The second meeting attracted thirty-eight new members; the third meeting, forty-one new members; and the fourth meeting, sixty-three. By the fifth meeting, women joined the ranks. This coed meeting drew forty-two new members, but after that, numbers of new members began to drop off dramatically. Altogether, the league's ranks comprised roughly 285 members, who met at Rouleau Hall, Kauth Block Hall, and, after the fourth meeting, exclusively at Pohjantähti Temperance Hall.[28]

Predictably, the group focused almost solely on socialist-unionist activities in Hancock. Whether the league was jumping on Copper Country Finnish socialist-unionists specifically after the strike or reacting to a general threat of a renewed Copper Country strike, it seemingly was working to thwart any future disturbances that might again bring about another strikelike event. Ever vigilant, the group utilized the power of the mining companies through the local company-influenced media to "make a petition for the city council of Hancock to keep an eye on the event." At this time, it was considered to be enough to write an article about maintaining surveillance on the Finnish socialists to the *Mining Gazette*.[29] The Hancock league was, however, a short-lived organization: the last meeting entry for the Hancock Anti-socialist League occurred only half a year later, on September 12, 1915.[30]

The mining companies, the Citizen's Alliance, Houghton County law enforcement officials, and the Copper Country oligarchy in general had turned back the WFM. Make no mistake though—the mining companies suffered financially as well as publicly because of the strike. What toll did the strike take on the mining companies? In the months following the strike, the companies made some changes that were beneficial to wageworkers. An eight-hour day became standard in many copper mines, though it was widely speculated that the eight-hour day was coming to the copper mines before the 1913–14 strike. Some companies instituted a better system for worker grievance reporting, and in some cases wages received a slight bump up. For the mining companies, dividends shrank precipitously. In 1912, the mining companies paid out $9 million, but in 1913, $7 million, and only $1.6 million in 1914.[31] The strike certainly had a great effect on the mining companies, but most historians count the strike a loss for organized labor because mining companies never recognized the WFM. Predictably, the *Miners' Bulletin* was not so defeatist in its summation of the strike: "Had it not been for the work of the Western Federation of Miners since coming into the district you would still be working from eleven to thirteen hours in super heated dungeons a mile below the surface of the earth. . . . You can now return to work with the feeling that the fight you have made for better pay, shorter hours and more humane working conditions has been granted." The WFM's epic confrontation with the entrenched copper bosses and the Copper Country oligarchy was expensive, and there was a large bill for creating an unsuccessful minirevolution: "Almost a half million dollars was poured into the copper country for your benefit, besides a trainload of clothing."[32]

There were a number of last-ditch efforts to salvage the battered and somewhat broken labor actions. These efforts included a federal investigation; a WFM and United Mine Workers of America (UMWA) affiliation; and last, but perhaps most interesting, the organization of a Coxey's Army–like group to give attention to the plight of Copper Country workers.

There were, in fact, a number of investigations by committees of various sorts during the 1913–14 strike. The Copper Country Commercial Club's investigation of the strike that began on September 19, 1913, was little better than a propaganda piece benefitting the mining companies. The tone of the club's report is perhaps best summed up by two of the report's opening sentences: "From the day of its inception the strike has been attended with rioting and bloodshed. Every day riotous mobs roam through the streets of our communities and are held in check only by the force of the National Guard of our state."[33] It was mailed out, however, to Governor Ferris as well as to newspapers and other organizations across the United States. Other investigations were more hospitable to organized labor, but still a part of the political machinery. There was an especially good investigation in regards to the workers' cause conducted by Secretary of Labor Royal C. Meeks in November 1913. This report was used to create a number of findings for a senatorial investigation, which was compiled in January 1914. In this investigation, Meeks sent John B. Densmore, a solicitor from the Labor Department, and John A. Moffitt, an immigrant inspector for the Department of Labor, to try to settle the strike.[34] These men were only on the side of labor inasmuch as they were trying to settle the strike, while the copper companies in the Keweenaw were trying to crush it. The WFM welcomed the men's suggestions for settling the strike, while the mining companies would have nothing to do with such talk.

The WFM and its Copper Country locals were most hopeful with the U.S. House of Representatives Subcommittee of the Committee on Mines and Mining. The members of the subcommittee visited the Copper Country in February of 1914, and their report, *Hearings before a Subcommittee of the Committee on Mines and Mining*, derived from House Resolution 387, "A Resolution Authorizing and Directing the Committee on Mines and Mining to Make an Investigation of Conditions in the Copper Mines of Michigan," was issued in March.[35] The report was about as long and ineffectual as its title, even though the WFM expected this report to turn the tide of the strike. It did not, however, though the pageantry and parading of federal officials in the Copper Country was quite a show. The subcommittee, consisting of Representatives Edward T. Taylor of Colorado (chairman), Samuel M. Taylor of Arkansas, John J. Casey of Pennsylvania, Joseph Howell of Utah, and Robert M. Switzer of Ohio, toured the Copper Country, took tours of the mines, talked with the companies, talked with the strikers, asked for forms to be filled out, had fact-finding trials, and generally were wined and dined, having a good time of it. Initially, the mining companies feared the negative publicity and expected federal mingling of this House investigation, but as it became clear that the investigation was just a spectacle, the mining companies began to relax and let the political process take place. The report did nothing to help the WFM or Michigan copper workers.

Also during the latter stages of the strike, labor officials were bandying about a reshuffling of the "organizational" deck. Throughout the strike, the UMWA sent organizers into the area, and not just organizers, but big-name organizers. At this time the UMWA, like the WFM, was a part of the American Federation of Labor (AFL) and had money and resources aplenty, even while the similarly disaster-prone Ludlow Strike was going on in Colorado. Many of the UMWA's big names were in the Copper Country: John Mitchell, former UMWA president and current second vice president of the AFL; John Walker, president of the Illinois UMWA and onetime UMWA national presidential candidate; and John P. White, then current president of the UMWA were all in the Copper Country. Certainly, the UMWA wanted to show solidarity with fellow Copper Country miners, but the prominent names being trotted out into the Keweenaw's copper-rich soil were not just for a show of solidarity.

This barrage of UMWA leadership and money was offered in the hopes of bringing the WFM into the UMWA fold. The reports from C&H labor spies indicated that the rank-and-file in the Copper Country were working under the assumption that this merger in March or April was going to occur. Key figures and organizers of the Copper Country WFM locals were seemingly already UMWA men, as one labor spy report indicated in mid-March:

> George Wolf was in Hancock last evening. Met all organizers and officers of the union and reported there were 987 of the imported men signed up to either go away or go out on strike the first of May. This George Wolf has fifteen men operating under him out of thirty-nine men in the strike district. Walker of the United Mine Workers sends the money to George and he pays them. All these men are working in the mines. They get their pay on the third of each month.[36]

This WFM and UMWA merger would likely have meant interesting things for the strike if it would have occurred earlier in the strike. While the WFM was a strong union, it was a strong union in western parts of the United States. The UMWA was especially strong in Appalachia and knew how to fight a protracted war against eastern U.S. capitalists. In the last months of the strike, according to labor spies, there was a plan to reboot the strike on May 1, 1914. This reorganization would have likely occurred under the UMWA, as most of the strength in money and spirit was coming organizationally from the UMWA.[37] For reasons still somewhat unclear, the WFM-UMWA merger did not occur. The failure to achieve the WFM-UMWA merger put organizational efforts on shaky ground—maybe even occasioning the WFM's last gasp during the 1913–14 strike.

As a last measure and in a moment of passion for the cause, efforts to organize a Coxey's Army in the Copper Country were envisioned. The basic idea behind a tactic of this sort had its roots in a populist movement founded during the economic panic of 1893. In 1894, Jacob Coxey began a march from Ohio to Washington, D.C., to protest unemployment. Along the way, thousands joined him, and there was a sort of mythical quality to the protest. People from other parts of the nation began their own marches, and this tactic as a protest of material conditions among the working class became a unique response to the poor prevailing economic conditions.[38]

The plans for a Copper Country Coxey's Army–like march began to be formulated in April, just before the end of the strike, and lasted until after the cessation of the official strike. Sadly, this tactic never got out of the planning stages. If a little high-minded, the efforts to organize a Coxey's Army were nonetheless very creative. Efforts to organize such a populist army began among the Finnish immigrant population, as one labor spy reported, "Mikko spoke to the Finns and advised them to stick to the union and to the socialist party. Wants one thousand men for Coxey's Army." The idea to organize such a working-class army was one thing; implementation was another. According to the same labor spy, "The Finn bartender from Croze saloon in Houghton was out to-day and said he was discharged from tending bar. Wants to know what is the matter with the Calumet fellows who don't organize a Coxey's Army. Said over one thousand had signed up in Hancock and South Range." By the end of April, the Coxey's Army idea had lost its luster, perhaps mostly due to the poor support in the Calumet and Laurium areas, as an April 25 labor spy report indicated: "Hietala, the district secretary, was out today for the purpose of getting the Calumet out to join Coxey's Army. Had very poor success. Calumet men won't join."[39]

None of these measures panned out. The congressional investigation was held, but it did not have the effect the WFM or its supporters in the Copper Country hoped for. The plans for affiliation with the UMWA never materialized, and Copper Country mineworkers were left wondering what a merger with that powerful organization might have meant. And the idea of a Coxey's Army—that had problems from the inception. Workers had just been on strike for almost nine months, and perhaps the thought of marching to Lansing and then Washington, D.C., was a little too much to ask.

No matter the tactic, facts were facts—the strike was unceremoniously broken and the WFM unrecognized. The WFM was even more "broke," as it sank a small fortune into the strike. "The Western Federation had lost hard fought battles before, but this one proved particularly devastating. The strike left the union buried in debt. It spent $800,000 in an attempt to organize the Michigan copper workers, including $125,000 borrowed from other labor organizations; $275,000 that had come as voluntary contributions; and nearly $400,000 of mandatory assessments paid in by WFM members," wrote Larry Lankton.[40]

Though the strike was off, a torch continued to burn for many who deplored wages, conditions, and labor-management relations in the Copper Country. The WFM National and its Sixteenth District Union agreed that calling off the strike had left some incomplete business in the Copper Country. Dan Sullivan, president of the Sixteenth District Union, and Charles Hietala, secretary of the same, authored a summation, thank-you, and defiant promise to various supporters of the strike, which included the UMWA, the AFL, and the Socialist Party of America (SPA): "The help which you gave has enabled us to stay with the struggle until our demands for improved working conditions were granted at least in part. . . . We wish to again express our appreciation and thanks to all who aided us and to assure you that while our victory at this time will be regarded as only partial our struggle for improved working conditions will continue until the banner of organized labor shall wave triumphant over the copper mines of Michigan."[41]

Still, many Finnish immigrant labor organizers planned and plotted ways to continue the challenge against the Copper Country bosses, and some believed that the WFM National did not fully commit to the strike.

In July 1914, Hietala implored the WFM national: "There are still men in the Copper Country who believe they were sold to the companies and believe that the Federation [WFM] had enough money to support them until the battle was won."[42] Like many socialist-unionist Finnish immigrants, Hietala remained true to the cause and was unwilling to give up on efforts in the Copper Country, as a final letter to the WFM national asserts:

> Now as to the organizing work in this district, I will say that in my opinion after 5–6 months the organizing work can be done with good success if the conditions little improve in the Iron district. At the present time every day number of men are coming from Iron Country to this district looking for work and that makes conditions to the local miners miserable or in other words hard to keep their jobs because hundreds of men are always looking for work round the mining company offices. The Anti-socialist movement will loose their foothold soonest the conditions little improve and they have already lost good number of their dues paying members according to their own newspaper reports.[43]

It was a hard and bitter truth, but the WFM had failed to organize the Michigan copper mines. The WFM had run out of money to support a strike, and increasingly, internal factions within the WFM began to argue over the future of the WFM. With the exception of a few holdout strikers, the copper mines were back in nearly full production by early May.[44]

Union sentiment was still very strong in the Copper Country; as steadfast supporters of the union were either unable or unwilling to give up the fight. Mining companies required workers to turn in their red WFM cards or "books" to regain employment in area mines, and many did. However, this did not mean that workers could not get another card. In many hearts, the union ideology burned bright. One example of this commitment was Herman Manley, who went back to work in the Tamarack Mine. He had lost his wife, who was pregnant, and one son in the Italian Hall tragedy. He had seen their caskets carried out of Calumet and buried in Lake View Cemetery, but he still believed in the union. Caring for a toddler-aged son, Manley went back into the mines, perhaps knowing only this vocation in America, and began working copper. He was working again in the mines, and he apparently had given up his WFM book, but he was not a wage-slave. According to a June 1914 labor spy report, "There is a man by the name of Manley working in North Tamarck, lost wife and child in Italian hall, got two books, a socialist."[45] Herman Manley believed. Whether it was a stubborn holding on to the union for his lost family members or a strong commitment to the collective ideology, Herman Manley believed the only way to a better life came through organized action.

The mining companies and the Citizens' Alliance were ever vigil for recurring attempts at organization, and there were several. The Quincy Mining Company remained vigilant because although the WFM had been defeated, the ideal persisted. Blacklisted workers, sympathizers, and those who were just fed up with the industrial milieu left the Copper Country's mining areas in droves, sometimes settling in rural areas on the mining companies' industrial periphery. At times, this settlement was too close for comfort, as we find with Paavola (formerly Concord City), a rural hamlet sandwiched in between the Quincy Mining Company's industrial core. In a letter from Quincy Mining Company general manager Charles Lawton to Quincy president William R. Todd, Lawton warned Todd that union men and socialists were leaving company property and heading to Paavola. Possibly fearing eviction from company houses, Finnish immigrant socialist-unionists retreated to this ethnic enclave to reorganize, reenergize, or simply escape. Paavola was unique in that it was almost adjacent to company property, and as it was not on company property, many of the strikers, members of the WFM, took refuge in Paavola. This troubled Lawton, as is clear from an April 4, 1914, letter to Todd: "In checking up on the voters of Franklin Township, we find that a great many of the Federation men who have left company houses, have gone over to Concord City to live, and still remain in Franklin Township. Therefore, the outlook for eliminating the Socialists and Federation men in the election of Monday next is not over bright. The idle labor vote seems to be very strong."[46]

Lawton had good reason to be worried about the concentration of workers with union and socialist sympathies in towns where they might use their votes to elect pro-union men to local office or punish anti-union politicians at the ballot box. Such was the case in Franklin Township, a stronghold of socialists and WFM members, where workers nominated a "Labor ticket" for the 1914 election. Labor's candidates included a number of Finnish workers such as Henry Kotila, who ran for justice of the peace, and Matti Paalakangas, a candidate for constable.[47]

While the prospect of workers electing their own candidates to office frightened employers and their allies in the press to attack the socialists as a "scourge," they were more concerned with Richard Rourke Jr., a bartender and county supervisor from Franklin Township.[48] Rourke was the incumbent during the April 1914 election, and he handily defeated his opponent by a 379 to 252 margin. Procompany candidates—always loyally referred to as the "regular nominees" in the mainstream press—won the remaining Franklin races. The *Daily Mining Gazette* celebrated the election of "regular nominees" throughout the Copper Country, except "in Franklin Township Supervisor Rourke was re-elected. He has socialistic tendencies, but is enrolled as a democrat."[49] Quincy general manager Charles Lawton showed mixed emotions about the election, mourning Rourke's election while celebrating the fact that the "full Socialist and Federation ticket was defeated with that exception [Rourke]. We therefore have the Supervisor's hands tied so that he cannot injure Quincy." Lawton continued by expressing an optimistic outlook for the future, a time in which the workers' parties would cease to function: "In another year, by the elimination of the Socialists and by the voting of our new men, I think we will be able to eliminate that member of the Socialist and Federation party."[50]

Workers also mobilized their vote throughout the Copper Country, running labor, socialist, or "workman's" tickets in the April 6 elections. In Allouez Township, workers won several races, as workman's candidates were elected as town clerk, treasurer, highway commissioner, and overseer of highways. The workers' ticket also captured three justice of the peace and three constable positions in Allouez, while workman's candidate Charles Johnson gained the Allouez seat on the Board of Review. Thus, while the *Daily Mining Gazette* reported that the "Socialists Fare Badly All Over," in Allouez, at least, election day provided Copper Country workers with a small measure of victory.[51] Still, victories for the workers' parties were few and far between. In Calumet, the "nomination ticket" defeated their WFM-supported foes, with James MacNaughton winning reelection as supervisor by a four-to-one margin over the socialist candidate.[52] Unable to mask its happiness at watching the workers' parties go down to defeat, the *Daily Mining Gazette* led off its election coverage with a headline reading: "Reds Repulsed in Their Attempts to Break into Copper Country Politics."[53]

As the WFM had withered with the loss of the strike, there was an organizational vacuum in the Lake Superior basin area. Into this void, and with more radical and more revolutionary gusto, the IWW set about trying to make inroads into the Copper Country. Radical sentiment after the loss of the Copper Country Strike had shifted west, and by 1916 the IWW had organized a districtwide strike of iron ore workers in northeastern Minnesota mines.

With Copper Country employers still on guard from events during the 1913–14 strike and flush with the support of the federal government to exploit at will during the First World War to boost wartime copper production, the Wobblies were really up against spectacular odds in their attempts to organize the Copper Country. Ever vigil, the Copper Country oligarchy was not going to make the mistake of letting an industrial union gain inroads into the Keweenaw, and a revival of a Citizens' Alliance–type group was in the making. "This organization is now being revived to get action before the suspected IWW forces become too menacing. During the past week activities of the agitators who have their headquarters in Kansankoti hall socialist headquarters in Hancock have become alarming."[54]

The first attempt at oppression by a new and improved citizens' alliance, re-named as a wartime "Home Guard," was directed at union media: "A great quantity of socialist and strike literature has been brought into the district lately and is secreted in the hall detectives claim and efforts to flood the district with it have been made but were stopped through prompt action of informal vigilance committees." Next came the stripping of freedom of assembly: "The civilian or Home Guard troop of cavalry at Calumet has twice patrolled the district once during the day and once at night to prevent holding of IWW meetings and circulation of the literature." However, despite the efforts to curtail the organization of Copper Country workers during WWI, union sentiment was a glowing ember: "The (IWW) organizers have for some time been making a house to house canvass in parts of the district in the interests of the IWW. The shortage of labor in the mines has helped the agitators in their work to a considerable extent, many of the men employed elsewhere and brought here by the companies found to be active members of the IWW. There are about twenty thousand men employed in the mining industry of Houghton Keweenaw and Ontonagon counties. As fast as IWW members are spotted among the mine crews they are discharged, but few, it is declared have left the district."[55]

Despite further attempts at organization in the Michigan copper mines over the years, various unions, their rank-and-file, and numerous ethnic groups and organizations were turned back for quite some time. It was not until the Franklin Roosevelt administration, in 1943, that organized labor would finally be recognized in Michigan's copper mines. The legend, mythology, and seeds of discontent that the 1913–14 Michigan Copper Strike left behind, however, were almost as epic as the strike itself. This strike—this protracted shutdown of an industry and at times a bitter class war—was a valiant effort to change the exploitive conditions of Copper Country living and working conditions. Copper Country workers grew to know and understand the ideals of organized labor, and some even experienced, for a short time, a radical social revolution, but it simply was just not enough to change the fundamental nature of industrial relations in the Copper Country. The tide had been turned back, and most significantly, Copper Country mineworkers were still non-union. This was a bitter pill for many to swallow.

Conclusion

AFTER THE GREAT STRUGGLE TO ORGANIZE THE COPPER COUNTRY WAS OVER, there was time to pause and consider the effects the 1913–14 Michigan Copper Strike had on Michigan and America. Perhaps the *Locomotive Firemen's Magazine*, the journal for the Brotherhood of Locomotive Firemen, which ran articles about the strike, put the strike in the most appropriate perspective. The newspaper argued that if the Citizens' Alliance was allowed to persist in its "insane attitude" and break the Western Federation of Miners (WFM), it would not stop until it successfully drove "union labor forever out of the copper country."[1]

The *Locomotive Firemen's Magazine*'s prediction proved all too prescient, as employers used their victory in the strike to their advantage, greatly impeding the Copper Country's labor movement, depriving the region's workers of union representation and a voice on the job. By April 1914, the Copper Country WFM had been destroyed, its leading activists were blacklisted by the region's mine companies, and all union members were forced to turn in their union cards to gain employment in the mines. That their defeat was the product of coercion rather than consent, and that it came at the hands of better-organized, better-financed, and more powerful interests than their own, surely made little difference to the defeated strike force.

This major setback for the Copper Country's labor movement was one illustration of the lasting significance of the great strike, but what elevates the strike to the level of national significance are several of its other leading features. This book was written partly in the hopes of thrusting the strike and its participants into the national spotlight. To be sure, several of the strike's key elements—the antilabor violence, the collective efforts of employers to break the strike, and the leading role of southern and eastern European immigrants—were shared by other prominent labor conflicts of the Progressive era. But much about the 1913–14 strike remains unique.

First, and ultimately most important, the Italian Hall tragedy occurred during and because of the strike. Even in the unlikely event that no one yelled "Fire!" and the deaths were nothing more than tragic accidents, those deaths would not have occurred without the strike. Moreover, while the victims of the tragedy came from different ethnic and age groups, all of the people who died in Italian Hall were members of the working class, and thus, as was true of most deaths that came during strikes, employers and their surrogates kept themselves and their families free from the bloodshed. Victims' families, strikers, and much of the nation's labor movement remembered the Christmas Eve disaster as an act of class violence. That the historian Arthur Thurner dismissed these views as little more than "a legend" is evidence that even in writing labor history, workers' voices are too often marginalized in favor of those from other social groups.[2]

Of course, the Italian Hall tragedy left scars throughout the Copper Country. The land, the mines, and the people all had their own scars and tales to tell. In time, some of the bitterness faded away as life in the Copper Country moved on, snowy winter after snowy winter, boom cycle after bust in the copper industry. Some scars, though, lasted a lifetime, as was the case with Melba Luoma, who was in Italian Hall that fateful night. Remembering her friend more than ninety years later, Lillian Gow stated of Luoma: "She lived the rest of her life with a great, big, black and blue mark on her arm. She was crushed, underneath this pile. . . . I suppose, all that pressure, and she carried that (mark) all her life."[3]

The strike also bankrupted the WFM, and the Copper Country mineworkers' defeat dramatically weakened that union. While damaging any institution that serves to increase the power of the marginalized in relation to the powerful is to be mourned, the damage done to the WFM and the end of that union's history in the Copper Country were exceptional tragedies. The WFM was the institution of choice for tens of thousands of America's most militant and most lionized workers, the hard-rock miners of the American West. After 1916, the WFM changed its name to the International Union of Mine, Mill, and Smelter Workers, a union with an impressive history of its own. But the union was never the same. After all, how could any institution live up to the reputation of the WFM, which had founded some of the most celebrated working-class institutions in U.S. history, including the Western Labor Union and American Labor Union? The WFM also deserves much of the credit for the founding the Industrial Workers of the World (IWW), the radical institution par excellence in American labor history. While the Wobblies remained relevant long after 1914, and miners and westerners more generally retain much of their militant spirit to this day, the decline of their original fighting union can only be seen for what it was: a tragic loss for the working class at large, a loss caused in part by the defeat of the Copper Country mineworkers in 1914.

The strike and its consequences were also significant to historians for the lessons they provide about early twentieth century labor relations. The strike witnessed a community polarized around divisions of class, as employers mobilized through their commercial club, the Citizens' Alliance, and the "kept press" against the region's unionized workers. The possibility of lost profits and control over the workplace posed by the WFM in the Copper Country was far too threatening for the region's copper barons to bear. While it is true that Copper Country employers were consistent in their use of paternalism to quiet working-class militancy—and thus the region's copper industry was in some ways unique—Copper Country employers replicated the actions of their counterparts across the United States in their attacks on workers and their unions. Indeed, when it came to dealing with militant workers and unions, employers in Michigan's copper industry dropped any pretense of benevolent dictatorship, preferring to break strikes with an iron fist. In this respect, at least, labor relations on the copper range resembled those of other American industries and regions during the late nineteenth and early twentieth centuries.

The strike also delivered important lessons about the nature of industrial capitalism. In the early twenty-first century, with all the talk of globalization, it is easy to forget that forces have been connecting people across oceans and seas and continents for centuries. One hundred years ago even the relatively isolated Copper Country, like the rest of the United States, was locked within a system of industrial capitalism that was not confined to a single region, nation, or continent. Thus subject to the forces of international capitalism, the 1913–14 strike was never confined to the Copper Country. Its workers, themselves immigrants from (mostly) across the Atlantic Ocean, were able to strike, to shut down Michigan's copper mines, and to exert a significant community presence through their parades, pickets, and mass meetings. But they had no power to provide jobs to members of the "reserve army of labor," who were recruited as scabs from other parts of the country and brought into the Copper Country, nor did the striking miners have the ability to halt the flow of eastern capital that was used to pay these men. Local workers and their union were also relatively powerless to prevent thrill-seeking criminals recruited by strikebreaking agencies from traveling into the region to guard the mines and break strikers' heads. Thus, even the most seemingly isolated of strikes was locked in a national and international socioeconomic system, one that influenced the strike's outcome and remained largely outside the control of the Copper Country's men and women.

The 1913–14 Copper Country Strike and Italian Hall tragedy remain the stuff of major controversy, especially in Michigan's Upper Peninsula. Longtime community members, seasoned historians, children participating in "History Day" discussions, and even visitors to the region can be heard repeating the oft-asked questions that surround this epic labor struggle and horrible tragedy: "Who shouted 'Fire!'?" "Which way did the doors open?" "How many people died at Italian Hall?" "Were the victims' deaths the product of premeditated mass murder or a terrible accident?" "Was the strike caused by outside agitators, a breakdown in paternalistic relations between boss and worker, years of organizing efforts by unionists and radicals, or long-standing class tensions between workers and employers that finally boiled over in 1913–14?" *Community in Conflict* was written in the hopes of shedding new light on these questions and contributing to these discussions, rather than offering any easy, definitive answers.

While it is questions such as those just listed that animate much of the historical discussion around the Copper Country, they are neither the most interesting nor important aspects of the Copper Country's past. Instead, what drove our research and what drives *Community in Conflict* are a number of historical processes through which workers and employers became aware of their oppositional interests and acted to protect those interests. Thus, Copper Country workers formed literally dozens of trade unions, industrial unions, socialist parties, revolutionary organizations, and radical ethnic clubs. But as should be apparent from reading the preceding chapters, workers did not confine their class-based activities to the workplace or picket line, but also expressed them through a rich cultural and social life, with workers meeting at their union halls and Labor Day parades, writing letters to their union or socialist periodical of choice, and forming a wide variety of class-based institutions.

Community in Conflict has not solved the mystery of who caused the Italian Hall disaster, nor was it written with that purpose in mind. In fact, it is unlikely that the mystery will ever be solved. We are, after all, in a much worse position to crack the case than were the WFM and the Calumet & Hecla (C&H) Mining Company, both of which launched investigations in the tragedy's immediate aftermath. Instead, our own investigations into that tragedy add further complexity to the case, informing us, among other things, that Copper Country mine bosses along with the Citizens' Alliance orchestrated a December campaign of violence and that their paid operative believed the culprit to have been a man named "Messner." Instead of purporting to "solve the case," this book represents an honest effort to fully investigate the complete historical record of Italian Hall, including "new" sources overlooked by earlier scholars. Ultimately, we cannot point the finger at a single individual or institution responsible for the Italian Hall tragedy, but we do recognize that the underlying causes of the disaster must be laid at the feet of the Copper Country mine bosses who refused to engage in collective bargaining with workers' representatives, preferring to meet the "threat" of unionism with an iron fist. That the WFM organized a Christmas Eve party to bring a little joy into the lives of the region's working-class children who suffered during a long winter where their parents had no money is testimony as to the scope of the struggle. That the party ended in a disaster for those same working people showed that nowhere, not even a Christmas celebration, was there a safe place for working-class families amid the antilabor crackdown that broke the Copper Country's mineworkers' unions in the winter of 1913–14.

The 100-year anniversary of the Copper Country Strike and Italian Hall tragedy has provided us with this opportunity to discuss and pay tribute to the men, women, and children who led the struggles for workers' rights in the late nineteenth and early twentieth centuries. That it took a full century for workers to be placed at the center of the region's history, including its epic 1913–14 labor war, is a useful lesson about the marginalization of working people within U.S. history and mainstream American discourse as a whole. If this book has restored the Copper Country's working-class majority to center stage of the region's history, then we have achieved our main purpose in writing this book. And if this book advanced the understanding of the complexities of working people's lives, the diverse forms of organizations they formed and struggles they waged, and the courageous stands they took in the face of overwhelming odds, then we have succeeded beyond our expectations.

Notes

INTRODUCTION

1. *Työmies*, December 25, 1913.
2. Woody Guthrie, "1913 Massacre," http://www.arlo.net/resources/lyrics/1913-massacre.shtml.
3. Lankton, *Cradle to Grave*. The idea of the three phases of production are developed throughout the book.
4. Indigenous peoples had used copper for hundreds if not thousands of years in ceremonial rites or for hunting purposes in this region of North America. It was not until the early nineteenth century that whites began exploiting the mineral wealth of Native American lands in this area. Lankton, *Cradle to Grave*; Arthur W. Thurner, *Strangers and Sojourners: A History of Michigan's Keweenaw Peninsula* (Detroit: Wayne State University Press, 1994). For an account of Native American use of copper in the region, see Susan Martin's archaeological work, *Wonderful Power: The Story of Ancient Copper Working in the Lake Superior Basin* (Detroit: Wayne State University Press, 1999).
5. Lankton, *Cradle to Grave*, 5–11.
6. Ibid., 148–152.
7. Ibid., 145.
8. Vernon H. Jensen, *Heritage of Conflict: Labor Relations in the Nonferrous Metals Industry up to 1930* (Ithaca, N.Y.: Cornell University Press, 1950), quoted in Lankton, *Cradle to Grave*.

CHAPTER 1. CONTEXT

1. *Solidarity* (Cleveland), April 11, 1914.

2. Stephen H. Norwood, *Strikebreaking and Intimidation: Mercenaries and Masculinity in Twentieth-Century America* (Chapel Hill: University of North Carolina Press, 2001), 154; Philip S. Foner, *The History of the Labor Movement in the United States*, Vol. 5, *The AFL in the Progressive Era, 1910–1915* (New York: International Publishers, 1980), 224–225.

3. U.S. Congress, *Conditions in the Copper Mines of Michigan: Hearings before a Subcommittee of the Committee on Mines and Mining* (Washington, D.C.: Government Printing Office, 1914), 8.

4. *Työmies*, December 31, 1913; Gary Kaunonen, *Challenge Accepted: A Finnish Immigrant Response to Industrial America in Michigan's Copper Country* (Lansing: Michigan State University Press, 2010), 152–153.

5. "Copper Region Calm with Militia There," *New York Times*, July 25, 1913; "Confer to End Copper Strike," *Los Angeles Times*, August 4, 1913; "Gov Ferris to Take Action," *Boston Daily Globe*, July 30, 1913.

6. "Xmas-Tree Panic Costs 80 Lives," *New York Times*, December 25, 1913.

7. Edward J. McGurty, "The Copper Miners' Strike," *International Socialist Review* 14, no. 3 (September 1913): 152.

8. Arthur Thurner, *Strangers and Sojourners: A History of Michigan's Keweenaw Peninsula* (Detroit: Wayne State University Press, 1994), 201; Carl Ross, *The Finn Factor in American Labor, Culture, and Society* (New York Mills, Minn.: Parta Printers, 1977), 125.

9. "Mitchell Praises Strikers," *New York Times*, August 24, 1913.

10. *Dubuque (Iowa) Telegraph-Herald*, November 6, 1913.

11. Cited in Jo Ann E. Argersinger, *The Triangle Fire: A Brief History with Documents* (Boston: Bedford/St. Martin's, 2009), 25. See also David Von Drehle, *Triangle: The Fire That Changed America* (New York: Atlantic Monthly Press, 2003).

12. Cited in Argersinger, *Triangle Fire*, 24.

13. Norwood, *Strikebreaking and Intimidation*, 147; Foner, *History of the Labor Movement in the United States*, 5:206–207.

14. Louis Adamic, *Dynamite! A Century of Class Violence in America, 1830–1930* (London: Rebel Press, 1984), 150–151; Norwood, *Strikebreaking and Intimidation*, 146–147. See also George McGovern and Leonard F. Guttridge, *The Great Coal Field War* (Boston: Houghton Mifflin, 1972).

15. *Masses*, June 1914.

16. Cited in Julia Pferdehirt, *More Than Petticoats: Remarkable Michigan Women* (Guilford, Conn.: TwoDot, 2007), 88; *Työmies*, December 25, 1913; *Miners' Magazine*, January 13, 1914.

17. "Xmas-Tree Panic Costs 80 Lives."

18. Larry Lankton, *Hollowed Ground: Copper Mining and Community Building on Lake Superior, 1840s-1990s* (Detroit: Wayne State University Press, 2010), 197–198; U.S. Congress, *Conditions in the Copper Mines*, 1163; Alice K. Hoagland, *Mine Towns: Buildings for Workers in Michigan's Copper Country* (Minneapolis: University of Minnesota Press, 2010).

19. "Moyer Wounded, Lays It to Plot," *New York Times*, December 28, 1913.

20. On the "labor wars," see Adamic, *Dynamite!*; Sidney Lens, *The Labor Wars: From the Molly Maguires to the Sit-Downs* (Garden City, N.Y.: Doubleday, 1973).

21. Patrick Renshaw, *The Wobblies: The Story of the IWW and Syndicalism in the United States* (New York: Anchor Books, 1968), 143–167.

22. Philip S. Foner, *The History of the Labor Movement in the United States*, Vol. 4, *The Industrial Workers of the World, 1905–1917* (1965; repr., New York: International Publishers, 1997), 499, 535–536; *Industrial Worker* (Seattle), May 9, 1923; Ralph Chaplin, *The Centralia Conspiracy* (Chicago: Industrial Workers of the World, 1924); Walker Smith, *The Everett Massacre* (Chicago: Industrial Workers of the World, 1917).

23. Philip Dray, *There Is Power in a Union: The Epic Story of Labor in America* (New York: Doubleday, 2010), 329.

24. William D. Haywood, "On the Paterson Picket Line," *International Socialist Review* 13 (June 1913): 848.

25. Philip S. Foner, *The History of the Labor Movement in the United States*, Vol. 3, *The Policies and Practices of the American Federation of Labor, 1900–1909* (1964; repr., New York: International Publishers, 1973), 32–36; David Roediger, "'Not Only the Ruling Classes to Overcome, but Also the So-Called Mob': Class, Skill, and Community in the St. Louis General Strike of 1877," *Journal of Social History* 19, no. 2 (Winter 1985): 213–239; William Millikan, *A Union against Unions: The Minneapolis Citizens Alliance and Its Fight against Organized Labor, 1903–1947* (St. Paul: Minnesota Historical Society Press, 2001); Reinhold Kramer and Tom Mitchell, *When the State Trembled: How A. J. Andrews and the Citizens' Committee Broke the Winnipeg General Strike* (Toronto: University of Toronto Press, 2010).

26. Foner, *History of the Labor Movement in the United States*, 4:191–194.

27. Cited in Robert Walter Bruere, *Following the Trail of the IWW: A First-Hand Investigation into Labor Troubles in the West—A Trip into the Copper and the Lumber Camps of the Inland Empire with the Views of the Men on the Job* (New York: New York Evening Post, 1918), 19.

28. Cited in Foner, *History of the Labor Movement in the United States*, 4:198.

29. U.S. Congress, *Conditions in the Copper Mines*, 1557.

30. Ibid., 1551.

31. Ibid., 1228–1229.

32. There exists a sizable literature on the history of labor spies. See Frank Morn, *"The Eye That Never Sleeps": A History of the Pinkerton National Detective Agency* (Bloomington: Indiana University Press, 1982); Robert P. Weiss, "Private Detective Agencies and Labour Discipline in the United States, 1855–1946," *Historical Journal* 29, no. 1 (1986): 87–107; Leo Huberman, *The Labor Spy Racket* (New York: Modern Age Books, 1937); Robert M. Smith, *From Blackjacks to Briefcases: A History of Commercialized Strikebreaking and Unionbusting in the United States* (Athens: Ohio University Press, 2003); Norwood, *Strikebreaking and Intimidation*; Rhodri Jeffreys-Jones, *Violence and Reform in American History* (New York: New Viewpoints, 1978), 100–114.

33. J. Anthony Lukas, *Big Trouble: A Murder in a Small Western Town Sets Off a Struggle for the Soul of America* (New York: Simon & Schuster, 1997), 84–85; Smith, *From Blackjacks to Briefcases*, 21.

34. Richard O. Boyer and Herbert M. Morais, *Labor's Untold Story: The Adventure Story of the Battles, Betrayals, and Victories of American Working Men and Women* (New York:

Cameron Associates, 1955), 151–157; Morn, *"Eye That Never Sleeps,"* 103; Vernon H. Jensen, *Heritage of Conflict: Labor Relations in the Nonferrous Metals Industry Up to 1930* (Ithaca, N.Y.: Cornell University Press, 1950; repr., New York: Greenwood Press, 1968), 202. In *Labor Before the Law,* Judy Fudge and Eric Tucker argue that the Thiel Detective Service also had great strength in Canada. Judy Fudge and Eric Tucker, *Labor Before the Law: The Regulation of Workers' Collective Action in Canada, 1900–1948* (Toronto: University of Toronto Press, 2004), 86.

35. Stephen H. Norwood, *Strikebreaking and Intimidation: Mercenaries and Masculinity in Twentieth Century America* (Chapel Hill: University of North Carolina Press, 2002), 4.

36. U.S. Congress, *Conditions in the Copper Mines of Michigan: Hearings Before a Subcommittee of the Committee on Mines and Mining* (Washington, D.C.: Government Printing Office, 1914), 1124. See also Norwood, *Strikebreaking and Intimidation,* 114–116, 149–154.

37. Joshua L. Rosenbloom, "Strikebreaking and the Labor Market in the United States, 1881–1894," *Journal of Economic History* 58, no. 1 (March 1998): 184.

38. F. C. Herr to C. L. Lawton, November 16, 1907, Quincy Mining Company Papers, Box 341, Folder 004, Spy Reports, The Burr-Herr Company Investigators, 1907, QN 321D, Copper Country Historical Archive, Michigan Technological University, Houghton.

39. Max Ross, Mgr., Youngstown Employment Agency, to Chas. L. Lawton, December 19, 1913, Quincy Mining Company Papers, Labor Spy Reports, July 1913–March 1914, Copper Country Historical Archive, Michigan Technological University, Houghton.

40. Calumet and Hecla Employee Records, "Ellis Spreadsheet," Copper Country Historical Archive, Michigan Technological University, Houghton, 2004.

41. *Conditions in the Copper Country,* 961–962.

42. Ibid., 963.

43. Ibid., 967.

44. Hugh E. Boyer, "The Decline of the Progressive Party in Michigan's Upper Peninsula: The Case of Congressman William J. MacDonald in 1914," *Michigan History* 13 (Fall 1987): 75–94.

45. Charles Moore, *History of Michigan* (Chicago: Lewis, 1915), 4:2278.

46. Thurner, *Strangers and Sojourners,* 200.

47. *Aberdeen (Wash.) Daily World,* November 24, 1911.

48. Robert Justin Goldstein, *Political Repression in Modern America: From 1870 to 1976* (Urbana: University of Illinois Press, 2001), 90.

49. Jack Morton, "Why Should I Be a Socialist?" *International Socialist Review* 15, no. 9 (March 1915): 543.

50. Robert Asher, "The Limits of Big Business Paternalism: Relief for Injured Workers in the Years Before Workmen's Compensation," in *Dying for Work: Workers' Safety and Health in Twentieth-Century America,* ed. David Rosner and Gerald Markowitz (Bloomington: Indiana University Press, 1989), 19.

51. State of Michigan, Industrial Accident Board, *Workmen's Compensation Law: Information to Employees* (Lansing, Mich.: Wynkoop Hallenbeck Crawford, State Printers, 1912), 5.

52. Lankton, *Hollowed Ground,* 185.

53. Ira Kipnis, *The American Socialist Movement, 1897–1912* (New York: Columbia University Press, 1952); Jeffrey A. Johnson, *"They Are All Red Out Here": Socialist Politics in the*

Pacific Northwest, 1895–1925 (Norman: University of Oklahoma Press, 2008); James R. Green, *Grass-Roots Socialism: Radical Movements in the Southwest, 1895–1943* (Baton Rouge: Louisiana State University Press, 1978); Philip S. Foner, *The History of the Labor Movement in the United States*, Vol. 2, *From the AF of L to the Emergence of American Imperialism* (New York: International Publishers, 1964), 367–392.

54. Kipnis, *American Socialist Movement*, 339.

55. Joseph Robert Conlin, *Bread and Roses Too* (Westport, Conn.: Greenwood Press, 1969), 128–129; Green, *Grass-Roots Socialism*, 200; Aaron Goings, "Red Harbor: Class, Violence, and Community in Grays Harbor, Washington" (Ph.D. diss., Simon Fraser University, 2011), 163–192; Kaunonen, *Challenge Accepted*, 49–66.

56. Green, *Grass-Roots Socialism*.

57. Paul Buhle, *Marxism in the United States* (London: Verso, 1987), 81.

58. Jon Bekken, "Socialist Press," in *Encyclopedia of American Journalism*, ed. Stephen L. Vaughn (New York: Routledge, 2008), 483–485.

59. J. F. Maki, "The Finnish Socialist Federation," in *The American Labor Year-Book, 1916* (New York: Rand School Press, 1916), 130–132, 148.

60. Leslie H. Marcy, "Calumet," *International Socialist Review* 14, no. 8 (February 1914): 454.

61. Ibid.

62. Thurner, *Strangers and Sojourners*, 123, 220.

63. Lankton, *Hollowed Ground*, 164.

64. Larry Lankton, *Cradle to Grave: Life, Work, and Death at the Lake Superior Copper Mines* (Oxford: Oxford University Press, 1991), 174.

65. *Solidarity*, n.d.

66. Cited in Lankton, *Hollowed Ground*, 174.

67. *Conditions in the Copper Mines*, 1033–1034.

68. Lankton, *Hollowed Ground*, 43–45, 171–172; *Conditions in the Copper Mines*, 70.

69. Ivan (John) Molek, *Slovene Immigrant History, 1900–1950: Autobiographical Sketches*, trans. Mary Molek (Dover, Del.: Mary Molek, 1979), 73.

70. Almont Lindsey, "Paternalism and the Pullman Strike," *American Historical Review* 44, no. 2 (January 1939): 272–289.

71. *Grays Harbor Post*, November 10, 1906.

72. Cited in Foner, *History of the Labor Movement in the United States*, 5:183.

CHAPTER 2. COMMUNITY

1. *Miners' Bulletin* (Hancock, Mich.), September 3, 1913.

2. Ibid.; *Daily Mining Gazette*, September 3, 1913.

3. Arthur Thurner, *Strangers and Sojourners: A History of Michigan's Keweenaw Peninsula* (Detroit: Wayne State University Press, 1994), 91.

4. Ibid., 88–121.

5. Melvyn Dubofsky, *We Shall Be All: A History of the Industrial Workers of the World* (Chicago: Quadrangle Books, 1969; repr., Quadrangle Books, 1973), 11.

6. Larry Lankton, *Cradle to Grave: Life, Work, and Death at the Lake Superior Copper Mines* (Oxford: Oxford University Press, 1991), 204–206; William B. Gates, *Michigan Copper and Boston Dollars: An Economic History of the Michigan Copper Mining Industry* (New York: Russell and Russell, 1951), 114–115.

7. Jonathan Garlock, *Guide to the Local Assembles of the Knights of Labor* (Westport, Conn.: Greenwood Press, 1982), 213.

8. Ibid.

9. Robert E. Weir, *Beyond Labor's Veil: The Culture of the Knights of Labor* (University Park: Pennsylvania State University Press, 1996), 182.

10. R. L. Polk & Company, *Houghton County Directory, 1895–1896* (Detroit: R. L. Polk & Company), 405, 426.

11. *Advance and Labor Leaf* (Detroit), April 27, 1889.

12. The Houghton County Trades and Labor Council appears under a number of different names during the early twentieth century, including the Portage Lake Trades and Labor Council and the Hancock Trades and Labor Council. To avoid confusion, we refer to the council as the Houghton-Hancock Trades and Labor Council (HTLC) throughout this book.

13. Committee on Labor of the House of Representatives, *Eight Hours for Laborers on Government Work: Hearings before the Committee on Labor of the House of Representatives, First Session Fifty-Seventh Congress* (Washington, D.C.: Government Printing Office, 1902), 275.

14. *Daily Mining Gazette*, July 13, 1913; R. L. Polk & Co., *Houghton County Directory, 1912* (Detroit: R. L. Polk & Company), 246, 366, 408, 429; Western Federation of Miners, Defense Funds, Michigan Defense Fund, Book I, 1913–1914, August 2, 1913—January 19, 1914, Copper Country Historical Archive, Michigan Technological University, Houghton.

15. *Keweenaw Miner*, August 25, 1911.

16. State of Michigan, *Twenty-First Annual Report of the Bureau of Labor and Industrial Statistics* (Lansing, Mich.: Robert Smith Printing, State Printers and Binders, 1904), 164–165.

17. State of Michigan, *Twenty-First Annual Report of the Bureau of Labor and Industrial Statistics*, 161–162; American Federation of Labor, *Report of Proceedings of the Twenty-Third Annual Convention of the American Federation of Labor* (Washington, D.C.: Law Reporter, 1903), 14.

18. American Federation of Labor, *Report of Proceedings of the Twenty-Third Annual Convention*, 13.

19. *Daily Mining Gazette*, September 8, 1908.

20. State of Michigan, *Fifteenth Annual Report of the Bureau of Labor and Industrial Statistics* (Lansing, Mich.: Robert Smith Printing, State Printers and Binders, 1897), 88; *Cigar Makers' Official Journal* (September 1900): 4.

21. *Daily Mining Gazette*, September 5, 1911.

22. *Cigar Makers' Official Journal* (April 1901): 30.

23. *Daily Mining Gazette*, September 8, 1908.

24. State of Michigan, *Twenty-First Annual Report of the Bureau of Labor and Industrial Statistics*, 181.

25. *Cigar Makers' Official Journal* (June 15, 1901): 9; State of Michigan, *Sixteenth Annual*

Report of the Bureau of Labor and Industrial Statistics (Lansing, Mich.: Robert Smith Printing, State Printers and Binders, 1899), 94; *Motorman and Conductor* (Detroit) (October 1905): 10; *Carpenter* 25, no. 9 (September 1905): 21; *Daily Mining Gazette*, September 8, 1908, September 7, 1909, September 3, 1911; Michigan Federation of Labor, *First Industrial History*, 95; State of Michigan, *Annual Report of the Michigan Bureau of Labor Statistics* (Lansing, Mich.: Wyncoop Hallenbeck Crawford, State Printers, 1907), 353–355, 370; *The Tailor: Official Organ of the Journeymen Tailors' Union of America* 24, no. 4 (November 1913): 38; "Strike Investigation—Telegrams, Corporate Correspondence, Spying Observations, Etc., 1913–14," Calumet and Hecla Mining Companies Collection, Box 351, Folder 001, Copper Country Historical Archive, Michigan Technological University, Houghton; A. H. Holland, *1887–8 Hand-Book and Guide to Hancock MICH.* (Marquette, Mich.: Mining Journal Book and Job Print, 1887), 26; R. L. Polk, *Houghton County Directory, 1910*, 406.

26. For a discussion of the need to buy union-label beer, see *Miners' Bulletin*, August 14, 1913.

27. *Daily Mining Gazette*, August 1, 1913; *Typographical Journal* (July 1903): 83; *Typographical Journal* (May 1914): 728; Western Federation of Miners, Defense Funds, Michigan Defense Fund, Book I, 1913–1914, August 2, 1913—January 19, 1914, 63, Copper Country Historical Archive, Michigan Technological University, Houghton; R. L. Polk, *Houghton County Directory, 1912*, 220; U.S. Bureau of the Census, *Twelfth Census of the United States Taken in the Year 1900*, State of Michigan, County of Houghton, Hancock Township. Charles M. Balconi's name was occasionally spelled "Balom" or "Balxomi."

28. *Cigar Makers' Official Journal* (September 15): 3.

29. *Cigar Makers' Official Journal* (December 1902): 7.

30. "Proceedings of the G.E.B.," *Tailor* 23, no. 9 (April 1913): 22; *Miners' Bulletin*, August 14, 1913.

31. "Strikes and Lockouts," *Motorman and Conductor* 13, no. 2 (January 1906): 6.

32. *Miners' Magazine*, July 7, 1910, 10.

33. R. L. Polk, *Houghton County Directory, 1907–1908*, 29.

34. *Daily Mining Gazette*, September 8, 1908.

35. State of Michigan, *Twenty-First Annual Report of the Bureau of Labor and Industrial Statistics*, 165.

36. *Typographical Journal* (October 1905): 411.

37. *Typographical Journal* (December 1910): 598, 621.

38. Charles Keifer, oral history interview, Hancock, Mich., Finnish American Historical Archive, Finlandia University, Hancock, Mich., 3–4.

39. *Michigan Federation of Labor: Official Year Book* (Detroit: Houghton-Jacobson Printing, 1907), 320–322.

40. *Työmies*, July 9, 1913.

41. *Cigar Makers' Official Journal* (April 1901): 5.

42. Ibid.; *Miners' Bulletin*, September 3, 1913.

43. *Daily Mining Gazette*, September 8, 1908.

44. *Copper Country Evening News*, February 28, 1905.

45. *Daily Mining Gazette*, September 7, 1909, September 4, 1910; *Wage-Slave*, April 17, 1908.

46. On the history of Labor Day, see Michael Kazin and Stephen J. Ross, "America's Labor

Day: The Dilemma of a Workers' Celebration," *Journal of American History* 78, no. 4 (March 1992): 1294–1323.

47. *Daily Mining Gazette,* September 7, 1909.

48. *Daily Mining Gazette,* September 1, 1912.

49. *Daily Mining Gazette,* September 6, 1910.

50. *Daily Mining Gazette,* September 1, 1908.

51. *Ontonagon (Mich.) Herald,* August 26, September 2, 9, 1911, August 31, September 7, 1912, August 23, 30, September 6, 1913.

52. *Daily Mining Gazette,* September 3, 1911.

53. *Ontonagon (Mich.) Herald,* September 9, 1911.

54. *Daily Mining Gazette,* September 3, 1911.

55. Ibid.

56. *Miners' Bulletin,* September 3, 1913.

57. *Daily Mining Gazette,* September 3, 1911.

58. *Daily Mining Gazette,* September 3, 1911.

59. U.S. Bureau of the Census, *Thirteenth Census of the United States Taken in the Year 1910,* State of Michigan, County of Houghton; "Local Unions," *Iron Molders' Journal* 43, no. 10 (October 1907): 767.

60. *American Federationist,* November 1902, 834.

61. Carl Ross, *The Finn Factor in American Labor, Culture, and Society* (New York Mills, Minn.: Parta Printers, 1977), 120.

62. Gary Kaunonen, *Challenge Accepted: A Finnish Immigrant Response to Industrial America in Michigan's Copper Country* (East Lansing: Michigan State University Press, 2010), 96.

63. *Tailor,* April 1913, 27; November 1913, 42.

64. U.S. Department of Labor, *Michigan Copper District Strike: Bulletin of the United States Labor Statistics* (Washington, D.C.: Government Printing Office, 1914), 133.

65. On the attitudes of the AFL toward organizing female laborers, see Alice Kessler Harris, *Out to Work: A History of Wage-Earning Women in the United States* (Oxford: Oxford University Press, 1982), 152–171. See also Philip S. Foner, *Women and the American Labor Movement: From the First Trade Unions to the Present* (New York: Free Press, 1979), 98–119.

66. *Ontonagon (Mich.) Herald,* September 7, 1913.

67. *Tailor,* November 1913, 31.

68. *Official Proceedings of the Twenty-First Convention of the Western Federation of Miners* (Denver, 1911), 195.

69. Ibid., 10.

70. *Miners' Magazine,* October 16, 1913. The Calumet Ladies' Auxiliary was first listed in the WFM's *Miners' Magazine* in its October 2, 1913, directory of local unions and officers.

71. *Miners' Magazine,* January 13, 1914.

72. *Miners' Magazine,* May 15, 1913.

73. *Motorman and Conductor* 13, no. 11 (October 1905): 10.

74. "Strikes and Lockouts," *Motorman and Conductor* 13, no. 2 (January 1906): 6.

75. *Copper Country Evening News* (Calumet, Mich.), February 25, 27, 1905.

76. *Copper Country Evening News*, February 25, 1905.

77. "Strikes and Lockouts," 6.

78. *Copper Country Evening News*, February 25, 1905.

79. Ibid.

80. *Copper Country Evening News*, February 25, 27, 1905.

81. *Copper Country Evening News*, February 27, 1905.

82. *Copper Country Evening News*, March 10, 1905.

83. *Copper Country Evening News*, March 23, 1905.

84. *Copper Country Evening News*, April 10, 1905.

85. *Motorman and Conductor* 8, no. 3 (February 1905): 27–28.

86. Ibid., 28.

87. "Strikes and Lockouts," 6.

88. *American Street Railway Investments, Published Annually by the Publishers of the Electric Railway Journal* (New York: McGraw, 1908), 15:157.

89. *Typographical Journal* (December 1910): 621.

90. Cited in Arthur Thurner, *Rebels on the Range: The Michigan Copper Miners' Strike of 1913–1914* (Lake Linden, Mich.: John H. Forster Press, 1984), 31

91. Manager, Chicago Branch of the Thiel Detective Service, Memo Re. Employees of the Quincy Mining Company, September 11, 1906, Quincy Mining Company Papers, Box 341, Folder 014, Copper Country Historical Archive, Michigan Technological University, Houghton.

92. *Copper Country Evening News*, February 25, 27, 1905.

93. *Iron Molders' Journal* 43, no. 11 (November 1907): 842.

94. *Conditions in the Copper Mines*, 675.

95. H. H. Baldwin to S. L. Lawton, May 24, 1912, Quincy Mining Company Papers, Box 341, Folder 005, Spy Reports, Thiel Detective Service Co., 1911–1913, QN 321E, Copper Country Historical Archive, Michigan Technological University, Houghton.

96. W. R. Todd to Chas. L. Lawton, January 7, 1913, Quincy Mining Company Papers, Box 341, Folder 005, Copper Country Historical Archive, Michigan Technological University, Houghton.

97. C. L. Lawton to W. R. Todd, January 9, 1913, Quincy Mining Company Papers, Box 341, Folder 6, Labor Spy Reports, 1911–1915, Copper Country Historical Archive, Michigan Technological University, Houghton.

98. Arthur Puotinen, "Early Labor Organizations in the Copper Country," in *For the Common Good: Finnish Immigrants and the Radical Response to Industrial America*, ed. Michael G. Karni and Douglas J. Ollila Jr. (Superior, Wis.: Työmies Society, 1977), 138–139.

99. *Copper Country Evening News*, May 11, 1905.

100. Attorney Steve Lehto made a similar observation in his book *Death's Door: The Truth Behind Michigan's Largest Mass Murder* (Troy, Mich.: Momentum Books, 2006).

101. The best estimates of Copper Country newspaper circulation come from *N. W. Ayer & Son's American Newspaper Annual & Directory: A Catalogue of American Newspapers* (Philadelphia: N. W. Ayer & Son Newspaper Advertising Agents, 1917), which listed the

circulation for the *Daily Mining Gazette* as 6,784, the *Copper Journal* of Hancock as 4,112, and the Calumet *News* as 5,283. See *N. W. Ayer & Sons American Newspaper Annual*, 420, 430, 432.

102. *Portage Lake Mining Gazette* (Houghton, Mich.), May 9, 1872.

103. Ibid.

104. Lankton, *Cradle to Grave*, 205.

105. Ibid.

CHAPTER 3. IMMIGRANTS

1. *Copper Country Evening News*, July 29, 1907; *Daily Mining Gazette*, July 30, 1907.

2. *Copper Country Evening News*, August 5, 1907.

3. Ibid.; Richard Hudelson and Carl Ross, *By the Ore Docks: A Working People's History of Duluth* (St. Paul: University of Minnesota Press, 2006), 65.

4. *Copper Country Evening News*, July 29, 1907.

5. *Miners' Magazine*, May 29, 1913.

6. Ibid.

7. Ibid.

8. *Miners' Magazine*, June 19, 1913. A similar meeting was held on June 15, 1913, with "miners and their families" being "addressed [by] English, Italian, Finnish, and Croatian speakers." See *Miners' Magazine*, June 26, 1913.

9. U.S. Congress, *Conditions in the Copper Mines of Michigan: Hearings before A Subcommittee of the Committee on Mines and Mining* (Washington, D.C.: Government Printing Office, 1914), 203.

10. Arthur Thurner, *Strangers and Sojourners: A History of Michigan's Keweenaw Peninsula* (Detroit: Wayne State University Press, 1994), 153.

11. Ibid., 153–155.

12. Arthur Puotinen, "Early Labor Organizations in the Copper Country," in *For the Common Good: Finnish Immigrants and the Radical Response to Industrial America*, ed. Michael G. Karni and Douglas J. Ollila Jr. (Superior, Wis.: Työmies Society, 1977), 130.

13. Labor Spy Report No. 5, Quincy Mining Company, August 13, 1906, Quincy Mining Company Papers, Box 341, Folder 013, Copper Country Historical Archive, Michigan Technological University, Houghton.

14. The best analysis of the varied meanings of race in the early twentieth-century United States can be found in David Roediger, *Working toward Whiteness: How America's Immigrants Became White, the Strange Journey from Ellis Island to the Suburbs* (New York: Basic Books, 2005).

15. Peter Kivisto, "The Decline of the Finnish American Left, 1925–1945," *International Migration Review* 17, no. 1 (Spring 1983): 68.

16. *Calumet and Red Jacket News*, March 22, 1889.

17. *Daily Mining Gazette*, July 7, 1906.

18. Puotinen, "Early Labor Organizations," 139.

19. Roediger, *Working toward Whiteness*, 64.

20. F. W. Rudler and G. G. Chisholm, *Europe* (London: Edward Stanford, 1885), 576; Augustus Henry Keane, *Ethnology* (London: C. J. Clay and Sons, 1901), 295, 301, 308.

21. Cited in Wayne Gudmundsom and Suzanne Winckler, *Testaments in Wood: Finnish Log Structures at Embarrass, Minnesota* (St. Paul: Minnesota Historical Society Press, 1991), 22.

22. Kivisto, "Decline of the Finnish American Left," 68; Thurner, *Strangers and Sojourners*, 153.

23. Kivisto, "Decline of the Finnish American Left," 68.

24. Alice K. Hoagland, *Mine Towns: Buildings for Workers in Michigan's Copper Country* (Minneapolis: University of Minnesota Press, 2010), 52.

25. C. L. Lawton to W. R. Todd, January 22, 1914, Quincy Mining Company Papers, Box 341, Folder 6, Labor Spy Reports, 1911–1915, Copper Country Historical Archive, Michigan Technological University, Houghton.

26. Some of the best works on Finnish American radicalism and working-class culture are Michael Karni, "The Founding of the Finnish Socialist Federation and the Minnesota Strike of 1907," in Karni and Ollila, *For the Common Good*, 65–86; Paul George Hummasti, *Finnish Radicals in Astoria, Oregon, 1904–1940: A Study in Immigrant Socialism* (New York: Arno Press, 1979); Reino Nikolai Hannula, *Blueberry God: The Education of a Finnish-American* (San Luis Obispo, Calif.: Quality Hill Books, 1979).

27. Michael M. Passi, "Introduction: Finnish Immigrants and the Radical Response to Industrial America," in Karni and Ollila, *For the Common Good*, 12.

28. Ibid.

29. Puotinen, "Early Labor Organizations," 131.

30. Dick Hoerder and Christiane Harzig, eds., *The Immigrant Labor Press in North America: 1840s-1970s, An Annotated Bibliography*, Vol. 1, *Migrants from Northern Europe* (Westport, Conn.: Greenwood Press, 1987), 205.

31. Puotinen, "Early Labor Organizations," 131–133; Gary Kaunonen, *A Finnish Immigrant Response to Industrial America in Michigan's Copper Country* (East Lansing: Michigan State University Press, 2010), 51, 65.

32. Suomalaisten Sosialistijärjestön Edustajakokouksen, *Pöytäkirja 1912* (Fitchburg, Mass.: Suomalainen Sosialisti Kustannus Yhtiö, 1912), 39.

33. Ibid.

34. *Solidarity*, September 20, 1913.

35. *Työmies*, December 20, 27, 1913.

36. Western Federation of Miners, Defense Funds, Michigan Defense Fund, Book I, 1913–1914, August 2, 1913—January 19, 1914, 1, 58, Western Federation of Miners Collection, Copper Country Historical Archive, Michigan Technological University, Houghton.

37. Ibid., 1, 53–54. On the history of Finnish radicals in Astoria, Oregon, see Hummasti, *Finnish Radicals in Astoria*.

38. *Wage-Slave*, May 1, 1908.

39. *Ontanogon (Mich.) Herald*, August 11, 1906.

40. *Wolverine Citizen* (Flint, Mich.), September 26, 1908.

41. Alex Susnar, "Report of South Slavic Socialist Federation to the National Committee of the Socialist Party of America, May 1913," http://www.marxists.org/history/usa/parties/lfed/southslavic/1913/0500-susnar-reporttonc.pdf.

42. Ivan Cizmic, "Yugoslav Immigrants in the US Labor Movement, 1880–1920," in *American Labor and Immigration History, 1877–1920s: Recent European Research*, ed. Dirk Hoerder (Urbana: University of Illinois Press, 1983), 184–189; Eric Foner, *The History of the Labor Movement in the United States*, Vol. 4, *The Industrial Workers of the World, 1905–1917* (New York: International Publishers, 1965), 495, 499; Paul Brissenden, *The IWW: A Study in Syndicalism* (1919, repr., 2nd ed. New York: Russell and Russell, 1957), 396; Kenyon Zimmer, "Anarchist Newspaper Circulation," http://katesharpleylibrary.pbworks.com/ Anarchist%20newspaper%20circulation.

43. *Conditions in the Copper Mines*, 690.

44. This group included Albert Webber, who, in January 1912, after having arrived in the United States only six weeks earlier, took control of the newspaper.

45. Cited in Cizmic, *History of the Croatian Fraternal Union*, 115.

46. Ibid.

47. Ibid., 95.

48. Ibid., 85, 123–126.

49. Prpic, *Croatian Immigrants*, 179.

50. Cited in Cizmic, *History of the Croatian Fraternal Union*, 114.

51. Ibid., 116.

52. Western Federation of Miners, Defense Funds, Michigan Defense Fund, Book I, 1913–1914, August 2, 1913—January 19, 1914, 77, Western Federation of Miners Collection, Copper Country Historical Archive, Michigan Technological University, Houghton.

53. Prpic, *Croatian Immigrants*, 142.

54. Julie Pferdehirt, *More Than Petticoats: Remarkable Michigan Women* (Guilford, Conn.: TwoDot, 2007), 80–93.

55. Ibid., 82.

56. "Class Struggle Notes: 'Big Annie,'" *International Socialist Review* 14, no. 6 (December 1913): 342.

57. Arthur Thurner, *Rebels on the Range The Michigan Copper Miners' Strike of 1913–1914* (Lake Linden, Mich.: John H. Forster Press, 1984), 92–93.

58. "Class Struggle Notes," 342.

59. John Bodnar, *The Transplanted: A History of Immigrants in Urban America* (Bloomington: Indiana University Press, 1985), 100–122.

60. Larry Lankton, *Beyond the Boundaries: Life and Landscape at the Lake Superior Copper Mines, 1840–1875* (Oxford: Oxford University Press, 1997), 194.

61. R. L. Polk & Co., *Houghton County Directory, 1907–1908*, 474, Copper Country Historical Archive, Michigan Technological University, Houghton.

62. Articles of Association for the Arbeiter Unterstuetzungs Verein of Calumet, Michigan, Liber 5, Copper Country Historical Archive, Michigan Technological University, Houghton, 372.

63. Articles of Association for the Germania Society of Hancock, Michigan, January 31, 1865, Liber 1, Copper Country Historical Archive, Michigan Technological University, Houghton, 123.

64. Dave Engel and Gerry Mantel, *Calumet: Copper Country Metropolis: 1898–1913* (Rudolph, Wis.: River City Memoirs-Maki, 2002), 112.

65. Articles of Association, Liebers 1–5, Copper Country Historical Archive, Michigan Technological University, Houghton.

66. Russell M. Magnaghi, *Miners, Merchants, and Midwives: Michigan's Upper Peninsula Italians* (Marquette, Mich.: Belle Fontaine Press, 1987), 68–71.

67. Articles of Association, Liebers 1–5, Copper Country Historical Archive, Michigan Technological University, Houghton.

68. Amanda Wiljanen Larson, *Finnish Heritage in America* (Marquette, Mich.: Belta Kappa Gamma Society, 1975), 39; Articles of Association for the Italian Mutual Fire Insurance Company, Red Jacket, July 1, 1901, Liber 4, Copper Country Historical Archive, Michigan Technological University, Houghton, 105–108; Thurner, *Strangers and Sojourners*, 142.

69. Articles of Association for the Croatian Benevolent Society, Calumet Township, Liber 4, Copper Country Historical Archive, Michigan Technological University, Houghton, 144.

70. Articles of Association for the Croatian Co-Op Store of Calumet, November 9, 1905, Liber 4, Copper Country Historical Archive, Michigan Technological University, Houghton, 419–420.

71. Articles of Association for the Societa Italiana di Mutua Beneficenza, Red Jacket, December 4, 1889, Liber 2, Copper Country Historical Archive, Michigan Technological University, Houghton, 306.

72. Articles of Association for the Scandinavian Union Store, Red Jacket, March 21, 1874, Liber 1, Copper Country Historical Archive, Michigan Technological University, Houghton, 163.

73. Hannula, *Blueberry God*, 216–217.

74. Armas K. E. Holmio, *History of the Finns in Michigan*, trans. Ellen M. Ryynanen (Detroit: Wayne State University Press, 2001), 334.

75. Ibid.

76. Thurner, *Rebels on the Range*, 103.

77. Magnaghi, *Miners, Merchants, and Midwives*, 40–44.

78. Ibid., 40; R. L. Polk, *Houghton County Directory, 1907–1908*, 90.

79. Engel and Mantel, *Calumet*, 112.

80. Carl Ross, *The Finn Factor in American Labor, Culture, and Society* (New York Mills, Minn.: Parta Printers, 1977), 121.

81. Leslie H. Marcy, "Calumet," *International Socialist Review* 14, no. 8 (February 1914): 460.

82. Michigan Bureau of Labor and Industrial Statistics, *Twenty-Fourth Annual Report of the Bureau of Labor and Industrial Statistics* (Lansing, Mich.: Wynkoop Hallenbeck Crawford, State Printers, 1907), 385.

83. Spy report, September 7, 1906, Quincy Mining Company Papers, Box 341, Folder 014, Copper Country Historical Archive, Michigan Technological University, Houghton.

84. H. H. Baldwin to S. L. Lawton, March 13, 1911, Quincy Mining Company Papers, Box 341, Folder 005, Spy Reports, Thiel Detective Service Co., 1911–1913, QN 321E, Copper Country Historical Archive, Michigan Technological University, Houghton.

85. O. O. Rindal, Superintendent, St. Paul Branch of the Pinkerton National Detective Agency, to C. L. Lawton, July 9, 1907, Quincy Mining Company Papers, Box 341, Folder 003, Spy Reports, Pinkerton Detective Agency, 1907, QN 321C, Copper Country Historical Archive, Michigan Technological University, Houghton.

86. *Daily Mining Gazette*, August 1, 1906.

87. Prpic, *Croatian Immigrants*, 204–205.

88. The best source on workers' housing in the Copper Country is Hoagland, *Mine Towns*.

89. U.S. Bureau of the Census, *Thirteenth Census of the United States Taken in the Year 1910*, State of Michigan, County of Houghton, Calumet Township; Sanborn Map Company, *Calumet 1907*, Proquest Sanborn Map Collection, presented in the Digital Sanborn Maps Collection, 1867–1970.

90. U.S. Bureau of the Census, *Thirteenth Census of the United States Taken in the Year 1910*, State of Michigan, Red Jacket Village.

91. Ivan (John) Molek, *Slovene Immigrant History, 1900–1950: Autobiographical Sketches*, trans. Mary Molek (Dover, Del.: Mary Molek, 1979), 81–82.

92. Larry Lankton, *Hollowed Ground: Copper Mining and Community Building on Lake Superior, 1840s-1990s* (Detroit: Wayne State University Press, 2010), 202; *Spokesman-Review* (Spokane, Wash.), February 28, 1914.

93. Thurner, *Rebels on the Range*, 245–247. See also Larry Lankton, *Cradle to Grave: Life, Work, and Death at the Lake Superior Copper Mines* (Oxford: Oxford University Press, 1991), 234; and Lankton, *Hollowed Ground*, 202.

94. U.S. Bureau of the Census, *Thirteenth Census of the United States Taken in the Year 1910*, State of Michigan, County of Houghton, Quincy Township; Thurner, *Rebels on the Range*, 245.

95. *Conditions in the Copper Mines*, 1290–1291.

96. Cited in Thurner, *Rebels on the Range*, 155.

97. C. L. Lawton to W. R. Todd, January 9, 1913, Quincy Mining Company Papers, Box 341, Folder 6, Labor Spy Reports, 1911–1915, Copper Country Historical Archive, Michigan Technological University, Houghton.

98. *Conditions in the Copper Mines*, 572–582.

99. Ibid., 888.

100. Ibid., 1085.

101. Elizabeth Jameson, *All that Glitters: Life, Work, and Death at the Lake Superior Copper Mines* (Oxford: Oxford University Press, 1991), 236.

102. Puotinen, "Early Labor Organizations," 143.

103. Gary Kaunonen, *Challenge Accepted: A Finnish Immigrant Response to Industrial America in Michigan's Copper Country* (East Lansing: Michigan State University Press, 2010), 115.

104. *Miners' Magazine*, January 16, 1913, 14.

105. Manager, Chicago Branch of the Thiel Detective Service, Memo Re. Employees of the Quincy Mining Company, September 7, 1906, Box 341, Folder 014, Copper Country Historical Archive, Michigan Technological University, Houghton.

106. Manager, Chicago Branch of the Thiel Detective Service, Memo Re. Employees of the Quincy Mining Company, August 29, 1906, Quincy Mining Company Papers, Box 341, Folder 014, Copper Country Historical Archive, Michigan Technological University, Houghton.

107. *Official Proceedings of the Fifteenth Convention of the Western Federation of Miners* (Denver: W. H. Kistler Stationery, 1907), 602.

108. Ibid., 602; Thurner, *Rebels on the Range*, 30; Magnaghi, *Miners, Merchants, and Midwives*,

20, 61.

109. *Official Proceedings of the Fifteenth Convention*, 601–602.

110. Engel and Martel, *Calumet*, 124.

111. Magnaghi, *Miners, Merchants, and Midwives*, 20, 61; Engel and Martel, *Calumet*, 124.

112. *Official Proceedings of the Fifteenth Convention*, 602.

113. Magnaghi, *Miners, Merchants, and Midwives*, 20, 61.

114. Engel and Martel, *Calumet*, 113.

115. Arnold R. Alanen, "Early Labor Strife on Minnesota Mining Frontier, 1882–1906," *Minnesota History* 52, no. 7 (Fall 1991): 261.

CHAPTER 4. TROUBLEMAKERS

1. *Miners' Magazine*, May 29, 1913.

2. Ibid.

3. *Memorial Record of the Northern Peninsula of Michigan* (Chicago: Lewis Publishing, 1895), 566–567.

4. *Official Directory and Legislative Manual of the State of Michigan for the Years 1887–8* (Lansing, Mich.: Secretary of State, 1888), 624.

5. U.S. Congress, House Committee on Mines and Mining, *Conditions in the Copper Mines of Michigan: Hearings before a Subcommittee of the Committee on Mines and Mining* (Washington, D.C.: Government Printing Office, 1914), 267; Arthur Thurner, *Rebels on the Range: The Michigan Copper Miners' Strike of 1913–1914* (Lake Linden, Mich.: John H. Forster Press, 1984), 114.

6. *Wage-Slave*, May 29 and June 19, 1908.

7. *Copper Country Evening News*, June 16, 1906.

8. Dave Engel and Gerry Mantel, *Calumet: Copper Country Metropolis: 1898–1913* (Rudolph, Wis.: River City Memoirs-Maki, 2002), 116.

9. U.S. Bureau of the Census, *Twelfth Census of the United States Taken in the Year 1900*, State of Michigan, County of Houghton; *Wage-Slave*, May 29, 1908; R. L. Polk, *Houghton County Directory*, 1899–1917; "Plumbers and Steam Fitters," *Plumbers Trade Journal, Gas, Steam, and Hot Water Fitters' Review* (December 15, 1907): 678.

10. *Daily Mining Gazette*, September 5, 1911; U.S. Bureau of the Census, *Thirteenth Census of the United States Taken in the Year 1910*, State of Michigan, County of Houghton; *Wage-Slave*, May 29, 1908; R. L. Polk, *Houghton County Directory, 1907–1908*, 309.

11. Western Federation of Miners, Defense Funds, Michigan Defense Fund, Book I 1913–1914, August 2, 1913—January 19, 1914, Copper Country Historical Archive, Michigan Technological University, Houghton.

12. U.S. Congress, *Conditions in the Copper Mines of Michigan: Hearings before a Subcommittee of the Committee on Mines and Mining* (Washington, D.C.: Government Printing Office, 1914), 690.

13. *Copper Country Evening News*, March 27, 1905.

14. *Wage-Slave*, May 29, 1908; R. L. Polk, *Houghton County Directory, 1912*, 688.

15. John Surbeck Papers, Accession No. KEWE-00257, Archival Collections, Keweenaw,

National Park Service, Calumet, Mich.

16. *History of the Bar and Bench of Utah* (Salt Lake City: Interstate Press Association Publishers, 1913), 157.

17. Engel and Mantel, *Calumet*, 85.

18. Arthur Puotinen, "Early Labor Organizations in the Copper Country," in *For the Common Good: Finnish Immigrants and the Radical Response to Industrial America*, ed. Michael G. Karni and Douglas J. Ollila Jr. (Superior, Wis.: Työmies Society, 1977), 144–147.

19. *Conditions in the Copper Mines*, 871–872.

20. *Wage-Slave*, March 20, April 24, and June 19, 1908. For a history of the Työmies Publishing Company, see Gary Kaunonen, *Challenge Accepted: A Finnish Immigrant Response to Industrial America in Michigan's Copper Country* (East Lansing: Michigan State University Press, 2010), 67–104.

21. *Wage-Slave*, May 1 and June 19, 1908.

22. *Wage-Slave*, May 1, 1908.

23. *Wage-Slave*, March 20, 1908.

24. Ibid.

25. Ibid.

26. Allen Ruff, *"We Called Each Other Comrade": Charles H. Kerr & Company, Radical Publishers* (Oakland, Calif.: PM Press, 2011), 161–175.

27. "News and Views," *International Socialist Review* 8, no. 9 (March 1908): 570.

28. "Socialist National Convention," *International Socialist Review* 8, no. 12 (June 1908): 723; James Langland, *The Chicago Daily News Almanac and Year Book for 1909* (Chicago: Chicago Daily News, 1909), 208.

29. "Alexander M. Stirton," *American Co-operator* 2, no. 16 (September 19, 1903): 16.

30. "From Star Dust to Socialism," *International Socialist Review* 6, no. 12 (June 1906): 760. Stirton continued his efforts as a pamphleteer after leaving the Copper Country. In 1910, he authored a short pamphlet entitled *Getting Recognition*, which was advertised in the *Industrial Worker*, June 4, 1910.

31. *Wage-Slave*, June 21, 1908. See also *Wage-Slave*, April 17, 1908.

32. *Wolverine Citizen* (Flint, Mich.), September 26, 1908.

33. *Michigan Manual, 2009–2010: Summary of Votes for Governor, 1835–2006* (Lansing, Mich.: Legislative Service Bureau, 2010), ix–9.

34. Cited in Louis Duchez, "Victory at McKees Rocks," *International Socialist Review* 10, no. 4 (October 1909): 294.

35. *Wage-Slave*, March 20, 1908.

36. "News and Views," *International Socialist Review* 10, no. 1 (July 1909): 85.

37. *Solidarity*, n.d.

38. *Official Proceedings of the Fifteenth Convention of the Western Federation of Miners* (Denver, Co.: W. H. Kistler Stationery, 1907), 299.

39. *Wage-Slave*, April 24, 1908.

40. Some of the best studies of the IWW are Melvyn Dubofsky, *We Shall Be All: A History of the Industrial Workers of the World* (New York: Quadrangle, 1973); Mark Leier, *Where the Fraser River Flows: The Industrial Workers of the World in British Columbia* (Vancouver:

New Star Books, 1990); Philip S. Foner, *The History of the Labor Movement in the United States*, Vol. 4, *The Industrial Workers of the World, 1905–1917* (1965; repr., New York: International Publishers, 1997); Fred Thompson and Jon Bekken, *The IWW: Its First 100 Years* (Cincinnati: Industrial Workers of the World, 2006); Salvatore Salerno, *Red November, Black November: Culture and Community in the Industrial Workers of the World* (Albany: State University of New York Press, 1989); Peter Cole, *Wobblies on the Waterfront: Interracial Unionism in Progressive-Era Philadelphia* (Urbana: University of Illinois Press, 2007); Paul Buhle and Nicole Schulman, eds., *Wobblies! A Graphic History of the Industrial Workers of the World* (London: Verso Press, 2005); Greg Hall, *Harvest Wobblies: The Industrial Workers of the World and Agricultural Laborers in the American West, 1905–1930* (Corvallis: Oregon State University Press, 2002).

41. Industrial Workers of the World, "Preamble of the Industrial Workers of the World," in *Rebel Voices: An IWW Anthology*, ed. Joyce L. Kornbluh, New and Expanded Edition (Chicago: Charles H. Kerr Press, 1998), 12–13.

42. William Haywood, "The General Strike," in Kornbluh, *Rebel Voices*, 51.

43. Thompson and Bekken, *IWW*, 42–45; Dubofsky, *We Shall Be All*, 202–209.

44. *Solidarity*, January 3, 1914.

45. William D. Haywood, "Solidarity in Prison," *International Socialist Review* 10, no. 12 (June 1910): 1066.

46. "Publisher's Department," *International Socialist Review* 10, no. 5 (November 1909): 472.

47. *Solidarity*, January 3, 1914; March 14, 1913.

48. *Industrial Worker*, October 19, 1910.

49. Paul Frederick Brissenden, *The IWW: The Story of American Syndicalism* (New York: Columbia University Press, 1920), 179.

50. *Official Proceedings of the Fifteenth Convention*, 137.

51. Ibid., 94.

52. *Industrial Worker*, April 30, 1910.

53. *Solidarity*, February 19, 1910.

54. *Official Proceedings of the Seventeenth Convention*, 245.

55. Ibid., 245–246.

56. *Solidarity*, March 26, 1910.

57. *Industrial Worker*, February 5, 1910.

58. Ibid.

59. *Solidarity*, January 3, 1914.

60. Ibid.

61. J. H. Halstead, District Manager of the Corporations Auxiliary Co., to C. L. Lawton, July 24, 1913, Quincy Mining Company Papers, Box 341, Folder 029—Corr.—Supt. (C. L. Lawton) Strike 1913–14, Copper Country Historical Archive, Michigan Technological University, Houghton.

62. C. L. Lawton to W. R. Todd, January 28, 1914, Quincy Mining Company Collection, Box 342, Folder 011, Collection #MS-001, Copper Country Historical Archive, Michigan Technological University, Houghton.

63. *Solidarity*, September 13, 1913, January 3, 1914; *Industrial Worker*, April 11, 1914.

64. Dr. Clarence Andrews, oral history interview, Hancock, Mich., Finnish American Historical Archive, Finlandia University, Hancock, Mich.

65. *Solidarity*, n.d.

66. *Solidarity*, n.d.

67. *Solidarity*, October 25, 1913.

68. Western Federation of Miners, Defense Funds, Michigan Defense Fund, Book I 1913–1914, 2 August 1913–19 January 1914, Copper Country Historical Archive, Michigan Technological University, Houghton, 56, 58.

69. *Solidarity*, April 11, 1914.

70. *Solidarity*, September 13, 1913.

CHAPTER 5. ORGANIZATION

1. Larry Lankton, *Cradle to Grave: Life, Work, and Death at the Lake Superior Copper Mines* (Oxford: Oxford University Press, 1991), 125.

2. Houghton County Mine Inspector's Report, *Accident 23* (Houghton, Mich.: Gazette Printing and Binding, 1895), 13–17; Lankton, *Cradle to Grave*, 122–124.

3. Houghton County Mine Inspector's Report, *Accident 23*, 15.

4. Ibid., 14–17.

5. U.S. Department of Labor, *Michigan Copper District Strike: Bulletin of the United States Labor Statistics* (Washington, D.C.: Government Printing Office, 1914), 106.

6. Ibid., 106–115; Lankton, *Cradle to Grave*, 38–39.

7. William B. Gates Jr., *Michigan Copper and Boston Dollars: An Economic History of the Michigan Copper Mining Industry* (Cambridge, Mass.: Harvard University Press, 1951), 215–220.

8. State of Michigan, *Twenty-Fifth Annual Report of the Bureau of Labor and Industrial Statistics* (Lansing, Mich.: Wynkoop Hallenbeck Crawford, State Printers, 1908), 296.

9. David Engel and Gerry Mantel, *Calumet: Copper Country Metropolis, 1898–1913* (Rudolph, Wis.: River City Memoirs–Maki, 2002), 139, 141, 153–154, quote from 154.

10. William Parsons Todd, oral history interview by Ralph Jalkanen, October 1974, oral history transcript, Finnish American Historical Archive, Finlandia University, Hancock, Mich., 1831–1833.

11. Ibid.

12. Ibid.

13. Lankton, *Cradle to Grave*, 95.

14. Arthur Thurner, *Rebels on the Range: The Michigan Copper Miners' Strike of 1913–1914* (Lake Linden, Mich.: John H. Forster Press, 1984), 33; Arthur Puotinen, "Early Labor Organizations in the Copper Country," in *For the Common Good: Finnish Immigrants and the Radical Response to Industrial America*, ed. Michael G. Karni and Douglas J. Ollila Jr. (Superior, Wis.: Työmies Society, 1977), 122–126, quote from 125. Organizers from the IWA had circulated among the employees and gained support for such demands as higher wages, an eight-hour workday, and improved safety conditions in the mines. Thurner's account of this strike is somewhat partial to the company, while Puotinen's highlights the

radical nature of the strike, citing the strike as a somewhat early watershed in Copper Country labor relations.

15. *Portage Lake Mining Gazette* (Houghton, Mich.), May 9, 23, 1872.

16. *Portage Lake Mining Gazette*, May 9, 1872.

17. Ibid.

18. Ibid.

19. Lankton, *Cradle to Grave*, 202–205, quote from 203.

20. Ibid., 203–204; Puotinen, "Early Labor Organizations in the Copper Country," 125.

21. Lankton, *Cradle to Grave*, 202–206; Puotinen, "Early Labor Organizations in the Copper Country," 129–132. These sources provide for a list of pre-1900 strikes: 1890, workers walked out at the Tamarack mine; 1892, small-scale strikes occurred at the Atlantic mine and at C&H when eighty workers walked off the job; 1893, C&H's stamp mill workers and trammers struck on separate occasions; 1894, Tamarack mine workers strike; 1896, workers strike at the Quincy mine; and 1897, workers strike at the Atlantic mine.

22. John P. Beck, "Homegrown," *Michigan History* 79, no. 5 (1995); 19–22.

23. Ibid., 21.

24. Lankton, *Cradle to Grave*, 208.

25. Beck, "Homegrown," 20–21.

26. *Labor World* (Butte, Mont.), June 20, 1902.

27. Elizabeth Jameson, *All That Glitters: Class, Conflict, and Community in Cripple Creek* (Urbana: University of Illinois Press, 1998), 288, 320; *Telegraph* (Nashua, N.H.), August 30, September 1, 2, 1904; *Lewiston (Me.) Evening Journal*, October 24, 1904; *Providence (R.I.) News*, October 31, 1904.

28. Cited in ibid., 29.

29. Engel and Mantel, *Calumet*, 100.

30. *Official Proceedings of the Fifteenth Convention of the Western Federation of Miners* (Denver: W. H. Kistler Stationery, 1907), 168.

31. *Official Proceedings of the Seventeenth Convention of the Western Federation of Miners* (Denver: W. H. Kistler Stationery, 1909), 296.

32. Ibid.

33. Ibid., 303.

34. Ibid.

35. Ibid., 303–304.

36. Manager, Chicago Branch of the Thiel Detective Service, Memo Re. Employees of the Quincy Mining Company, October 25, 1906, Quincy Mining Company Papers, Box 341, Folder 15, Copper Country Historical Archive, Michigan Technological University, Houghton.

37. Ibid.

38. Ibid.

39. Manager, Chicago Branch of the Thiel Detective Service, Memo Re. Employees of the Quincy Mining Company, September 11, 1906, Quincy Mining Company Papers, Box 341, Folder 014, Corr-Spy Reports, "K" August–September 1906, QN 321 N, Copper Country Historical Archive, Michigan Technological University, Houghton.

40. Manager, Chicago Branch of the Thiel Detective Service, Memo Re. Employees of the Quincy Mining Company, October 6, 1906, Quincy Mining Company Papers, Box 341, Folder 015—Corr-Spy Reports, "JAP" September–November 1906, ZN 3210, Copper Country Historical Archive, Michigan Technological University, Houghton.

41. Manager, Chicago Branch of the Thiel Detective Service, Memo Re. Employees of the Quincy Mining Company, September 11, 1906.

42. List of strikes at the Quincy Mining Company, 1901–1905, Quincy Mining Company Papers, Copper Country Historical Archive, Michigan Technological University, Houghton; *Copper Country Evening News*, March 20, 21, 1905.

43. Lankton, *Cradle to Grave*, 204–206.

44. Strike resolution presented "To the Quincy Mining Company" by the striking employees of the Quincy Mining Company, July 27, 1906, Quincy Mining Company Collection, Box 487, Folder 1, Copper Country Historical Collections, Michigan Technological University, Houghton.

45. No. 5 to Quincy Mining Company, Business Correspondence, August 10, 1906, Quincy Mining Company Collection, Box 341, Copper Country Historical Archive, Michigan Technological University, Houghton.

46. Ibid.

47. Puotinen, "Early Labor Organizations in the Copper Country," 137–138.

48. Ibid.; Lankton, *Cradle to Grave*, 208–209.

49. Puotinen, "Early Labor Organizations in the Copper Country," 138–139.

50. Ibid.

51. Unknown operative, Thiel Detective Service, to Quincy Mining Company, "Re: Employees," October 15, 1906, Quincy Mining Company Collection, Box 341, Copper Country Historical Archives, Michigan Technological University, Houghton.

52. Unknown operative, Thiel Detective Service, to Quincy Mining Company, "Re: Employees," October 6, 1906, Quincy Mining Company Collection, Box 341, Copper Country Historical Archives, Michigan Technological University, Houghton.

53. Ibid.

54. For an in-depth examination of the Finnish immigrant contribution to attempts to organize the Copper Country's workers, see Gary Kaunonen, *Challenge Accepted: A Finnish Immigrant Response to Industrial America in Michigan's Copper Country* (Lansing: Michigan State University Press, 2010).

55. Albert Gedicks, *Working Class Radicalism among Finnish Immigrants in Minnesota and Michigan Mining Communities* (Ann Arbor, Mich.: University Microfilms International, 1980), 123–124; Lankton, *Cradle to Grave*, 209.

56. Lankton, *Cradle to Grave*, 220.

57. Todd, oral history interview, 1839–1841. Todd believed that the introduction of the one-man drill into the Copper Country was the sole instigator of the 1913–14 strike.

58. Thurner, *Rebels on the Range*, 45; U.S. Department of Labor, *Michigan Copper District Strike: Bulletin of the United States Labor Statistics* (Washington, D.C.: Government Printing Office, 1914), 11–21.

59. Mass City Miners Union No. 215 to Elton W. Walker, "Correspondence," April 21, 1913, Calumet and Hecla Mining Companies Collection, Box 352, Folder 006, Copper Country Historical Archive, Michigan Technological University, Houghton.

60. C. E. Mahoney to Elton W. Walker, "Correspondence," April 28, 1913, Calumet and Hecla Mining Companies Collection, Box 352, Folder 006, Copper Country Historical Archive, Michigan Technological University, Houghton.

61. "Union Mass Meeting," Image Copper Country Historical Archive's Keweenaw Digital Archive, Image #:Acc-400–12–13–1988–01–08–01, Michigan Technological University, Houghton.

62. Gedicks, *Working Class Radicalism*, 124–125.

63. Charles Lawton to William R. Todd, "Correspondence," June 12 and 16, 1913, Quincy Mining Company Collection, Box 342, Folder 011, Copper Country Historical Archive, Michigan Technological University, Houghton.

64. Lawton to Todd, "Correspondence," June 18, 1913, Quincy Mining Company Collection, Box 342, Folder 011, Copper Country Historical Archive, Michigan Technological University, Houghton.

65. Lawton to Todd, "Correspondence," July 2, 1913, Quincy Mining Company Collection, Box 342, Folder 011, Copper Country Historical Archive, Michigan Technological University, Houghton.

66. Lawton to Todd, "Correspondence," July 5 and 10, 1913, Quincy Mining Company Collection, Box 342, Folder 011, Copper Country Historical Archive, Michigan Technological University, Houghton.

67. Lawton to Todd, "Correspondence," July 11, 1913, Quincy Mining Company Collection, Box 342, Folder 011, Copper Country Historical Archive, Michigan Technological University, Houghton.

68. Lawton to Todd, "Correspondence," July 15, 1913, Quincy Mining Company Collection, Box 342, Folder 011, Copper Country Historical Archive, Michigan Technological University, Houghton.

69. James MacNaughton to Quincy Shaw, "Correspondence," July 15, 1913, Calumet and Hecla Mining Companies Collection, Box 350, Folder 001, Copper Country Historical Archive, Michigan Technological University, Houghton.

70. Lawton to Todd, "Correspondence," July 14, 1913, Quincy Mining Company Collection, Box 342, Folder 011, Copper Country Historical Archive, Michigan Technological University, Houghton.

71. MacNaughton to Shaw, "Correspondence," July 23, 1913, Calumet and Hecla Mining Companies Collection, Box 350, Folder 001, Copper Country Historical Archive, Michigan Technological University, Houghton.

72. MacNaughton to Shaw, "Correspondence," July 24, 1913, Calumet and Hecla Mining Companies Collection, Box 350, Folder 001, Copper Country Historical Archive, Michigan Technological University, Houghton.

CHAPTER 6. UNION

1. Utah Phillips and Ani DiFranco, "I Will Not Obey," on *Fellow Workers*, Righteous Babe Records, Buffalo, N.Y., 1999.

2. *Miners' Bulletin*, various issues, 1913.

3. Western Federation of Miners, "In Unity Is Strength," 1913, Keweenaw Digital Archives, Image #:Acc-400–12–13–1988–01–08–15, Copper Country Historical Collections,

Michigan Technological University, Houghton, http://digarch.lib.mtu.edu/showbib. aspx?bib_id=628915#.

4. For an extensive history on the WFM and the IWW, see Elizabeth Jameson, *All that Glitters: Class, Conflict, and Community in Cripple Creek* (Urbana: University of Illinois Press, 1998), quote from 179; and Fred Thompson and Patrick Murfin, *The I.W.W.: Its First Seventy Years* (Chicago: Kerr Publishers, 1975).

5. Louis Adamic, *Dynamite: The Story of Class Violence in America*, (Oakland, Calif.: AK Press, 2008), 91–127.

6. Ibid., 105–177.

7. Douglas J. Ollila Jr., "From Socialism to Industrial Unionism (IWW): Social Factors in the Emergence of Left-Labor Radicalism among Finnish Workers on the Mesabi, 1911–19," in *The Finnish Experience in the Western Great Lakes Region: New Perspectives* (Turku, Finland: Institute for Migration, 1975), 156–158.

8. Gary Kaunonen, *Challenge Accepted: A Finnish Immigrant Response to Industrial America in Michigan's Copper Country* (East Lansing: Michigan State University Press, 2010). The section on Finns is a general characterization of the Finnish immigrant population in the Copper Country.

9. J. Peter Campbell, "The Cult of Spontaneity: Finnish-Canadian Bushworkers and the Industrial Workers of the World in Northern Ontario, 1919–1934," *Labour/Le Travail* 41 (Spring 1998): 121.

10. Larry Lankton, *Cradle to Grave: Life, Work, and Death at the Lake Superior Copper Mines* (Oxford: Oxford University Press, 1991), 221–223.

11. Charles Lawton to William R. Todd, "Correspondence," July 17, 1913, Quincy Mining Company Collection, Box 342, Folder 011, Copper Country Historical Archive, Michigan Technological University, Houghton.

12. Ibid.

13. Antti Sarell, "The Copper Country Strike: Its Features So Far," *Työmiehen Joulu 1913*, trans. Jarno Heinilä, 2006, Hancock, Mich.: Työmies Publishing Company, 1913, 2.

14. *Miners' Bulletin*, April 14, 1914.

15. Lankton, *Cradle to Grave*, 219–222

16. Calumet and Hecla Mining Company, "Men Working Underground at C&H Mine, by nationalities," July 14 and September 29, 1913, Calumet and Hecla Mining Companies Collection, Box 350, Copper Country Historical Archive, Michigan Technological University, Houghton.

17. *Miners' Bulletin*, September 13, 1913.

18. *Työmies*, December 11, 1913.

19. *Työmies*, July 24 and 25, 1913.

20. *Työmies*, July 24, 1913.

21. Sanborn Insurance Company, Calumet, Mich., Map, sheet 2, 1908; Arthur Thurner, *Rebels on the Range: The Michigan Copper Miners' Strike of 1913–1914* (Lake Linden, Mich.: John H. Forster Press, 1984), 133; *Miners' Bulletin*, various issues. Thurner identifies the FSF'S Socialist Hall as WFM headquarters in South Range (130–132).

22. *Miners' Bulletin*, various issues.

23. Arthur Puotinen, "Early Labor Organizations in the Copper Country," in *For the Common*

Good: Finnish Immigrants and the Radical Response to Industrial America, ed. Michael G. Karni and Douglas J. Ollila Jr. (Superior, Wis.: Työmies Society, 1977), 154; *Työmies*, December 11, 1913.

24. Keweenaw Miners Union, "Correspondence," July 26, 1913, Calumet and Hecla Mining Companies Collection, Box 351, Folder 004, Copper Country Historical Collections, Michigan Technological University, Houghton.

25. Jim MacNaughton to Quincy Shaw, "Correspondence," August 26, 1913, Calumet and Hecla Mining Companies Collection, Box 350, Folder 005, Copper Country Historical Collections, Michigan Technological University, Houghton.

26. *Keweenaw Miner*, September 12, 1913.

27. Jim MacNaughton to Quincy Shaw, "Correspondence," n.d., Calumet and Hecla Mining Companies Collection, Box 350, Folder 008, Copper Country Historical Collections, Michigan Technological University, Houghton.

28. *Miners' Bulletin*, September 11, 1913.

29. Ibid.

30. Sanborn Insurance Company, Calumet, Mich., Map, sheet 2, 1908; Thurner, *Rebels on the Range*, 133; *Miners' Bulletin*, various issues.

31. *Miners' Bulletin*, November 1, 1913.

32. George Nichols to Houghton County Board of Supervisors, "Arrests Report," 1914, Calumet and Hecla Mining Companies Collection, Copper Country Historical Archive, Michigan Technological University, Houghton.

33. Frank Aaltonen, "Heroines of the Copper Country," *Työmiehen Joulu*, (1913), 23–24.

34. *Miners' Bulletin*, August 14, 1913.

35. *Miners' Bulletin*, August 23, 1913, and various other issues.

36. *Miners' Bulletin*, various issues.

37. *Miners' Bulletin*, December 16, 1913.

38. Articles of Association, Houghton County, Book 5, Copper Country Historical Archive, Michigan Technological University, Houghton, 463–464.

39. Jukka S., "March of the Copper Territory Strikers," trans. Anna Leppänen, *Työmies*, 1913.

40. Sarell, "Copper Country Strike," 15.

41. Ibid.

42. *Miners' Bulletin*, August 14, 1913.

43. *Miners' Bulletin*, September 18, 1913.

44. Sarell, "Copper Country Strike," 19–20.

45. *Miners' Bulletin*, August 14, 1913.

46. *Miners' Bulletin*, December 16, 1913.

47. *Miners' Bulletin*, November 11, 1913.

48. *Miners' Bulletin*, August 14, 1913.

49. Alvah L. Sawyer, *A History of the Northern Peninsula of Michigan and Its People* (Chicago: Lewis Publishing, 1911), 3:1503–1504.

50. *Hancock (Mich.) Evening Journal*, August 3, 1907.

51. Ibid.

52. Jim MacNaughton to Quincy Shaw, "Correspondence," September 29, 1913, Calumet and Hecla Mining Companies Collection, Box 350, Folder 005, Copper Country Historical Collections, Michigan Technological University, Houghton.

53. *Miners' Bulletin*, November 1, 1913.

54. *Miners' Bulletin*, September 9, 1913.

55. *Miners' Bulletin*, November 15, 1913.

56. Lankton, *Cradle to Grave*, 229.

57. Nick Hendrickson and John Palosaari, oral history interview by Arthur Puotinen, July 14, 1973, oral history transcript, Finnish American Historical Archive, Finlandia University, Hancock, Mich., 23.

58. Ibid.

59. *Miners' Bulletin*, December 9, 1913.

60. *Miners' Bulletin*, September 27, 1913.

61. Though the quote in various forms is widely attributed to Goldman, scholar Alix Kates Shulman points out that Goldman likely never uttered the exact quote and attributes the quote to Goldman T-shirt artist Jack Frager. Goldman was thought to have taken umbrage at the stoic nature of some early twentieth-century revolutionary movements, giving a stern rebuke of the cloisterlike attitudes of some members, but the famous quip was, according to Frager, never actually uttered in full by Goldman. Wikiquote, "List of Misquotations," http://en.wikiquote.org/wiki/List_of_misquotations.

62. U.S. Department of Labor, *Michigan Copper District Strike: Bulletin of the United States Labor Statistics* (Washington, D.C.: Government Printing Office, 1914), 66–67.

63. Sarell, "Copper Country Strike," 13.

64. Lankton, *Cradle to Grave*, 222–225; U.S. Department of Labor, *Michigan Copper District Strike*, 67.

65. Sarell, "Copper Country Strike," 14–15.

66. John F. Kennedy, "Speech, 1962," http://thinkexist.com/quotation/those_who_make_peaceful_revolution_impossible/11217.html.

CHAPTER 7. COMPANY

1. Antti Sarell, "The Copper Country Strike: Its Features So Far," *Työmiehen Joulu 1913*, 19; *Työmies*, December 19, 1913.

2. Larry Lankton, *Cradle to Grave: Life, Work, and Death at the Lake Superior Copper Mines* (Oxford: Oxford University Press, 1991), 224–225.

3. Quincy Shaw to James MacNaughton, "Personal Letter," October 16, 1913, Calumet and Hecla Mining Companies Collection, Box 350, Folder 002, Copper Country Historical Archive, Michigan Technological University, Houghton.

4. State of Michigan, *Proceeding of the Court of Inquiry (Jackson County), People v. Blackman and Jackson 1912*, Calumet and Hecla Mining Companies Collection, Box 352, Folder 003, Copper Country Historical Collections, Michigan Technological University, Houghton.

5. Ibid.

6. Arthur Thurner, *Rebels on the Range: The Michigan Copper Miners' Strike of 1913–1914*

(Lake Linden, Mich.: John H. Forster Press, 1984), 87.

7. Thurner, *Rebels on the Range*, 92–95.

8. Ibid.

9. U.S. Bureau of Naturalization Examiner to the General Manager, Calumet and Hecla Mining Co., "Personal Letter," October 14, 1913, Calumet and Hecla Mining Companies Collection, Box 351, Folder 001, Copper Country Historical Archive, Michigan Technological University, Houghton.

10. U.S. Bureau of Naturalization Examiner to A. E. Petermann, Calumet and Hecla Mining Co., "Personal Letter," October 17, 1913, Calumet and Hecla Mining Companies Collection, Box 351, Folder 001, Copper Country Historical Archive, Michigan Technological University, Houghton.

11. R. L. Polk & Co., *Houghton County Directory, 1912*, 474, Copper Country Historical Archive, Michigan Technological University, Houghton.

12. Ibid.

13. George Nichols to Houghton County Board of Supervisors, "Arrests Report," 1914, Calumet and Hecla Mining Companies Collection, Copper Country Historical Archive, Michigan Technological University, Houghton.

14. R. L. Polk & Co., *Houghton County Directory, 1912, 1917*, 474, Copper Country Historical Archive, Michigan Technological University, Houghton; Calumet and Hecla Company Records, Employee Files, Copper Country Historical Archive, Michigan Technological University, Houghton; Heritage Quest Online, *Thirteenth Census of the United States, 1910* and *Fourteenth Census of the United States, 1920*, www.heritagequestonline.com.

15. R. L. Polk & Co., *Houghton County Directory, 1912 and 1917* and Heritage Quest Online, *Thirteenth Census of the United States, 1910* and *Fourteenth Census of the United States, 1920*, www.heritagequestonline.com.

16. Larry Lankton, *Cradle to Grave*, 214.

17. James MacNaughton to Quincy Shaw, "Correspondence," December 8, 1913, Calumet and Hecla Mining Companies Collection, Box 350, Folder 006, Copper Country Historical Archive, Michigan Technological University, Houghton.

18. Thiel Detective Service Co. to C. L. Lawton, General Manager Quincy Mining Co., Business Correspondence, August 5, 1913, Quincy Mining Company Collection, Box 341, Copper Country Historical Archive, Michigan Technological University, Houghton.

19. Ibid.

20. James MacNaughton to Quincy Shaw, "Various Coded Western Union Messages," July 23 to July 30, 1913, Calumet and Hecla Mining Companies Collection, Box 350, Folder 001, Copper Country Historical Archive, Michigan Technological University, Houghton.

21. James MacNaughton to Quincy Shaw, "Western Union Coded Message," July 23, 1913, Calumet and Hecla Mining Companies Collection, Box 350, Folder 001, Copper Country Historical Archive, Michigan Technological University, Houghton.

22. MacNaughton to Shaw, "Various Coded Western Union Messages."

23. *Työmies*, August 22, 1913.

24. Ibid.

25. Ibid.

26. Ibid.

27. Charles Lawton to William R. Todd, "Correspondence," September 24, 1913, Quincy Mining Company Collection, Box 342, Folder 11, Copper Country Historical Archive, Michigan Technological University, Houghton.

28. U.S. Department of Labor, *Michigan Copper District Strike: Bulletin of the United States Labor Statistics* (Washington, D.C.: Government Printing Office, 1914), 63–64.

29. William Parsons Todd, oral history interview by Ralph Jalkanen, October 1974, oral history recording and interview transcript, Finnish American Historical Archive, Finlandia University, Hancock, Mich., 1848–1850.

30. George E. Nichols, Special Prosecutor Houghton County, "Correspondence with Board of Supervisors Houghton County," February 17, 1914, Calumet and Hecla Mining Companies Collection, Copper Country Historical Collections, Michigan Technological University, Houghton; Waddell-Mahon Company, "Medallion—Material Culture," artifact stored in the Keweenaw National Historical Park's Museum, Archive, and Historical Services Division building.

31. Nichols, "Correspondence."

32. Ibid.

33. Frank Aaltonen, "Heroines of the Copper Country," *Työmiehen Joulu* (1913), 23–24.

34. Ibid.

35. Charles Lawton to William R. Todd, "Correspondence," September 22, 1913, Quincy Mining Company Collection, Box 342, Folder 11, Copper Country Historical Archive, Michigan Technological University, Houghton.

36. Charles Lawton to William R. Todd, "Correspondence," December 15, 1913, Quincy Mining Company Collection, Box 342, Folder 11, Copper Country Historical Archive, Michigan Technological University, Houghton.

37. *Työmies*, October 27, 1913.

38. Sarell, "Copper Country Strike," 15.

39. *Miner's Bulletin*, October 2, 1913.

40. Charles Lawton to William R. Todd, "Correspondence," October 6, 1913, Quincy Mining Company Collection, Box 342, Folder 11, Copper Country Historical Archive, Michigan Technological University, Houghton.

41. Charles Lawton to William R. Todd, "Correspondence," October 8, 1913, Quincy Mining Company Collection, Box 342, Folder 11, Copper Country Historical Archive, Michigan Technological University, Houghton.

42. Sarell, "Copper Country Strike," 15–16.

43. Ibid.

44. *Miners' Bulletin*, August 19, 1913

45. Ibid.

46. Arthur Puotinen, "Early Labor Organizations in the Copper Country," in *For the Common Good: Finnish Immigrants and the Radical Response to Industrial America*, ed. Michael G. Karni and Douglas J. Ollila Jr. (Superior, Wis.: Työmies Society, 1977), 153.

47. Nichols, "Correspondence"; Thomas Raleigh to O. F. Bailey, "Correspondence," Calumet and Hecla Mining Companies Collection, Box 353, Folder 003, Copper Country Historical Collections, Michigan Technological University, Houghton.

48. U.S. Department of Labor, *Michigan Copper District Strike*, 70.

49. Anthony Lucas, "Fazekas Shooting," Calumet and Hecla Mining Companies Collection, Box 352, Folder 004, Copper Country Historical Archive, Michigan Technological University, Houghton.

50. Anthony Lucas, "Fazekas Shooting," Calumet and Hecla Mining Companies Collection, Box 352, Folder 004, Copper Country Historical Archive, Michigan Technological University, Houghton; U.S. Department of Labor, *Michigan Copper District Strike*, 66–67.

51. Anthony Lucas, "Fazekas Shooting."

52. Ibid.

53. Nichols, "Correspondence."

54. Sarell, "Copper Country Strike," 19–20.

55. Arthur Thurner, *Rebels on the Range: The Michigan Copper Miners' Strike of 1913–1914* (Lake Linden, Mich.: John H. Forster Press, 1984), 100–101.

56. Charles Lawton to William R. Todd, "Correspondence," December 8, 1913, Quincy Mining Company Collection, Box 342, Folder 11, Copper Country Historical Archive, Michigan Technological University, Houghton.

57. James MacNaughton to Quincy Shaw, "Western Union Coded Message," December 8, 1913, Calumet and Hecla Mining Companies Collection, Box 350, Folder 008, Copper Country Historical Archive, Michigan Technological University, Houghton.

58. "Bill" to Albert E. Petermann, "Correspondence," December 3, 1913, Calumet and Hecla Mining Companies Collection, Box 354, Folder 002, Copper Country Historical Archive, Michigan Technological University, Houghton. Petermann seems to have edited the letter. Evidence for this assertion is the crossing out of text from the article, and then in handwritten pen or pencil, others words are scribbled over the original text.

59. Charles Lawton to William R. Todd, "Correspondence," December 9, 1913, Quincy Mining Company Collection, Box 342, Folder 11, Copper Country Historical Archive, Michigan Technological University, Houghton.

60. Lankton, *Cradle to Grave*, 234–235.

61. *Miners' Bulletin*, December 13, 1913.

62. Nichols, "Correspondence."

63. State of Michigan, *People of the State of Michigan vs. John Huhta, Nick Verbanac, Hjalmar Yalonen and Joseph Juntunen,* Case #4691, Copper Country Historical Collections, Michigan Technological University, Houghton.

64. "Labor Spy Report," Calumet and Hecla Mining Companies Collection, Box 351, Folder 001, Copper Country Historical Archive, Michigan Technological University, Houghton.

65. "Labor Spy Report," March 3, 1914, Calumet and Hecla Mining Companies Collection, Box 351, Folder 001, Copper Country Historical Archive, Michigan Technological University, Houghton.

66. "Labor Spy Report," March 11, 1914, Calumet and Hecla Mining Companies Collection, Box 351, Folder 001, Copper Country Historical Archive, Michigan Technological University, Houghton.

67. Thurner, *Rebels on the Range*, 130–133.

68. Ibid., 133–135.

69. Puotinen, "Early Labor Organizations," 121; Thurner, *Rebels on the Range*, 130–133; *Työmies*, December 11, 16, 1913.

70. Lillian Lahti Gow, interview by Jo Urion, transcript by Melissa Davis, Keweenaw National Historical Park, April 14, 2004, 14.

71. Ibid., 15–16.

72. Charles Lawton to William R. Todd, "Correspondence," December 12, 1913, Quincy Mining Company Collection, Box 342, Folder 011, Copper Country Historical Collections, Michigan Technological University, Houghton.

73. Ibid.

74. Lawton to Todd, "Correspondence," December 15, 1913.

CHAPTER 8. TRAGEDY

1. *Calumet News*, October 13, 1908.

2. *Calumet News*, October 13, 1908; Arthur Thurner, *Rebels on the Range: The Michigan Copper Miners' Strike of 1913–1914* (Lake Linden, Mich.: John H. Forster Press, 1984), 140–144.

3. "Italian Hall Disaster," Image#: Acc-400-12-13-1988-01-09-05 *Keweenaw Digital Archives: Michigan's Copper Country in Photographs*, Copper Country Historical Collections, Michigan Technological University, Houghton, http://digarch.lib.mtu.edu/showbib. aspx?bib_id=629109#.

4. James MacNaughton to Quincy Shaw, "Personal Letter," December 3, 1913, Calumet and Hecla Mining Companies Collection, Box 353, Folder 002, Copper Country Historical Archive, Michigan Technological University, Houghton.

5. *Miners' Bulletin*, November 11, 1913.

6. *Miners' Bulletin*, November 14, 1913. Italics in original.

7. *Miners' Bulletin*, November 29, 1913.

8. "Bill" to A. E. Petermann, "Personal Letter," December 3, 1913, Calumet and Hecla Mining Companies Collection, Box 353, Folder 002, Copper Country Historical Archive, Michigan Technological University, Houghton.

9. Ibid.

10. Ibid.

11. Ibid.

12. *Lapatossu*, "Monkey Cartoon," December 15, 1913.

13. *Miners' Bulletin*, December 16, 1913.

14. James MacNaughton to Quincy Shaw, "Personal Letter," December 17, 1913, Calumet and Hecla Mining Companies Collection, Box 350, Folder 006, Copper Country Historical Archive, Michigan Technological University, Houghton.

15. Charles Lawton to William R. Todd, "Correspondence," December 17, 1913, Quincy Mining Company Collection, Box 342, Copper Country Historical Archive, Michigan Technological University, Houghton.

16. "Labor Spy Report," December 1913, Calumet and Hecla Mining Companies Collection, Box 350, Folder 008, Copper Country Historical Archive, Michigan Technological University, Houghton. The best estimate of a date of this report is December 16 or 17, as there are no previous reports in the folder, and this entry from the labor spy precedes

reports for December 18, 1913.

17. Personal letters of A. E. Petermann, Calumet and Hecla Mining Companies Collection, Box 351, Folder 001, Copper Country Historical Archive, Michigan Technological University, Houghton.

18. *Daily Mining Gazette* (Houghton, Mich.), December 20, 1913. Italics added.

19. Nathan Drew to Albert E. Petermann, "Personal Correspondence," Calumet and Hecla Mining Companies Collection, Box 351, Folder 009, Copper Country Historical Archive, Michigan Technological University, Houghton.

20. *Miners' Bulletin*, November 14, 1913.

21. *Miners' Bulletin*, December 24, 1913.

22. Ibid.

23. Operative #1, "Labor Spy Report," January 23, 1914, Calumet and Hecla Mining Companies Collection, Box 350, Folder 009, Copper Country Historical Archive, Michigan Technological University, Houghton.

24. *Työmies*, December 26, 1913, "83 MURDERED," translation, Calumet and Hecla Mining Companies Collection, Box 353, Folder 001, Copper Country Historical Archive, Michigan Technological University, Houghton.

25. Larry Molloy, *Italian Hall: The Witnesses Speak* (Hubbell, Mich.: Great Lakes GeoScience, 2004), 23.

26. Houghton County, State of Michigan, "Coroner's Inquest Transcript," December 31, 1913, Labor and Political Collection, Italian Hall Materials, Manuscript Box K-17, Finnish American Historical Archive, Finlandia University, Hancock, Mich., 133–134.

27. Molloy, *Italian Hall*, 70–72, 88–90.

28. Joyce Sneller Seng, "Recollections of John Sneller," National Park Service, Keweenaw National Historical Park, Calumet Visitors Center, "Italian Hall Exhibit," July 5, 2012; U.S. Census Bureau, "Fourteenth Census of the United States—1920," www.ancestry.com. In 1920, the Sneller family lived on a farm in Allouez Township and consisted of eight members: father Joseph and mother Francis Sneller, both Croatian immigrants; John, fourteen; Frank, twelve; William, ten; Francis, eight; Anna, five; and Victor Albert, one.

29. Allied Printing, Houghton, Mich., "No. 13, Niemalä Stereoscope," Immigration History Research Center Photograph Collection, University of Minnesota, Minneapolis, 1913.

30. Seng, "Recollections of John Sneller."

31. David Juntti, "Recollections of Edwin J. Juntti," National Park Service, Keweenaw National Historical Park, Calumet Visitors Center, "Italian Hall Exhibit," December 2011–January 2012; "Michigan Deaths, 1971–1996," "Social Security Death Index," and "Edwin J. Juntti Family Tree," www.ancestry.com.

32. Houghton County, State of Michigan, "Coroner's Inquest Transcript," 63.

33. Molloy, *Italian Hall*, 92.

34. Houghton County, State of Michigan, "Coroner's Inquest Transcript," 35–36.

35. Ibid., 37–38.

36. Ibid., 131.

37. Ibid., 165–166, 168.

38. Ibid.

39. Ibid., 157–158.

40. Jenevive Sandretto, "Deposition," December 29, 1913, Calumet and Hecla Mining Companies Collection, Box 352, Folder 004, Copper Country Historical Archive, Michigan Technological University, Houghton.

41. Mari Chopp, "Deposition," December 29, 1913, Calumet and Hecla Mining Companies Collection, Box 352, Folder 004, Copper Country Historical Archive, Michigan Technological University, Houghton.

42. Herman Kallungi, interview by Harold L. Mathieu, July 18, 1973, oral history interview transcript, Finnish American Historical Archive, Finlandia University, Hancock, Mich., 34–36.

43. *Työmies*, December 25, 1913.

44. *Työmies*, December 26, 1913, "83 MURDERED."

45. *Miners' Bulletin*, December 28, 1913.

46. *Työmies*, December 27, 1913.

47. Unknown operative, "Labor Spy Reports," December 25 and 27, 1913, Calumet and Hecla Mining Companies Collection, Box 350, Folder 008, Copper Country Historical Archive, Michigan Technological University, Houghton.

48. *Calumet News*, "Afternoon Edition," December 24, 1913.

49. *Calumet News*, "Afternoon Edition," December 26, 1913.

50. Ibid.

51. On December 31, 1913, *Työmies* printed another list of those who died at Italian Hall, using the coroner's report as a source. The newspaper makes no mention of the credibility of this source as compared with its earlier accounts of the Italian Hall deceased.

52. Houghton County, State of Michigan, "Coroner's Inquest Transcript," 179. Italics added.

53. The figure for O'Brien's donation comes from an unknown labor spy, "Labor Spy Report," April 12, 1914, Calumet and Hecla Mining Companies Collection, Box 350, Folder 008, Copper Country Historical Archive, Michigan Technological University, Houghton; the quote comes from "Labor Spy Report," March 7, 1914, Calumet and Hecla Mining Companies Collection, Box 351, Folder 001, Copper Country Historical Archive, Michigan Technological University, Houghton.

54. Ed Stewart, "Neil's Story," unpublished family memoir of Neil Manley (Manni in Finnish), n.d., Finnish American Historical Archive, Finlandia University, Hancock, Mich.

55. Charles Lawton to William R. Todd, "Correspondence," December 27, 1913, Quincy Mining Company Collection, Box 342, Folder 011, Copper Country Historical Archive, Michigan Technological University, Houghton.

56. Unknown operative, "Labor Spy Report," December 25, 1913, Calumet and Hecla Mining Companies Collection, Box 350, Folder 008, Copper Country Historical Archive, Michigan Technological University, Houghton.

57. Molloy, *Italian Hall*, iii-iv.

58. *Työmies*, December 25 and 26, 1913.

59. *Työmies*, December 27, 1913; Arne Halonen, "The Role of Finnish-Americans in the Political Labor Movement" (Master's thesis, University of Minnesota, 1945), 86; Thurner, *Rebels on the Range*, 165–166. Oppman and Mikko, who likely provided union media sources with information on the events at Italian Hall, at the very least interviewed Anna

Lustig (who lost a child in the events), an eyewitness to events. Lustig was one of the strongest voices in stating that a person with a Citizens' Alliance button cried "Fire!"

60. *Miners' Bulletin,* December 28, 1913.

61. Ibid.; Thurner, *Rebels on the Range,* 165–167.

62. *Miners' Bulletin,* December 28 and 31, 1913; Unknown operative, "Labor Spy Report," Box 350, Folder 008, Calumet and Hecla Mining Companies Collection, Box 350, Folder 008, Copper Country Historical Archive, Michigan Technological University, Houghton; Thurner, *Rebels on the Range,* 165–167.

63. S. W. "Harry" Goldsmith to "Art," "Personal Letter," January 15, 1914, Calumet and Hecla Mining Companies Collection, Box 351, Folder 001, Copper Country Historical Archive, Michigan Technological University, Houghton.

64. Ibid.

65. Ibid.

66. Ibid.

67. Ibid.

68. Ibid.

69. Operative #2, "Labor Spy Report," January 16, 1914, Calumet and Hecla Mining Companies Collection, Box 350, Copper Country Historical Archive, Michigan Technological University, Houghton.

70. Robert J. Foster to Albert E. Petermann, "Business Correspondence," March 26, 1914, Calumet and Hecla Mining Companies Collection, Box 350, Copper Country Historical Archive, Michigan Technological University, Houghton.

71. Unknown operative, "Labor Spy Report," January 16, 1914, Calumet and Hecla Mining Companies Collection, Box 350, Copper Country Historical Archive, Michigan Technological University, Houghton.

CHAPTER 9. FIRE!?

1. Larry Molloy, *Italian Hall: The Witnesses Speak* (Hubbell, Mich.: Great Lakes GeoScience, 2004), 88–89.

2. Ibid., 70–72.

3. *Työmies,* December 26, 1913, "83 MURDERED," translation, Calumet and Hecla Mining Companies Collection, Box 353, Folder 001, Copper Country Historical Archive, Michigan Technological University, Houghton.

4. William R. Todd to Charles Lawton, "Personal Letter," December 26, 1913, Quincy Mining Company Collection, Box 341, Copper Country Historical Archive, Michigan Technological University, Houghton.

5. Unknown operative, "Labor Spy Report," June 6, 1914, Calumet and Hecla Mining Companies Collection, Box 352, Folder 006, Copper Country Historical Archive, Michigan Technological University, Houghton.

6. Steve Lehto, *Shortcut: The Seeberville Murders and the Dark Side of the American Dream* (Troy, Mich.: Momentum Books, 2012), 93–94.

7. Ibid.

8. *Ibid., n.473. Italics added.*

9. Molloy, *Italian Hall*, 71.

10. Houghton County, State of Michigan, "Coroner's Inquest Transcript," December 31, 1913, Labor and Political Collection, Italian Hall Materials, manuscript box K-17, Finnish American Historical Archive, Finlandia University, Hancock, Michigan, 157–158; *Työmies*, "83 MURDERED."

11. *Calumet News*, "Afternoon Extra," December 24, 1913.

12. *Calumet News*, December 26, 1913.

13. Operative #1, "Labor Spy Report," January 5, 1917, Calumet and Hecla Mining Companies Collection, Box 350, Folder 009, Copper Country Historical Archive, Michigan Technological University, Houghton.

14. Robert J. Foster to A. E. Petermann, "Business Correspondence," January 17, 1914, Calumet and Hecla Mining Companies Collection, Box 350, Folder 009, Copper Country Historical Archive, Michigan Technological University, Houghton.

15. Operative #1, "Labor Spy Report," January 7, 1914, Calumet and Hecla Mining Companies Collection, Box 350, Folder 009, Copper Country Historical Archive, Michigan Technological University, Houghton.

16. Operative #1, "Labor Spy Report," January 9, 1914, Calumet and Hecla Mining Companies Collection, Box 350, Folder 009, Copper Country Historical Archive, Michigan Technological University, Houghton.

17. Operative #1, "Labor Spy Report," January 12, 1914, Calumet and Hecla Mining Companies Collection, Box 350, Folder 009, Copper Country Historical Archive, Michigan Technological University, Houghton.

18. Operative #1, "Labor Spy Report," January 13, 1914, Calumet and Hecla Mining Companies Collection, Box 350, Folder 009, Copper Country Historical Archive, Michigan Technological University, Houghton.

19. Ibid.

20. Chelsea Pavolich, "Recollections of Annie Pavolich," National Park Service, Keweenaw National Historical Park, Calumet Visitors Center, "Italian Hall Exhibit," March 22, 2012; U.S. Census Bureau, "Thirteenth Census of the United States—1910," www.ancestry.com. Annie Pavolich's maiden name was Grentz. The Grentz family lived in Calumet Township and had attended festivities at Italian Hall. The family consisted of six people, and in 1910, at the age of ten, Annie was the oldest of the Grentz children. Her mother and father were Slovenian immigrants. Her father worked as a trammer in an area copper mine.

21. Operative #1, "Labor Spy Report," January 13, 1914.

22. Operative #1, "Labor Spy Report," January 15, 1914, Calumet and Hecla Mining Companies Collection, Box 350, Folder 009, Copper Country Historical Archive, Michigan Technological University, Houghton.

23. Ibid.

24. *Miner's Bulletin*, January 7, 1914.

25. Operative #1, "Labor Spy Report," January 16, 1914, Calumet and Hecla Mining Companies Collection, Box 350, Folder 009, Copper Country Historical Archive, Michigan Technological University, Houghton.

26. Ibid.

27. Ibid.

28. Ibid.

29. Ibid.

30. Operative #1, "Labor Spy Report," January 17, 1914, Calumet and Hecla Mining Companies Collection, Box 350, Folder 009, Copper Country Historical Archive, Michigan Technological University, Houghton.

31. Ibid.

32. Ibid.

33. Operative #1, "Labor Spy Report," January 17 and 18, 1914, Calumet and Hecla Mining Companies Collection, Box 350, Folder 009, Copper Country Historical Archive, Michigan Technological University, Houghton.

34. Operative #1, "Labor Spy Report," January 19, 1914, Calumet and Hecla Mining Companies Collection, Box 350, Folder 009, Copper Country Historical Archive, Michigan Technological University, Houghton.

35. Ibid.

36. Operative #1, "Labor Spy Report," January 22, 1914, Calumet and Hecla Mining Companies Collection, Box 350, Folder 009, Copper Country Historical Archive, Michigan Technological University, Houghton.

37. Ibid.

38. Operative #1, "Labor Spy Report," January 23, 1914, Calumet and Hecla Mining Companies Collection, Box 350, Folder 009, Copper Country Historical Archive, Michigan Technological University, Houghton.

39. Ibid.

40. Operative #1, "Labor Spy Report," January 24, 1914, Calumet and Hecla Mining Companies Collection, Box 350, Folder 009, Copper Country Historical Archive, Michigan Technological University, Houghton.

41. Operative #1, "Labor Spy Report," January 25, 1914, Calumet and Hecla Mining Companies Collection, Box 350, Folder 009, Copper Country Historical Archive, Michigan Technological University, Houghton.

42. Ibid.

43. Ibid.

44. R. L. Polk & Co., *Houghton County Directory, 1912*, "Calumet," (Detroit: R.L. Polk & Company), 95, 163–65.

45. Operative #1, "Labor Spy Report," January 26, 1913.

46. Unknown operative, "Labor Spy Report," March 3, 1914, Calumet and Hecla Mining Companies Collection, Box 350, Folder 008, Copper Country Historical Archive, Michigan Technological University, Houghton.

47. Unknown operative, "Labor Spy Report," March 14, 1914, Calumet and Hecla Mining Companies Collection, Box 350, Folder 009, Copper Country Historical Archive, Michigan Technological University, Houghton.

48. Unknown operative, "Labor Spy Report," April 3, 1914, Calumet and Hecla Mining Companies Collection, Box 350, Folder 009, Copper Country Historical Archive, Michigan Technological University, Houghton.

49. Unknown operative, "Labor Spy Report," April 3 and 10, 1914, Calumet and Hecla Mining Companies Collection, Box 350, Folder 009, Copper Country Historical Archive,

Michigan Technological University, Houghton.

50. Unknown operative, "Labor Spy Report," April 13, 1914, Calumet and Hecla Mining Companies Collection, Box 350, Folder 009, Copper Country Historical Archive, Michigan Technological University, Houghton.

51. Unknown operative, "Labor Spy Report," May 30, 1914, Calumet and Hecla Mining Companies Collection, Box 350, Folder 009, Copper Country Historical Archive, Michigan Technological University, Houghton.

CHAPTER 10. CAVE-IN

1. *Miners Bulletin*, December 31, 1913.

2. Larry Lankton, *Cradle to Grave: Life, Work, and Death at the Lake Superior Copper Mines* (Oxford: Oxford University Press, 1991), 237–238; Arthur Puotinen, "Early Labor Organizations in the Copper Country," in *For the Common Good: Finnish Immigrants and the Radical Response to Industrial America*, ed. Michael G. Karni and Douglas J. Ollila Jr. (Superior, Wis.: Työmies Society, 1977), 160.

3. Charles Lawton to William R. Todd, "Correspondence," December 26, 1913, Quincy Mining Company Collection, Box 342, Folder 011, Copper Country Historical Collections, Michigan Technological University, Houghtonh.

4. Graham Romeyn Taylor, "Moyer's Story of Why He Left the Copper Country," *Survey*, January 10, 1914, 433–435.

5. Ibid.

6. Ibid.

7. Ibid.

8. Ibid.

9. Ibid.

10. Charles Lawton to William R. Todd, "Correspondence," December 27, 1913, Quincy Mining Company Collection, Box 342, Folder 011, Copper Country Historical Collections, Michigan Technological University, Houghton.

11. Taylor, "Moyer's Story," 435.

12. Nichols, to Houghton County Board of Supervisors, "Arrests Report Correspondence," Copper Country Historical Collections, Michigan Technological University, Houghton, Michigan, 1914.

13. Ibid. Italics added.

14. Unknown operative, "Labor Spy Report," Calumet and Hecla Mining Companies Collection, Box 352, Copper Country Historical Archive, Michigan Technological University, Houghton.

15. Puotinen, "Early Labor Organizations," 159–161.

16. Charles Lawton to William R. Todd, "Correspondence," December 26, 1913, Quincy Mining Company Collection, Box 342, Folder 011, Copper Country Historical Collections, Michigan Technological University, Houghton.

17. "Boats Tied Up," *International Socialist Review* (September 1913): 184.

18. University of Arizona, "The Bisbee Deportation of 1917—An Overview," web exhibit,

http://www.library.arizona.edu/exhibits/bisbee/history/overview.html.

19. *Miners' Bulletin*, January 21, 1914.

20. *Työmies*, December 27, 1913.

21. Puotinen, "Early Labor Organizations," 162; Arthur Thurner, *Rebels on the Range: The Michigan Copper Miners' Strike of 1913–1914* (Lake Linden, Mich.: John H. Forster Press, 1984), 229–232.

22. *Miners' Bulletin*, March 12, 1914.

23. *Miners' Bulletin*, April 1, 1914.

24. *Miners' Bulletin*, April 14, 1914.

25. Puotinen, "Early Labor Organizations," 162–163.

26. *Miners' Bulletin*, April 14, 1914.

27. Armas K. E. Holmio, "Notes on the Finnish Anti-socialist League," Anti-Sosialistien Liitto Papers, Manuscript Box O-43, Finnish American Historical Archive, Finlandia University, Hancock, Mich.

28. Anti-sosialistien Liitto, *Pöytäkirja*, April 9, 1914–May 12, 1915, tran. Anna Leppänen and Gary Kaunonen (2008), Manuscript Box O-43, Finnish American Historical Archive, Finlandia University, Hancock, Mich.

29. Ibid.

30. Ibid.

31. Lankton, *Cradle to Grave*, 240–241; Thurner, *Rebels on the Range*, 229–232.

32. *Miners' Bulletin*, April 14, 1914.

33. Committee of the Copper Country Commercial Club, *Strike Investigation: By the Committee of the Copper Country Commercial Club of Michigan 1913* (Houghton, Mich., 1913), 1–2.

34. U.S. Department of Labor, *Strike in the Copper Mining District of Michigan* (Washington, D.C.: Government Printing Office, 1914).

35. House of Representatives, Subcommittee of the Committee on Mines and Mining, *Hearings before a Subcommittee of the Committee on Mines and Mining*, House Resolution 387 (Washington, D.C.: Government Printing Office, 1914).

36. Unknown operative, "Labor Spy Report," March 13, 1914, Box 351, Calumet and Hecla Mining Companies Collection, Box 352, Copper Country Historical Archive, Michigan Technological University, Houghton.

37. Unknown operative, "Labor Spy Reports," March–May 1914, Boxes 351 and 352, Calumet and Hecla Mining Companies Collection, Box 352, Copper Country Historical Archive, Michigan Technological University, Houghton.

38. Matthew Robert Isham, "From Coxey's Army to Occupy Wall Street," Richards Civil War Era Center, Penn State University, http://www.psu.edu/dept/richardscenter/2011/10/from-coxeys-army-to-occupy-wall-street.html.

39. Unknown operative, "Labor Spy Reports," April, Box 352, Calumet and Hecla Mining Companies Collection, Box 352, Copper Country Historical Archive, Michigan Technological University, Houghton.

40. Lankton, *Cradle to Grave*, 239.

41. *Miners' Bulletin*, April 14, 1914.

42. Thurner, *Rebels on the Range*, 230.

43. Charles E. Hietala to Ernest Mills, Business Correspondence, June 7, 1915, Papers of the Western Federation of Miners/International Union of Mine, Mill and Smelter Workers, Box 1, Folder 29, University Archives, University of Colorado–Boulder.

44. Lankton, *Cradle to Grave*, 239.

45. Unknown operative, "Labor Spy Report," June 4, 1914, Calumet and Hecla Mining Companies Collection, Box 352, Folder 006, Copper Country Historical Archive, Michigan Technological University, Houghton.

46. Charles Lawton to W. R. Todd, Business Correspondence, April 4, 1914, Quincy Mining Company Collection, Box 342, Copper Country Archives, Michigan Technological University, Houghton

47. *Daily Mining Gazette*, March 28, 1914.

48. *Daily Mining Gazette*, April 7, 1914.

49. Ibid.

50. Charles Lawton to W. R. Todd, Business Correspondence, April 7, 1914, Quincy Mining Company Collection, Box 342, Copper Country Archives, Michigan Technological University, Houghton.

51. *Daily Mining Gazette*, April 7, 1914.

52. Ibid.

53. Ibid.

54. "Trouble in the Copper Country with I.W.W. Agitators," *Engineering and Mining Journal* 104, no. 3 (July 1917): 148.

55. Ibid.

CONCLUSION

1. "Michigan Copper Mine Strikers Standing Firm," *Locomotive Firemen's Magazine* 56, no. 1 (January 1914): 78.

2. Arthur Thurner, *Rebels on the Range: The Michigan Copper Miners' Strike of 1913–1914* (Lake Linden, Mich.: John H. Forster Press, 1984), 153.

3. Melba Luoma, "Oral History Transcript," interview by Jo Urion, transcribed by Melissa Davis, Keweenaw National Historical Park Archive, April 14, 2004.

Bibliography

MANUSCRIPT COLLECTIONS

Anti-Sosialistien Liitto Papers, Finnish American Historical Archive, Finlandia University, Hancock, Michigan.

Articles of Incorporation, Liebers 1–5, Copper Country Historical Archive, Michigan Technological University, Houghton.

Calumet and Hecla Mining Companies Collection, Copper Country Historical Archive, Michigan Technological University, Houghton.

Finnish-American Historical Archives, Finlandia University, Hancock, Michigan.

Quincy Mining Company Papers, Copper Country Historical Archive, Michigan Technological University, Houghton.

R. L. Polk & Co., *Houghton County Directory*, 1899–1917, Copper Country Historical Archive, Michigan Technological University, Houghton.

John Surbeck Papers, Archival Collections, Keweenaw, National Park Service, Calumet, Michigan.

Western Federation of Miners Collection, Copper Country Historical Archive, Michigan Technological University, Houghton.

CENSUS

U.S. Bureau of the Census. *Fourteenth Census of the United States Taken in the Year 1920.* Microfilm.

U.S. Bureau of the Census. *Thirteenth Census of the United States Taken in the Year 1910.* Microfilm.

U.S. Bureau of the Census. *Twelfth Census of the United States Taken in the Year 1900.* Microfilm.

NEWSPAPERS

Aberdeen (Wash.) Daily Bulletin

Aberdeen (Wash.) Herald

Advance and Labor Leaf (Detroit)

Calumet and Red Jacket News (Red Jacket, Mich.)

Chicago Tribune

Cigar Makers' Official Journal (Chicago)

Coast Seamen's Journal (San Francisco)

Copper Country Evening News (Calumet, Mich.)

Daily Mining Gazette (Houghton, Mich.)

Daily Washingtonian (Hoquiam, Wash.)

Dubuque (Iowa) Telegraph-Herald

Grays Harbor Post (Aberdeen, Wash.)

Industrialisti (Duluth, Minn.)

Industrial Solidarity (Chicago)

Industrial Union Bulletin (Chicago)

Industrial Worker (Spokane, Wash.)

Industrial Worker (Seattle)

Keweenaw Miner (Mohawk, Mich.)

Labor Defender (Chicago)

Labor World (Butte, Mont.)

Lewiston Evening Journal (Lewiston, Me.)

Miners' Bulletin (Hancock, Mich.)

Miners' Magazine (Denver)

Motorman and Conductor (Detroit)

New York Times

Ontonagon (Mich.) Herald

Oregonian (Portland, Ore.)

Portage Lake Mining Gazette (Houghton, Mich.)

Providence (R.I.) News

Seattle Post-Intelligencer

Solidarity (New Castle, Pa.)

Sosialisti (Duluth, Minn.)

Spokesman-Review (Spokane, Wash.)

Telegraph (Nashua, N.H.)

Toveri (Astoria, Ore.)

Toveritar (Astoria, Ore.)

Town Development (New York City)

Työmies (Hancock, Mich.)

Typographical Journal (Indianapolis)

Wage-Slave (Hancock, Mich.)

Wolverine Citizen (Flint, Mich.)

PUBLICATIONS

Adamic, Louis. *Dynamite! A Century of Class Violence in America, 1830–1930.* London: Rebel Press, 1984.

Adamic, Louis. *Dynamite: The Story of Class Violence in America.* Oakland, Calif.: AK Press, 2008.

Alanen, Arnold R. "Early Labor Strife on the Minnesota Mining Frontier, 1882–1906." *Minnesota History* 52, no. 7 (Fall 1991): 246–263.

"Alexander M. Stirton." *American Co-Operator* 2, no. 16 (September 19, 1903): 16.

Alter, Peter T. "The Creation of a Multi-Ethnic Peoplehood: The Wilkeson, Washington Experience." *Journal of American Ethnic History* 15, no. 3 (Spring 1996): 3–21.

American Federation of Labor. *Report of Proceedings of the Twenty-Third Annual Convention of the American Federation of Labor.* Washington, D.C.: Law Reporter, 1903.

The American Labor Yearbook, 1916. New York: Ran School of Social Science, 1916.

American Street Railway Investments, Published Annually by the Publishers of the Electric Railway Journal. Vol. 15. New York: McGraw, 1908.

Andrews, Clarence. Oral history interview. Finnish American Historical Archive, Finlandia University, Hancock, Mich.

Argersinger, Jo Ann E. *The Triangle Fire: A Brief History with Documents.* Boston: Bedford/St. Martin's, 2009.

Asher, Robert. "The Limits of Big Business Paternalism: Relief for Injured Workers in the Years Before Workmen's Compensation." In *Dying for Work: Workers' Safety and Health in Twentieth-Century America*, ed. David Rosner and Gerald Markowitz, 19–33. Bloomington: Indiana University Press, 1989.

Beck, John P. "Homegrown." *Michigan History* 79, no. 5 (1995): 19–25.

Bekken, Jon. *"Socialist Press."* In *Encyclopedia of American Journalism*, ed. Stephen L. Vaughn, 483–485. New York: Routledge, 2008.

Berkman, Alexander. *The Russian Tragedy.* Comp. William G. Nowlin Jr. Montreal: Black Rose Books, 1976.

Bernstein, Irving. *A History of the American Worker, 1920–1933: The Lean Years.* Boston: Houghton-Mifflin, 1960.

Bird, Stewart, Dan Georgakas, and Deborah Shaffer. *Solidarity Forever: An Oral History of the IWW*. Chicago: Lake View Press, 1985.

"Boats Tied Up." *International Socialist Review* 14 (September 1913): 184.

Bodnar, John. *The Transplanted: A History of Immigrants in Urban America*. Bloomington: Indiana University Press, 1985.

Boyer, Hugh E. "The Decline of the Progressive Party in Michigan's Upper Peninsula: The Case of Congressman William J. MacDonald in 1914." *Michigan History* 13 (Fall 1987): 75–94.

Boyer, Richard O., and Herbert M. Morais. *Labor's Untold Story: The Adventure Story of the Battles, Betrayals, and Victories of American Working Men and Women*. New York: Cameron Associates, 1955.

Braverman, Harry. *Labor and Monopoly Capital: The Degradation of Work in the Twentieth Century*. New York: Monthly Review Press, 1974.

Brissenden, Paul. *The IWW: A Study in Syndicalism*. 1919. Reprint. 2nd ed. New York: Russell and Russell, 1957.

Brown, K. Marianne Wargelin. "Three 'Founding Mothers' of Finnish America." In *Women Who Dared: The History of Finnish-American Women*, ed. Carl Ross and K. Marianne Wargelin Brown, 136–157. St. Paul: Immigration History Research Center, University of Minnesota, 1986.

Brown, Ronald C. *Hard-Rock Miners: The Intermountain West, 1860–1920*. College Station: Texas A&M Press, 1979.

Bruere, Robert Walter. *Following the Trail of the IWW: A First-Hand Investigation into Labor Troubles in the West—A Trip into the Copper and the Lumber Camps of the Inland Empire with the Views of the Men on the Job*. New York: New York Evening Post, 1918.

Brundage, David. *The Making of Western Labor Radicalism: Denver's Organized Workers, 1878–1905*. Urbana: University of Illinois Press, 1994.

Buhle, Mari Jo. *Women and American Socialism, 1870–1920*. Urbana: University of Illinois Press, 1981.

Buhle, Paul. *Marxism in the United States*. London: Verso, 1987.

Buhle, Paul, and Nicole Schulman, eds. *Wobblies! A Graphic History of the Industrial Workers of the World*. London: Verso Press, 2005.

Burr, Christina. "Defending 'The Art Preservative': Class and Gender Relations in the Printing Trades Unions, 1850–1914." *Labour/Le Travail* 31 (Spring 1993): 47–73.

Calvert, Jerry W. *The Gibraltar: Socialism and Labor in Butte, Montana, 1895–1920*. Helena: Montana Historical Society Press, 1988.

Campbell, Peter J. "The Cult of Spontaneity: Finnish-Canadian Bushworkers and the Industrial Workers of the World in Northern Ontario, 1919–1934." *Labour/Le Travail* 41 (Spring 1998): 117–146.

Chaplin, Ralph. *The Centralia Conspiracy*. Chicago: Industrial Workers of the World, 1924.

———. *Wobbly: The Rough-and-Tumble Story of an American Radical*. Chicago: University of Chicago Press, 1948.

Cizmic, Ivan. *History of the Croatian Fraternal Union of America, 1894–1994*. Zagreb, Croatia: Golden Marketing, 1994.

———. "Yugoslav Immigrants in the US Labor Movement, 1880–1920." In *American Labor and Immigration History, 1877–1920s: Recent European Research*, ed. Dirk Hoerder, 184–189.

Urbana: University of Illinois Press, 1983.

Clark, Norman H. *Mill Town: A Social History of Everett, Washington, from Its Earliest Beginnings on the Shores of Puget Sound to the Tragic and Infamous Event Known as the Everett Massacre*. Seattle: University of Washington Press, 1970.

"Class Struggle Notes: 'Big Annie.'" *International Socialist Review* 14, no. 6 (December 1913): 342.

Clawson, Mary Ann. *Constructing Brotherhood: Class, Gender, and Fraternalism*. Princeton, N.J.: Princeton University Press, 1989.

Cole, Peter. *Wobblies on the Waterfront: Interracial Unionism in Progressive-Era Philadelphia*. Urbana: University of Illinois Press, 2007.

Committee of the Copper Country Commercial Club, *Strike Investigation: By the Committee of the Copper Country Commercial Club of Michigan 1913*. Houghton, Mich., 1913.

Committee on Labor of the House of Representatives. *Eight Hours for Laborers on Government Work: Hearings before the Committee on Labor of the House of Representatives, First Session Fifty-Seventh Congress*. Washington, D.C.: Government Printing Office, 1902.

"Confer to End Copper Strike." *Los Angeles Times*, August 4, 1913.

Conlin, Joseph Robert. *Big Bill Haywood and the Radical Union Movement*. Syracuse, N.Y.: Syracuse University Press, 1969.

——. *Bread and Roses Too: Studies of the Wobblies*. Westport, Conn.: Greenwood Publishing, 1969.

Copeland, Tom. *The Centralia Tragedy of 1919: Elmer Smith and the Wobblies*. Seattle: University of Washington Press, 1993.

"Copper Region Calm with Militia There." *New York Times*, July 25, 1913.

Coulter, John Lee. "The Cooperative Farmer." *World's Work* 23, no. 1 (November 1911): 59–63.

Dawley, Alan. *Class and Community: The Industrial Revolution in Lynn*. Cambridge, Mass.: Harvard University Press, 1976.

Decaux, Len. *Labor Radical: From the Wobblies to the CIO*. Boston: Beacon Press, 1970.

——. *The Living Spirit of the Wobblies*. New York: International Publishers, 1978.

DeLeon, Solon. *The American Labor Press Directory*. New York: Department of Labor Research, Rand School of Social Science, 1925.

DeLeon, Solon, and Nathan Fine, eds. *The American Labor Yearbook*. New York: Rand School of Social Science, 1929.

Derickson, Alan. "Down Solid: The Origins and Development of the Black Lung Insurgency." *Journal of Public Health Policy* 4, no. 1 (March 1983): 25–44.

Dowell, E. F. *A History of Criminal-Syndicalist Legislation in the United States*. Baltimore: John Hopkins University Press, 1939.

Dray, Philip. *There Is Power in a Union: The Epic Story of Labor in America*. New York: Doubleday, 2010.

Dubofsky, Melvyn. *"Big Bill" Haywood*. Manchester: Manchester University Press, 1987.

——. *We Shall Be All: A History of the Industrial Workers of the World*. Chicago: Quadrangle Books, 1969. Reprint, Chicago: Quadrangle Books, 1973.

——. *We Shall Be All: A History of the Industrial Workers of the World*. Ed. Joseph A. McCartin. Urbana: University of Illinois Press, 2000.

——. "Wobblies Past and Present: A Response." *Labor History* 40, no. 3 (August 1999):

365—369.

Duchez, Louis. "Victory at McKees Rocks." *International Socialist Review* 10 (October 1909): 289–300.

Ealham, Chris. *Anarchism and the City: Revolution and Counter-Revolution in Barcelona, 1898—1937.* Oakland, Calif.: AK Press, 2010.

Emmons, David M. *The Butte Irish: Class and Ethnicity in an American Mining Town, 1875—1925.* Urbana: University of Illinois Press, 1990.

Engel, Dave, and Gerry Mantel. *Calumet: Copper Country Metropolis: 1898–1913.* Rudolph, Wis.: River City Memoirs-Maki, 2002.

Faue, Elizabeth. *Community of Suffering and Struggle: Women, Men, and the Labor Movement in Minneapolis, 1915–1945.* Chapel Hill: University of North Carolina Press, 1991.

Feurer, Rosemary. *Radical Unionism in the Midwest, 1900–1950.* Urbana: University of Illinois Press, 2006.

Flynn, Elizabeth Gurley. *The Rebel Girl: An Autobiography, My First Life (1906–1926),* 1955. New ed. New York: International Publishers, 1973.

Folsom, Franklin. *Inpatient Armies of the Poor: The Story of Collective Action of the Unemployed.* Boulder: University Press of Colorado, 1991.

Foner, Philip S. *The History of the Labor Movement in the United States.* Vol. 2, *From the AF of L to the Emergence of American Imperialism.* New York: International Publishers, 1964.

———. *The History of the Labor Movement in the United States.* Vol. 3, *The Policies and Practices of the American Federation of Labor, 1900–1909.* New York: International Printers, 1981.

———. *The History of the Labor Movement in the United States.* Vol. 4, *The Industrial Workers of the World, 1905–1917.* New York: International Publishers, 1965.

———. *The History of the Labor Movement in the United States.* Vol. 5, *The AFL in the Progressive Era, 1910–1915.* New York: International Publishers, 1980.

———. *Women and the American Labor Movement: From the First Trade Unions to the Present.* New York: Free Press, 1979.

Frank, Dana. *Purchasing Power: Consumer Organizing, Gender, and the Seattle Labor Movement, 1919–1945.* Cambridge: Cambridge University Press, 1994.

"From Star Dust to Socialism." *International Socialist Review* 6, no. 12 (June 1906): 760.

Fudge, Judy, and Eric Tucker. *Labor Before the Law: The Regulation of Workers' Collective Action in Canada, 1900–1948.* Toronto: University of Toronto Press, 2004.

Gambs, John S. *Decline of the IWW.* New York: Columbia University Press, 1932.

Garlock, Jonathan. *Guide to the Local Assembles of the Knights of Labor.* Westport, Conn.: Greenwood Press, 1982.

Gates, William B., Jr. *Michigan Copper and Boston Dollars: An Economic History of the Michigan Copper Mining Industry.* Cambridge, Mass.: Harvard University Press, 1951.

Gedicks, Albert. *Working Class Radicalism among Finnish Immigrants in Minnesota and Michigan Mining Communities.* Ann Arbor, Mich.: University Microfilms International, 1980.

Goings, Aaron. "Hall Syndicalism: Radical Finns and Wobbly Culture in Grays Harbor, Washington." *Journal of Finnish Studies* 14, no. 1 (Summer 2010): 18–28.

———. "Red Harbor: Class, Violence, and Community in Grays Harbor, Washington." Ph.D. diss., Simon Fraser University, 2011.

Goldman, Emma. *My Disillusionment in Russia*. Garden City, N.Y.: Doubleday, Page, 1923.

Goldstein, Robert Justin. *Political Repression in Modern America: From 1870 to 1976*. Urbana: University of Illinois Press, 2001.

"Gov Ferris to Take Action." *Boston Daily Globe*, July 30, 1913.

Green, Archie. *Wobblies, Pile Butts, and Other Heroes: Laborlore Explorations*. Urbana: University of Illinois Press, 1993.

Green, James R. *Grass-Roots Socialism: Radical Movements in the Southwest, 1895–1943*. Baton Rouge: Louisiana State University Press, 1978.

———. *The World of the Worker: Labor in Twentieth-Century America*. 1980. Reprint, Urbana: University of Illinois Press, 1998.

Green, Victor. *A Singing Ambivalence: American Immigrants Between the Old World and the New, 1830–1930*. Kent, Ohio: Kent State University Press, 2004.

Greenwald, Maurine Weiner. "Working-Class Feminism and the Family Wage Ideal: The Seattle Debate on Married Women's Right to Work, 1914–1920." In *Women in Pacific Northwest History*, rev. ed., ed. Karen Blair, 94–134. Seattle: University of Washington Press, 2001.

Gudmundsom, Wayne, and Suzanne Winckler. *Testaments in Wood: Finnish Log Structures at Embarrass, Minnesota*. St. Paul: Minnesota Historical Society Press, 1991.

Gutman, Herbert G. *Work, Culture, and Society in Industrializing America*. New York: Alfred A. Knopf, 1976.

Hall, Covington. *Labor Struggles in the Deep South & Other Writings*. Ed. David R. Roediger. Chicago: Charles H. Kerr Press, 1999.

Hall, Greg. *Harvest Wobblies: The Industrial Workers of the World and Agricultural Laborers in the American West, 1905–1930*. Corvallis: Oregon State University Press, 2001.

Hall, Joan Houston, ed. *Dictionary of Regional English*, Vol. 4. Cambridge, Mass.: Harvard University Press, 2002.

Hannula, Reino Nikolai. *Blueberry God: The Education of a Finnish-American*. San Luis Obispo, Calif.: Quality Hill Books, 1979.

Hawley, Lowell Stillwell, and Ralph Bushnell Potts. *Counsel for the Damned: A Biography of George Francis Vanderveer*. Philadelphia: J. B. Lippincott, 1953.

Haywood, William D. *The Autobiography of Big Bill Haywood*. New York: International Publishers, 1929.

———. "The Fighting IWW." *International Socialist Review* 8, no. 3 (September 1912): 246–247.

———. "On the Paterson Picket Line." *International Socialist Review* 13 (June 1913): 847–851.

———. "The General Strike." In *Rebel Voices: An IWW Anthology*, ed. Joyce L. Kornbluh, 51–52. Chicago: Charles H. Kerr Press, 1998.

———. "Solidarity in Prison." *International Socialist Review* 10, no. 12 (June 1910): 1065–1068.

Herringshaw, Thomas William. *American Blue-book of Biography: Prominent Americans of 1912—An Accurate Biographical Record of Prominent Citizens of All Walks of Life*. Chicago: American Publishers' Association, 1913.

History of the Bar and Bench of Utah. Salt Lake City: Interstate Press Association Publishers, 1913.

Hoagland, Alison K. *Mine Towns: Buildings for Workers in Michigan's Copper Country*. Minneapolis: University of Minnesota Press, 2010.

Hobsbawm, Eric J. *Workers: Worlds of Labour*. New York: Pantheon Books, 1984.

Hodges, Adam J. "Thinking Globally, Acting Locally: The Portland Soviet and the Emergence of American Communism, 1918–1920." *Pacific Northwest Quarterly* 98, no. 3 (Summer 2007): 115–129.

Hoerder, Dick, and Christiane Harzig, eds. *The Immigrant Labor Press in North America: 1840s—1970s, An Annotated Bibliography.* Vol. 1, *Migrants from Northern Europe.* Westport, Conn.: Greenwood Press, 1987.

Hoglund, A. William. *Finnish Immigrants in America, 1880–1920.* Madison: University of Wisconsin Press, 1960.

Holmio, Armas K. E. *History of the Finns in Michigan.* Trans. Ellen M. Ryynanen. Detroit: Wayne State University Press, 2001.

Huberman, Leo. *The Labor Spy Racket.* New York: Modern Age Books, 1937.

Hudelson, Richard, and Carl Ross. *By the Ore Docks: A Working People's History of Duluth.* St. Paul: University of Minnesota Press, 2006.

Hummasti, Paul George. *Finnish Radicals in Astoria, Oregon, 1904–1940: A Study in Immigrant Socialism.* New York: Arno Press, 1979.

———. "'The Working Man's Daily Bread': Finnish-American Working Class Newspapers, 1900–1921." In *For the Common Good: Finnish Immigrants and the Radical Response to Industrial America,* ed. Michael G. Karni and Douglas J. Ollila Jr., 167–197. Superior, Wis.: Tyomies Society, 1977.

Impola, Helvi, and Miriam Leino Eldridge. "The Life and Songs of Arthur Kylander." *New World Finn* 2 (October–December 2001): 14.

Industrial Workers of the World. *IWW Songs to Fan the Flames of Discontent.* Facsimile Reprint of the Popular Nineteenth Edition, 1923. Chicago: Charles H. Kerr Press, 1989.

———. "Preamble of the Industrial Workers of the World." In *Rebel Voices: An IWW Anthology,* ed. Joyce L. Kornbluh, 12–13. Chicago: Charles H. Kerr Press, 1998.

Jameson, Elizabeth. *All That Glitters: Class, Conflict, and Community in Cripple Creek.* Urbana: University of Illinois Press, 1998.

———. "We Shall Be All: Thirty Years Later." *Labor History* 40, no. 3 (August 1999): 349–356.

Janes, George Milton. *American Trade Unionism.* Chicago: A. C. McClurg, 1922.

Jeffreys-Jones, Rhodri. *Violence and Reform in American History.* New York: New Viewpoints, 1978.

Jensen, Joan M. *Army Surveillance in America, 1775–1980.* New Haven, Conn.: Yale University Press, 1991.

Jensen, Vernon. *Heritage of Conflict: Labor Relations in the Nonferrous Metals Industry up to 1930.* Ithaca, N.Y.: Cornell University Press, 1950. Reprint, New York: Greenwood Press, 1968.

Johansson, Ella. "Men without Bosses: Encounters with Modernity in the Logging Camps of Northern Sweden, 1860–1940." In *Sustainability, the Challenge: Power, People, and the Environment,* ed. L. Anders Sandberg and Sverker Sorlin, 141–148. Montreal: Black Rose Books, 1998.

Jones, Mary Harris. *Autobiography of Mother Jones.* Chicago: Charles H. Kerr Press, 1925.

Karni, Michael. "The Founding of the Finnish Socialist Federation and the Minnesota Strike of 1907." In *For the Common Good: Finnish Immigrants and the Radical Response to Industrial America,* ed. Michael G. Karni and Douglas J. Ollila Jr., 65–86. Superior, Wis.: Tyomies Society, 1977.

Karni, Michael G., and Douglas Ollila, eds. *For the Common Good: Finnish Immigrants and the Radical Response to Industrial America.* Superior, Wis.: Tyomies Society, 1977.

Karni, Michael G., Matti E. Kaups, and Douglas J. Ollila. *The Finnish Experience in the Western Great Lakes Region: New Perspectives.* Turku, Finland: Institute for Migration Studies, 1975.

Karvonen, Hilja. "Three Proponents of Women's Rights." In *Women Who Dared: The History of Finnish-American Women,* ed. Carl Ross and K. Marianne Wargelin Brown, 123–135. St. Paul, Minn.: Immigration History Research Center, 1986.

Kaunonen, Gary. *Challenge Accepted: A Finnish Immigrant Response to Industrial America in Michigan's Copper Country.* East Lansing: Michigan State University Press, 2010.

——. *The Finns of Michigan.* East Lansing: Michigan State University Press, 2009.

Kazin, Michael, and Stephen J. Ross. "America's Labor Day: The Dilemma of a Workers' Celebration." *Journal of American History* 78, no. 4 (March 1992): 1294–1323.

Keane, Augustus Henry. *Ethnology.* London: C. J. Clay and Sons, 1901.

Kero, Reino. "Migration Traditions from Finland to North America." In *A Century of European Migrations, 1830–1930,* ed. Rudolph J. Vecoli and Suzanne M. Sinke, 111–133. Urbana: University of Illinois Press, 1991.

Kessler-Harris, Alice. *Out to Work: A History of Wage-Earning Women in the United States.* Oxford: Oxford University Press, 1982.

Kipnis, Ira. *The American Socialist Movement, 1897–1912.* New York: Columbia University Press, 1952.

Kivisto, Peter. "The Decline of the Finnish American Left, 1925–1945." *International Migration Review* 17, no. 1 (Spring 1983): 65–94.

Kolehmainen, John Ilmari. *A History of the Finns in Ohio, Western Pennsylvania, and West Virginia.* Painesville: Ohio Finnish-American Historical Society, 1977.

Kornbluh, Joyce L., ed. *Rebel Voices: An IWW Anthology.* Chicago: Charles H. Kerr Press, 1998.

Kostiainen, Auvo. "A Dissenting Voice of Finnish Radicals in America: The Formative Years of *Sosialisti-Industrialisti* in the 1910s." *American Studies in Scandinavia* 23 (1991): 83–94.

——. "Finnish-American Workmen's Associations." In *Old Friends—Strong Ties: The Finnish Contribution to the Growth of the USA,* ed. Vilho Niitemaa et al., 205–234. Turku, Finland: Institute of Migration 1976.

——. "The Finns and the Crisis Over 'Bolshevization' in the Workers' Party, 1924–1925." In *The Finnish Experience in the Western Great Lakes Region: New Perspectives,* ed. Michael G. Karni, Matti E. Kaups, and Douglas J. Ollila, 171–185. Turku, Finland: Institute for Migration Studies, 1975.

——. *The Forging of Finnish-American Communism, 1917–1924: A Study in Ethnic Radicalism.* Turku, Finland: Turin Yliopisto, 1978.

——. "For or Against Americanization? The Case of the Finnish Immigrant Radicals." In *American Labor and Immigration History, 1877–1920s: Recent European Research,* ed. Dirk Hoerder, 259–275. Urbana: University of Illinois Press, 1983.

Langland, James. *The Chicago Daily News Almanac and Year Book for 1909.* Chicago: Chicago Daily News, 1909.

Lankton, Larry. *Beyond the Boundaries: Life and Landscape at the Lake Superior Copper Mines, 1840–1875.* Oxford: Oxford University Press, 1997.

———. *Cradle to Grave: Life, Work, and Death at the Lake Superior Copper Mines*. Oxford: Oxford University Press, 1991.

———. *Hollowed Ground: Copper Mining and Community Building on Lake Superior, 1840s–1990s*. Detroit: Wayne State University Press, 2010.

Larson, Amanda Wiljanen. *Finnish Heritage in America*. Marquette, Mich.: Belta Kappa Gamma Society, 1975.

Leary, James P. "Yksi Suuri Union: Field Recordings of Finnish American IWW Songs." *Journal of Finnish Studies* 14, no. 1 (Summer 2010): 6–17.

Lehto, Steve. *Death's Door: The Truth behind Michigan's Largest Mass Murder*. Troy, Mich.: Momentum Books, 2006.

———. *Shortcut: The Seeberville Murders and the Dark Side of the American Dream*. Troy, Mich.: Momentum Books, 2012.

Leier, Mark. *Bakunin: The Creative Passion*. New York: St. Martin's Press, 2006.

———. *Where the Fraser River Flows: The Industrial Workers of the World in British Columbia*. Vancouver: New Star Books, 1990.

Lembcke, Jerry, and William M. Tattam. *One Union in Wood: A Political History of the International Woodworkers of America*. New York: International Publishers, 1984.

Lens, Sidney. *Labor Wars: From the Molly Maguires to the Sit Downs*. Garden City, N.Y.: Doubleday, 1973.

Lindsey, Almont. "Paternalism and the Pullman Strike." *American Historical Review* 44, no. 2 (January, 1939): 272–289.

Long, Priscilla. *Where the Sun Never Shines: A History of America's Bloody Coal Industry*. New York: Paragon House, 1989.

Lukas, J. Anthony. *Big Trouble: A Murder in a Small Western Town Sets Off a Struggle for the Soul of America*. New York: Simon and Schuster, 1997.

Luoma, Melba. Interview by Jo Urion, April 14, 2004. Transcribed by Melissa Davis. Keweenaw National Historical Park Archive, Calumet, Mich.

Magnaghi, Russell M. *Miners, Merchants, and Midwives: Michigan's Upper Peninsula Italians*. Marquette, Mich.: Belle Fontaine Press, 1987.

Maki, J. F. "The Finnish Socialist Federation." In *The American Labor Year-Book, 1916*, 130—132. New York: Rand School Press, 1916.

Marcy, Leslie H. "Calumet." *International Socialist Review* 14, no. 8 (February 1914): 453–461.

Marx, Karl. *Capital*. Vol. 1. Trans. Ben Fowkes. London: Penguin Books, 1990.

McCartin, Joseph A. "Introduction." In *We Shall Be All: A History of the Industrial Workers of the World*, by Melvyn Dubofsky, vii–xi. Abridged ed. Urbana: University of Illinois Press, 2000.

McClelland, John. *Wobbly War: The Centralia Story*. Tacoma: Washington State Historical Society, 1987.

McGovern, George S., and Leonard F. Guttridge. *The Great Coalfield War*. Boston: Houghton Mifflin, 1972.

McGurty, Edward J. "The Copper Miners' Strike." *International Socialist Review* 14, no. 3 (September 1913): 150–153.

Memorial Record of the Northern Peninsula of Michigan. Chicago: Lewis Publishing, 1895.

Meyers, Jeanne. "Ethnicity and Class Conflict at Maillardville/Fraser Mills: The Strike of 1931." Master's thesis, Simon Fraser University, 1983.

"Michigan Copper Mine Strikers Standing Firm." *Locomotive Firemen's Magazine* 56, no. 1 (January 1914): 77–78.

Michigan Federation of Labor. *First Industrial History and Official Year Book of the Michigan Federation of Labor.* Lansing, Mich.: The Federation, 1915.

——. *Official Year Book.* Detroit: Houghton-Jacobson, 1907.

Michigan Manual, 2009–2010: Summary of Votes for Governor, 1835–2006. Lansing, Mich.: Legislative Service Bureau, 2010.

Millikan, William. *A Union against Unions: The Minneapolis Citizens' Alliance and Its Fight against Organized Labor, 1903–1947.* St. Paul: University of Minnesota Press, 2001.

Molek, Ivan (John). *Slovene Immigrant History, 1900–1950: Autobiographical Sketches.* Trans. Mary Molek. Dover, Del.: Mary Molek, 1979.

Molloy, Larry. *Italian Hall: The Witnesses Speak.* Hubbell, Mich.: Great Lakes GeoScience, 2004.

Montgomery, David. *The Fall of the House of Labor: The Workplace, the State, and American Labor Activism, 1865–1925.* Cambridge: Cambridge University Press, 1987.

——. "What More to Be Done?" *Labor History* 40, no. 3 (August 1999): 356–361.

——. *Workers' Control in America: Studies in the History of Work, Technology, and Labor Struggles.* Cambridge: Cambridge University Press, 1979.

Moody, Kim. *US Labor in Trouble and Transition: The Failure of Reform from Above, the Promise of Revival from Below.* London: Verso, 2007.

Moore, Charles. *History of Michigan.* Vol. 4. Chicago: Lewis Publishing, 1915.

Moravets, F. L. "Lumber Production in Oregon and Washington, 1869–1948." Forest Survey Report, 100. U.S. Forest Service, Pacific Northwest Forest and Range Experimentation Station Forest Survey, 1949.

Morn, Frank. *"The Eye That Never Sleeps": A History of the Pinkerton National Detective Agency.* Bloomington: Indiana University Press, 1982.

Morton, Jack. "Why Should I Be a Socialist?" *International Socialist Review* 15, no. 9 (March 1915): 542–544.

"Moyer Wounded, Lays It to Plot." *New York Times,* December 28, 1913.

Murphy, Mary. *Mining Cultures: Men, Women, and Leisure in Butte, 1914–1941.* Urbana: University of Illinois Press, 1987.

Nelson, Bruce. *Divided We Stand: American Workers and the Struggle for Black Equality.* Princeton, N.J.: Princeton University Press, 2001.

——. *Workers on the Waterfront: Seamen, Longshoremen, and Unionism in the 1930s.* Urbana: University of Illinois Press, 1990.

Nelson, Eugene. *Break Their Haughty Power: Joe Murphy in the Heyday of the Wobblies.* San Francisco: ISM Press, 1996.

Newbill, James G. "Yakima and the Wobblies, 1910–1936." In *At the Point of Production: The Local History of the IWW,* ed. Joseph Robert Conlin, 167–190. Westport, Conn.: Greenwood Press, 1981.

"News and Views." *International Socialist Review* 8, no. 9 (March 1908): 570.

"News and Views." *International Socialist Review* 10, no. 1 (July 1909): 85.

Niemala, Juha. "Hiska Salomaa (1891–1957)." In *The American Midwest: An Interpretive Encyclopedia*, ed. Richard Sission, Christian K. Zacher, and Andrew Robert Lee Cayton, 396. Columbus: Ohio State University Press, 2007.

Norwood, Stephen H. *Strikebreaking and Intimidation: Mercenaries and Masculinity in Twentieth-Century America*. Chapel Hill: University of North Carolina Press, 2001.

N. W. Ayer & Son's American Newspaper Annual & Directory: A Catalogue of American Newspapers. Philadelphia: N. W. Ayer & Son Newspaper Advertising Agents, 1917.

Oberdeck, K. J. "'Not Pink Teas': The Seattle Working-Class Women's Movement, 1905–1918." *Labor History* 32, no. 2 (Spring 1991): 193–230.

"Officers of the Friends of Soviet Russia." *Soviet Russia* 6, no. 7 (April 15, 1922): 203.

Official Directory and Legislative Manual of the State of Michigan for the Years 1887–8. Lansing, Mich.: Secretary of State, 1888.

Official Proceedings of the Fifteenth Convention of the Western Federation of Miners. Denver: W. H. Kistler Stationery, 1907.

Official Proceedings of the Seventeenth Convention of the Western Federation of Miners. Denver: W. H. Kistler Stationery, 1909.

Official Proceedings of the Twenty-First Convention of the Western Federation of Miners. Denver: W. H. Kistler Stationery, 1911.

Orth, Samuel P. *The Armies of Labor: The Chronicle of the Organised Wage-Earners*. New Haven, Conn.: Yale University Press, 1919.

Ottanelli, Fraser M. *The Communist Party of the United States*. New Brunswick, N.J.: Rutgers University Press, 1991.

Palmer, Bryan. *A Culture in Conflict: Skilled Workers and Industrial Capitalism in Hamilton, Ontario, 1860–1914*. Montreal: McGill-Queen's University Press, 1979.

———. *James P. Cannon and the Origins of the American Revolutionary Left, 1890–1928*. Urbana: University of Illinois Press, 2007.

———. "Rethinking the Historiography of United States Communism." *American Communist History* 2 (December 2003): 139–173.

Passi, Michael M. "Introduction: Finnish Immigrants and the Radical Response to Industrial America." In *For the Common Good: Finnish Immigrants and the Radical Response to Industrial America*, ed. Michael G. Karni and Douglas J. Ollila Jr., 9–22. Superior, Wis.: Tyomies Society, 1977.

Peck, Gunther. *Reinventing Free Labor: Padrones and Immigrant Workers in the North American West, 1880–1930*. Cambridge: Cambridge University Press, 2000.

Penti, Marsha. "Piikajutut: Stories Finnish Maids Told." In *Women Who Dared: The History of Finnish-American Women*, ed. Carl Ross and K. Marianne Wargelin Brown, 55–72. St. Paul: Immigration History Research Center, University of Minnesota, 1986.

Pferdehirt, Julie. *More Than Petticoats: Remarkable Michigan Women*. Guilford, Conn.: TwoDot, 2007.

Phelan, Craig. *Divided Loyalties: The Public and Private Life of Labor Leader John Mitchell*. Albany: State University of New York Press, 1994.

Phillips, Anne, and Barbara Taylor. "Sex and Skill: Notes towards a Feminist Economics." *Feminist Review* 6 (1980): 79–88.

"Plumbers and Steam Fitters." *Plumbers Trade Journal, Gas, Steam, and Hot Water Fitters' Review*

(December 15, 1907): 678.

Preston, William, Jr. *Aliens and Dissenters: Federal Suppression of Radicals, 1903–1933.* Cambridge, Mass.: Harvard University Press, 1963.

———. "Shall This Be All? U.S Historians versus William D. Haywood, et al." *Labor History* 12, no. 3 (Summer 1971): 435–453.

"Principles of Revolutionary Syndicalism (Extracts)." *Anarcho-Syndicalist Review* 55 (Winter 2011): 2.

Prpic, George Jure. *The Croatian Immigrants in America.* New York: Philosophical Library, 1971.

"Publisher's Department." *International Socialist Review* 10, no. 5 (November 1909): 472.

Puotinen, Arthur. "Early Labor Organizations in the Copper Country." In *For the Common Good: Finnish Immigrants and the Radical Response to Industrial America*, ed. Michael G. Karni and Douglas J. Ollila Jr., 119–166. Superior, Wis.: Työmies Society, 1977.

Raatajain Lauluja. Duluth, Minn.: Workers Socialist Publishing, 1923.

Rajala, Richard A. "Bill and the Boss: Labor Protest, Technological Change and the Transformation of the West Coast Logging Camp, 1890–1930." *Journal of Forest History* 33 (October 1989): 168–179.

———. "A Dandy Bunch of Wobblies: Pacific Northwest Loggers and the Industrial Workers of the World, 1900–1930." *Labor History* 37 (Spring 1996): 205–234.

The Rank and File versus Dictatorship. Spokane, Wash.: Industrial Workers of the World, 1925.

"Red Cedar Shingle and Shakes: The Labor Story, Interviews with Elwood R. Maunder." *Journal of Forest History* 19, no. 3 (July 1975): 112–127.

Renshaw, Patrick. "The IWW and the Red Scare, 1917–1924." *Journal of Contemporary History* 3, no. 4 (October 1968): 63–72.

———. *The Wobblies: The Story of Syndicalism in the United States.* New York: Anchor Books, 1967.

Richardson, Henry P. "Scientific Organizing and the Farmer." *International Socialist Review* 15, no. 9 (March 1915): 554–558.

Rissanen, Aku. *Suomalaisten Sosialistiosastojen ja Työväenyhdistysten viidennen: Pöytäkirja, 1–5, 7–10 p. kesäkuuta, 1912.* Fitchburg, Mass: Suomalainen Sosialisti Kustannus Yhtiö, 1912.

Robbins, William G. *Hard Times in Paradise: Coos Bay, Oregon.* Seattle: University of Washington Press, 1988.

———. *Lumberjacks and Legislators: Political Economy of the U.S. Lumber Industry.* College Station: Texas A&M Press, 1982.

———. "The Social Context of Forestry: The Pacific Northwest in the Twentieth Century." *Western Historical Quarterly* 16, no. 4 (October 1985): 413–427.

Rocker, Rudolf. *Anarcho-Syndicalism.* London: Pluto Press, 1989.

Roediger, David. "'Not Only the Ruling Classes to Overcome, but Also the So-Called Mob': Class, Skill, and Community in the St. Louis General Strike of 1877." *Journal of Social History* 19, no. 2 (Winter 1985): 213–239.

———. *Working toward Whiteness: How America's Immigrants Became White, the Strange Journey from Ellis Island to the Suburbs.* New York: Basic Books, 2005.

Rosemont, Franklin, ed. *Joe Hill: The IWW and the Making of a Revolutionary Working-Class Counterculture.* Chicago: Charles H. Kerr Press, 2003.

———. *Juice Is Stranger Than Friction: Selected Writings of T-Bone Slim*. Chicago: Charles H. Kerr Press, 1992.

Rosenbloom, Joshua L. "Strikebreaking and the Labor Market in the United States, 1881–1894." *Journal of Economic History* 58, no. 1 (March 1998): 183–205.

Ross, Carl. "The Feminist Dilemma in the Finnish Immigrant Community." In *Women Who Dared: The History of Finnish-American Women*, ed. Carl Ross and K. Marianne Wargelin Brown, 71–83. St. Paul: Immigration History Research Center, University of Minnesota, 1986.

———. *The Finn Factor in American Labor, Culture, and Society*. New York Mills, Minn.: Parta Printers, 1977.

Rudler, F. W., and G. G. Chisholm. *Europe*. London: Edward Stanford, 1885.

Ruff, Allen. *"We Called Each Other Comrade": Charles H. Kerr & Company, Radical Publishers*. Oakland, Calif.: PM Press, 2011.

Salerno, Salvadore, ed., *Direct Action and Sabotage: Three Classic IWW Pamphlets from the IWW*. Chicago: Charles H. Kerr Press, 1997.

———. "No God, No Master: Italian Anarchists and the Industrial Workers of the World." In *The Lost World of Italian American Radicalism: Politics, Labor, and Culture*, ed. Philip J. Cannistraro and Gerald Meyer, 171–188. Westport, Conn.: Praeger, 2003.

———. *Red November, Black November: Culture and Community in the Industrial Workers of the World*. Albany: State University of New York Press, 1989.

Salerno, Salvadore, Franklin Rosemont, David Roediger, and Archie Green, eds. *The Big Red Songbook*. Chicago: Charles H. Kerr Press, 2007.

Sanborn Map Company. *Calumet 1907*. Proquest Sanborn Map Collection, presented in the Digital Sanborn Maps Collection, 1867–1970.

Sarell, Antti. "The Copper Country Strike: Its Features So Far." *Työmiehen Joulu 1913*. Trans. Jarno Heinilä, 2006. Hancock, Mich.: Työmies Publishing Company, 1913.

Saxton, Alexander. *The Indispensable Enemy: Labor and the Anti-Chinese Movement in California*. Berkeley: University of California Press, 1971.

———. *The Rise and Fall of the White Republic*. London: Verso, 1990.

Scott, James C. *Weapons of the Weak: Everyday Forms of Peasant Resistance*. New Haven, Conn.: Yale University Press, 1985.

Sellars, Nigel. *Oil, Wheat, and Wobblies: The Industrial Workers of the World in Oklahoma, 1905–1930*. Norman: University of Oklahoma Press, 1998.

Shenk, Gerald R. *"Work or Fight!" Race, Gender, and the Draft in World War One*. New York: Palgrave Macmillan, 2005.

Smith, Robert M. *From Blackjacks to Briefcases: A History of Commercialized Strikebreaking and Unionbusting in the United States*. Athens: Ohio University Press, 2003.

Smith, Walker. *The Everett Massacre*. Chicago: Industrial Workers of the World, 1917.

"Socialist National Convention." *International Socialist Review* 8, no. 12 (June 1908): 723.

Souchy, Augustin. *Beware Anarchist! A Life for Freedom: The Autobiography of Augustin Souchy*. Ed. and trans. Theo Waldinger. Chicago: Charles H. Kerr Press, 1992.

State of Michigan. Industrial Accident Board. *Fifteenth Annual Report of the Bureau of Labor and Industrial Statistics*. Lansing, Mich.: Robert Smith Printing, State Printers and Binders, 1897.

———. *Proceedings of the Court of Inquiry (Jackson County), People v. Blackman and Jackson 1912.* Calumet and Hecla Mining Companies Collection, Box 352, Folder 003. Copper Country Historical Collections, Michigan Technological University, Houghton.

———. *Twenty-First Annual Report of the Bureau of Labor and Industrial Statistics.* Lansing, Mich.: Robert Smith Printing, State Printers and Binders, 1904.

———. *Workmen's Compensation Law: Information to Employees.* Lansing, Mich.: Wynkoop Hallenbeck Crawford, State Printers, 1912.

State of Washington, Bureau of Labor. *Eighth Biennial Report of the Bureau of Labor Statistics and Factory Inspection, 1911–1912.* Olympia, Wash.: E. L. Boardman, Public Printer, 1912.

———. *Eleventh Biennial Report of the Bureau of Labor Statistics and Factory Inspection, 1917–1918.* Olympia, Wash.: Public Printer, 1918.

———. *Fifth Biennial Report of the Bureau of Labor Statistics and Factory Inspection, 1905–1906.* Olympia, Wash.: C. W. Gorham Public Printer, 1906.

———. *Fourth Biennial Report of the Bureau of Labor Statistics and Factory Inspection, 1901–1902.* Olympia, Wash.: Blankenship Saterlee, 1904.

———. *Ninth Biennial Report of the Bureau of Labor Statistics, 1913–1914.* Olympia, Wash.: Public Printer, 1914.

———. *Sixth Biennial Report of the Bureau of Labor of the State of Washington, 1907–1908.* Olympia, Wash.: Public Printer, 1908.

Stevenson, Archibald E. *Revolutionary Radicalism: Its History, Purpose and Tactics, with an Exposition and Discussion of the Steps Being Taken to and Required to Curb It, being the Report of the Joint Legislative Committee Investigating Seditious Activities, Filed April 24, 1920, in the Senate of the State of New York.* New York: J. B. Lyon, 1920.

"Strikes and Lockouts." *Motorman and Conductor* 13, no. 2 (January 1906): 6.

Sulkanen, Elis, ed. *Amerikan Suomalaisen Tyovaenliikkeen Historia.* Fitchburg, Mass.: Amerikan Suomalainen Kansanvallen Liitto ja Raivaaja Publishing, 1951.

Suomalaisten Sosialistijärjestön Edustajakokouksen. *Pöytäkirja 1912.* Fitchburg, Mass.: Suomalainen Sosialisti Kustannus Yhtiö, 1912.

Taft, Philip. "Violence in American Labor Disputes." *Annals of the American Academy of Political and Social Science* 364 (March 1966): 127–140.

Taylor, Paul S. *The Sailors' Union of the Pacific.* New York: Arno Press, 1971.

Tentler, Leslie Woodcock. *Wage-Earning Women: Industrial Work and Family Life in the United States, 1900–1930.* Oxford: Oxford University Press, 1979.

Thompson, E. P. *The Making of the English Working Class.* New York: Vintage Books, 1966.

Thompson, Fred. *The IWW: Its First Fifty Years, 1905–1955.* Chicago: Industrial Workers of the World, 1955.

———. "They Didn't Suppress the Wobblies." *Radical America* 1, no. 2 (September–October 1967): 3–5.

Thompson, Fred, and Jon Bekken. *The IWW: Its First 100 Years.* Cincinnati: Industrial Workers of the World, 2006.

Thompson, Fred, and Patrick Murfin. *The IWW: Its First Seventy Years.* Chicago: Industrial Workers of the World, 1975.

Thompson, Paul. "Playing at Being Skilled Men: Factory Culture and Pride in Work Skills among Coventry Car Workers." *Social History* 13, no. 1 (January 1988): 45–69.

Thorpe, Wayne. *"The Workers Themselves": Revolutionary Syndicalism and International Labour, 1913–1923.* Amsterdam: Kluwer Academic/International Institute of Social History, 1990.

Thurner, Arthur. *Rebels on the Range: The Michigan Copper Miners' Strike of 1913–1914.* Lake Linden, Mich.: John H. Forster Press, 1984.

———. *Strangers and Sojourners: A History of Michigan's Keweenaw Peninsula.* Detroit: Wayne State University Press, 1994.

Tillotson, Shirley. "'We May All Soon Be First-Class Men': Gender and Skill in Canada's Early Twentieth Century Urban Telegraph Industry." *Labour/Le Travail* 27 (Spring 1991): 97–125.

Tipton, Julianna Niemim. "Bits and Pieces of My Childhoods." In *East Aberdeen Finns: Grays Harbor County, Washington.* Finnish-American Historical Society of the West 25, no. 1 (December 1998): 29.

Todd, Williams Parson. Interview by Ralph Jalkanen, October 1974. Oral history interview transcript. Finnish American Historical Archive, Finlandia University, Hancock, Mich.

Todes, Charlotte. *Lumber and Labor.* New York: International Publishers, 1931.

"Trouble in the Copper Country with I.W.W. Agitators." *Engineering and Mining Journal* 104, no. 3 (July 1917): 148.

Twenty-Five Years of Industrial Unionism. Chicago: Industrial Workers of the World, 1930.

Twining, Charles E. *Phil Weyerhaeuser, Lumberman.* Seattle: University of Washington Press, 1985.

Tyler, Robert L. "Comment." In *Failure of a Dream? Essays in the History of American Socialism,* ed. John H. M. Laslett and Seymour Martin Lipset, 204–212. Rev. ed. Berkeley: University of California Press, 1984.

———. *Rebels of the Woods: The IWW in the Pacific Northwest.* Eugene: University of Oregon Books, 1967.

Tyomies-Eteenpain, 1903–1973: Seventieth Anniversary Souvenir Journal. Superior, Wis.: Tyomies Society, n.d.

Tyomies Kymmenvuotias, 1903–1913. Hancock, Mich.: Tyomies Kustannusyhtio, 1913.

U.S. Commissioner of Labor. *Twenty-Third Annual Report of the Commissioner of Labor, 1908, Workmen's Insurance and Benefit Funds in the United States.* Washington, D.C.: Government Printing Office, 1909.

U.S. Commission on Industrial Relations. Final Report and Testimony, submitted to Congress by the Commission on Industrial Relations Created by the Act of August 23, 1912. Washington, D.C.: Government Printing Office, 1916.

U.S. Congress. *Conditions in the Copper Mines of Michigan: Hearings before a Subcommittee of the Committee on Mines and Mining.* Washington, D.C.: Government Printing Office, 1914.

U.S. Department of Labor. *Michigan Copper District Strike: Bulletin of the United States Labor Statistics.* Washington, D.C.: Government Printing Office, 1914.

U.S. Department of Labor. *Strike in the Copper Mining District of Michigan.* Washington, D.C.: Government Printing Office, 1914.

van der Walt, Lucien, and Michael Schmidt. *Black Flame: The Revolutionary Class Politics of Anarchism and Syndicalism.* Oakland, Calif.: AK Press, 2009.

Van Tine, Warren R. *Making of the Labor Bureaucrat: Union Leadership in the United States,*

1870–1920. Amherst: University of Massachusetts Press, 1973.

Von Drehle, David. *Triangle: The Fire That Changed America*. New York: Atlantic Monthly Press, 2003.

Watkins, T. H. *The Hungry Years: A Narrative History of the Great Depression*. New York: MacMillan, 2000.

Weinstein, James. *The Decline of American Socialism*. Piscataway, N.J.: Rutgers University Press, 1984.

Weir, Robert E. *Beyond Labor's Veil: The Culture of the Knights of Labor*. University Park: Pennsylvania State University Press, 1996.

Weiss, Robert P. "Private Detective Agencies and Labour Discipline in the United States, 1855—1946." *Historical Journal* 29, no. 1 (1986): 87–107.

Williams, Michael. *Americans and Their Forests: A Historical Geography*. Cambridge: Cambridge University Press, 1989.

Williamson, Thames. *Problems in American Democracy*. Boston: D. C. Heath, 1922.

Wyman, Mark. *Hard Rock Epic: Western Miners and the Industrial Revolution*. Berkeley: University of California Press, 1989.

"Xmas-Tree Panic Costs 80 Lives." *New York Times*, December 25, 1913.

Zinn, Howard, Dana Frank, and Robin D. G. Kelley. *Three Strikes: Miners, Musicians, Salesgirls, and the Fighting Spirit of Labor's Last Century*. Boston: Beacon Press, 2001.

Index